Everyday Communalism

Everyday Communalism

Riots in Contemporary Uttar Pradesh

Sudha Pai
Sajjan Kumar

OXFORD
UNIVERSITY PRESS

Oxford University Press is a department of the University of Oxford.
It furthers the University's objective of excellence in research, scholarship,
and education by publishing worldwide. Oxford is a registered trademark of
Oxford University Press in the UK and in certain other countries.

Published in India by
Oxford University Press
2/11 Ground Floor, Ansari Road, Daryaganj, New Delhi 110 002, India

ISBN-13: 978-0-19-946629-0
ISBN-10: 0-19-946629-7

Typeset in ITC Giovanni Std 9.5/13
by The Graphics Solution, New Delhi 110 092
Printed in India by Rakmo Press, New Delhi 110 020

Contents

Figures and Tables

Figures

Tables

Preface

One of the most important developments in the 2000s has been the resurgence of communalism and incidents of Hindu–Muslim riots in the state of Uttar Pradesh (UP). While the state experienced a wave of communal riots following the Ram Temple movement and the destruction of the Babri Masjid on 6 December 1992, the second half of the 1990s was a relatively peaceful period with no major riots. This book attempts to understand the reasons for a new 'saffron wave' and communal tension and riots in UP after a long interval. It examines the creation of deep-seated polarization by the Bharatiya Janata Party (BJP)–Rashtriya Swayamsevak Sangh (RSS) leading to Hindu–Muslim riots in Mau in 2005, Gorakhpur in 2007, and Muzaffarnagar in 2013. More importantly, it moves beyond the riots to analyse the 'new ways and means' whereby communalism in the present phase is being manufactured by the Hindu right in UP. The study argues that the state is experiencing a post-Ayodhya phase of communalism currently, markedly different from the earlier phase of the late 1980s and early 1990s. A fusion of rising cultural aspirations and deep economic anxieties in UP, which remains an economically backward state, and where a deepening agrarian crisis, unemployment, poverty, and inequalities are widespread, has created fertile ground for a new kind of communal mobilization.

To analyse this new phenomenon we offer a model of 'institutionalized everyday communalism'. The defining feature of this model is that rather than instigating major and violent state-wide riots as in the earlier phase, the BJP–RSS have attempted to create and sustain constant, low-key communal tension together with frequent, small, low-intensity incidents out of petty everyday issues that institutionalize communalism at the grass roots; to keep the 'pot boiling'. While earlier big riots constituted a major episode lasting a few days, the riots in the 2000s have been preceded by a long period of sustained mobilization at the grass roots and once the riots are over, they are used to install a new antagonistic relationship that remains on the ground causing constant tension. The phenomenon of everyday communalism is analysed based on extensive fieldwork in selected districts, towns, and villages within eastern and western UP that experienced major riots. Further, the book examines how this strategy of everyday communalism, and the riots which followed, was deftly combined by a new generational BJP leadership with the use of electoral politics, to mount a communally charged and divisive electoral campaign in the 2014 national elections to gain 73 Lok Sabha seats in UP and obtain power at the centre. The agenda of the BJP–RSS is hence twofold: political, to gain state power and establish majoritarian rule, but equally important, cultural, because India is viewed as fundamentally 'Hindu' in a civilizational sense, while Muslims and other non-Hindus were and will remain alien, and the Indian state a 'culturally alien' construction imposed on India by anglicized intellectuals. It is through this lens of the new 'avatar'of the BJP, its ideology and strategies, and its impact on society and polity, that an attempt is made to understand the current round of communalism in UP.

In sum, the book addresses some significant larger questions regarding communalism and its impact on our democratic structure not only in UP, but also in the country. Has the multiple, mobilizational politics of identity in UP driven by political parties and their agendas created a specific variant of communalism different from other states? Why has UP become a communal cauldron at this particular juncture? Is it the decline of secular formations such as political parties and institutions that has provided space to the BJP–RSS? Why does the Hindu and Muslim middle and lower-middle class respond to the provocation by the BJP–RSS both in terms of voting and creation of communal confrontation at the societal level such as 'Love Jihad' and stories of forced conversions? Are economic changes in UP including the changes induced by globalization, the underlying factors responsible for communal strife in the state? These are important questions as the present communal conflict in UP has the potential to change the democratic system based on values of equality and fraternity to one of majoritarianism.

This book could not have been written without the help of many individuals, only some of whom we are able to personally acknowledge here. In the conceptualization of the study and its scope, discussions were held with many colleagues and friends, particularly Professor C.P. Bhambhri, Professor Badri Narayan, and Rakesh Batabyal. We are grateful to the Centre for the Study of Developing Societies (CSDS), particularly Director Sanjay Kumar and Himanshu Bhattacharya, for providing us data on the 2017 UP assembly elections, which was very helpful. Extensive fieldwork was possible due to contacts provided by many individuals. In western UP Shahid Siddiqui, who belongs to the region, put us in touch with many journalists of Hindi newspapers and heads of organizations that had knowledge about and had witnessed the Muzaffarnagar riots, and had later provided help to the Muslim families living in the camps. Many local political workers of different political parties and local journalists were also willing to talk about the long-term mobilization prior to the Muzaffarnagar riots in the region. The fieldwork in eastern UP was more difficult as there is little secondary material available; here Professor Badri Narayan and the Govind Ballabh Pant Institute, Uttar Pradesh, provided much help on the ground. Most important are the respondents in the selected towns and villages in both eastern and western UP who spared time to talk and give us rich information that enabled us to formulate the model of 'institutionalization of everyday communalism' and write in detail about the riots in our selected districts. We remain grateful to them, as without their inputs much of the details provided on communalism at the grass roots would not have been available to the reader. Professor Niraja Gopal Jayal generously read parts of the manuscript and gave comments, which were both helpful and provided confidence that the book was moving in the right direction.

We would also like to acknowledge the help of the librarian and staff of Jawaharlal Nehru University, New Delhi, for help in locating material, both print and digital, which gave us access to important documents and information we could not have located on our own.

We are personally grateful to Oxford University Press for their valuable inputs, guidance, and help through the stages of production of the book.

Sudha Pai
Sajjan Kumar
May 2017

Abbreviations

ABVP	Akhil Bharatiya Vidyarthi Parishad
AIBMM	All-India Backward Muslim Morcha
AICC	All India Congress Committee
BHU	Banaras Hindu University
BJP	Bharatiya Janata Party
BJS	Bharatiya Jan Sangh
BJYM	Bharatiya Janata Yuva Morcha
BKD	Bharatiya Kranti Dal
BKU	Bhartiya Kisan Union
BLD	Bharatiya Lok Dal
BMAC	Babri Masjid Action Committee
BMU	Bharatiya Mazdoor Union
BPL	below poverty line
BRGF	Backward Regions Grant Fund
BSP	Bahujan Samaj Party
CPI	Communist Party of India
CPI(M)	Communist Party of India (Marxist)
CrPC	Code of Criminal Procedure
DM	District Magistrate
HYV	Hindu Yuva Vahini
ICDS	Integrated Child Development Services Scheme
INC	Indian National Congress
IPC	Indian Penal Code
IRS	institutionalized riot system
JP	Janata Party
JUH	Jamiat Ulema-e-Hind

KCC	Kisan Credit Cards
MAJGAR	Muslims, Ahirs, Jats, Gujjars, and Rajputs
MBCs	most backward classes
MNREGA	Mahatma Gandhi National Rural Employment Guarantee Act
MSME	Ministry of Small and Medium Enterprises
NCMEI	National Commissioner for Minorities' Educational Institutions
NDA	National Democratic Alliance
NHRC	National Human Rights Commission
OBC	other backward class
PAC	Provincial Armed Constabulary
PCR	police control room
PPI	Peace Party of India
PSP	Praja Socialist Party
PUCL	People's Union for Civil Liberties
QED	Quami Ekta Dal
RJBBM	Ram Janma Bhoomi Babri Masjid
RLD	Rashtriya Lok Dal
RSS	Rashtriya Swayamsevak Sangh
RUC	Rashtriya Ulema Council
SAP	state advised price; Structural Adjustment Programme
SC	Scheduled Caste
SDM	Sub-Divisional Magistrate
SEIAA	State Level Environment Impact Assessment Authority
SHO	Station House Officer
SIT	Special Investigation Team
SP	Samajwadi Party; Superintendent of Police
SSP	Samyukta Socialist Party
STF	Special Task Force
UP	Uttar Pradesh
UPPCB	UP Pollution Control Board
UPUDF	Uttar Pradesh United Democratic Front
VHP	Vishva Hindu Parishad

Introduction
Everyday Communalism in Uttar Pradesh

One of the most important developments in the 2000s has been the resurgence of communalism and incidents of Hindu–Muslim riots in the state of Uttar Pradesh (UP). While the state experienced a wave of communal riots from the late 1980s onwards due to the Ram Janma Bhoomi Babri Masjid (RJBBM) dispute and the destruction of the Babri Masjid on 6 December 1992, the second half of the 1990s was a relatively peaceful period with no major riots. There was little response to various attempts by both Hindu and Muslim leaders to mobilize their respective communities during the 1990s. Examples are the attempt by the Vishva Hindu Parishad (VHP) to launch the Mathura and Kashi temple movements around 1995–6, their pressure to pass new laws to hand over the Ayodhya site to the Ram Janmabhoomi Nyas, or the scrapping of the Place of Worship (Special Provisions) Act. Similarly Muslim leaders, who had once launched the Shah Bano movement aggressively and formed the Babri Masjid Action Committee, were on the defensive or were marginalized. The Bharatiya Janata Party (BJP) included most of the issues raised by the VHP in its electoral agenda for the 1996 Lok Sabha elections but they elicited little response from the people in UP (Engineer 1997: 323). Pointing out that the number of riots had come down drastically in the post-Babri period and even the small incidents that occurred were due to local reasons, Asghar Ali Engineer argued that 'organizing riots does not seem to be a paying proposition, at least for the present' (Engineer 1997: 326).

However, in the 2000s a new 'saffron wave' was witnessed in UP. Riots took place in the eastern districts of Mau in 2005, Gorakhpur in 2007, and in the capital city of Lucknow in 2006; communal tension started in some western districts from 2011 onwards leading to the violent riots in Muzaffarnagar and surrounding districts in September 2013 whose aftermath is still being felt (Graff and Galonnier 2013b). These incidents show that the BJP has revived its fundamentalist agenda in UP and brought communalism back to the centre stage in the state and the country. The immediate reason was the shocking defeat of the National Democratic Alliance (NDA) in the 2004 Lok Sabha elections that led to demands within the BJP to return to their core agenda of Hindutva, which had been set aside during the 'responsible national government' led by Atal Behari Vajpayee. However, even before that, the Gujarat riots of 2002 had revealed the desire of a section of the party to return to its programme of communal polarization of the late 1980s/early 90s. At the same time, some commentators have argued that in the 2000s with the rise of the 'Arab Spring' and Muslim fundamentalism in West Asia there are visible signs of Muslim restiveness described as 'India's Muslim Spring' due to which we are witnessing greater confrontation between the two communities and religion-based politics (Suroor 2014).

The present study is an attempt to understand the reasons for the resurgence of communalism and riots in UP in the 2000s after a long interval. The significance of our study lies in its attempt to examine the creation of deep-seated polarization between the Hindu and Muslim communities by the BJP–RSS (Rashtriya Swayamsevak Sangh [RSS]) leading to Hindu–Muslim riots. More importantly to move beyond them to analyse the 'new ways and means' whereby communalism in the present phase is being manufactured by the Hindu right in UP. We argue that UP is experiencing a post-Ayodhya phase of communalism which is markedly different from the earlier phase during the RJBBM period of the late 1980s and early 1990s. A fusion of rising cultural aspirations and deep economic anxieties in UP, which remains an economically backward state, and where a deepening agrarian crisis, unemployment, poverty, and inequalities are widespread, has created fertile ground for a new kind of communal mobilization. These shifts are not limited to India, as observers such as Pankaj Mishra have pointed out; they are witnessed across the globe in the 2000s seen in the rise of

Donald Trump in the US, the vote for Brexit in the UK, along with support among Muslim youth for the ISIS (P. Mishra 2017). Everywhere, right-wing forces are successfully tapping into the anxiety–aspiration matrix affecting a large majority on account of the precarious changes in the capitalist economy. This has brought to the fore uncertainties and unsettling of identities making them vulnerable to the populist discourses of the right promising them a sense of rootedness. It is in this larger context that the emergence of the Hindutva rightwing and everyday communalism in UP needs to be located.

In order to describe and analyse this new phenomenon we offer a model of 'institutionalized everyday communalism' described in detail a little later. The central and defining feature of everyday communalism in the 2000s is that rather than instigating major and violent state-wide riots as in the earlier phase, the BJP–RSS has attempted to create and sustain constant, low-key communal tension. This together with frequent, small, low-intensity incidents out of petty everyday issues that institutionalize communalism at the grass roots, keep the 'pot boiling'. While earlier big riots constituted a major episode lasting a few days, the riots in the 2000s have been preceded by a long period of sustained mobilization at the grass roots and once the riots are over, they are used to install a new antagonistic relationship that remains on the ground causing constant tension. This strategy is viewed as politically more manageable, to be carried out by the local cadres without the top leadership being involved, and only at times when mobilization reaches a peak does it create large riots as in Mau in 2005 or Muzaffarnagar in 2013.

This model has many new and significant elements, which show the manner in which communalism is being manufactured and institutionalized today. Elements such as a shift in the location of riots from earlier classic and endemic sites to new ones, the recruitment of local BJP–RSS cadres/leaders who carry out sustained everyday grass roots mobilization using local, mundane issues and imaginary threats, and the spread of communalism and riots into villages in the rural and semi-rural areas. A key feature of everyday communalism, which has contributed to its success, is the second round of experimentation with 'non-Brahminical Hindutva' in eastern UP under the leadership of Yogi Adityanath since the early 2000s, from where it has spread to other regions including western UP. The idea is not new and arose during the 1990s when the BJP leadership realized that in order to expand its vote share there was need to subalternize the Hindutva agenda recognizing the political and identitarian assertion and rising aspirations of the numerically large other backward classes (OBCs) and Dalits. While the idea lost importance during the Atal Behari Vajpayee regime, it has resurfaced in the 2000s as the attempt to institutionalize everyday communalism and create antagonism towards the Muslim community holds great appeal to this section both in the social and electoral realm. Our study suggests that this strategy particularly appeals to a younger, post-globalization generation within the majority community in UP.

Further, we examine how this strategy of everyday communalism and the riots which followed, particularly in the case of western UP, were deftly combined by the BJP leadership with use of electoral politics, to mount a communally charged and divisive electoral campaign in the 2014 national elections. This enabled them to gain 73 Lok Sabha seats in UP and obtain power at the centre. The agenda of the BJP–RSS is hence twofold: political, to gain state power and establish majoritarian rule, but equally important cultural, because India is viewed as fundamentally 'Hindu' in a civilizational sense, Muslims and other non-Hindus, were and will remain alien and the Indian State a 'culturally alien' construction imposed on India by anglicized intellectuals (Hansen 1999: 11).

Our study also examines the phenomenon of everyday communalism in two differing contexts in UP which would enhance our understanding of how it works and its impact. There are common features that enable the institutionalization of everyday communalism in the districts of eastern and western UP arising out of the interplay of political and economic factors and sociocultural aspirations of both the communities, including increasingly the subaltern castes that are sought to be brought into the fold of the BJP. However, there are also important regional specificities. The districts of Mau and Gorakhpur and Muzaffarnagar and Shamli in eastern and western UP, respectively, and towns and villages within them that formed the epicentre of the riots, were selected for analysis based on extensive fieldwork. The attempt has been to map the spread of communalism in the 2000s from the east towards the west and understanding the distinctiveness of each region.

The attempt to institutionalize everyday communalism was witnessed first in eastern UP where Mahant Adityanath and his organization the Hindu Yuva Vahini (HYV), formed in Gorakhpur in 2002, has been active in fomenting communal tension around small incidents leading to the violent riots of 2005 and 2007. The eastern part of the state has emerged as the prime experimental laboratory of 'communalization of everyday life' on a continuous basis, under the Mahant. Here the 'everydayness' of the new communal discourse seems to be more entrenched in the cultural realm, even though there are underlying socio-economic factors such as poverty and declining livelihoods due to decline of the weaving industry and rise of mafia dons, which make both communities vulnerable to mobilization.

In western UP, economic fault-lines are more important as the Jats identity themselves primarily through their occupational identity as peasants, and are deeply unhappy over the deepening agrarian crisis in the region and the lack of reservation in government jobs. However, in recent years caste and religious identities have become important, causing conflict with the Muslim community. Simultaneously, a perception has grown that a section of the Muslims have taken to non-agricultural business and prospered, creating antagonism. Hence, as our study shows the main aim of the BJP has been to mobilize the Jats and break the alliance between them and the Muslims, an attempt that began through grass roots mobilization much before the Muzaffarnagar riots of 2013 and the national elections of 2014.

The goal of everyday communalism in both regions is to establish a permanent anti-Muslim bias as the platform of contemporary 'Hindutva' and legitimize it as normal in the eyes of the people. We argue that this was possible due to mobilization by a resurgent BJP under a new leadership that has redefined 'Hindutva' ideology, and introduced change in the discourse and strategies of mobilization. Second, economic changes due to globalization and the rise of a young, aspirational, middle and lower middle class within sections of both the Hindu and the Muslim communities, which has made this possible. It is through this lens of the new 'avatar'of the BJP, its ideology and strategies, and its impact on society and polity, that an attempt is made to understand the current round of communalism in UP.

Communalism: The Indian Debate

The term 'communalism' has a different meaning and usage in India compared to Europe where it means consciousness or feeling of oneness among members that makes them feel they belong to a distinct group. In India communalism is a narrow and negative concept that has come to be used in a derogatory sense meaning antagonism between people belonging to different religions. It is used to describe 'religious communities' or persons belonging to a single religion who develop a 'community of religious interests'; that followers of a particular religion have common interests different from those who follow a different religion. In our study, communalism is used as meaning an inherently divisive ideology that captures the imagination of communities and creates antagonism and hostility between them. How do organizations/parties/leaders foster communalism in a society? By drawing on historical memories of war and conquest, divisive ideas such as religion, nationalism, cultural practices, customs, etc.

Communal mobilization in our study means the strategies and means devised and used by parties or organizations to create divisions between communities and create riots. Both state and society have a role in fostering or preventing communalism and communal mobilization leading to riots. The state has a role to both prevent the development of communalism and communal divides by fostering secularism and actions, which lead to secularization of society. It also has the responsibility of protecting the minority community particularly when a riot occurs. Society has the responsibility of creating a composite culture, and a sense of freedom, harmony, and equal rights where diverse religious communities live together within a nation-state. Thus, communalism is a subversive ideology that encourages separatism, hatred, violence, and fratricide and is often used by the political elite to exploit the sentiments of the people.

A number of historians have argued that this notion of separate religious 'communities' in India was created by the colonial state. Romila Thapar points out that there were no overarching religious communities in the pre-colonial days, where the sense of religious identity seems to have been related more to a particular sect, than to a dominant Hindu community (Thapar 1989: 209). The colonial period brought new values and ideas that led to a different understanding of religious communities, leading to the notion of a Hindu community or ideology of Hindu fundamentalism (Thapar 1989: 211). Similarly, Gyanendra Pandey and Sandra Freitag have shown how this process under specific contexts in north India, by giving centrality to the colonial state, led to community identities becoming more fully formed, focused, and organized during the colonial period (Freitag 1989; Pandey 1990).

The new notion of communities arose in the latter half of the nineteenth century and early twentieth century due to a number of developments that promoted communal ideas. The political competition leading to reformulation of Hinduism from a segmented community to a single community united across language and region, attempted in various socio-religious reform movements in the nineteenth century. The writings/work of Swami Dayanand Saraswati, Bal Gangadhar Tilak, Bankim Chandra Chatterjee and others which gave a definite shape to the Hindu ideology through glorification of ancient Hindu culture. The resurgence of militant Hinduism advocated by communal organizations—such as the RSS, the Hindu Mahasabha, etc.—who put forward the concept of Hindi, Hindu, and Hindustan and conversion of religious minorities. Furthermore, there was a need in the nineteenth century to postulate an overarching and distinct Hindu and a Muslim community as political representation and mobilization or the 'politics of numbers' became important (Gupta 1985). New entities arose such as the nation, which could be defined in various ways: as a political entity inclusive of all those living within its geographical boundaries or as a cultural entity consisting of all those who belonged to a particular culture, religion, or language community.

Nationalism, Thapar points out, could develop as a project of radical social transformation together with cultural homogenization, unified languages, and education systems, which happened in nineteenth century Western Europe. On the other hand, it could be one of conservative modernization and consolidating existing forms of social domination and exclusion. It was the latter that happened in India, with the Muslims constituting the 'other' and the lower castes remaining at the bottom of an unequal social hierarchy. In fact, every nation-state across the world has been founded upon a series of exclusions of 'others' and was stabilized through governmentalities establishing nationality both territorially and in the mental boundaries of its citizens.

In studies of Hindu–Muslim relations, the term 'communalism' since the colonial period has been preferred to ethnicity, reserving the latter term mainly to study primarily linguistic or racially distinct groups. It is used here as well in this manner. Scholars such as Horowitz have argued that all conflict based on ascriptive identities—race, language, religion, tribe, or caste—can be described as ethnic (Horowitz 1985: 41). In this broader usage, ethnic conflicts could range from Hindu–Muslim conflict in India, black–white conflict in the US, or Tamil–Sinhala conflict in Sri Lanka, that is, for religious, racial, linguistic, and sectarian conflict. Supporters of this argument hold that not all forms of ethnic conflict mentioned above seem to be different in terms of length, passion, violence, or intensity. Second, their emphasis is on the ascriptive and cultural core of the conflict which they argue needs to be distinguished from the largely non-ascriptive and economic core of class conflict. In sum, ethnic conflict might in some places have an economic basis but it is not its fundamental feature. Irrespective of internal class differentiation in an ethnic group race, language, or religion can be the defining characteristic of its politics. In contrast, class conflict is largely economic in nature; but if a person remains within the class in which he was born then class conflict could acquire ascriptive overtones. Based on the work of Horowitz it is now generally agreed that the latter characteristics do not apply to homogeneous societies but to societies which are 'ranked' such as South Africa during its period of Apartheid and India with its caste system (Horowitz 1985: 21).

After independence, the resurgence of severe communalism in the country, particularly Hindu communalism and major riots, in the late 1980s and 1990s sparked a debate on the subject. One set of scholars have argued that the dominant position that Hindu nationalism or 'Hindutva' came to occupy in the 1990s was because it could draw upon historical and cultural 'reserves' from the past of religious nationalism that have always accompanied in an overt or covert manner various forms of Indian nationalism (Van de Veer 1994). This strand has held that both in the colonial and postcolonial period from time to time communalism has reared its head at points of weakness of the Indian body politic. Examples of this are the Partition, the collapse of the single-party system that provided a stable and secular system, or the economic crisis of 1991 and the opening of the economy (Van de Veer 1994).

A few scholars argue that revival of 'Hindutva' in the 1980s was possible due to years of systematic, well–organized, and imaginative political strategies (Jaffrelot 1996). The wings of the Sangh Parivar such as the RSS, VHP, Bajrang Dal, and various Vidya Niketans and Shishu Mandirs have been able to spread the Hindu ideology through material, social, and spiritual mobilization (S. Gupta 2007). However, Thomas Blom Hansen has pointed out that while much effort has been made to spread the 'Hindutva' ideology, the larger goal in the 1990s has been—as it has been from the beginning—to transform the wider sphere of 'public culture' through political discourse, commercial and cultural expressions, and representations of the state and civic organizations. The Hindu nationalists desire to transform Indian public culture into a sovereign, disciplined, national culture rooted in what is claimed to be a superior ancient Hindu civilization. This can only happen when its rightful heirs the Hindu majority resurrect a strong sense of 'Hindutva' or Hinduness (Hansen 1999: 4).

This means that beneath the religious mobilization that is attempted, communalism is an ideology. As Bipan Chandra wrote in the late 1980s:

> Communalism is basically an ideology. Rioting and other forms of violence are its contingent or conjectural forms. A communal riot or an act of communal terrorism with the suddenness of its outbreak and its toll of tens or hundreds dead hits the headline and compels us to pay attention; but in fact it is an episodic consequence of the spread of communal ideology. It is a *concrete manifestation and product of the prior communalization of the people* (emphasis mine). Communal ideology can prevail without violence but violence cannot exist without communal ideology. (Chandra 2012 [1987])

This perspective is visible in the writings of many scholars on communalism in India such as Asghar Ali Engineer (1983, 1992, 1997), A.G. Noorani (2003, 2014), and Omar Khalidi (1995, 2004) among others.

Communalism is also viewed in India as a manifestation of the contradictions of development in the political processes of a society, especially one with a democratic political structure, moving towards modernity. The process of development leads to secularization of individual attitudes and communalization of different groups in society. However, simultaneously the capitalist path leads to economic inequalities as various groups expect to receive a share in the benefits of development. Political parties mobilize people at the same time promising benefits, but the political system cannot keep up with expectations of the people leading to discontentment. Political leaders with vested interests do not blame the system for its failure to achieve goals of development, but exploit the social contradictions consciously and in a systematic manner. By raising the issue of backwardness and relative deprivation repeatedly, they create a sense of insecurity in the minds of the members of a community. This makes them act as a community, not as individuals, and to support a group identity leading to a chain reaction among communities, and recruitment of individuals to join political parties or communal clashes. Once in power, political leaders ensure its continuity by spreading communalism. The processes of urbanization, industrialization, and migration contribute by making social groups conscious of their class and communal identities. This alliance between religion and politics in a community leads to communalism. Thus, communalism is more political and economic in nature than social as widely believed. The social aspect is associated largely to mark the boundaries of a group. Many scholars believe that fast growth keeping up with people's expectations alone can check the growth of these manifestations.

It has also been pointed out that this resurgence in the Hindi heartland in the 1980s is due to 'pressure from below'. This has led to a rise of the lower castes who have challenged the caste and class position that the upper castes have long occupied, which has given them control over not merely the social hierarchy but also political and economic power making them a dominant elite (Pai 2002). The minorities have also become more demanding. They expect the government to provide not just protection to life and property as in the past, but also education, jobs, and well-being as equal citizens of the country. The emergence of a post-independence, educated, politically conscious, and more aggressive middle and lower-middle class among the lower castes and minorities has created anxieties among the upper castes/classes, which explains their response to the call of 'Hindutva' over the last few decades and a desire to create a strong Hindu nation based on order and collective strength. The Hindu middle classes at the same time with exposure to global culture and consumerism following globalization have also felt the desire to be recognized and respected in the community of nations as a strong nation with economic power and political standing (Fernandes 2007). However, the Hindu nationalist groups could not capture political power by mobilizing only the poorer sections; as our work will reveal, it was among the rising, urban, middle classes belonging to the upper, middle, and the lower castes/classes that they found a constituency. Against this understanding of communalism as an ideology, we move to a discussion on the site selected for our study.

Situating UP in History: Nationalism versus Communalism

UP provides us a special social laboratory to understand the theoretical and empirical ramifications of the communal question, its relationship to nationalism, and the role of societal and political forces in making communal conflict possible in India, for a number of reasons. As Gyanesh Kudaisya (2007) has pointed out, there have been multiple imaginings of the erstwhile United Provinces as the 'heartland' of India, one important aspect being as a Muslim 'powerhouse' due to its long Islamic tradition. This was particularly true of the 1930s ending with the tragic event of Partition (S. Mishra 2001).

The rise of the BJP and its construction of the ideology of Hindutva in the 1980s in UP has rekindled an interest among scholars in exploring the roots of this phenomenon in the colonial period. This has led to new literature in recent years on the 'creation' of Hindu and Muslim identities, their relationship, and the reasons for the rise of communalism in the colonial period. Much scholarship suggests that until the late eighteenth century, the categories described as Hindu and Muslim in north India were malleable, not clearly defined, and marked by immense internal differentiation. The emergence of religious communalism was a gradual and progressive development in this region, reaching a peak only in the late colonial period, an end-product of the experience of colonialism and the fundamental socioeconomic changes that it unleashed in Indian society. However, this subject has not been free from controversy, especially in the context of UP. Scholars such as Francis Robinson, writing in the early 1970s argued that there were 'fundamental' religious differences between Hindus and Muslims in the nineteenth century 'before' community-based mobilization began. These differences were based on issues such as idol worship, cow protection, and monotheism, which created a 'basic antipathy' between the two communities, set them apart, made assimilation unthinkable, and contributed to the rise of communalism (Robinson 1975).

However, more recent literature has held that religious communities began to be defined more sharply during the colonial period, making communalism largely a 'colonial construct' in north India (Pandey 1990: 3). It contained both modern and traditional aspects, making it a hybrid phenomenon. Communalism arose out of the false totalities of ready-made religious communities of 'Hindu', 'Muslim', and 'Sikh', which ignored existing internal differentiation within these communities (Pandey 1990). Brass has argued that while there were differences between the Hindu and the Muslim communities that cannot be ignored, the roles played by particular elite groups also played a very important role. Brass talks about the balance between the rates of social mobilization and assimilation between different communities, the setting up of political organizations for promoting group identities and interests, and the influence of colonial policies as important factors (Brass 1991). Jaffrelot's study also points out that Hindu nationalism was constructed and crystallized as an ideology between the 1870s and the 1920s (Jaffrelot 1996).

Certain developments in the internal dynamics of UP aided the growth of both Hindu and Muslim communalism. Numerous actions of the colonial government contributed to this: labelling breakdowns of law and order as 'Hindu–Muslim riots'; the colonial construction of the Indian past as chaotic and full of communal tension while projecting the colonial state as the upholder of law and order; the Census; and missionary activities. Equally important were the tensions within both communities at the time. The context for Hindu revivalism was provided by the emergence of a vital mercantile culture in the early nineteenth century together with the rapid expansion of the railways and communication networks (posts and telegraphs); the emergence of the professions; the founding of public bodies; and the growth of the press and vernacular newspapers in the northern plains. Prominent members of the Arya Samaj, who owned many of the important publishing houses and newspapers published in UP in the early twentieth century, carried out a massive campaign against Muslims and Islam in print. The central role played by the rising Hindu middle class in towns such as Lucknow made religious categories politically salient in new ways in the colonial milieu. There was a marked increase in the religious rituals and activities of the Arya Samaj and the Hindu Mahasabha (Freitag 1989), together with a more aggressive Hinduism based on Vaishnav reforms and an attempt by many lower castes to move upwards in the caste hierarchy (Dalmia 1997). Gooptu has shown how increased population, economic dislocation, and absence of opportunities in the villages led to the migration of thousands of low-caste Hindus to a ghettoized existence in towns, resulting in their consolidation as defenders of Hinduism against Muslims. This new force, she suggests, provided the material required for organized Hindu communalism (Gooptu 1997). Thus, by the early twentieth century, being Hindu or Muslim became politically significant in ways quite different from the time when the nawabs of Oudh held power.

In the 1920s, militant Hindu assertion reached new heights, leading to communal clashes in the United Provinces. The 'rediscovery' of Hindu and Muslim religious values took place at the same time as the growth of political nationalism, leading to the strengthening of separate identities. Communalism was the 'other' of nationalism, its opposite and chief adversary (Pandey 1990). Consequently, by the 1930s, nationalism came to be viewed as secular and democratic, and was defined largely in opposition to a growing politics of communalism or the 'politics of religious communities', leading to tension and strife (Pandey 1990). At independence, the Congress party had senior leaders such as Purshottam Das Tandon, the Khare brothers, and later Kamlapathi Tripathi with a strong Hindu orientation. However, Nehru's leadership and the enshrinement in the constitution of secularism and the right to practice and propagate religion, helped establish peace. Hence, communalism in UP as experienced in the post-independence period is rooted in the late colonial period arising concurrently with nationalism. In short, the germs of communalism are found in the late colonial period, and resurfaced on a large scale in the late 1980s.

Consequently a significant feature of UP have been two tendencies visible after Partition in its society and polity: a secular one represented by Nehru and other leaders within the Congress party and outside. Socialist forces under leaders such as Rammanohar Lohia opposed communal ideas, both Hindu and Muslim. Left parties were also active in eastern UP and parts of western UP after independence, but declined later. Politically from the 1950s to the 1980s the Congress party was in power in UP and it was a phase of comparative peace and harmony, when it is argued a composite culture began to develop, punctuated at times by tension. However, the tendency towards communalism at the societal level remained dormant at the subterranean level where Hindu communal ideas mingled with strong and powerful socially conservative forces existing at the state level. It was the weakening and collapse of the Congress party in the 1980s and the formation of the BJP and its politics of communal mobilization that brought it to the fore in the early 1990s and now during more recent times. While such tendencies undoubtedly exist in other states particularly in the Hindi heartland, in UP they have been central to the functioning of its society and polity.

Uttar Pradesh as a location for examining the phenomena of communalism is also important today because new historical research on the erstwhile United Provinces has attempted to re-examine the manner in which Pakistan was created in the late colonial period. More particularly for our study, the role played in this project by Muslims living in the United Provinces. The best-known work has been that of Ayesha Jalal who describes Jinnah as the 'sole spokesperson' of the Indian Muslims and claims that Pakistan was not Jinnah's real demand but a 'bargaining counter' to acquire for the Muslims political equality with the numerically preponderant Hindus in an undivided postcolonial India (Jalal 1994). An assumption in Jalal's work is that this was a strategy pursued by Jinnah which he kept hidden even from his close colleagues or the public and led finally to Pakistan.

In contrast, a recent study by Venkat Dhulipala challenges these long-held assumptions. He argues that the idea of Pakistan was developed and debated in the public sphere and popular enthusiasm generated for its successful achievement in the United Provinces of Agra and Oudh; whose Muslims, he argues, played a critical role in its creation despite their awareness that they would not be part of Pakistan (Dhulipala 2015). He underlines that it was here that the idea of Pakistan found its earliest, most sustained, and overwhelming support much before it found support in the Muslim majority provinces from which it was created (Dhulipala 2015: 4). Most important, he holds that far from being vague ideas that accidentally became a nation-state, Pakistan was popularly imagined in UP as a sovereign Islamic state, a 'New Medina' as it was called by some of its proponents. It was not envisaged as a refuge for Indian Muslims, but as an Islamic utopia that would be the harbinger for renewal and rise of Islam in the modern world. It was to act as the powerful new leader and protector of the entire Islamic world and thus emerge as a worthy successor to the defunct Turkish Caliphate as the foremost Islamic power in the twentieth century (Dhulipala 2015).

Dhulipala shows how once the Muslim League introduced the Resolution for Pakistan at Lahore in 1940, it was talked about, debated, and fought over in the popular press, through books and pamphlets, in public meetings, and political conferences held in cities, towns, bazaars, and *qasbah*s (small towns) across India, but most particularly in the United Provinces (Dhulipala 2015: 17). The debates were both for and against the formation of an 'autonomous and sovereign' Muslim homeland that would leave a large section of the Muslims in the United Provinces outside it. Those in favour repeated the ideas of the Muslim League that Pakistan would possess adequate territory and natural resources, a hardworking, enterprising, and martial population, and adequate resources and immense potential for developing into a great power (Dhulipala 2015: 18). There was, Dhulipala alleges, collaboration between the elites in the League and sections of the Ulama in the United Provinces such as the Deobandi ulama led by Maulana Shabbir Ahmad Usmani that developed steadily after the Lahore Resolution which proved critical for creating Pakistan (Dhulipala 2015: 21). Based on the work of Francis Robinson, he points to the existence of an 'incipient' print capitalism involving the mass publication of the Quran and new methods of Muslim mass education through revamped madrassas and the rise of a new autonomous Muslim self that began to directly access the holy texts. This enabled Muslims to be part of politics and to read in the Urdu press the debates about Pakistan and be part of it. Paul Brass attributes the popularity of the idea of Pakistan in UP to the Ashraf Muslims quest for political power through symbol manipulation and myth creation while claiming to defend the rights of north Indian Muslims (Brass 1974). Dhulipala points to Robinson's work which argues that the acute sense of separate religio-political identity and a new sense of self-conscious community among the ordinary UP Muslims in the late nineteenth and early twentieth centuries provided the fundamental rationale and impetus to the Pakistan movement (Dhulipala 2015: 12).

The relevance of Dhulipala's work is that during our field study in western UP, there are statements by respondents or other villagers that Muslims 'should go to Pakistan' if they cannot live within the social values espoused by the majority Hindu community. The ruling BJP at the centre under Narendra Modi has whipped up the sentiment of Hindu nationalism against Pakistan through its 'surgical strikes' particularly in western UP where a substantial number of families of army men reside. Party members and MPs have questioned the patriotism of the Muslim community on many occasions implying that they support Pakistan.[1] Through such tactics the party hopes to gain the support of the Hindus in the 2017 assembly elections in UP. This shows that the much written about 'composite culture' described as developing during the Nehruvian period, particularly in the Hindi heartland, had stored beneath it unhappy memories of Partition riots which could be revived six decades after independence by the communal mobilization of the BJP, creating antagonism afresh between the Hindu and Muslim communities. This is evident today in the response to Love Jihad, the ban on beef, and cow vigilantism in UP particularly in the western districts. This makes our choice of UP significant as the site for understanding communalism in the country.

Situating UP in the 2000s

In contemporary Indian politics, UP is a key state where some of the most important sociopolitical movements that have introduced fundamental shifts in India's democracy have taken place, which are closely related to the resurgence of communal politics since the 1980s and once again in the 2000s. The state had experienced a strong backward class movement beginning in the mid-1960s, which sped up in the early 1990s. This led to the implementation of the Mandal Report granting reservations to the OBCs making them important in state politics. Besides this, the Hindutva movement and the RJBBM dispute led to serious communal riots in the late 1980s/early 1990s and Dalit assertion, a product of democratization, which since the 1980s has questioned the position of the upper castes who have supported the Hindutva movement. Each of these movements has also thrown up well-established political parties leading to heightened competition reflected in the electoral politics of the state.

---

[1] Recently BJP MP Parvesh Verma, while addressing a rally at Baghpat made derogatory statements against the Muslim community saying, 'Muslims have never voted for us and they never will … because the BJP is a patriotic party.' *India 90 Home News*, 'Why Every Terrorist is Muslim and why Muslims do not Vote for BJP: BJP MP Finds Connect,' Aadi Ikram Zaki Iqbal, 20 December 2016, downloaded on 23 December 2016.

After independence, at least three major phases of communal politics in UP can be identified that make it the most significant site for understanding communalism in India and which are analysed in our study. The Nehruvian period of comparative communal harmony from the early 1960s to the mid-1970s when Hindu–Muslim relations improved, Muslim artisanal and other business began to improve in UP, and the number of riots fell, providing hope that the communalism of the colonial and Partition period had been left behind. The late 1970s experienced the beginnings of communal tension, but it is the second phase from the 1980s onwards and the early 1990s that witnessed heightened communal tension and violent riots over the Babri Masjid dispute due to the formation of the right-wing Hindu nationalist party the BJP in 1980, and collapse of the idea of Nehruvian secularism. This period constituted a turning point in communal politics; the destruction of a place of worship shocked the Muslim community and the riots were reminiscent of those during Partition. In UP, Meerut and surrounding districts experienced communal conflict in 1987 when the locks of the Babri Masjid were opened by the Rajiv Gandhi government; the Rath Yatra in 1990 and the destruction of the Babri Masjid in December 1992 sparked off riots in Faizabad district that spread to all regions of the state and across the country.

During the second half of the 1990s following the destruction of the Babri Masjid, the decline of the BJP, and the weakening of caste and communal identity politics, communal disharmony in UP abated. It was argued that 'UP was not Gujarat'. It had two lower-caste parties—the Samajwadi Party (SP) and the Bahujan Samaj Party (BSP)—which had strong minority and lower-caste bases and had successfully 'contained' the BJP by defeating it in the 1993 assembly elections, channelling politics towards Mandalization and Dalitization, and challenging the position of the upper castes in the society and polity (Pai 1998). The 2000s constitute the third phase when, after a period of decline, the BJP under a new leadership decided to revive its organizational and social base, and create a Hindu vote bank through communal mobilization in UP, an important state with 80 seats in parliament for any party aiming to capture power at the centre. The BJP managed to do both, winning 75 seats in UP and a majority at the centre. It is on the third phase that our study, based on fieldwork in our selected regions of eastern and western UP, will concentrate.

At least two features of UP society and polity can be identified that help explain the persistence of communalism and communal riots after independence in the state and which have provided the fertile soil in which the construction of communalism and religion-based mobilization of the BJP has often succeeded. These are economic backwardness in the post-Independence period including during the period of globalization and the divisive politics of caste and communal identity.

The collapse of the single dominant party system of the Congress in UP in the late 1980s provided room for the rise of the politics of identity based on caste and communalism led by the BSP, SP, and the BJP. Identity politics led mass and electoral politics throughout the 1990s. While scholars have pointed to a weakening of identity politics by the late 1990s and the re-emergence of the agenda of development, the former has continued into the 2000s taking new forms. A new relationship has emerged between caste and development that has enabled mobilization along primordial lines to continue. Simultaneously in the 2000s, significant changes have taken place within the BJP, which are responsible for the resurgence of communalism in western and eastern UP. It experienced a generational change in 2009 when a new leadership led by Narendra Modi—a move carefully planned over a period of time with the support of the Sangh Parivar—replaced the older leaders/founders—Atal Behari Vajpayee and L. K. Advani. Among the younger generation leaders in the BJP, Modi was able to take control of the party due to his three consecutive victories in the Gujarat assembly elections and his close association with the RSS. He brought in supporters to UP who had worked with him in strengthening the BJP in Gujarat, the most important being Amit Shah, who was later appointed the president of the party. By centralizing power in his hands, Modi introduced substantial changes in the BJP's organization and leadership structure (Pai and Kumar 2015: 1).

Most important, Modi decided to redefine 'Hindutva'—conceived in the 1980s/90s as a sociocultural and religious ideology for political mobilization—by including the agenda of economic development to create a strong and stable nation, with greater inclusiveness through improving the lives of all castes and communities, not only Hindus. This was in keeping with the broadening of the social base of the BJP by the 2000s. In the 1990s, the party particularly in north India was identified with the Hindu upper castes/classes. Today it is far more plebian;

through social engineering, it has been able to gain the support of large sections of the OBCs and the Dalits. It does not mean that the BJP has abandoned or did not use its strategy of communal mobilization to create communal polarization, engineer riots, or secure the Hindu vote in 2014, but it was combined with a discourse of development which appealed to a larger section of the electorate.

The revival and redefinition of 'Hindutva' enabled Modi to take firm control of the BJP with the help of the RSS, revamp the organization, and mount a well-planned, highly competitive, and aggressive campaign for the 2014 elections. In UP, the party under Modi's leadership used a two-pronged campaign ideology: promises of rapid development based on the Gujarat model and communal strategies used to create a broad Hindu vote bank encompassing the upper castes, the backwards, and the Dalits. Hence, an ideological combination of social conservatism, and promises of rapid development for all together with a social base among the backwards, has made Hindutva more appealing and acceptable to a larger number of Hindus belonging to all socio-economic levels, that is, a 'Maha Hindu' identity across UP (Narayan 2014: 29). It is the upwardly mobile, new middle classes, the new rich, the better-off lower castes, anxious to obtain recognition, who are the most prone to fall prey to religious and ethnic intolerance. Hansen has termed it as 'conservative populism' which has attracted the better off within every stratum (Hansen 1999.). A victory based on this kind of communal mobilization, the BJP feels, will allow it to take further its cultural project of making India Hindu.

Persisting economic underdevelopment, and a high level of inequalities within the population even in areas such as the comparatively better-off western districts, underlies much of the communal mobilization tension and riots in UP. Despite a long period of political stability under Congress rule in the immediate post-independence period, economic development in UP was very slow, industrial investment took place only in pockets, implementation of land reform was poor, and the state fell much behind many large states such as Maharashtra. This particularly affected the Dalits and the Muslims who remained the poorer and disadvantaged sections in the state. As Jean Dreze has pointed out, UP carries the 'burden of inertia' (Dreze and Gazdar 1996). Due to the Green Revolution and some progress in industry, for the first time in the 1980s, there was structural change away from agriculture to industry and poverty levels fell, particularly in the poorer districts of eastern UP. However, the 1990s were a period of de-stabilizing change due to the collapse of single-party dominance resulting in hung assemblies, endemic political instability, and poor governance leading to high fiscal deficits putting the state in a 'debt trap' (Pai 2007).

The state of the economy in UP during the 2000s has also impacted communal politics giving it a different dimension. While the country has experienced globalization since 1991 bringing in much development, UP remains mired in caste and communal politics. As a result, while studies do point to some improvement in agriculture and non-farm employment, in Human Development UP remains behind the better-developed states of Maharashtra, Gujarat, and Tamil Nadu that have made better use of the opportunities provided by globalization (Singh and Mehrotra 2014). With rising levels of political consciousness, this has created much frustration and unhappiness within the emerging educated middle- and lower-middle class communities (Jeffrey 2010) which the BJP harnessed to gain votes in the 2014 elections. Studies point to problems in the sugar industry in recent years that have affected farmers in the western districts, especially Muzaffarnagar, often called the 'sugar bowl', as they have not been paid by industry with cane crushing being slow and prices low (Damodaran and Singh 2007: 3953). Traditional industries such as the brassware, leather, and lock industry are also not performing as well as in the past. In eastern UP the traditional weaving and carpet making industry and other smaller crafts and forms of employment are also in decline, creating problems (Wood 2014). The impact of these changes on the Hindu and Muslim communities underlie much of the unhappiness which makes them prone to jealousy, competition, and open to communal mobilization against each other.

In western UP, the Jats and the Muslims—the two groups which clashed violently in the riots in 2013—have historically lived side-by-side in harmony. While mobilization during the Babri Masjid dispute in the early 1990s created fault lines, it is the deepening of the agrarian crisis and resulting unhappiness among the Jats and simultaneously a strong perception of improvement in the condition of sections of the Muslim community that underlies their conflict (Pai 2013b). In eastern UP the rise of political consciousness among the Pasmanda (backward) Muslims, a steep decline of their handloom industry, the lack of

alternative employment together with criminalization of politics leading to the rise of dons in the Hindu and Muslim community makes
them prone to the mobilization of the HYV of Mahant Adityanath.
Thus, in the 2000s, the political economy of communalism emerged
in a substantial manner and became more important than in the 1980s
and 90s. These characteristics of UP politics will provide the larger
context within which the specific features of communalism in the state
and their linkages with economic underdevelopment and patterns of
political mobilization and electoral politics in the state can be studied.

At the societal level, an important development which has contributed to the dominance of the BJP in the 2000s is the change in the
manner in which religious communities, particularly those belonging
to the minority group, are identified. We are witnessing the emergence
of distinct religious communities as unified 'totalities in politics and
as undifferentiated units of development policies and discourse' that
are sought to be culturally essentialized and frozen in time and space
(Sheth 2009: 76). This has produced a 'severe breach in the secularizing
process of democracy' (Sheth 2009: 71). Sheth has argued that it was
hoped that the victory of the Congress party in 2004 would mend the
breach in the process of political secularization created by communal
politics of the 1990s (Sheth 2009: 75). However, the Congress leadership post-2004 shifted the focus of social policies from backwardness
and reservation—which it had championed earlier—to communality
of groups in which religious minorities were viewed as culturally unified political entities that competed with each other rather than citizens
organized around secular interests or groups sharing common social,
economic, or educational deprivation (Sheth 2009). At the heart of this
shift was the Sachar Committee Report, which introduced new debates
and policies and special schemes for minority community. This shift
Sheth argues had long-term negative implications on the secularization
process as it made the minority community into one undifferentiated
total whole. Another difference between the early 1990s and the current phase of communalism is increasing Muslim political ambitious-
ness and a new autonomous politics witnessed in the formation of new
Muslim parties in UP. This brought back the control of the religious
leaders of the community and undermined the backward groups and
suppressed their demands and movement. This new form of discourse
has provided space for the contemporary phase of the politics of

communalism by the BJP–RSS and has resulted in a battle between majoritarian and minoritarian communalism.

Closely related is the fact that in contrast to the 2000s, secular forces were much stronger in the country during the late 1980s and 1990s, intellectuals and observers wrote against the movements led by the Hindutva forces and the destruction of the Babri Masjid in December 1992. There was space for such criticism and opposition. Much of the debate on secularism was written in the late 1980s and 1990s. Today, secular intellectuals are quiet; they have little support. The decline of the secular forces underlie the communal riots in various parts of UP during the 2000s and following the victory of the BJP in 2014 has encouraged the right-wing fringe organizations such as the VHP and Bajrang Dal to do moral policing, hold Hindu *sammelans* (summits), and make allegations of 'Love Jihad', conversions by the Muslim community, etc. Today as a result, the Hindutva forces are attempting to create divides between Hindus and Muslims reducing the latter to second-class citizens, but are also saffronizing the institutions of the state. Thus, we are confronting a more aggressive RSS, which the BJP finds difficult to control at times. While the earlier phase of the Ram Mandir was a phase of building of the BJP and its sociopolitical support base, the present seems to be one of consolidation. In this game UP will occupy centre stage.

Framing the Problem

In the existing social science literature, communalism and communal conflicts in India have been studied using four overarching, broad theoretical frameworks: essentialism, instrumentalism, constructivism, and institutionalism. The first two were the earliest frameworks deployed to understand communal violence. Essentialism argues that present-day communal violence can be traced back to primordial, historical memories and older animosities between two groups (Geetz 1973). The main proposition of instrumentalism is that elite groups strategically manipulate communal identities to obtain power creating political, economic, and cultural differences and conflict (Brass 1974). Essentialism is useful in explaining the reoccurrence of communal riots in UP and is found as an underlying idea in many studies. The same is true of instrumentalism as most scholars would agree that riots are a result of elite mobilization to create divides among communities. However, a purely instrumental conception of communalism cannot explain why communal identities are mobilized by leaders. The institutionalists posit a close relationship between communal conflict or its absence and the nature of political institutions including the system of representation. Simple transfer of the Westminster system from Britain, a small and homogenous country, to highly diversified countries such as India can create an unhappy and antagonistic minority community leading to conflict. However, a problem with these frameworks is that they cannot explain that if identities are so deep-seated why violence takes place at certain points of time and not others. In addition, why it happens in some regions/cities and not in others within a country or, even in districts within a province in which the two conflicting groups are found.

In this study it is the framework of constructivism that will be deployed to understand this phenomenon in UP. It is selected, as it is multidisciplinary, drawing on history, politics, social anthropology, and even psychology, making it possible to deploy it in various ways to understand a multifaceted phenomenon. This perspective is seen in the work of Eric Hobsbawm (1983) and Benedict Anderson (1983) who argue that identities that seem well established were constructed and reconstructed in recent times. In postcolonial societies such as India, constructivists argue that cleavages between the Hindu and Muslim were a creation of the colonial power, which became master narratives. This was not the truth, but was constructed and promoted as such by the British partly because it suited them and also because they believed the natives could not form a modern nation (Brass 1997; Hansen 1999; Pandey 1990). In addition, it is agreed that in developing societies it is the process of modernization that promotes the construction of new identities and conflicts over them. Alexis de Tocqueville points out that those pre-modern societies undergo a profound democratic revolution in which the traditional and divine legitimization of power and naturalness of hierarchy is replaced by the new revolutionary creed of democracy. This moment is one of great difficulty as the old has been removed and the new has yet to establish itself fully, when a society dominated by multiple relations of inequality adopts a democratic system of government. He suggests that it produces a transitional society 'without foundations', that is, without stable legitimacy and certainties creating for a time a period of confusion and anxiety. A new form of secular power emerges that no one understands and in which dissolution of old markers of certainty takes place. The process of modernity plays a significant role here; unequal relations and old ideas of social antagonism and oppression remain. It is in this space that new identities of 'we' and an antagonistic 'they' are created, and it is around these new processes of identification and representation that struggles take place. It is through this process that concepts such as nation or people are forged which can cause conflicts.

In the post-independence period, the framework of constructivism has been used by many scholars though in different ways. A study, which has examined the Hindu nationalist movement in detail, argues that the construction of communalism is the result of systematic, painstaking, organizational work over time and imaginative sociopolitical strategies (Jaffrelot 1996). In a similar vein, another study analysing the electoral incentives for Hindu–Muslim violence argues that ethnic riots are not a spontaneous upsurge of anger. They are planned by politicians 'for a clear electoral purpose ... in order to build a winning coalition' and also where and when ethnic violence against minorities will occur and whether the state will choose to stop it (Wilkinson 2004). In contrast, analysing violence in pairs of cities—where riots takes place and where riots do not take place—Ashutosh Varshney points to a link between the structure of civic life in a city and the occurrence of communal riots. Local organs of the state, such as the police, function better where there is associational life in cities and quotidian in villages, while a multi-ethnic society with few interconnections across ethnic boundaries is very vulnerable to ethnic disorder and violence (Varshney 2013).

Writing on UP, Paul Brass has shown how the perspective of constructivism is useful in understanding identity formation and helps account for the dispersion of rioting in India in time and space and its concentration in particular sites (Brass 2003). Arguing that riots are a form of 'collective action', Brass bases his work on theories of social movement and collective action drawing on Tilly, Tarrow, and others. Describing 'riot production' in a single town, Aligarh, where riots have persisted, he holds that it is not just the historical background of Hindu–Muslim violence in the town or the circumstances surrounding the riot, rather the decisive factor is the often large-scale political movements and 'action' that takes place before the precipitating incidents and immediately after—action that is often planned and organized and that fills the intermediate space and time between past history and immediate circumstance (Brass 2003: 11). Similarly, in a later work focusing on Meerut, Brass has developed a framework of 'institutionalized riot system' that, he argues, creates riots at intervals making them endemic in the city from 1961 onwards (Brass 2006). In both works, Brass points to issues of persistence, differential incident/timing, classification/meaning, and power which are of relevance in understanding communal riots in UP today. These are questions that raise issues of causality, function, and discourse requiring diverse approaches that constructivism enables us to address.

Finally, while constructivism provides a framework to the study of communalism, its impact and aftermath also needs to be understood. When communal riots are a recurrent phenomenon as in UP what is their impact on Hindu–Muslim relations both immediately and in the long run are seminal questions. Writing on the impact of the Gujarat riots 2002 not only in that state but elsewhere, Dipankar Gupta argues that it is necessary to understand the 'internalization of strained conditions under which communities learn to live with each other in a "new normal"' (D. Gupta 2011: 4–5). As in the past, this new normal is mindful too, he points out, of distances, differences, and tensions between groups, but bears the signs of fresh historical circumstances. Social relations that have been recently disrupted by political philippics may exhibit an overt sense of peace but everybody is careful about keeping it that way. He holds that the much talked about coexistence between Hindus and Muslims is really an outcome of 'antagonistic tolerance' rather than warm feelings of brotherhood. Violence is under the surface and socialization is all about how to live with this presence of violence. At the end of the day, a new normal emerges and with it a new negotiated boundary between communities that may differ in significant ways from the earlier one that has already been disrupted (D. Gupta 2011). Hence, the history of human relations, Gupta argues, is a movement from one tense negotiated contract to another, from one contested normal to the next. The violence is not sudden or spontaneous but planned because a group of social actors see a clear interest based on caste, community, class, religion, or primordial honour (D. Gupta 2011). They see an immediate political advantage to upset the existing normal and set a new normalcy under a fresh set of terms conditions and negotiating spaces, which is greatly to their advantage. Multiple religious identities are able to coexist with each other as long as the 'power asymmetries' between them are so vast that there is no room for contest, religious boundaries cordon off people of different faiths. Political mobilization is what makes it possible to break these and create a new set of relations (D. Gupta 2011: 7).

Institutionalized 'Everyday' Communalism in UP in the 2000s

In our study we use a model of 'institutionalized everyday communalism' that takes forward the institutionalized riot system (IRS) developed by Paul Brass in his study of communal riots in Meerut city in UP. He argues that in this system riots are not spontaneous, but involve calculated and 'learned forms of collective action' by individuals such as recruitment of participants, rumours and messages, and various provocative acts. Such a system becomes institutionalized due to frequent rehearsals and can be activated when needed particularly during elections, or remain dormant for some time. Complicity of the police and state administration is also an important component (Brass 2006: 65–6). In this model changes in society, which make people vulnerable to provocative acts, is not given importance.

While our model shares some features of the IRS, a central differentiating element is the deliberate, planned, long-term, and continuous 'everyday' grass roots communal mobilization by local leaders belonging to the area. These leaders are recruited for the purpose, using small, mundane but provocative local incidents to gradually create animosity and social jealousies between Hindus and Muslims who have lived together for a long time. Institutionalized everyday communalism has roots in 'communal commonsense' which aims to create a permanent anti-Muslim societal prejudice and make it acceptable in the popular discourse. A related key component is that this is possible in societies undergoing rapid and at times destabilizing social change such as an agrarian crisis, high levels of unemployment, shift to a post-identity or post-globalization stage leaving its members, particularly the younger generation, frustrated, open, and vulnerable to communal mobilization.

Our model of everyday communalism has a structure, albeit loosely held together and not always organized in exactly the same manner in different regions such as eastern and western UP. It consists of three concentric circles or layers. The innermost consists of the core BJP leadership providing leadership in terms of ideology, strategy, and methods of grass roots mobilization for a region such as western or eastern UP. This is required, as the BJP believes that each region has its distinct politics, culture, and economy that is different and needs to be paid attention to accordingly. The second circle is made up of local leaders recruited for the purpose of institutionalizing communal tension in inter-community relationships over a period of time. They belong to the area and are familiar with the people and their needs and interests. Good examples are the members of the HYV in eastern UP under Mahant Adityanath, and Jat leaders in western UP such as Umesh Malik and Sanjeev Baliyan recruited to gain support of the Jat community. In both cases, they are local MPs or MLAs and in charge of the ground-level cadres who assist them by providing them information and organizing meetings, etc. Apart from them, this level everywhere also has political and sociocultural organizations such as the RSS, VHP, and Bajrang Dal apart from a host of other local organizations that come up particularly during elections or periods of intense mobilization. It is at this level that the work of institutionalizing everyday communalism is carried out through agitations for cow protection, Love Jihad, beef politics, *ghar vapasi*, and anti-conversion and random other agitations against people, art, events, etc. This group often trains a larger fuzzier group, often the educated, unemployed youth in backward states such as UP who are treated as a reservoir of support during agitations and lie dormant during lean times. The outer most, third circle of this model consists of the social media such as Twitter, which provide support to the strategy of everyday communalism through constant propaganda and messages targeted at the host population of the region. A recent book shows in detail—what is well known—that the BJP has an elaborate and social media cell for this purpose, which is particularly active during elections (Chaturvedi 2016).

Some of the elements that distinguish our model from the IRS are discussed as follows:

Location

The locations at which riots take place have undergone a marked change in the contemporary period. UP has a number of towns where riots have occurred very often such as Moradabad, Saharanpur, Meerut, Aligarh, Kanpur, Varanasi, and Lucknow, and so forth, where the construction of communalism has taken place in specific contexts built over a long period of time. In the 1960s and 70s communal riots arose mainly out of economic competition and attempts by Hindus to take over industry owned by Muslims and therefore occurred more frequently in places where Muslims were seen to have improved their local business and economic conditions than in places where they were in a poor condition (Khalidi 1995: 23). Much literature shows that they typically took place in towns in which they prospered in artisanal industries such as brassware, locks, carpets, bangles, handlooms, silk weaving, and wood working, and so forth (Chakravarti 1993; Rajgopal 1987; Saberwal and Hasan 1984; Siraj 1993).

In contrast, in the 2000s riots have spread into newer areas in western and eastern UP which did not experience large-scale and violent riots earlier. They are the product of conscious selection, planned and sustained, quiet, communal mobilization by the BJP–RSS. None of our selected districts of Muzaffarnagar, Shamli, Mau, and Gorakhpur experienced a full-scale communal riot lasting a number of days until the 2000s; not even during the RJBBM movement, with the exception of a riot in Muzaffarnagar in 1988. Hence, the construction of communalism here is recent, is taking place in new social and economic contexts, and is the handiwork of a new generation leadership within the BJP. Our fieldwork shows that communal mobilization at the grass roots by young, local leaders selected by the BJP–RSS began first in eastern UP in the late 1990s but more actively after the formation of the HYV by Yogi Adityanath in 2002 particularly in the stretch from Gorakhpur to Bahraich. In western UP, mobilization began in 2004 when the NDA lost the election and more particularly in 2009 when the party came under the control of Narendra Modi and Amit Shah. The attempt in both regions was to build the base of the party and gain the support of the Hindu community. Communalism in these districts exhibit features different from the classic districts where communal riots have become endemic, as well as from the riots during the RJBB period of the early 1990s, which are briefly described subsequently.

Spatial Spread

Earlier riots were confined largely to towns and cities. In the 2000s in western UP, communal riots have spread for the first time on a large scale into rural areas, with villages constituting the epicentre breaking down relations between Hindus and Muslims who have lived side-by-side for a long time. In western UP this seems to have been possible due to 'r-urbanization', that is, spread of better facilities and communication into the rural areas, resulting in a close nexus between towns and villages, including for employment or business. In eastern UP the small towns are rapidly expanding with increasing population and demographic changes with little to offer in terms of facilities and employment. Such towns and villages provide a fertile ground for the construction of everyday communalism, which over time can create a conflagration such as the Mau, Gorakhpur, or Muzaffarnagar riots.

Change in Form

The form of construction of communalism and thereby of communal riots has undergone a marked change in UP in recent years. What we are witnessing is a 'new refinement' of the model of Hindutva used in the Gujarat riots of 2002 (Deshpande 2015). Rather than large-scale, statewide, mobilization as in the early 1990s around the RJBBM issue, what is attempted is a series of low-key, restrained, and carefully calibrated communal incidents to avoid large-scale riots. Through them, there is a constant reproduction of a string of 'communal moments' suitable to create divides and for parties to mobilize votes and win elections (Narayan 2014: 30). The aim is to install a 'normalized' anti-Muslim prejudice and establish a far more durable system of normalized oppression where Muslims are compelled to become permanent participants in their own subordination; the key element being the imposition of conditionalities limiting the extent and quality of their citizenship (Deshpande 2015). These small incidents were responsible for making UP a 'tinder box' and eventually sparked off major riots in eastern and western UP. The 'new' form of low-key mobilization has continued afterwards in UP and elsewhere in the country—despite the BJP gaining a majority at the centre—through strategies such as 'Love Jihad', conversions, attacks on Christian churches, the beef ban, the alleged exodus of Hindus from Kairana and cow vigilantism, which has kept the communal pot boiling.

The aim is clearly political and cultural—to create a Hindu nation in which the Muslims would have to confirm to the majority culture, values, and ideas; in short, a majoritarian democracy based on religion.

Subaltern Component

Everyday communalism in the 2000s is based on an ideology of 'non-Brahminical Hindutva' as it has a subaltern component in the ranks of the perpetrators and supporters. While in the 1980s and 90s the support base of the BJP was the upper castes, today the attempt is to co-opt the marginalized and vulnerable. In the 1990s for the Dalits and Backwards the Hindu upper castes were the 'other' to be challenged, today the attempt is to Hinduize the former and bring them closer to the latter and render the Muslim the alien for all sections of a united Hindu community. The non-Yadav and non-Jatav sections are targeted, as they are not attracted to the SP and the BSP. In western UP media reports show that a ninth of all communal incidents since May 2014 were Dalit–Muslim confrontations in villages (*The Indian Express* 2014). Similarly, as our study will show, during the Mau riots Dalits clashed with the Muslims in large numbers.

Cultural Aspirations and Economic Anxieties

Rather than identity which was important in defining social relations earlier, today social jealousies, cultural aspirations, and economic anxieties are the driving forces behind the construction of everyday communalism. This is particularly true among the lower caste/class younger generation of both the Hindu and Muslim communities.

Everyday Communalism and Electoral Politics

The institutionalization of everyday communalism and electoral politics are closely related; the former is a longer-term process and cultural goal while the latter is more immediate and provides the power to take cultural goals forward. Two stages are evident in the communal mobilization in eastern and particularly western UP: an initial stage of sustained, everyday grass roots mobilization over a period of time, which eventually is used to create a communal electoral campaign during an election, which the party hopes to win.

The 'New Normal'

Our model of IEC indicates that once the riots are over in both eastern and western UP, a new normal[2] emerges in the relationship between the Hindus and the Muslims as they return to their daily lives. A return to the older relationships is not possible and each time there is a small clash, relationships are recast and a new normal emerges which is more suspicious, distant, and in which old and painful memories remain. Often older economic relationships are re-established out of necessity; for example, Muslims have returned to work on the fields of the Jats in western UP and artisans to the looms owned by Hindu businessmen in eastern UP, but social intercourse remains minimal. This new normal is visible in our selected villages and towns in the social relationships between the majority and minority community.

Selected Regions in UP

The two regions of eastern and western UP that have been selected for analysis of communal disturbances in the 2000s reveals that these are the regions where the phenomenon of everyday communalism at the grass roots has, over time, led to major communal riots. The districts selected are Mau and Gorakhpur districts in eastern UP in 2005 and 2007, and Muzaffarnagar and Shamli districts in 2013 in western UP. Within these districts, villages and towns where the riots were severe have been selected for a detailed study based on field work.

While a major reason underlying communal tension and riots in UP since the late 1980s and its resurgence in the 2000s, has been the construction of the ideology of Hindutva and based on it religious mobilization by the BJP, there are major differences in the history, social composition, economy, and politics of the two selected regions. This will provide an opportunity to examine the contrasting context, methods, and strategies through which communalism has taken root and Hindu–Muslim relations are constructed and reconstructed over

---

[2] This term is borrowed from Dipankar Gupta's study (2011) of the Gujarat riots where he uses it to describe how relationships between communities are constructed and reconstructed due to communal tension and riots and how both sides attempt to return to their old relationships, which is no longer possible. Hence, a new normal emerges each time, which is different.

time. Two important differences are the much lower number of communal riots in eastern UP since independence and second, the eastern
region is much poorer in contrast to western UP. What is common
to both regions is the attempt to establish a normalized and controlled anti-Muslim prejudice as the basic platform of contemporary
'Hindutva'.

In both the eastern and western districts the rebuilding of the Ram
Mandir after the demolition of the Babri Masjid was a sensitive issue
in the 1980s and early 1990s. From time to time, this has been evoked
by the BJP during communal mobilization leading to riots in many
places such as Ayodhya, Colonelganj, Gorakhpur, Mau, Azamgarh,
and Varanasi, and so forth. However, communalism has exhibited new
features in eastern UP in the 2000s. Most important being the creation
of an independent power centre of Hindutva mobilization—outside
the control of the BJP leadership and RSS—by the aggressive BJP MP
of the Gorakhpur constituency, Yogi Adityanath and the HYV, a youth
militia founded by him. The Yogi has been inciting communal polarization, attempting to institutionalize everyday communalism in the
stretch from Bahraich to Gorakhpur by raising issues such as increase
in madrassas, Love Jihad, and the use of loudspeakers during prayers
by either community. Second, is the political economy of the region
which underlies communal tension; most of the Muslims are artisans
or handloom weavers, an industry that is in decline throwing many of
them out of work. At the same time, the Muslims of the area though
poor, are politically conscious and active due to the strong Pasmanda
of movement of backward sections of the community that has swept
the region. Apart from this, communalism here is linked with the mafia
associated with political parties; within the Muslim community, it is
alleged, Muktar Ansari and his supporters have played a leading role
in riots.

In western UP the reasons for the resurgence of communalism in
the 2000s lie in the changed social and material relations between the
Hindus, particularly the Jats who constitute an important landowning
caste, and the Muslims who form a numerically strong community in
the region. Historically, the two communities had good social relations
and were part of the political alliance created by Charan Singh in the
1960s through a backward-class movement and prosperity in the wake
of the Green Revolution. The deepening agrarian crisis, which has

affected the region since the late 1980s, has made the once-prosperous Jats unhappy and aggressive, evident in their demand for reservation. Simultaneously, the rise of a small entrepreneurial section within the Muslim community—who traditionally did not own land—that has taken to business in some of our sample villages has created the perception that they have prospered, creating strong social jealousies. This has led to marked deterioration of relations between the Jats and the Muslims, a rift which began in the Babri Masjid period when they found themselves in opposing parties. This changed political economy of the region has provided fertile ground for the communal mobilization of the BJP–RSS cadres and local leaders in the towns and villages of the region since the early 2000s, most particularly after Narendra Modi became the leader of the party in 2009 culminating in the 2013 Muzaffarnagar riots.

In the western region, apart from interviews of community leaders in Muzaffarnagar town, five villages were selected for detailed fieldwork. The selected villages fall into two groups: three Jat-dominated villages—Lisadh, Kutba, and Fugana—where a large number of Muslims were either killed or they fled to refugee camps; second two Muslim-dominated villages—Loi and Khampur—to which Muslims fled from Fugana and other villages. This method provided us both the Jat and the Muslim perspective on the riots. In eastern UP, Mau and Gorakhpur towns were selected and important and influential leaders from both communities were interviewed, from the central and semi-urban areas of these towns where severe rioting took place. Unlike in western UP, here riots did not spread extensively into the countryside. While structured interviews and group discussions were carried out in both regions, equally useful were the narratives provided by the respondents on the reasons, both immediate and longer term, underlying the riots, events, and the role of communities in them.

Thus, the attempt is to examine two variants of communalism and understand the manifestations of Hindu nationalists in the 2000s within an 'anthropology of the political field' (Hansen 1999: 13) in eastern and western UP. This will provide an in-depth understanding of the construction of communalism, the nature of communal discourse in the specific context of UP, and a better understanding of the communal disturbances in the 2000s arising from socio-economic and political change, globalization, and emergence of an aspirational middle class within both communities. Such a study would also contribute to a better understanding of communalism in the all-India context and its impact on the functioning of our democratic system.

Organization of the Study

The rest of the volume, after a background of the post-independence period provided in Chapter 1, is divided into two parts each of which has two chapters. The first part analyses the specificities of everyday communalism and riots in eastern UP, while the second does the same for western UP in the 2000s. In each part, one chapter explores the longer-term reasons underlying the resurgence of communalism and its specific features, while the other describes the actual riots and their impact. As already discussed, the attempt is to understand the phenomenon of everyday communalism leading to riots in two differing contexts in UP and their meaning for democratic politics in this key state.

The first chapter provides a historical narrative of Hindu–Muslim relations in UP from independence till the period of the RJBBM riots in the early 1990s. While there are historical narratives by scholars on the rise of communalism in the erstwhile United Provinces, not enough attention has been paid to the post-independence period. Our analysis reveals that the decade of the 1950s witnessed the gradual emergence of a composite culture and was a period of relative peace possible due to the adoption of a secular and democratic constitution that promised protection to minorities and the leadership provided by Nehru and other nationalist leaders. The Muslim community largely supported the Congress viewing it as a secular party, which would protect their interests in post-independent India, though they did experiment with political organizations of their own such as the Muslim Mushawarat. The period also witnessed some improvement in the economic condition of sections of the Muslim community in UP. However, beginning in the mid-1960s, communal forces long kept under check by Nehru's leadership revived causing serious stress to India's secular fabric. One of the reasons was the formation of the right-wing party the Bharatiya Jan Sangh in UP, the precursor of the BJP, which created antagonism. The brief period of inter-religious peace proved to be short, the promise of increasing communal harmony and secularization of the society and the polity does not seem to have materialized. There began a trajectory of estrangement of the Muslim community from the mainstream, a feeling of being deprived and a sense of insecurity due to the re-appearance of communal tension and riots which reached a peak by the early 1990s due to the destruction of the Babri Masjid.

Moving to the first part of the volume, in Chapter 2 our narrative travels to eastern UP where the beginnings of the phenomenon of everyday communalism can be traced to the late 1990s/early 2000s. Two developments are responsible for the renewed incidents of com-munal violence in the 2000s in eastern UP. These are the emergence of new patterns of communal mobilization by the BJP–RSS and the HYV which has affected Hindu–Muslim relations in the region; and signifi-cant changes in the economy of the region particularly in towns such as Mau leading to confrontation between the two communities. Here the confrontation has been between Yadavs/OBCs and Muslims in some areas and between Dalits and Muslims in others. At least four signifi-cant, political strands underlie the communal tension and riots in the region. First, there has been a shift from class-based mobilization by left and socialist parties to identity politics, and to the criminalization and rise of both Hindu and Muslim mafia dons in the Mau–Azamgarh area. Then, the emergence of the Pasmanda (backward Muslim) move-ment, leading to a rise in political consciousness, fragmented Muslim identity, and the rise of an autonomous Muslim politics in the region; and changes due to globalization in the weaving industry in the Mau region that have affected the Muslim Ansari community resulting in confrontation between them and Hindu traders. Most importantly, these provided a fertile ground for an aggressive everyday communal mobilization by an independent power centre under Yogi Adityanath who is also trying to create a more broad and inclusive Hindu identity by bringing Dalits and backwards into the saffron fold and pitching them against the Muslims. Since the riots in 2007 in Gorakhpur, there are no big riots but low-key simmering communal tension and small, but violent incidents has been a fairly constant feature of this region especially prior to elections.

Against this exploration of changing politics in eastern UP, Chapter 3 is based on fieldwork in the towns of Mau and Gorakhpur and pro-vides a rich description of everyday communalism and the communal riots in 2005 and 2007, respectively. In Mau, incidents of everyday communalism take a sociocultural form. It is well known that the Bharat Milap ceremony during the Ram Leela, which takes place in a part of the city close to a Masjid, has often led to communal incidents. However, our discussions with local leaders and respondents show that the actual reasons lie in the undercurrent of tensions. These tensions arise out of the desire to protect religio-cultural practices, economic distress due to the decline of the weaving industry, heightened political consciousness and the role of the mafia within both the Hindu and Muslim community, which the BJP was able to exploit and engineer the riots in 2005. Our field discussions revealed that during the riots, parts of the town where the minority community resides and the shops and businesses owned by them were targeted and destroyed. In Gorakhpur, in contrast, communalism has a more distinctly political colour being the result mainly of the presence of the Gorakhpur Math and sustained religion-based mobilization by Yogi Adityanath and his HYV responsible for creating communal polarization, tension, and incidents which culminated in the 2007 riots. A characteristic of communalism in both towns is the attempt to saffronize the Dalits taking them away from the BSP.

The second part of the volume focuses on the attempts to institutionalize everyday communalism and riots in western UP, the more developed part of the state. The first chapter, Chapter 4, analyses the reasons underlying revival of communalism—after a period of comparative peace in the 1990s—in western UP, culminating in one of the largest and extremely violent riots in recent decades in UP in Muzaffarnagar and surrounding districts in 2013. It argues that two developments—both operating over a period of time—played a key role. The first was the organized and sustained construction of everyday communalism by the BJP–RSS in the region at the grass roots from the early 2000s onwards, followed by the long and divisive electoral campaign for the 2014 national elections under the leadership of Narendra Modi. The second was the breakdown of the earlier, relatively harmonious, socio-economic relationship between Hindus—primarily Jats—and Muslims in western UP, which made them highly prone to communal tension and riots. The agrarian crisis, which began in the late 1980s and deepened in the 2000s making agriculture no longer profitable made the Jats unhappy and aggressive. The emergence of a small entrepreneurial class particularly among the Muslims who traditionally did not hold land and took to petty business, created the perception particularly among the younger Jats, that they had become prosperous creating social jealousies and making them vulnerable to the communal mobilization of the BJP. These shifts allowed the BJP through well-organized, planned, and sustained mobilization to deepen the social and political divide between the Jats and Muslims, leading to communal tension and the terrible Muzaffarnagar riots. While the former constitutes the political and aggressively visible form, the latter constitutes the underlying political economy aspect.

Against this backdrop, Chapter 5, based on extensive fieldwork in the selected districts of Muzaffarnagar and Shamli and towns and villages within them in western UP, describes the communal incidents from 2011 onwards and the riots in September 2013. The focus is on the immediate provocative incidents and the violence between the two major communities involved: the Jats and the Muslims. Contrasting narratives about the riots emerged from discussions with community leaders in Muzaffarnagar town and the Jat dominated and Muslim majority villages in our sample that formed the epicentre of the riots, which indicate the high level of aggression and antagonism leading to a pogrom in some of the villages. Our fieldwork narrative also revealed the deeply implicating role of political parties during the riots. The local leaders and cadres of the BJP were aware of and in some cases involved in the rioting, while the leaders of the SP remained largely silent hoping to gain the support of the Muslims of the region in the approaching 2014 elections. As the support base and cadre of the BSP straddles both the Hindu—that is, Dalit—and Muslim communities, local leaders found it difficult to deal with the rioters. Many respondents narrated in detail the complicity on the part of the ruling party the SP, and the bias and negligence of the police and local administration to check the communal incidents or protect villagers during the riots in September 2013. Our visit revealed the poor quality of the camps set up for Muslims who fled from their native villages. Collectively, these elements indicate the successful creation in our sample villages, of a system of institutionalized everyday communalism, which is visible even two years after the riots.

Based on the ideas and framework discussed earlier, our study hopes to address some significant larger questions regarding communalism and its impact on our democratic structure not only in UP, but in the country. Has the multiple, mobilizational politics of identity in UP driven by political parties and their agendas created a specific variant of communalism different from other states? Why has UP become a communal cauldron at this particular juncture? Is it the decline of secular formations such as political parties and institutions that have provided space to the BJP–RSS? Why does the Hindu and Muslim middle and lower middle class respond to the provocation by the BJP–RSS both in terms of voting and creation of communal confrontation at the societal level such as 'Love Jihad' and stories of forced conversions? Are economic changes in UP including the changes induced by globalization, the underlying factors responsible for communal strife in the state? These are important questions as the present communal conflict in UP has the potential to change the democratic system based on values of equality and fraternity to one of majoritarianism.

Communal Politics in Uttar Pradesh from Independence to the 1990s

1

A Background

While much has been written on communal politics and Hindu–Muslim relations in the colonial period in the United Provinces and the impact of Partition, not much attention has been devoted to the changes that took place in the first four decades after independence. Scholars are now trying to understand the reasons underlying the resurgence of major riots in post-independence India only after the emergence of the RJBBM dispute, the destruction of the Masjid in 1992, and the major riots in many parts of the country that followed. The resurgence of communalism in the 2000s has been another factor. The immediate decades after Independence were an important formative period in the life of the new nation emerging from colonialism, which was particularly true of the state of Uttar Pradesh (UP). Uttar Pradesh along with a few other states in the country was profoundly affected by Partition and the riots that followed, and this had an impact on Hindu–Muslim relations in the state. It is well known that Muslim separatism and the Pakistan movement developed roots in north India particularly in UP, from where it spread to the Muslim majority provinces of Bengal, Punjab, Sindh, and the North-West Frontier Province. It is here that the Aligarh movement began, the Muslim League began to organize, and the movement of 1937 led to the birth of Pakistan. Hence, understanding communal politics in the first four decades after Independence in UP is of importance and is attempted here.

We argue that the immediate post-Independence period needs to be analysed because the reasons for the resurgence of communalism and riots in UP during the RJBBM phase, and more importantly for our study in the 2000s, lie not only in the memories of clashes during the colonial period or the terrible riots during Partition. Equally importantly, they lie in the limitations in the capacity of the process of secularization of the newly formed Indian state and society, to construct a secular polity, syncretic culture, and accommodative relations between the majority and minority community. There was a window of opportunity at independence due to the inheritance from the national movement of the idea of building a composite social culture, which created an air of optimism that India was making a fresh beginning after long years of colonialism under tall leaders such as Nehru, Ambedkar, and Patel.

The decade of the 1950s did witness improvement in the relationship between the majority and minority community. It was a period of relative peace. This was possible due to the adoption of a secular and democratic constitution that promised protection to minorities, and the leadership provided by Nehru and other nationalist leaders. The Muslim community supported the Congress viewing it as a secular party, which would protect their interests in post-independent India. There was also some improvement in the economic condition of sections of the Muslim community in UP. However, by the mid-1960s communal forces long kept under check by Nehru's leadership surged forward causing serious stress to India's secular fabric. The brief period of inter-religious peace was short-lived, the promise of increasing communal harmony and secularization of society and the nation-state does not seem to have materialized. There began a trajectory of estrangement of the Muslim community from the mainstream, a feeling of being deprived and a sense of insecurity due to the reappearance of communal tension and riots which reached a peak by the early 1990s and as subsequent chapters will show, have reappeared in recent years.

Nevertheless, this trajectory of communal relationships has been a complex process; two factors seemed to be at work almost simultaneously: integration and alienation clearly reflected in UP (M. Hasan 1988). The process of integration with Muslims beginning to feel settled was slow as the better-off, educated, professional, and business Muslim families left for Pakistan, while those left behind were rendered economically depressed, politically leaderless, and socially fragmented. The community was also divided into many segments: the conservative

Muslim Ulema, the small educated middle class, the rural poor, the artisanal class, and so on. Consequently, the Muslim community in UP lost the position of dominance that it had enjoyed during the colonial period and it took time to adjust and accommodate itself within the new democratic and secular framework.

However, the process of adjustment remained incomplete as by the end of the Nehruvian period communal tension and riots re-emerged. A major reason was disillusionment within the Muslim community, which felt the Congress party had not fulfilled its promises of looking after the legitimate needs of the community and providing it protection of life and property. Another was the emergence of a right-wing party, the Bharatiya Jan Sangh (BJS), with roots in the Rashtriya Swayamsevak Sangh (RSS) that opposed many demands of the Muslim community. Committed to the cause of building a resurgent Hindu nation and a revived Hindi–Hindu culture, the ideology of the RSS and the BJS was fuelled by the stereotype of an aggressive Islam. Both organizations repudiated secularism, denounced the Congress for its policy of appeasement under the 'camouflage of secularism', and proposed that 'Indianisation' of the Muslim outlook was the only solution of the socio-religious as well as the political aspect of the communal problem (Madhok 1970: 82).

Both the attempts at integration and alienation are reflected in developments between 1967 and 1980: in assembly and national elections in which the Muslims began to move away from the Congress to other parties, and more importantly, attempted to experiment with alternative sociopolitical organizations such as the Majlis-e-Mushawarat and a small political party in UP. These experiments were not successful as they had within them diverse Muslim groups, but they created political consciousness within the community. The 1970s witnessed more serious riots in which economic factors and social jealousies aimed at the improved position of the Muslims played a role exacerbated by the Hindu and Muslim communal groups and the partisan attitude of the police. The period of the Emergency further alienated Muslims who together with the scheduled castes (SCs) had formed the mainstay of the Congress party, contributing to its sharp decline in the 1980s (Rudolph and Rudolph 1981). While many Muslims had come to realize the importance and necessity of secularism as it provided them security, the developments of the 1970s made it possible for communally oriented

Muslim leaders to occupy the political space; the increasing number of riots granted them legitimacy. These Muslim leaders emphasized the need to preserve religious identity and culture and by opposing modern education and the more reformist and integrative process were successful in insulating the community from the process of social change and modernization (M. Hasan 1988: 34).

As a consequence of changes in the politics of both the majority and minority community, the 1980s and early 1990s witnessed the re-emergence of the worst communal riots in UP and elsewhere after independence. The collapse of the Congress party which had upheld a moderate, inclusive, and centrist form of politics, provided room for the rise of a fundamentalist, right-wing, Hindu nationalist party the BJP, a successor to the BJS. Although it emerged out of the Janata party, like the BJS it had its roots in the RSS and its aim was to build a strong Hindu vote bank using its divisive ideology of Hindutva. The earlier essentially democratic and secular method of mobilization by political parties was replaced by that of religious identity. Consequently, the 1980s were a period of rising communal tension and competitive communal politics between the Congress and the BJP over the RJBBM dispute which led eventually to the destruction of the Babri Masjid at Ayodhya on 6 December 1992. The destruction of the Masjid by a 300,000-strong mob, which left 1,700 dead and 5,500 injured in the worst communal violence after Partition was a turning point in Hindu–Muslim relations (Thakur 1993: 645). While there had been communal incidents and riots earlier in the first four decades after independence, the destruction of a Muslim place of worship constituted a serious incident that shocked the Muslim community and the riots that followed were reminiscent of those in the post-Partition period. It constituted a watershed in the relationship between the two communities and although after 1993 there was no major communal riot in UP until almost 2005, the destruction of the Masjid has had a seminal impact on Hindu–Muslim relations. The polarizing effect it had, enabled the BJP to renew its programme of communal mobilization based on Hindutva once again in the early 2000s.

Using this lens, the chapter attempts to understand the process of social and political change within the Muslim community and its relationship with the majority community in UP between the 1950s and early 1990s. Prior to that an attempt is first made to analyse the impact of Partition on the Muslim community in UP, the socio-economic condition of the community particularly of the artisanal class and the poorer and backward sections in the post-independence period, which enables us later to link it to the political economy of communalism during in this period. The period up to the early 1990s is divided into three phases for the purpose of analysis. First, the early Nehruvian period until 1964 which witnessed relative communal peace. Then a more turbulent period from 1964 to 1980 which witnessed the 1967 elections, resurgence of communal politics, and the imposition of Emergency. The final period was from 1980 to 1990 which witnessed the formation of the BJP, the rise of Hindu fundamentalism, and revival of the RJBBM dispute and demolition of the Masjid, which witnessed the worst riots in post-independence India and introduced different political equations between the majority and minority community. Our analysis forms a backdrop to the more contemporary period of riots in the 2000s in UP which is the major focus of this study.

Muslim Community in UP at Independence

Muslims constitute the second largest religious community in India, constituting 19.26 per cent of the population of UP (Census of UP 2011). However, they are concentrated in some regions of the state, namely, western and eastern UP. Muslim separatism in the erstwhile United Provinces had quite distinct features and was different from that of Bengal and Punjab. The predominant view of Hindu–Muslim relations in nineteenth and twentieth century India is that the Muslims were backward compared to the Hindus, who had quite early moved ahead of the Muslims in the race for western education and government employment. Muslim separatism from this point of view is well reflected in the writings of Wilfred Cantwell Smith (Smith 1946: 256), who argued that it was a combination of Muslim backwardness within a minority position that produced a more intense separatist identification among Muslims in the former United Provinces.

On the other hand, scholars such as Paul Brass and Omar Khalidi have pointed out that while notions of Muslim backwardness may have been true elsewhere in the country such as Bengal, this was not true in the special environment of the United Provinces. Based on an examination of the census and other documents on the differential rates of change in social mobilization and assimilation within the Hindu and Muslim communities, Brass says that Muslims were modernizing at a faster rate than Hindus and 'the myth of Muslim backwardness were articulated by the aristocracy of north India, in an effort to retain their domination in the areas where Muslim had over-representation' (Brass 1974).[1] It was the Muslims who were the more advanced community, constituting in some respects a dominant, urban, administrative, and cultural elite well represented in schools and colleges and among the English-educated classes and in government jobs (Brass 1970: 167–86).[2] In fact, Khalidi holds that Muslim separatism acquired its strength in the United Provinces because Muslim political leaders consistently struggled to maintain their privileges (Khalidi 2004). It was the failure of this strategy after 1936 with the formation of the Congress government in the province that led Muslim leaders to support the movement for a separate homeland long before the demand was supported in other regions. Ultimately, the sheer numerical superiority of the Hindus in the province ensured that no matter how slowly they mobilized, they would ultimately displace Muslims from their privileged position in public life after 1936. Consequently, in UP Muslims have been a relatively small and scattered minority after Partition. However, due to these shifts, at independence there was a legacy of Hindu–Muslim antagonism due to changes in the late colonial period, which have affected relations in post-independence India.

Partition leading to unprecedented migration of Indian Muslims totalling six million had a far-reaching impact on their social structure and the process of social stratification in the immediate post-independence period (Imam 1975). The migration was mainly from the states of UP, Bihar, MP, and Rajasthan, regions where Muslims are educationally backward today (Khalidi 1997). The urban migrants to Pakistan were mostly educated intelligentsia, industrial and trading families, service personnel, doctors, and lawyers and the majority was young, leaving behind a socially fragmented and economically depressed Muslim community (Khalidi 1997; M. Hasan 1988: 19). There had been few links between the Muslim elites that had occupied

---

[1] A similar argument has been advanced by Robinson (1973).

[2] On the issue of Muslim backwardness in various regions and in the United Provinces, see Seal (1968) and Low (1968: 14).

high positions in the government, army, police, and judiciary and the poorer artisanal or labouring class left behind with whom they never had anything in common.

In UP, the rural areas were not affected as much by the Partition as the Muslim rural aristocracy did not migrate; they remained behind. Though shaken they did not lose their economic stake (Imam 1975: 85). Politically, they lost their eminence as the British, after the mutiny through land revenue settlements, had created big Muslim zamindars and taluqdars in Oudh and some parts of western UP (Metcalfe 1979). These big landowners lost their lands due to zamindari abolition but managed to keep their home farms and were given compensation; the poorer peasantry, though small in number, suffered economically because of the forcible grabbing of their land in the wake of Partition and the enforcement of the Evacuee Property Act. Zamindari abolition reduced the influence of the Muslim zamindars more than that of their Hindu counterparts because of the smaller number of Muslim peasants in the state and the greater number of rentiers among the Muslim land-lords (Brass 1974: 235). Many shifted from rural to urban areas for fear of communal riots and the sense of insecurity in rural areas; especially in eastern UP where the population was small and scattered (Imam 1975: 95). The loss of land by the zamindars also meant being cut off from the peasantry and loss of both prestige and power. A section shifted to urban cities and took up jobs but many were not prepared to do this and suffered due to the 'feudal ethos' which led to luxurious living which soon made them poor (Khalidi 1997: 193). Zarina Bhatty describes Muslim zamindars in a village in UP as 'lacking power, their manoeuvrability was limited and consequently they lost a good part of their lands to the tenants who acquired legal rights over the lands that they were cultivating' (Bhatty 1973: 98). A small number who were active in the national movement and were part of the Congress were able to adjust and join politics in UP such as the Kidwai family of Oudh who adapted by handling their tenants well and family members took to professions or business (Bhatty 1973: 87–98).

Consequently, after the Partition with the disintegration of the Muslim League and elimination of separate electorates, Muslims were no longer able to organize politically. With the introduction of universal franchise and joint electorates they lost their position as a privileged minority, which they had enjoyed under the British since 1909. After independence the Congress was supported by the Jamiat-e-ulema Hind, an organization of Ulema associated with Deoband situated in Saharanpur on the matter of places of worship, religious endowments, personal law, and other issues related to Muslim culture. They were slow in adjusting to these developments as they had been nurtured with ideas of political separatism and religious fundamentalism. The idea of a secular state was contrary to the fundamentals of Islam, it rested on the denial of sovereignty of God and to be secular was being *ghair mazhabi or la dini* (irreligious) (M. Hasan 1988: 821). However while some continued to cling to the idea of an Islamic state, the large majority came to regard the democratic framework and secularism as a boon, since their welfare depended on the secularity of the state. The Jamiyat al-ulema propounded the theory of a social contract between Hindus and Muslims to establish a secular state, while the Jamaat-i-Islami after years of diffidence, declared in 1970 that in the prevailing circumstances in contrast to fascist modes of government the secular democratic mode in India was much better and should endure.[3] As Percival Spear observed, 'informed Muslim opinion is clear that it wants nothing better than the liberty to work out its own destiny within the Indian secular society' (Spear 1967).

At the same time it is important to understand that the Muslim community after independence does not constitute, whether in UP or elsewhere in the country, a homogenous bloc. Features of the Hindu caste system, such as hierarchical ordering of social groups, endogamy, and hereditary occupation have been found to be amply present among the Indian Muslims as well. The Census of India, 1901 listed 133 social groups wholly or partially Muslim. The 1911 Census listed some 102 caste groups among Muslims in Uttar Pradesh, at least 97 of them came from the non-Ashraf category. Briefly put, today one can discern three groups among Muslims. First, the Ashrafs, those without any social disabilities and who trace their origins to foreign lands such as Arabia or Persia. Then there are the Ajlafs, those who are deemed equivalent to Hindu OBCs and who are the low-ranking converts from Hinduism. Finally the Arjzals, who are deemed equivalent to the Hindu SCs consisting mainly of the carpenters, artisans, graziers, and functional groups. Since the Constitutional (Scheduled Caste) Order, 1950,

[3] Quoted in Wright (1979: 86).

popularly known as the Presidential Order (1950), restricts the SC status only to Hindu groups having 'unclean' occupations, 14 of their non-Hindu equivalents are bracketed with the middle-caste converts and declared OBC (Sachhar Committee Report 2006).

As a consequence of these social groupings, after independence, Theodore Wright identified four categories of Muslims by the 1970s. Traditionalists, who accepted the whole classical tradition of the Quran and Hadith by the Ulema and were represented by the Jamiat-ul-Ulema-i-Hind. The revivalists or fundamentalists who argued that Muslims having suffered at the hands of the West due to defeat because they are no longer good Muslims, must return to the fundamentals of Islam. The modernists, according to whom Islam has declined due to failure of Muslims to adapt their religion to the demands of modern science and life while retaining its ethical core. Sir Syed Ahmed Khan (Aligarh University) is a good example. Finally, the secularists, usually Marxists and well educated Muslims by birth who reject Islam and all religion as incompatible with science, but retain an emotional attachment to Muslim culture and are identified as Muslim by Hindus (Wright 1977: 1208).

Thus, partition and migration of the educated class to Pakistan created problems within the Muslim community in UP due to which it remained backward after independence. The cumulative impact was a social vacuum in the Muslim community, which was 'more uneven and unnatural, indeed deeper and wider' (Imam 1975: 85), especially in areas such as UP. Imam points out that the loss of a bourgeoisie and educated leadership created 'widespread confusion, insecurity and alienation ... as a community; they lost self-confidence and hope in their future' (Imam 1975: 87). Much data exists today which shows that Muslims suffer from greater deprivation and disadvantage as compared to other religious minorities. Various reports such as the Gopal Singh Committee (1983), the Rajendra Sachar Committee Report (2006) and the Ranganath Mishra Commission Report (2007) clearly indicate that Muslims are lagging behind in the field of education, economy, and employment. The poorer sections are beset by poverty and lack of education and jobs in public and private spheres; the better-off sections are affected by fear-psychosis, issues of personal law, Urdu, status of Aligarh Muslim University, and minimal representation in the armed forces and civil services (Wilkinson 2008). Large sections live as 'structurally segregated' groups, which deprives them of access to modern education and occupation (Sheth 2009).

The Nehruvian Period: Relative Communal Harmony

The Nehruvian period, despite the Partition and the riots that followed, was one of relative communal harmony and gradual improvement in the relationship between the majority and minority community in UP. This period provided a prospect of creating a more cohesive and harmonious society. There were signs of a more composite culture and a process of integration with the larger society. This was due to the tall leadership of Nehru and the presence of the Congress viewed as a secular party, which would protect the interests of the minorities. Nehru's vision during the national movement was to build a modern state, in which caste and religious conflicts would end and a new secular order would bring people together under a socialist system; 'New Temples', that is, heavy industry would bring modernity and prosperity to all. Partition and the riots that followed in north India from 1946 to 1948 did come as a shock and destroyed many aspirations and illusions. However, the assassination of Mahatma Gandhi in January 1948 put an end to the mass violence. Strong leaders such as Sardar Patel, the Union Home minister, also described as the 'Iron Man of India' deployed the machinery of the state including the army to restore order and the confidence of the people. Equally important, in the constituent assembly after much debate it was decided to provide under Article 25 that '...all persons are equally entitled to freedom of conscience and the right to move freely to profess, *practice and propagate* religion....' (Morris-Jones 1957).

However, it is important to underline that initially Nehru faced a number of problems from within his own party in maintaining secular politics. The Congress party was singularly lacking in coherence, signified by the presence of communal and revivalist elements entrenched in the states and districts, and their uneasy relationship with Nehru who was committed to the establishment of a secular state and society. It surged ahead without isolating such elements and without evolving instruments to widen the social basis of secularism and thus assuage the fears of the minorities while satisfying the rising aspirations of various social groups. In UP the leadership of the Congress party was largely

Brahmins with a conservative mindset and a Hindi–Hindu orientation such as Purshottamdas Tandon and Kamlapati Tripathi. These leaders were more inclined to support Sardar Patel who was viewed as more sympathetic to a right-wing orientation than Nehru was. Nehru was no doubt aware of these limitations, but it is held, he dithered on vital issues. He took certain steps or failed to take others, which did not fit squarely with his promotion of secularism (Kriplani n.d.).

Unlike in south India, UP had not experienced a non-Brahmin or strong SC movement that could question the predominant position of the upper castes or throw up a strong anti-caste leader such as Ambedkar or Periyar. The Hindi Pracharini Sabha had been active in Benares, whose members later did not allow Urdu to gain the status of a second language in the state creating much unhappiness within the Muslim community (Pai 2002). The Hindu orientation is evident in the suggestions in the UP legislative assembly on the new name to be given after independence to the erstwhile United Provinces: Braj-Kashi, Ram Pradesh, Ram-Krishna Bhoomi, Aryavarta, etc., reacting angrily to which Nehru ruled that the new province would be simply called Uttar Pradesh from its geographical position (Kudaisya 2007: 3–31). The progressive orientation of the Congress in UP was also depleted at independence with the departure of the socialists belonging to the Congress Socialist Party. The Congress Socialist Party had been a part of it during the national movement under both Acharya Narendra Dev, who wanted more radical land reforms and joined the SP, and Acharya Kriplani who left to form the Kisan Mazdoor Praja party in the late 1940s (Moore and Freydig 1955: 53–61). The Communist party of India was also active in UP but was weaker than other parties such as the BJS. The formation of the BJS meant that Nehru's capacity to push forward secular policies was hampered.

Some scholars have also pointed out that Nehru was weak in his action against communalism. An easy way out of the communal impasse was to woo minorities even if it meant heightening their community consciousness. In his keenness to win their confidence, Nehru allowed Muslims a voice in whether or not to provide equality to all women or, to promulgate a common civil code, thus precluding either (M. Hasan 1988: 43). He stated in 1954 that while he thought a unified civil code was inevitable, the time was not ripe to push it through. He did not ban communal parties and allowed the banning of cow slaughter in UP,

Bihar, MP, and Rajasthan. The Congress party ruled all these states (M. Hasan 1988). It was only after Nehru defeated Purshottamdas Tandon and became the president of the Congress and the death of Patel in 1951 that he became the undisputed leader of the party. Moreover, by the 1950s developments in external affairs softened communal relations. The Nehru–Liquat Ali Khan pact helped improve Indo-Pak relations. Thereafter, Nehru as PM was able to impose his views without encountering any real opposition from within. His personal standing allowed Muslims to join the party and he had around him a number of respected 'nationalist' Muslim leaders such as Maulana Azad and Rafi Ahmad Kidwai that enabled him to gain the confidence of the Muslim community.

It is also essential to recognize that while UP remained a conservative state there were strands of thinking that were markedly secular and progressive and which sought to improve the social life of the province. Intellectuals such as Humayun Kabir contributed to building harmonious relations. He argued that Muslims in India entered in small groups and have been influenced by the syncretic culture of the Hindus. Hence, they are different from Muslims in the rest of the world. Here, the 'process of growth, both among the Hindus and the Muslims for almost nine centuries was one of contact, assimilation and synthesis' (Kabir 1969: 16). Another strand was the Socialist movement which in India and in UP was a 'specific form of left nationalism' (Tolpadi 2010: 71–7). It grew, ideologically and politically, as an integral part of the nationalist struggle led by the Congress Socialist party, the official organ of the Socialists until independence. Among the Socialists, Rammanohar Lohia took a secular stand against caste, class, communal, and patriarchal ideas. Anand Kumar describes his thought as an attempt at 'de-Hinduising', 'decolonising', and 'de-westernising' the country and argued that there was no need to wait for the rise of an industrial proletariat or progressive middle class to attack the structures of exclusion and oppression in society (Kumar 2010: 69). Lohia was also closely associated with the leaders of the backward class and SC movements in the country and the members of the First Backward class Commission. He emphasized on the need for unity between the poor *dwija* (twice born) and the socially depressed and marginalized, which included poor Muslims and stood for a 'new caste policy' that would bring about a horizontal solidarity of all poor persons across the divides of caste and religion (Kumar 2010: 66). This synchronized view sought to bring all sections together including the Hindus, Muslims, and Christians as well as caste groups.

Despite these progressive trends, by the early 1960s there was a change in the attitude within the Muslim community towards the majority community and the Indian state. In the 1950s, the number of violent communal disorders had fallen steadily, reaching the low watermark of 26 in 1960. The number went up to 92 in 1961; the worst year was 1964 with over 1,170 incidents, mostly in Bengal. From 1965 to 1967, there were 515 officially recorded outbursts. Muslims suffered the most in 35 such incidents at the hands of rampaging communal mobs headed not very infrequently by RSS volunteers (Brass 1974: 291). A number of developments contributed to this. First, the death of Nehru increased the feeling of disillusionment within the Muslim community, which felt the Congress party had not helped the minority community. Then, the re-emergence of communal tension and violence, and the activities of the BJS seen in disputes over revival of the cow protection movement, the Hindi–Urdu controversy, and the playing of music before mosques. Equally important were disputes over protection to cows, religious processions, and the playing of music before mosques. The first major riot took place in Jabalpur in 1961 February; it shook up the nation and was followed by riots in Ranchi in 1968, Ahmadabad in 1969, and Bhiwandi in 1970 (Graff and Galonnier 2013a). In UP the first communal riot broke out in Meerut between 5 and 8 October 1961, after a Hindu student was severely beaten by Muslim boys during clashes at the Aligarh Muslim University (Graff and Galonnier 2013a). Consequently, rioting broke out in several parts of the city. Violence lasted several days, claiming between 13 and 17 lives (Brass 2006: 66–8).

Nehru's last years were fraught with difficulties due to the war with China in 1962, rising tensions within the Congress, failure of the Third Five Year Plan, and rising communal violence. The short tenure of Lal Bahadur Shastri (from May 1964 to January 1966) and the early years of Indira Gandhi's government were marked by agitations, war with Pakistan, the threat of famine, and a grave economic crisis. The Jamaat-i-Islami and the Itehadul Muslimeen derived strength and sustenance from the wave of communal violence, which swept through much of north India (M. Hasan 1988: 824). It led a perceptive Muslim observer to conclude that, 'Muslim communalism is now coming to surface again. Its fundamental idea...is that true Muslim society can exist only in a society where the government is in the hands of Muslims and is carried out according to Islamic law' (M. Hasan 1988: 825). On the other hand, the BJS and the RSS were able to strongly mobilize Hindu nationalist feelings during the war with China and later Pakistan. They repudiated secularism and denounced the Congress for its policy of appeasement of the minorities (M. Hasan 1988). 'The strength and influence of the avowedly and objectionably militant Hindu parties have grown alarmingly,' warned a commentator (Inder Malhotra, *Statesman*, New Delhi, October 1968). In addition, Muslims were worried about the possible 'suspension' of the special minority status of the Aligarh Muslim University and particularly the constant suspicion which surrounded Muslim civilians and military personnel during the 1965 war with Pakistan despite their loyalty (Graff and Galonnier 2013a). The formation of the VHP on 29 August 1964 contributed to the feelings of unease.

The communal upsurge in the 1960s was part of the sharpening of existing caste, class and community cleavages and reflected the limitations of the secularization process. For a weakened Congress party winning elections and devising electoral strategies became its prime concern, while populist slogans, radical rhetoric and diffused socioeconomic policies were its answers to the growing caste/class tensions and increased communal animosities. Consequently, from the mid-1960s, inter-communal politics took two forms: electoral competition and rising communal disharmony leading at times to riots.

Alternative Muslim Politics and Changed Communal Relations: 1964–1980

The period from 1964 to 1980 witnessed new patterns of politics with implications for communal relations in UP. The first was the emergence of the right-wing BJS formed in 1951 and the Muslim Majlis Mushawarat, a pressure group formed in 1964 (Burger 1969; Khalidi 2004). The second was the re-emergence of communal riots both of which were responsible for more competitive, at times communal, electoral politics.

New Muslim Organizations in the 1960s: The Majlis-e-Mushawarat

Underlying the formation of new Muslim organizations were significant socio-economic developments that contributed to experimentation with alternative politics. The 1960s witnessed gradual improvement in the economic position of sections of the backward classes of Muslims composed of mainly weavers, artisans, craftsmen, and some menial workers (Aslam 1990: 150). This was due to some progress in the brassware industry in Moradabad, lock factories in Aligarh, the power loom industry in Meerut, Mubarakpur, Ambedkar Nagar, and Badohi, and the bangle makers of Firozabad. The result was the rise of a neo-elite leadership in the Muslim BC community. They began to question not only identity and emotional issues but also the need for education, employment, removal of discrimination and backwardness, rather than attention only to issues such as Urdu, personal law, or Aligarh University, etc. As Mohammad Aslam points out there was a shift in the power structure within the Muslim community which was already divided by caste and class; it became even more complex, heterogeneous, and fragmented in terms of regional identity even within UP. Politicization of the weavers and artisans brought greater fragmentation in 'Muslim politics' as well as greater secularization; in the sense that there was a shift from emphasis on religio-cultural demands to economic demands, which Aslam argues was a 'healthy and positive development' (Aslam 1990: 141). For the first time questions of political economy began to affect communal politics and Hindu–Muslim relations. Another reason for the attempt to form new organizations was the re-emergence of communal riots, which particularly affected these new classes.

The Majlis-e-Mushawarat was formed on 9 August 1964 a few months after the death of Nehru, by Maulana Abdul Hasan Ali Nadvi and Dr S. Mahmood, a former member of parliament, to articulate Muslim 'interests' (Quraishi 1971: 1229–34). The immediate provocation was the communal riots in the early 1960s in Calcutta, Jamshedpur, Rourkela, and Jabalpur; unhappiness with the Congress, which had not provided education, security, and employment as promised and the formation of the BJS. However, more importantly Muslim leaders wanted to influence the1967 general elections by means of concerted action on the part of the community (M. Hasan 1997: 219). The Majlis was not meant to be a political party but a 'pressure group' to influence the central and state governments to undertake policies suited to minority interests (Sayeed 1989: 544). It decided to extend support to individual candidates belonging to different parties who were sympathetic to the needs of the Muslim community (Sayeed 1989). In UP, Dr Abdul Jalil Faridi, the main founder of the Majlis, established a new party the UP Majlis in 1968.

The organization and functioning of the Majlis marked a departure from earlier Muslim movements and heralded a new beginning for the community as it decided to be part of the secular constitutional framework and work within it. At the inaugural conference held in Lucknow on 9 August 1964, the Majlis adopted 'The National Resolution', calling out to all Muslims to participate in the building of a secular nation:

> Although it was the responsibility of the majority that it should have won the confidence of minorities and sympathised with them, unfortunately *a considerable section of majority* expresses its lack of confidence in Muslim minority on untenable grounds. Therefore, it is all the more necessary for Muslims *to remove useless misunderstandings* and complaints of that section of majority so that *the beloved motherland* may obtain peace and tranquillity and may proceed by leaps and bounds on the road to progress. (Quraishi 1971: 1230, emphasis added)

The Majlis also put forward a *People's Manifesto* on 22 July 1966 calling upon Muslims to give up futile protests and publicity of miseries and 'try to regain the lost energies and strive for a change in the prevailing conditions' (Quraishi 1971: 1230). It suggested reforms that would help the community such as reform of the educational system, proportional representation, a minority board to look after minority interests, a welfare state which would provide jobs and social security, and protection to the life and property of the minorities among others (Quraishi 1971: 1231).

However, the Majlis in UP and elsewhere was a loose confederation of diverse political interest groups. It was made up of erstwhile members of the Muslim League who had remained in India. Besides this, the ideologically oriented and well-disciplined Jamaat-e-Islami, which due to its efforts to reform the Muslim social structure had gained appeal among the younger generation; and a group of leaders associated with the Congress during the national movement and members of the Jamiat-Ulama-e-Hind who hoped to recapture their lost position of influence with the government and immunity from suspicion and hostility (Quraishi 1971: 1229–30). These three groups were joined by those independent Muslims who had for long felt the desperate need for the community to have leadership in order to avert the prospective loss of identity in the wake of industrial progress, large-scale urbanization, and democracy. However, it was not a harmonious amalgamation of Muslim opinion that could gain community support and votes. It was a loose organization and there was room for a variety of opinions and serious conflicts (Quraishi 1971: 1229–30).

While the Majlis succeeded in stirring up 'political and social consciousness' among Muslims (Tyabji 1971: 128). Its electoral success was limited except in UP and Bihar where it had developed some support but it was more due to unhappiness of the Muslims with the Congress than the image of the Majlis (Ahmad 1974). The electoral adventurism of the Majlis failed due to the absence of a unified leadership, differences between various groups, the fragmentary nature of the Muslim community and its regional and local specificity, and the small and scattered Muslim votes in most electoral constituencies. Scholars have pointed out that the Majlis had inherent problems that came to the surface once it began to work (Quraishi 1971: 1230). Hasan points out that the path of 'contest mobility' was clearly strewn with difficulties because democratic political institutions did not always lend themselves to being used by minority groups in defence of their interests. The Majlis learnt this by being stigmatized as a sinister, incipient revival of the old Muslim League and its demands pushed more votes towards candidates whose appeal was to Hindi and Hindu revivalism (M. Hasan 1997). The danger signs were already there. The alienation of the minorities and the consequent weakening of the secular elements amongst them, the newly acquired militancy of parochial and sectarian tendencies, the growing intrusion of religion into politics, and the widening gulf that separated Hindus and Muslims, lent credence to the view that 'the secularism of India is an aspiration not yet a reality' (Smith 1965: 10). These aspects become clear when we discuss the pattern of electoral politics in UP a little later.

The Bharatiya Jan Sangh and Right-wing Politics in UP

In this situation the presence of the BJS, a right-wing party formed in 1951 in north India, greatly impacted communal politics in UP. It had its roots in a militant, but non-political Hindu organization the Rashtriya Swayamsevak Sangh (RSS) founded in 1925 whose aim was to build a nationalist cadre that would unite and defend the 'Hindu nation' (Anderson 1972: 726). RSS leaders Hedgewar and Golwalkar had refused to allow the RSS as an organization and its *Pracharaks* (full time cadre) from joining any political party; it was to be an apolitical organization (Anderson 1972: 678). It was the ban imposed on the RSS and arrest of its senior leaders following the assassination of Mahatma Gandhi and the lifting of the ban a year and half later, that led many to argue that there was need of a political party if the movement was to survive.[4] Also, Sardar Patel's idea of allowing the RSS into the Congress—RSS leaders had hoped thereby to influence the Congress— was not supported by Nehru in the CWC in 1948, who stipulated that that they could join only if they gave up their RSS membership (Anderson 1972: 724–7). The sections who were interested in forming a party hence received a better hearing, which would not have been possible prior to 1948.

The new party could be formed only after its relationship with the RSS was resolved.[5] The final decision was a compromise, the BJS would be formed as a political party while the RSS workers and supporters would remain a separate and 'cultural' unit (Anderson 1972: 724). These developments were of great importance for the new nation formed at independence and also for present-day politics.[6] Golwalkar and other senior leaders of the RSS were ideologically convinced that politics as such is not an effective way to 'change character', rather 'character change' was to be the primary goal of the RSS. Golwalkar insisted that the BJS and the RSS remain separate organizations (Anderson 1972: 725). Hence, from its inception, the BJS was distinct, but drew on

[4] For details of the early years of the RSS, see Anderson 1972.

[5] As the formation of the BJS has been dealt with by many scholars and is well known, the details are not given here.

[6] After capture of power by the BJP in 2014, a major goal of the party and the Sangh Parivar is cultural change, that is, making India a Hindu country.

the RSS for its organizational cadre; both ideologically and organizationally the former was to remain dependent on the latter. This ensured
that the influence of the RSS on both policy and personnel would
be significant (Anderson 1972). On 21 October 1951, the All-India
Bharatiya Jan Sangh was formed at Delhi with Mookerjee as president.
He announced that his party would be 'open to all citizens of India
irrespective of caste, creed or community' though he also mentioned
the necessity of honouring the culture of Bharat (Anderson 1972: 725).

The BJS had a different social base in UP from other parties. Its support base was the conservative ex-taluqdars, former zamindars, and
Hindu professional and business classes from both rural and urban
areas. At the same time, it was often described as a small Hindu shopkeepers and businessmen's party in the smaller towns in UP (Brass
1962: 1111–18). From the beginning, it was social and cultural issues
that formed the core of the ideology of the BJS. In the existing literature,
it was described as 'communal', that is, representing narrow, selfish, and
aggressive attitudes within the Hindu community. It stood for a strong
nation and national unity for which it held that a unitary government
with a strong centre and small local bodies was required. Its early publications and electoral manifesto put emphasis on the rebuilding of India
as a 'modern, progressive and strong State on the basis of Bharatiya
culture and true Bharatiya nationalism' (Burger 1969: 35). While there
were a few Muslim members, the party mainly attracted conservative
Hindus and often obtained votes by calling for Hindu unity. It opposed
'appeasement of Muslims' and from its inception stood for 'Akhand
Bharat' (united India), that is, the union of India and Pakistan (Burger
1969: 34). It wanted Hindi to be the national language and supported
development of regional languages except Urdu, which was excluded
as it was associated with the Muslim community. These divisive ideas
within the party found reflection in the electoral politics and contributed to the Hindu–Muslim relations of the period.

Inter-communal Relations Reflected in Electoral Politics

Electoral politics in UP was marked by the dominance of the Congress
party throughout this period apart from a brief interlude after the 1967
assembly elections and the Janata regime from 1977 to 1980. However,
beneath the single dominant party system both the Hindu right-wing

forces represented by the BJS and Muslim politics reflected in UP by the Majlis played an important role shaping inter-community politics in the state.

A number of studies have shown that the Muslims in UP voted heavily in favour of the ruling Congress in the first three elections (Wright 1989: 247). This was because the electoral behaviour of Muslims was largely guided by the issues of security and physical protection after the trauma of Partition and the resulting fear psychosis. However, it must be mentioned that a number of positive features are visible in the early years in UP. First, in 1952 Muslim candidates contesting elections on the Congress party ticket constituted the largest proportion among Muslim candidates and succeeded in getting elected in larger proportions than the candidates put up by other parties (Ahmad 1974). Second, despite some studies pointing to a strong communal consciousness among Muslims while voting (Imtiaz Ahmad 1967: 523; S.K. Gupta 1962). Paul Brass in his study of Kanpur found that voting was non-communal in the 1957 and 1962 elections (Brass 1985). Third, a study argues that Muslims did not vote as a monolithic entity in politics, rather competitive electoral processes helped to break down their communal solidarity (Krishna 1967: 187). Finally due to these trends there were indications of integration, Muslim candidates contesting elections on national party tickets improved their share of the total votes polled by Muslim candidates from 65.41 per cent to 75.20 per cent in 1962 (Krishna 1967). There were also indications of the conscious decision to reject overtly communal organizations and an unmistakable preference for secular parties (Krishna 1972).

However, by the mid-1960s Muslims in various parts of the country including UP, began to question the wisdom of continuing their alliance and dependence on the Congress party. The Congress they felt had shown insensitivity to their specific needs such as unequal educational opportunities and employment, discrimination in government employment and poor representation in administrative services, the police, and the army (*The Hindustan Times*, New Delhi, 12 June 1961). In addition, communal riots began to be more frequent and there was a sense of insecurity. By 1968, Rasheeduddin Khan argued that Muslims were in a 'quandary ... they appear out of grips with evolving reality of a contemporary India' (Khan 1968: 25).

Consequently, a different trend is discernible in Muslim electoral politics and voting behaviour from the mid-1960s. In the 1967 elections, the Majlis-e-Mushawarat described earlier, supported candidates in eight states: UP, Andhra, Bihar, Maharashtra, Madhya Pradesh, Mysore, Rajasthan, and West Bengal.[7] From the beginning, it was doubtful if the Majlis commanded the fairly large Muslim support it claimed to represent (Quraishi 1971: 1232). Consequently, its performance was not spectacular in terms of absolute numbers, but it was successful in influencing Muslim voters so that the bulk of them did not vote for the Congress. In UP, 39 Majlis-supported candidates from various parties won the assembly election. The Majlis was keen to join the coalition governments formed in UP after the 1967 elections, but the inclusion of the BJS led to it remaining outside (Hassnain 1968: 96).

In this situation, the Majlis organization became badly divided in UP with one section arguing for direct participation in politics through the formation of a political party, which was opposed by the national leadership who transformed the Muslim Majlis-e-Mushawarat into a loose federation of Muslim associations hoping to regain its political influence. However, on 3 June 1968, the Working Committee of the UP unit of the Majlis unanimously resolved to form a political party called the Muslim Majlis and fought the 1969 elections, which further divided it over its future direction (Quraishi 1971: 1233). Eventually the unstable coalition governments of the period in UP drove the Muslims back to the Congress in the 1972 and 1974 elections. Thus, the Mushawarat could not sustain a separate political party; it could only bargain successfully with the Congress as a pressure group.

Different viewpoints have been expressed regarding the rise of the Majlis and what it meant for the electoral process and the role of the Muslims in the process. Hassnain has held that the failure of the Mushawarat was one of the 'greatest tragedies in the political and social life of the Muslims' (Hassnain 1968: 73). He feels that the members tried to improve the relations of Muslims with the Hindus including reaching out to the BJS but did not succeed. An important reason was the stranglehold of the conservative leaders and the Jamaat-e-Islami who worked against the organization and by their activities would pitch them against the Hindus in north India

---

[7] For details of their activities in the various states, see Quraishi (1968).

(Hassnain 1968). A more positive opinion was voiced by Gopal Krishna who observed that the formation of the majlis signalled that Indian Muslims who had generally kept aloof were showing signs of interest in becoming part of the constitutional and democratic electoral process. Rather than remaining a monolithic entity, Muslim political leaders were promoting the slow integration of their community into the emerging secular society (Krishna 1967: 179–90). However, Imtiaz Ahmad argued that while it is true that Muslims were beginning to participate in electoral politics, this did not necessarily imply that they were becoming increasingly secularized politically or that communal solidarity was being subjected to pressure by electoral competition (Ahmad 1967: 521–3). Rather he feels that the evidence shows that Muslims particularly in north India were trying to consolidate themselves politically so as to be able to influence the political process directly (Ahmad 1967: 521).

In contrast, the BJS was the only party that was able to steadily increase the seats and votes it obtained between 1952 and 1967 in the UP legislative assembly elections; it increased its strength nearly six times while the seat and vote percentage of the Congress declined (V.B. Singh 1971: 307–16). The opposition parties—the Samyukta Socialist Party (SSP), Praja Socialist Party (PSP), Swatantra and the Communists (Communist Party of India [CPI] and Communist Party of India (Marxist) [CPI(M)])—also lost seats and votes over this period. As Burger has pointed out it was 'remarkable' that the strength of the BJS in the assembly elections rose steadily, which demonstrated that there was a right-wing constituency available that grew with the steady decline of the Congress and other parties (Burger 1969). Many developments had favoured it in the mid-1960s. Issues like the banning of cow slaughter which had led to demonstrations, mass agitations, and even police firing; a state-wide strike by the state government employees just before the 1967 election; the 25 per cent surcharge on land revenue in UP re-imposed in 1965 by the state government after the Indo-Pak conflict which the BJS committed itself to removing. Besides this, there were other issues such as the teachers' strike, the student's strike, the rising prices of essential commodities, an acute shortage of food grains, and administrative corruption (V.B. Singh 1971: 316). However, in the 1969 mid-term polls the BJS suffered a sudden and serious setback which raised doubts about its appeal and popularity, and its organizational base in the state. Its seats were reduced sharply by half and its votes by as much as 4 per cent (V.B. Singh 1971).

The more fundamental reason for the decline of the BJS was a shift in the larger socio-economic and political arena in the mid-1960s in UP (Pai 1999). The Green Revolution spawned a rich peasant class especially in western UP leading to the formation of the Bharatiya Kranti Dal (BKD) under the leadership of Charan Singh, which made agrarian politics important in UP. It was only after the death of Charan Singh in 1987 and the decline of agrarian politics together with the collapse of the Congress party in UP by the late 1980s that right-wing politics based on religion became important once again. But, in the shorter term, in the 1974 assembly elections the Congress under the leadership of Mrs Gandhi was able to come back to power obtaining 215 seats and 34.04 per cent of the votes. The space for the BJS shrank it could get only 61 seats and 18.15 per cent of the votes compared to the BKD, which obtained 106 seats and 22.53 per cent of the votes. However, right-wing politics espoused by the BJS did not disappear; the party retained its social base to emerge later as the BJP in the 1980s.

The Impact of the Emergency on Muslim Politics: 1974 to 1980

The period from 1974 to 1980 witnessed important developments, which had an impact on Muslim politics and communal relations: the return of the Congress under Mrs Gandhi in the 1974 assembly elections in UP; declaration of the national Emergency and the alleged excesses during it on Muslims leading to their alienation from the Congress. A major political reason that contributed to the victory of the Congress in the national elections in 1971 and the 1974 UP assembly elections, was the absence of serious communal riots during the rule of Mrs Indira Gandhi. There was also the promise of 'Garibi Hatao' in the party manifesto, based on a 'genuine radical programme of economic and social development' upholding the interests of the small farmer and landless labourer, and small entrepreneur against the big capitalist (Frankel 1978: 397–8). Mrs Gandhi offered a 'strong and stable government' and asked for support against the 'dark and evil forces of Right reaction' intent on destroying democratic and socialist objectives (Frankel 1978). The left-oriented programme of Mrs Gandhi, appealed to both the Hindu and the Muslim community, which voted for the Congress in large numbers. The verdict was suggestive of a differentiated, secular, and national, rather than de-regionalized politics (Frankel 1978: 419). It was during the Emergency that the 42nd Amendment Act of 1976 inserted the term 'Secular' into the Preamble of the Constitution. It implied equality of all religions and religious tolerance; that all citizens irrespective of their religious beliefs are equal in the eyes of the law.

While the elections of 1974 marked the return of Congress dominance in UP under Mrs Gandhi's leadership, it could not fulfil the radical promises it had made to the people, evident from the imposition of Emergency. By the mid-1970s there were intractable problems faced by her government: slow economic growth of 3–4 per cent, high poverty levels of 40–50 per cent in both rural and urban areas, the Bangladesh crisis, the oil crisis, famine, and so on. From the early 1970s these developments contributed to the formation of violent oppositional organizations/movements such as the Nirman Yuvak Samiti in Gujarat and Chhattra Sangharsh Samiti in Bihar followed by Jayaprakash Narayan's call for 'Total Revolution' in 1974 (Frankel 1978: 526). Initially the imposition of Emergency was a relief for Muslims, who feared the BJS's influence within the Jayaprakash Narayan movement. However, especially in UP and Bihar, the Emergency had its dark side; there were excesses, which changed perceptions (Dayal and Bose 1977; Kochanek 1976). In Delhi—two campaigns by Sanjay Gandhi and his followers— slum clearance and sterilization in the Turkman Gate area in April 1976 and at Muzaffarnagar on 18 October 1976, and confrontations between the armed police, firings on crowds of Muslims were important in alienation of the Muslim community (Wright 1977: 1210). In January 1977, Mrs Gandhi declared mid-term elections in which the Congress was badly beaten by the newly formed Janata party.

The Emergency was responsible for the Muslims and SCs, two groups who had formed the main support of the Congress, deserting it contributing to its eventual collapse in 1980. All over the country, but especially in states such as UP where Muslims are found in large numbers, the Janata Party (JP) put up candidates and won a good number. In the Hindi belt all Congress Muslim candidates lost; in UP 149 lost in the constituencies of Rampur, Moradabad, Bareilly, Muzaffarnagar, Meerut, Pilibhit, and Unnao (Wright 1977: 1217). Theodore Wright has argued that it was not simple desertion or anger with the Congress; rather the 1977 Lok Saha election constitutes a 'watershed in Hindu–Muslim communal relations which heralds a new era in which religion will cease to be a key cleavage in Indian politics?' (Wright 1977). It marked 'a complete reversal of the power configuration within the Muslim community of north India as it had crystallized under Indira Gandhi rule'. The secularists among the Muslim leaders lost out, a loose coalition of revivalists and traditionalists and a few modernists represented the new Muslim minority in the JP regime (Wright 1977: 1218). In the UP state assembly elections that followed, the JP obtained 352 seats and 48.4 per cent of the votes while the Congress was reduced to 47 seats though it did gain 34.53 per cent of the votes.

However, writing in 1977 Asghar Ali Engineer differed in his assessment of the Muslim pattern of voting during this period in UP and the country. He argued that there was a strong perception that Muslims, though they constituted about 11 per cent of the population, had earlier voted en bloc for the Congress (Engineer 1977: 458–9). He held that many studies had shown that Muslim electoral behaviour is not very different from that of other communities. Whenever there was discontent in the country and people have voted against the Congress, Muslims have done the same; the Muslim vote is as 'unpredictable' as that of any other community. Yet he agrees Muslims suffer from 'insecurity'. The RSS and the BJS have made them wary and they distrust these two. In 1977, the Muslims voted against the Congress as they were angry over the misdeeds during the 18 months of Emergency (Engineer 1977: 458). As the JP promised to set up a commission to solve the problems of the minorities and give Urdu its rightful legal status, Muslim leaders decided to give them a chance. Thus, Engineer held that 'in the North there is a major crack in the Muslim monolith, in central and south India there are smaller breaches' (Engineer 1977: 459) The Muslims like all other communities fully supported the triumph of the JP in north India.

Communal Riots: Mid-1960s to 1980

The competitive politics of the 1960s and 70s, rapid social and economic change, and growing feelings of insecurity within the Muslim community in UP is reflected in the communal riots of the period. There were a number of communal incidents during this period but none of them were serious compared to those in the 1980s and 90s.

Two kinds of communal riots were visible during this period: first, arising out of economic competition and jealousies between the majority and minority community and second, the political uncertainty, poor governance, and competition among political parties during the brief phase of the JP rule.

Political Economy of Riots: Ferozabad

The communal riots in Ferozabad following the decline of its once prosperous bangle industry in June 1972 provides a good example of communal riots in many small, once prosperous, colonial Muslim artisanal towns that after independence have in many cases passed into Hindu hands and where Muslims not been able to switch over to some other industry (Chopra and Singh 1972: 1711–13). During the 1970s, nearly all communal riots occurred in towns where Muslims had been able to attain a measure of economic success through their traditional, artisanal, and entrepreneurial skills. Good examples are Aligarh, Varanasi, Moradabad, Azamgarh, Meerut, and elsewhere. This Hindu petty bourgeoisie often ascribed this 'economic resurgence' to Islamic fundamentalism, a new sense of confidence among Muslims, and money from the Gulf States, though the link was at best tenuous (J. Alam 1983:38–9; Engineer 1983: 15–18).

Ferozabad, with a population of 133,534 in 1972, 40 per cent of whom were Muslims, originally consisted of craftsmen who ran independent units manufacturing bangles. A study by Suneet Chopra and N.K. Singh shows that these units, after a series of riots after Partition, were burnt down and taken over by Hindus, reducing Muslim craftsmen to mere workers in the factories (Chopra and Singh 1972). These units, after a series of riots after Partition, were burnt down and taken over by Hindus, reducing Muslim craftsmen to mere workers in the factories. This created both poverty and feelings of insecurity among the Muslim artisans, leaving them vulnerable to communal mobilization. The new factory owners transformed the process of glass smelting by bringing smelters and turners together in the factories, but they did not centralize the whole process. Instead, they preferred to farm out some processes, like joining, cutting, and gilding. Consequently, a fragmented and dependent workforce—largely Muslim—continued to exist in the ghettoes, jealously guarding their communal identity and their craft, which gave them their livelihood. Nevertheless, the influx of industrial workers made inroads into the ancestral preserves of the craftsmen, giving them a feeling of insecurity. Even the workers' aristocracy, comprising some 200 highly skilled men earning over Rs 60 a day, no longer remained exclusively Muslim. The change did not bring prosperity to the town due to lack of diversification and the bangle industry remaining stagnant. With the rising price of raw materials, the factory owners found it more profitable to sell their coal quota in the black at four times the purchase price, and at least 30 of the 80 factories in the town became mere fronts for resale of raw materials, barely running for 15 days in a whole year. Consequently, the labour by the 1970s was divided and insecure with low earnings, appalling working conditions leading to diseases such as tuberculosis, and extensive use of child labour (Chopra and Singh 1972: 1711).

In this atmosphere, the news of a proposed new Aligarh University Bill created a sense of alarm and was viewed as a threat to the Muslim community. The craftsmen understood nothing about the issue and it was their illiteracy and religious faith in the absence of a working class movement that led them to support their community (Chopra and Singh 1972). Once the Muslim craftsmen had responded defensively to the news, a bandh was organized on 18 June 1974 supported by Muslim traders and factory owners for completely different reasons; with the stoppage resented by the Hindu factory owners. The Glass Industrial Syndicate declared the bandh 'communal' although the posters that appeared were addressed to all communities. At this juncture, the local branches of the RSS began mobilizing Hindus on a communal basis and decided to teach the Muslims a good lesson 'should anything happen during the bandh'. The local Congress organization and leader's son joined them and attempts were made to create communal tension following the Friday prayer at the local Jama Masjid. Despite this, several thousand Muslims participated in the prayer, and thereafter except for a few hundred, the rest dispersed quietly to their homes with some elderly persons urging even those that remained to go away (Chopra and Singh 1972).

However, some of the younger Muslim boys allegedly began shouting anti-national slogans when they had passed the Hindu quarter. Even then, the study argues, in the absence of general tension or mass participation on either side, events could very well have been controlled at this stage if they had been handled tactfully (Chopra and Singh 1972: 1712). It was the lathi charge by the Provincial Armed Constabulary (PAC) deployed and eventually firing by a head constable, in which a boy was killed, that led to the crowd throwing stones and heavy brick batting. The furious mob then raided the eastern police station, where the head constable had taken refuge, setting fire to it. Thereafter, the police opened fire once again—killing half a dozen or so Muslims on the spot. Curfew was imposed, and it was to continue for a full 87 hours. Meanwhile, a Hindu was stabbed. Despite the curfew, the police went on a rampage shooting Muslims, raiding and looting their homes, making false arrests, assaulting their women, and setting fire to their buildings including the Jama Masjid and the Islamia College. Rumours of killings of Hindus made the situation worse. However, according to the study, the Muslims were the victims of the systematic attack on them. Hindus, including goldsmiths, were not harmed while Muslim shops were looted and burnt. The local Congress establishment, it is alleged, was involved in helping the Hindus and supporting the police (Chopra and Singh 1972).

What is of importance in the study by Chopra and Singh is their finding that while the attack was on the minority community as a whole, it was directed with special vengeance at the craftsman and the worker. The reason given, which was true, was that the workers were proposing to go on strike for higher wages. The craftsmen especially in Ahmadnagar area had their tools looted; in the case of the workers, the Glass Workers' Union office was attacked, for no obvious reason other than that the union president was a Muslim. The pattern was not new: Mhow, Jabalpur, Varanasi, Ranchi, and Ahmedahad were precedents. Thus, there was a political economy and identity angle to communal riots in UP during the 1970s which badly affected the Muslim community (Chopra and Singh 1972).

Riots during Janata Party Rule: Recurring Patterns

The period of JP rule in UP witnessed riots. After an initial period of euphoria following the victory of the Janata coalition, differences arose between its various constituents creating considerable political uncertainty. A major reason for conflict between constituents of the JP was the issue of 'dual membership' of the BJS members who refused to give up their membership of the RSS while being part of the JP. In May 1979, the Minister of State for Home announced in parliament that there had been a three-fold rise in riot deaths since 1977; with UP heading the casualty list: 19 in 1977 to 65 in 1978 (*The Times of India*, New Delhi, 4 May 1979). In all the riots that took place, studies by scholars and reports point to attempts by the RSS to create polarization and tension, though in many cases members of the Congress were also involved. While there was a cultural angle in all these riots, there were strong economic underpinnings that were equally important.

Communal riots took place in two towns in which such incidents have become endemic in post-independence India: Aligarh and Varanasi (Graff and Galonnier 2013a). In Aligarh, riots took place in 1978 and in Varanasi in October 1977. While the first clashes occurred in Varanasi on 22–23 October after an altercation between Hindu students and a Muslim weaver, it was the attempt on 22 October to take a Durga Puja procession through a Muslim area that created tension (Akbar 1978: 47; Khan and Mittal 1984: 308). A similar incident took place on 29 March 1978 in Sambhal, a tehsil (subdistrict) of Moradabad district in which 70 per cent of the population is Muslim. A Holi procession led by a local Hindu Congressman and a beauty contest in which two Muslim girls had participated enraged Manzar Shafi, a Muslim League leader. Tensions increased following a gherao (protest demonstration) led by sweepers who had not been paid for three months. Aided by goondas (criminals) Manzar Shafi took this opportunity to call for a bandh (general strike). Violence flared up when a Hindu shopkeeper a paanwallah (betel seller) refused to follow the strike. About 25 persons were killed in these riots; among them 22 were Hindu victims (Sharma 1978: 59; Ghosh 1987: 227–8).

The riots in Aligarh on 5 October and once again on 6 November 1978 were more serious and violent and a report (Editorial, *Economic and Political Weekly*, November 1978: 1869–70) alleged that Vidya Bharati, an RSS organization, which tried to give a Hindu orientation to the educational system, was involved as well as its local leaders. The report also points to the biased role of the PAC and of local criminal elements. The annual report (1979) of the National Minorities Commission established that trouble started after the stabbing of Bhure Lal—a wrestler in a Hindu akhara (traditional physical training centre) and a notorious criminal—by Muslim criminals on 3 October. However, a report by the People's Union for Civil Liberties (PUCL) (1978),[8] emphasized that communal agitation in the city had been stirred up for months earlier by RSS groups over the issue of Aligarh Muslim University's minority status and also criticized local Hindu nationalist leader K.K. Navman for his involvement in the violence. Large-scale rioting erupted again in the city one month later, on 6 November with 15 to 20 persons killed. Tension had spread over the construction of a new cinema hall in the area of Manik Chowk, which Muslim residents had opposed. On 5 November, a speech by the BJS leader, Balraj Madhok had already inflamed the situation and a quarrel between two Muslim youth triggered violence. The riots spread to localities which had been spared in October with Muslims suffering heavily and retaliation against low-caste Hindu (Brass 2003: 90–6). However, they were small riots compared to those that followed in the 1980s.

Communal Riots in the 1980s and 1990s: The RJBBM Dispute

The late 1980s constitute a turning point in the trajectory of communal politics and Hindu–Muslim relations in UP and the country. For the first time since independence major communal riots that spread across UP and many parts of the country took place that were reminiscent of the riots at Partition. During the 1980s close to 4,000 people were killed in communal riots, which were four times the figure of the 1970s (*India Today*, 15 June 1987: 37). According to another estimate from February 1986 to 1987 nearly 'sixty major' and 'minor' riots took place in UP killing over 200 people leaving more than 1,000 injured and causing damage to property to the tune of 1.5 crore (*Sunday*, 21–27 June 1987: 12). Eventually religion-based mobilization led to the destruction of the Babri Masjid on 6 December 1992 leading to more riots. Second, while earlier riots were largely driven by economic competition, social jealousies, and cultural differences, this was the first time that deliberate, cultural mobilization of the Hindu community was carried by right-wing forces on a large scale targeting the minorities based on the

[8] See reports of the PUCL (1978), Sampradayikta Virodhi Committee (1978), and National Minorities' Commission (1979) provided in Graff and Galonnier (2013a).

ideology of Hindutva. Equally important was the new pattern of communal mobilization by all parties during the decade of the 1980s most notably of course the BJP, which led to competitive communalism and violent conflict.

A number of significant developments were responsible: the collapse of the Congress party which provided room for the formation of the BJP. A deep economic crisis and the need for a Structural Adjustment Programme (SAP) in 1991, the assassination of Rajiv Gandhi during the 1991 national elections, and the lack of a strong government at the centre, all of which contributed to a heightened feeling of crisis. Underlying these developments was the breakdown of the consensus on secularism and socialism, which had held the country together. This provided the context in which it was possible for the BJP to revive the RJBBM dispute and around it carry out a programme of communal mobilization centred in UP, but which affected the entire country.

New Patterns of Communal Mobilization by Political Parties

The Congress Party and Communal Tension in the 1980s and 90s

Although the Congress party was able to gain a majority in the 1980 national elections after the collapse of the Janata party, it played a substantially different role in the 1980s first under Mrs Indira Gandhi and then Rajiv Gandhi. Realizing that despite gaining a big majority the social base of the party was not as strong as earlier and with the emergence of a right-wing party, the BJP, Mrs Gandhi made a conscious decision to shift to the right. She did this in order to appeal to the emerging Hindu middle class in terms of both the economy and politics (Engineer 1991a: 1649). She went on conspicuous visits to temples and was lenient towards Hindu revivalism. This had an impact on the party in UP also. Having lost the support of the minorities and Dalits during the Emergency, she turned to the Hindus for support against the Muslims. Mrs Indira Gandhi was, in the words of Syed Shahabuddin, 'strategically secular' and could be 'tactically communal when the occasion so demanded' (Shahabuddin 1986). The Congress defeat in AP and Karnataka also brought a change in attitude towards the RSS leading to a deal in 1980 with Bala Saheb Deoras, the RSS chief. During the

1980s, the Sikhs also turned against the Congress. Mrs Gandhi extended her patronage to the VHP and inaugurated the Bharat Mata temple at Haridwar built by it, a well-calculated move to create a Hindu vote bank (Shakir 1988: 52). Operation Blue Star over the Golden temple issue followed this in June 1984, the assassination of Indira Gandhi on 31 October, and the anti-Sikh riots after that. The last phase of Mrs Gandhi's government witnessed an unprecedented intensification of religious fervour and religiosity, an exacerbation of sectarian feuds, and an increased polarization of society along communal grounds.

Rajiv Gandhi's campaign prior to the 1984 elections also portrayed an element of anti-minorityism: his constant reference to the Anandpur Sahib Resolution as a threat to unity and integrity of the country appealed to Hindus in north India which yielded rich dividends while the Muslims felt neglected. During Rajiv Gandhi's regime three controversies with strong communal overtones and the reaction of the Congress leadership to them, portrayed his retreat from a secular position. First, the Shah Bano incident in which Gandhi supported the conservative section of the Muslims by passing the Muslim Women (Protection of Rights on Divorce) Act in 1986. Then it was the banning of the *Satanic Verses* which led to horrendous anti-Muslim riots in Meerut, Hashimpura, and adjoining areas in UP; many were killed and some victims blinded. Finally, there was the RJBBM dispute described below (Thakur 1993: 648–50). Through this competitive communalism the Congress hoped to gain Hindu support, but these events actual helped the BJP to take its mobilization forward.[9] The widely shared Muslim perception of these shifts was of a virtual breakdown of the secular consensus embodied in the model of integration worked out by Nehru.

The BJP and the Politics of Religious Mobilization

However, it was the BJP which openly espoused the politics of communal mobilization based on its ideology of Hindutva. The BJP formed on 5 April 1980 emerged out of the short-lived JP and the erstwhile BJS. While it initially adopted the ideology of Gandhian Socialism it soon

---

[9] L.K. Advani admitted that the Shah Bano case was a 'watershed event' in mobilizing Hindu sentiment behind his party. *Sunday Times of India*, 14 October 1990.

shifted to Integral Humanism. But sensing the mood in the country, by the middle of the decade, the party leadership decided that communal mobilization based on Hindutva would improve its position in Parliament and in UP (Sen 1998: 303–4). By selecting the RJBBM dispute to fuel its mobilization it hoped to create a single, Hindu, upper-caste vote bank across north India particularly UP and also create a feeling of the Muslim as the 'other' in this region.

From 1979 onwards, events in the Muslim world had also impacted on the community in India: revolution in Iran under Imam Khomeini, the occupation of Afghanistan by the Soviet Army, and an attack on the holy shrine of Mecca. These developments made the cadres of the newly formed BJP and its affiliates alert to opportunities to weaken Muslims. Two examples of which they made use were the mass conversion to Islam in 1981 of Dalits at Meenakshipuram in Tamil Nadu (Ahmad 1982; *Sunday*, 7 September). Second was a speech by the president of the Jamaat-e-Islami during an international gathering in Hyderabad, where he made a strong appeal to Muslim families to have more children. The response was an impressive Hindu rally, the Hindu Sammelan, held in Delhi in October 1981. At the rally, a number of leaders called for a necessary rethinking of the Hindu society and was followed by efforts in various places to bring back the Muslim 'converts' to the Hindu fold and by the Ekatmata Yagna Yatra when, in November 1983, urns filled with Holy Ganga water crisscrossed India in motored caravans.

These developments coincided with rumours in UP and elsewhere in the country of sudden increase in the money sent back by Indian migrants working in the Gulf region due to the emergence of newly built colourful mosques and new wealth in the hands of some small-scale Muslim entrepreneurs and even workers. This created jealousies and Moradabad witnessed the first communal riot during the 1980s on 13 August, on the festival of Id-ul-Fitr. The rising prosperity of the Muslim population within the brassware industry (because of exports to the Middle East) had created deep resentment among Hindu middlemen, particularly those who were refugees from East Pakistan. Tensions had also increased between Valmikis (a sub-caste of Dalits) and Muslims after the kidnapping of a young Dalit girl during a marriage ceremony by four Muslim youths in March 1980. On 13 August, when a large number of Muslims were offering prayers at the city Mosque, a small incident sparked off a major riot, paramilitary forces were deployed, and police fired killing a large number. While government put the figure at 400 killed in the riots a Muslim group claimed that 1,500 to 2,000 had died in the violence. As the government did not try to curb the violence it spread throughout UP, first to Aligarh and Allahabad, and then to other cities (Delhi, and even Mhow).[10]

The Babri Masjid Dispute, Communal Mobilization and Riots

While these controversies created antagonisms, it was the RJBBM dispute which had a deeper impact and was responsible for communalization of the society and polity in UP and elsewhere. The mosque emerged as the most bitterly contested terrain after Partition mainly because the dispute was used by the Hindutva forces in their strategy of communal mobilization. Since it is a matter of faith rather than history, it has been more open to politicization and manipulation by all sections of the Sangh Parivar. But, while it was consistently used by the BJP in its strategy of communal mobilization in the 1980s and early 90s, political leaders belonging to both Hindu and Muslim communities and all political parties in UP including the Congress, contributed to communal polarization and made 'political profit' from the religious tension it unleashed (Thakur 1993: 655). Much has been written on the RJBBM controversy, its history, sequence of events in the colonial era and after independence, the adoption of this dispute by the BJP,[11] the Rath Yatra by L.K Advani, and its final demolition which is not dealt with in detail here.[12] Rather we are concerned with its impact on Hindu–Muslim relations and communal politics.

Few Indians knew about the existence of the mosque and it was only in the late 1980s that the Sangh Parivar realized the symbolic importance of the RJBBM to both communities (S. Srivastava 1991: 17). In

---

[10] Compiled by Graff and Galonnier (2013a).

[11] The two parties in the dispute are the Vishva Hindu Parishad (VHP) and the All-India Babri Masjid Action Committee with two questions forming the core of the dispute: was the mosque built on the ruins of a temple and is Ayodhya the birthplace of Ram. Both sides point to folklore, historical evidence, and archaeological records, and have been unwilling to cede ground to the other making it a fertile issue for communal mobilization (Thakur 1993).

[12] Akbar (1988); Dubashi (1992); Engineer (1990, 1992); Narain (1993); Noorani (2003, 2014); Pandey (1989); S. Srivastava (1991); Udaykumar (1997).

July 1986, the VHP tried to make it a national issue through forming the Sri Rama Janma Bhoomi Mukti Yajna Samiti and held a number of chariot yatras in some UP towns to rouse Hindus about the dispute. It was at the Palampur session in 1989 that the BJP, through a resolution, consolidated the Ayodhya movement.[13] With an eye on the forthcoming 1989 elections, a detailed strategy was planned to demolish the mosque and build a Ram temple with consecrated bricks to be brought by *karsevaks* largely from the RSS–VHP–BJP cadres from across the country so as to give the party a foothold everywhere (Mishra 2007: 2582).

History, myths, symbols, and cultural narratives were used to construct a people's past memories, present identity, and discursive space for changes in the knowledge of the past which gains divine sanction when religious symbols are used. In addition, an allegedly homogeneous notion of the Hindu race was projected which spoke many languages but were all part of Bharat Varsh. So a monolithic Hinduism and homogeneous Hindu *samaj*, the pure old glory of Hinduism is pitted against the Other, Islam and Muslims (Lutgendorf 1991: 23, 34).

These strategies were successful because a new political leadership had emerged within both the Hindu and Muslim communities who, unlike the earlier generations were not cautious and prone to mobilize, creating trouble. On the Muslim side, important leaders of the period were the Shahi Imam of the Jama Masjid in Old Delhi, Syed Abdullah Bukhari, and Syed Shahabuddin an MP from Bihar (Kishanganj) and a former diplomat (Graff and Galonnier 2013a). On the other were the leaders of the BJP–RSS who used the movement from the beginning for political gains. Realising that the Congress party was in deep trouble, the former used the concept of 'pseudo-secularism' to gain political legitimacy among the middle- and upper-caste Hindus (Engineer 1991a: 1652). They carried out aggressive propaganda that the Congress was using the concept of 'pseudo-secularism', which they traced to Nehru for appeasement of the minorities in order to exploit them as their vote banks. They pointed out that psuedo-secularism helped only the minorities and India could be a genuinely secular country only if it opted to be a Hindu Rashtra. Constant repetition of this idea by leaders such as Advani and its consequent use by the media gave it great appeal among middle-class Hindus in urban areas.

[13] For the BJP version, see BJP (1993).

The actions of the Congress party, already in deep organizational decline in the late 1980s under Rajiv Gandhi due to the beginnings of an economic crisis, contributed to further communalization of the dispute. As Asghar Ali Engineer argued, 'The Ram Janma Bhoomi controversy came as a political gift from the Congress, which decided to exploit Hindu religious sentiments for electoral purposes' (Engineer 1990). On 1 February 1986, the District and Sessions Judge of Faizabad passed an order to unlock the RJBBM allowing priests to enter and a few days prior to the 1989 elections Rajiv Gandhi himself performed Shilanyas on 9 November 1989 on the disputed land which was temporarily declared to be undisputed (Gopal 1991). The UP Congress also used Arun Govil, the man who played Ram in the famous TV serial Ramayan, in their campaign for the 1988 Allahabad by-election (Badhwar and Pachauri 1989: 29). It was in this charged atmosphere that V.P. Singh on 7 August 1990 heading a weak national government the National Front with BJP support decided to introduce the Reservation Bill popularly called the Mandal Report in the Lok Sabha which would give reservations to the BCs. It was Singh's rejoinder to the growing dominance of the BJP based on upper-caste support (Engineer 1991b: 155). In UP, which was witnessing a strong BC movement, Mulayam Singh Yadav was even more aggressive in his pro-Muslim attitude. This can be seen from his speeches in September–October which became counter-productive and further communalized the Hindus and led to a series of communal riots in Aligarh, Agra, Khurja, and Bulandshahr in which the Muslims suffered badly as the PAC did not help them (Engineer 1991b: 155). These developments encouraged the VHP–BJP–RSS combine to take forward its Ramjanmabhoomi campaign (Engineer 1991b).

As a result of these developments the 22–24 November 1989 Lok Sabha election witnessed the worst ever communal violence in independent India's electoral history that took a massive toll of 800 lives in UP (Engineer 1991b). In May 1987, the city of Meerut and the nearby areas of Moradnagar and Maliana were the scene of riots and violence. In Meerut city on 14 February 1986, Muslims hoisted black flags in the city to protest against the opening of the lock that sealed the Babri Masjid in Ayodhya. They set fire to Hindu shops, leading to a small-scale riot. On 30 March 1987, a large number of Meerut's Muslims participated in a rally held by the Babri Masjid Action Committee (BMAC) in Delhi, where the Shahi Imam Syed Abdullah Bukhari delivered inflammatory speeches. As a result, on 14 April and again on 16 May, and 18 and 19 May there were serious riots in Meerut and surrounding areas. Imposition of curfew did not help and in many cases, the police sided with the Hindus. Two massive riots with killings occurred at Moradnagar where around a hundred Muslims in the Hashimpura area were arrested taken to the Ganga canal area, shot by the PAC and dumped in the canal on 22 May. Survivors allege that more than 100 persons were killed. A similar incident took place in Maliana close to Meerut where Muslim houses were looted and burned in which it is alleged Dalits took part. On 8 October 1988 communal riots took place in Muzaffarnagar town. Hindu communal organizations held a bandh (general strike) to counter a rally that was scheduled by the BMAC for 14 October. Some Muslim shopkeepers refused to close their shops and violence flared up, many shops belonging to Muslims were burnt and Muslims killed. On 11 October, a peace committee, mainly composed of Muslims, organized a demonstration in the town but they were attacked, and both Hindus and Muslims lost their lives in the confrontation. In Badaun on 28 September 1989, riots took place on the day a Bill was introduced in the UP legislative assembly to make Urdu the second official language of UP. On 27 September, college students belonging to the Akhil Bharatiya Vidyarthi Parishad (ABVP) created communal tension and the resulting riot claimed 27 lives; some accounts assessed the total at more than 60 killed with violence spreading to the countryside. A very serious riot broke out during December 1990 in Bijnor, Khurja over the Babri Masjid/Ramjanmabhoomi issue in which both Hindu and Muslim shops were attacked and looted. During early 1991, the towns of Saharanpur, Kanpur, Meerut, and Varanasi experienced riots over a number of days (Engineer 1991b).

In this state of affairs, BJP leader L.K. Advani launched a nationwide campaign in support of the movement for the construction of a temple to Ram in Ayodhya by carrying out a Rath Yatra in a jeep painted to look like a war chariot in September 1990. The idea was to unite the Hindu upper and lower castes to promote national unity and create a single Hindu vote bank across north India and capture power at the centre and in UP. Adopting the slogan *Mandir wohi banayege* he called upon the people to show *Ram Bhakti* (Ram worship) and *lokshakti* (people power). On the ground, it caused communal polarization and riots. In October 1990 in Ayodhya when a 100,000-strong gathering of karsevaks (holy volunteers) tried to storm the Babri Masjid, about 30 were killed by the police and hundreds more died in the ensuing communal riots (Thakur 1993: 654). There was a second round of Kar Seva in December in UP and violent riots began in Bijnor and continued into the whole of eastern UP, Bundelkhand and spread to all regions; curfew had to be clamped in no less than 30 districts.[14] Following the arrest of Advani in Bihar on 23 October 1990 riots were witnessed in several places in UP and in Jaipur, Jodhpur, Ahmedabad, Baroda, and Hyderabad (Engineer 1991a: 1651). The period prior to the 1991 Lok Sabha elections in UP and elsewhere, there was 'unparalleled communalization of the Indian polity in the post-independence period…which shook the very foundations of Indian secularism' (Engineer 1991a: 1649–50).

The BJP's politics of communal mobilization prior to the 1991 UP assembly elections provoked Hindu–Muslim polarization. Many of its candidates in the 1991 election were closely associated with religious personalities 'Sadhu Sants' involved in the Ayodhya issue of whom five were elected to Parliament (Pai 1988: 1842). In the early 1990s, the Hindutva ideology appealed to not only the upper castes but to the dominant agricultural castes in the region such as the Jats, Rajputs, and Gujjars. The BJP obtained 211 seats and 33 per cent of the votes compared to 7.6 per cent in the 1989 assembly elections (Pai 1988). The BJP performed well in all the five regions and successfully mobilized a large chunk of the upper-caste Hindu vote across the state based upon the Ayodhya issue. Its success was most marked in the western region, which has traditionally been the area where new social forces have made their presence felt and has experienced sharp electoral swings. It was able to defeat candidates from the JD and later SP, whose agrarian and backward-caste agenda was not relevant at that point (Pai 1988).

The final stage in the conflict was the destruction of the Masjid on 6 December by a 300,000 strong mob plunging the country into the worst riots after Partition. By this time the BJP was in power in UP under the leadership of Kalyan Singh who used the absence of widespread communal riots during his tenure from 1991 onwards as evidence of fair government. In reality, preparations were on for the destruction of the Masjid and the relative calm was attributable to a refusal by

[14] For details of riots in all the various regions of UP, see Asghar Ali Engineer (1991a).

Muslims to be provoked into an unwise confrontation with an unsympathetic administration (Thakur 1993: 654). The Congress which was in power at the centre under P.V. Narasimha Rao did not act prior to or during the demolition of the Mosque despite advance information that an attempt would be made as early as in October (Udaykumar 1997: 16). It was only after the demolition that the Bajrang Dal, RSS, VHP, and two Muslim organizations were banned as communal organizations. Following the demolition of the mosque the mob that destroyed it built a makeshift temple on the ruins and installed images of Ram. On 2 January 1993 the district administration of Ayodhya lifted the ban and permitted Hindus to worship at the Ram shrine on the site of the demolished mosque (Udaykumar 1997: 20). There is little doubt that the manner in which the Congress dealt with the RJBBM dispute contributed to its decline in the Hindi heartland and elsewhere. The V.P. Singh government established a special bench in January 1990 and the Allahabad High Court declared that no construction could be undertaken until all civil suits were decided; despite much litigation, no settlement could be reached.[15]

The demolished Babri Masjid was no longer a rallying point. Muslims themselves were in a state of shock and deep anger, but they remained realistic enough to understand that confrontation did not pay. Their leaders were now reduced to silence and introspection. The following years were rather quiet. Sporadic incidents occurred, of course, but, except in Kanpur where the army had to be called in, these events were more or less trivial, or stopped in time by the police (Engineer 1994). UP witnessed no major riots during the rest of the 1990s or during the NDA government headed by Atal Behari Vajpayee at the centre upto 2004.

* * *

Our narrative shows that in the first two decades after independence, despite Partition and the communal riots that accompanied them, the beginnings of a composite and syncretic culture in the relationship between the majority and minority community was visible in UP. A process of integration and inclusion began which was recognized by many within both communities as a positive sign. It was a legacy of

[15] For details, see Udaykumar (1997: 15).

the national movement, tall leaders such as Nehru and the adoption of a secular, democratic constitution which allowed freedom to practice and propagate religion. Also, because the initial years of independence were free of any major communal riots, whether in UP or elsewhere, the Muslim community believed the government established by the Congress, which had led the national movement, would be able to provide protection of life, liberty, and property to the minority community. Despite the loss of its educated and professional class, which had migrated to Pakistan, the community began to gradually adjust and recoup its losses and there was steady improvement in the economic condition of sections of the Muslim community.

However, as our narrative suggests the Nehruvian period was unusual in terms of communal harmony; quite early it became evident that this accord could not be sustained. By the mid-1960s, problems between the two communities surfaced and communal riots re-emerged. The reasons lie partly in historical memories of riots during the colonial period, of Partition and partly in the situation after independence. A major reason for the continuation of riots in post-independence UP—and which will be more evident in the coming chapters—is that divisive features of both state and society were responsible for the re-emergence of communalism and riots particularly after the death of Nehru. Society remained divided into caste, class, and community, contributing to communal riots and concerns were voiced from the mid-1960s onwards at organized communal violence from time to time, which posed a threat to secularism. The secularity of the state was not established, it never punished those guilty of communal discord and violence; the instruments of the state especially the police and lower judiciary remained biased and communal. As a result, communalism and communal riots have always been as much a problem of law and order as social divisions which the state has failed to control.

Certain features of UP society have also been responsible. Located in the Gangetic plains of north India where social change in the colonial period was slow, it has a conservative society with a Brahminical culture. Our study points to the existence of a fairly strong, right-wing constituency within the leaders of the Congress party and in society, witnessed in the rapid progress made by the BJS and the RSS. It is a state where communal mobilization by the BJS but more particularly by the BJP, of not only the upper but also the middle castes from the

1980s onwards has proved successful. Consequently, the conservative Muslim leadership, particularly the Ulema, has also been successful in preventing social reform within the Muslim community and the rise of a modern educated leadership that could have helped prevent confrontation and conflict.

A consequence of this was the gradual communalization of electoral politics in UP from the mid-1960s witnessed in the attempt to create Muslim organizations and parties by Muslim leaders as a counterpoise to the BJS. While the general elections during the first decade were free of communal tension, with the Muslim community voting for the Congress, gradually competitive communal politics crept in with both sides keen to outdo the other. It also introduced the phenomenon of 'strategic' voting on the part of the Muslim community who began to vote keeping their narrower economic interests and safety in mind. The BJS while it did not indulge in open communal mobilization as in the case of the BJP later, it did cater to the Hindu community particularly the business class.

A second reason was the political economy of communalism which took a particular shape in the 1960s and 70s. A large section of the Muslim community left behind in UP, particularly in the rural areas, was poor, illiterate, and landless and unable to catch up with the majority community after independence. They owned little land and became landless labour on the fields of big landowners making them vulnerable to economic pressures. The artisanal section, which had prospered during the colonial period and in the early years of independence, due to their skills faced communal violence from the mid-1960s onwards in towns where they had traditionally practiced their craft due to competition with Hindu craftsmen and traders. There were attempts to take over the ownership of these businesses by Hindu merchants, which caused long-term damage to the Muslim community from which they have not yet recovered.

However, while the 1960s and 70s witnessed the return of communal riots in UP. The 1980s did constitute a turning point in communal relations in India and UP in particular, with the formation of the BJP, a right-wing party, based on the ideology of Hindutva, which is inherently divisive. The shift in the mid-1980s towards a more strident, open, and at times violent form of communal mobilization, particularly during the 1991 elections to create an upper caste Hindu vote bank under a more radical leadership that revived the RJBBM dispute. The decision of the Congress leadership also to move to the right, set the stage for a far more confrontational and violent phase. While it is true that after the destruction of the Masjid, UP did not experience any serious communal riots during the 1990s, the return of communal riots in an equally violent form in the 2000s, suggests that the 1980s and early 90s opened a new and more acrimonious chapter in Hindu–Muslim relations in UP and in the country. It is against this trajectory of Hindu–Muslim relations which seemed set for a new and harmonious beginning at independence, but returned in a more virulent communal form by the 1980s/90s, that the remaining chapters of our study attempt to understand the communal riots in selected districts of western and eastern UP in the 2000s.

Appendix A.1

Hindu–Muslim Communal Riots in India I (1947–86), by Violette Graff and Juliette Galonnier

Monday, 15 July 2013
Online Encyclopaedia of Mass Violence
URL: http://www.massviolence.org/Article?id_article=736
PDF version: http://www.massviolence.org/PdfVersion?id_article=736

Incidents of Violence in UP, 1947 to 1986

3 October 1961: Aligarh (Western Uttar Pradesh)
5–8 October 1961: Meerut (Western Uttar Pradesh)
22–23 October 1977: Varanasi (Eastern Uttar Pradesh)
29 March 1978: Sambhal (Western Uttar Pradesh)
13–14 August 1980: Moradabad (Western Uttar Pradesh)
29 September–2 October 1982: Meerut (Western Uttar Pradesh)
Upto 1986 there was only one major communal riot in eastern UP in Varanasi in 1977, five in western UP and none in any other part of the state.

Hindu–Muslim Communal Riots in India II (1986–2011) *Violette Graff and Juliette Galonnier*

Tuesday 20 August 2013, last modified 16 June 2015

Stable URL: http://www.massviolence.org/Article?id_article=738, accessed on 21 May 2016
PDF version: http://www.massviolence.org/PdfVersion?id_article=738

Incidents of Violence in UP, 1986 to 2011:

18–23 May 1987: Meerut (Western Uttar Pradesh)
8–11 October 1988: Muzaffarnagar (Western Uttar Pradesh)
28 September 1989: Badaun (Western Uttar Pradesh)
30 September 1990: Colonelganj (Eastern Uttar Pradesh)
30 October–2 November 1990: Ayodhya (Eastern Uttar Pradesh)
30 October–2 November 1990: Bijnor (Western Uttar Pradesh)
7–10 December 1990: Aligarh (Western Uttar Pradesh)
10–15 December 1990: Kanpur (Central Uttar Pradesh)
16 December 1990: Agra (Western Uttar Pradesh)
15–23 December 1990: Khurja (Western Uttar Pradesh)
31 January–5 February 1991 Khurja (Western Uttar Pradesh)
27 March 1991: Saharanpur (Western Uttar Pradesh)
19 May 1991: Kanpur (Central Uttar Pradesh)
20 May 1991: Meerut (Western Uttar Pradesh)
8 and 13 November 1991: Varanasi (Eastern Uttar Pradesh)
6–11 December 1992: Kanpur (Central Uttar Pradesh)
13–14 October 2005: Mau (Eastern Uttar Pradesh)
3 March 2006: Lucknow (Central Uttar Pradesh)
27–29 January 2007 Gorakhpur (Eastern Uttar Pradesh)

There were five incidents of communal riots in eastern UP and nine in western UP out of a total of 18 between 1987 to 2007. There were four in central UP four of which were in Kanpur and one in Lucknow.

Note: Violette Graff and Juliette Galonnier's encyclopaedia ends at 2011; there were, according to their estimate, no major Hindu–Muslim communal riots during 2007 and 2011 in UP. Between 2011 and 2016, there was only one major riot in September 2013 in Muzaffarnagar, western UP and its aftermath. However, there were numerous smaller incidents in western and eastern UP described in our chapters.

PART I

Eastern Uttar Pradesh

Culture, Political Economy, and the New
Discourse of Everyday Communalism

2 Politics, Culture, and the Political Economy of Everyday Communalism in Eastern Uttar Pradesh

As we have seen, communal tension and riots remain a pervasive feature of Indian and particularly UP society. However, the social and political context in which communal tension and riots take place varies in different regions of UP. This is particularly true of western and eastern UP, the two regions selected in our study. In the east, history, demography, and the economy together with politics have created a region where the nature and form of communalism is distinct from the western region. The number of Muslims in the population is less; there have been fewer major communal riots since Independence and relations between Hindus and Muslims are better than in the west. After Independence, until the riots related to the Babri Masjid dispute, there was only one major riot in eastern UP, in Varanasi on 22–23 October 1977, compared to five in western UP (Graff and Galonnier 2013a). During the period of the Babri Masjid dispute there were riots in Colonelganj on 30 September 1990, in Ayodhya from 30 October to 2 November 1990, and Varanasi from 8 to 13 November 1991 (Graff and Galonnier 2013b, see Chapter 1—Appendix). However, after the destruction of the Babri Masjid in 1992 there were no major riots in eastern UP during the 1990s.

During the 2000s, riots have reappeared in UP beginning in the eastern districts of Maunath Bhanjan (Mau henceforth) and Gorakhpur on 13–14 October 2005 and 27–29 January 2007, respectively, and moving towards the west from 2011 onwards. In this chapter, the attempt is to understand the reasons underlying the reappearance of communal tension and riots in the eastern districts particularly in our selected districts of Mau and Gorakhpur. The renewed communal incidents in UP during the 2000s date from the defeat of the BJP in the 2004 Lok Sabha elections and the unexpected victory of the Congress despite the 'Shining India Campaign' through which the former had hoped to gain another term at the centre. In UP, the BJP was shocked as it gained only 10 seats, down from 22 in 1999. In the 2007 assembly elections in UP it gained 51 seats as against the 89 it had won in 2002, its lowest score in many years. Throughout the 1990s, it was the SP and BSP who drove mass and electoral politics in the state. In the early 2000s with the continued decline of the two national parties—the Congress and the BJP—a bi-polar competition was witnessed between the SP and the BSP in eastern UP, where both have had a strong presence.

In this context, the 2000s constitute for the BJP a post-Ayodhya phase when the ideas and issues used in the RJBBM movement in the early 1990s are viewed as no longer effective having reached a phase of exhaustion. The continued failure of the Congress to revive its organization and base and the weakening of identity politics in the 2000s, allowed space for the revival and strengthening of the BJP in eastern UP. Clearly new strategies were required and the eastern districts provided space for experimentation. Therefore a key feature of communalism in the region—which our study also shows in the western region and seems to constitute the hallmark of this phase—is that long before the riots in Mau and Gorakhpur, the BJP–RSS attempted to institutionalize a system of low key, simmering communal tension and small incidents. This resulted in 'everyday communalism', which only sometimes leads to big riots. The aim is to create anxiety and fear in the minds of the Muslims by making them the 'other' in the eyes of the majority community. There have been no big riots since the Gorakhpur riots of 2007 but the attempt to sustain communal tension has continued. In fact, in Gorakhpur it was a continuation of daily small conflicts that briefly fed a riot. The aim as in western UP is essentially to build a vote bank and capture state power, though as our study will show, communal mobilization in eastern UP has distinct cultural features, which makes the underlying ideas and strategies different from those employed in western UP.

At the same time, it is essential to note that it was the SP under the leadership of Mulayam Singh Yadav—described as 'Maulana' Mulayam for his protection to Muslims during the RJBBM movement—that was in power when the Mau and Gorakhpur riots took place in eastern UP and the Muzaffarnagar riots in September 2013 in western UP. Commentators have pointed out that whenever the SP is in power, the BJP has been able to foment riots during the 2000s. They point to a tacit understanding that the former would gain the Muslim votes, the latter the Hindu votes. This shows the decay of the SP from a socialist to a feudal and corrupt family party, with strong links to communal leaders and mafia dons to whom tickets are given on the basis of winnability.

We argue that in eastern UP it is the emergence in recent years of three mobilizational strands that have provided fertile ground for grass roots communal politics by the BJP and its affiliates in the region, including in our selected districts. The Pasmanda movement of the poorer and backward Muslims that has swept eastern UP and Bihar since the early 1990s has constructed a new identity and heightened political consciousness that has empowered them to challenge the dominance of the upper caste/class Ashraf elite. The movement coincided with the acceptance of the Mandal report, which granted them reservation as a backward class. Consequently, they have emerged as a significant political mass and political parties in eastern UP are keen to gain their support. During the same period, globalization, decline, and a deep crisis in the handloom weaving industry has impacted on the livelihood of the Ansari Muslims. Political empowerment has been accompanied by loss of livelihood leaving them unhappy and hostile, rendering them vulnerable to mobilization and conflicts with Hindu traders. Simultaneously, the continuing economic backwardness of the region and decay of political parties into feudal and corrupt organizations interested only in capture of power has promoted criminalization of politics with strong links between mafia dons and politicians, which enable the former to protect their economic interests, support and encourage communalism.

The BJP and its affiliates during the 2000s have been able to take full advantage of these changes in the polity and economy of the region. The eastern region has witnessed, since the late 1990s, the rise of a new Hindutva communal power centre, fairly independent of and which often challenges the BJP–RSS organization, headed by Yogi Adityanath, Mahant (head) of the Gorakhnath temple in Gorakhpur. While the temple has existed in Gorakhpur for a long time, it is the present

Mahanth Adityanath and his aggressive organization the HYV who are playing an active role in creating, particularly in the area stretching from Gorakhpur to Bahraich, grass roots communalism to build a strong and inclusive Hindu identity. They are doing this by bringing Dalits and backwards into the saffron fold and pitching them against the Muslims. The mobilization has been attempted in a targeted manner; there was confrontation during the Mau and Gorakhpur communal riots between the Dalits and the Muslims in which the Yadavs and other OBCs were closely involved. While the socio-economic and political movements in the region mentioned above constitute the longer term, underlying, causal factors, it is Yogi Adityanath and his organization that has been the visible, political driving element in the 2000s, able to exploit these changes and undertake communal mobilization in the region.

In this chapter, an attempt is made to discuss these distinct socio-cultural and political features of eastern UP and to understand the nature of communalism in the region during the 2000s. It forms a background to the fieldwork in the two selected districts of Gorakhpur and Mau provided in the next chapter.

Castes and Communities in Eastern UP: Demography and Economy

Historically, eastern UP popularly called Poorvanchal, was the region ruled by the king of Kashi (Benares) made up of the regions of Mirzapur, Chandauli, Ballia, Mau, Ghazipur, Sonbhadra, Deoria, Kushinagar, Azamgarh, Jaunpur, Bhadohi, some main parts of Gorakhpur, Basti, and also Sant Kabir Nagar (Bayly 1992). Ruled by Brahmins and Rajputs, after the decline of the Mughal Empire, the militant Bhumihar Brahmins strengthened their sway in the area south of Avadh and in the fertile rice growing areas of Benares, Gorakhpur, Deoria, Ghazipur, Ballia, and Bihar and on the fringes of Bengal. The Nawab of Oudh eventually ceded the Kingdom of Kashi to the British in 1775 (Bayly 1992). Today Poorvanchal made up of 24 districts consists mainly of four divisions: the eastern-Awadhi and the western-Bhojpuri region, the Baghelkhand region in the south, and the Nepal terai region in the north.

Mau was earlier part of Azamgarh district. On 19 November 1988, the birth anniversary of Indira Gandhi, it was carved out as a separate district by the endeavours of then Congress MP Kalpanath Rai. During the period of the freedom struggle, the residents of Mau had given their full support to the national movement. Mahatma Gandhi visited Doharighat in October 1939. In the salt law Satyagraha, many persons from Mau took an active part. Also during the 1942 Quit India Movement, police firing killed and injured many persons. The Nawab of Awadh ceded one of the major districts of eastern UP, Gorakhpur, to the British East India Company in 1801. Gorakhpur city is the administrative headquarters of Gorakhpur district and division. It is well connected by bus services being within 90 km of the Nepal border, 273 km from Lucknow, 140 km from Faizabad, and 60 km from Kushinagar. An Air Force station was established in 1963. Gorakhpur is a Lok Sabha parliamentary constituency. It has four assembly constituencies Caimpiyarganj, Pipraich, Gorakhpur rural, and Sahajanwa.

The eastern districts form an agricultural region which historically has been a rare combination of extreme poverty and dense population with heavy pressure on agricultural land. While they have undergone considerable economic and social change, it has been much slower than in the west. These districts have very fertile soil, adequate rainfall, and abundant labour. However, the landowning pattern has been skewed, the upper- and middle castes owning large plots and the lower castes/classes marginal or dwarf plots. During the colonial period, beginning in 1874, eastern UP emerged as a major producer of sugar. The Gorakhpur–Basti region experienced a boom in the 1930s, but the unequal agrarian structure did not allow for the rise of an independent peasant class in spite of the spread of commercial crops in the 1930s as in west UP. It was the zamindar and the middleman who profited from sugarcane cultivation making it a debt-servicing crop rather than a surplus accumulator for the peasants (Amin 1982: 39–87).

In contrast to the western region, in the post-independence period the green revolution was late in eastern UP and covered a much smaller area (Pai 1993). While the first phase touched mainly the western region, the early 1980s witnessed a 'second round of the Green Revolution' in which the principal crop was rice, just as wheat had fuelled the first round in the 1960s (Dasgupta 1980; Pai 1993). Agricultural growth spread into the poorer peasant-dominated central and eastern region. Due to spread of HYVs of rice, consolidation of holdings, and introduction of tube wells and rural electricity, considerable agricultural transformation took place. In the 1980s UP as a whole registered a growth rate of 4.92—much higher than in the 1970s. The eastern region experienced higher productivity growth (5.81 per cent) per annum during the 1980s (Lieten and Srivastava 1999: 48). As a result the eastern districts can no longer be described as constituting an economic 'drag' on UP (Papola 1989). Some eastern districts have experienced agricultural prosperity though not on the same scale as in western UP earlier. However, in the 1990s due to globalization and neglect of agriculture the eastern districts together with large parts of UP experienced agrarian decline. The 1990s also witnessed endemic political instability and short-lived governments in UP which underlies much of the continuing backwardness in the state and contributed to the rise of the mafia in eastern UP (Shankar 2007: 81). The 2000s have experienced continuing agrarian distress which has affected particularly the Gorakhpur region while the decline of the weaving industry has impacted the Mau region.

The Muslims of Eastern UP

The Muslims of eastern UP have a distinct social identity different from that of the west. The large majority belong to the Ajlaf or middle- and lower-middle castes/classes with low ritual status and some from the Arjal or lower caste/class approximating to the Dalits in the Hindu community (A. Alam 2009). Most are handloom weavers/artisans with unique weaving skills, but who form the depressed, downtrodden, poorly educated, and marginal sections of Indian Muslim society. In the 1930s, influenced by the national movement and left movements in the region, the weavers who shared an occupational/class identity, mobilized and asserted themselves as a caste group, seeking special recognition as Momins or Ansaris[1] within a broader Muslim identity (Rai 2012: 61). This was visible in the formation of the All India Momin Conference or Jamiat-ul-Ansar in the late colonial period that seriously challenged the Muslim League's attempt to speak on behalf of all Indian Muslims. In the 1931 Census they asked their community to register as Momins. Santosh Rai describes this as part of the 'little tradition' which may not necessarily be compatible with the textual religious tradition

---

[1] The name or title of Ansari ('supporters') originated in Arabia at the time of the prophet Mohammad, Haynes (2012).

of the upper-caste Muslims. The weaving localities of eastern UP were sites of nationalist mobilization but their politics were not just about aligning with parties like the Indian National Congress (INC) or the Muslim League in the colonial and postcolonial period they had 'local meanings' shaped by local circumstances (Rai 2012).

These developments enabled the Ansaris to come together as a backward caste group and create a viable handloom industry after independence. In the 1990s during the Mandal agitation which gave them reservation as OBCs, the Ansaris experienced rising social and political consciousness leading to the formation of the Pasmanda Muslim Mahaz (hereafter Mahaz) demanding a better position and treatment from the upper-caste/class Muslims internally, and externally measures such as reservation from the Indian State (Rai 2012). Simultaneously in 1994, Ejaz Ali formed the All-India Backward Muslim Morcha (AIBMM) an umbrella group of over 40 BC Muslim organizations for the Arjal or Dalit Muslims.[2] The Morcha has demanded that the Arjal be recognized not as OBCs under Mandal but as SCs, as they find themselves disadvantaged against the Hindu and Muslim OBCs. The Mahaz in 2004, transformed itself into the All India Pasmanda Muslim Mahaz, an umbrella organization for all lower caste groups fighting for their rights; it also supports the demands of the Arjal Muslims.

A study has argued that the rise of Pasmanda consciousness suggests a new kind of Muslim politics, which is more about secularism and redistributive justice including reform of Personal Law, quality education, business skills, and protection of their handlooms, than about identity and representation and has implications for their relationship with the Hindu community in eastern UP, including in more recent years, the Dalits (A. Alam 2009). Ejaz Ali, leader of the Morcha, points out that communalism is a basic issue with which the Dalit Muslim movement has to contend with, as Dalits irrespective of religion, are made to attack and kill each other in the name of religion.[3] If all Dalits, irrespective of religion join hands, he feels they

---

[2] Interview of Ejaz Ali by Yoginder Sikand published in *Outlook*, 20 June 2002. Web edition, downloaded from https://www.outlookindia.com/website/story/dalit-muslims/216144 on 26 September 2016.

[3] See detailed interview of Ejaz Ali in Sikand (2004: 69–86).

could become a solid political force, as they form a large majority of the Indian population. It would resolve the allegation that during Hindu–Muslim riots, attacks on Muslims are by Dalits who are instigated by right-wing caste-Hindu groups. The Pasmanda consciousness has led to building of new identities to demand social justice and autonomous politics, both of which affect communal politics and are discussed in our study.

The Ansari weaving community has been badly affected during the 2000s by the decline and deep crisis in the handloom industry which has been affected by the entry of power looms, globalization, and the entry of cheap cloth from other countries, particularly China. This has affected the day-to-day relations between the Ansaris and the Hindu traders in the region. Certain economic features in eastern UP have traditionally made Hindu–Muslim relations different. In the western districts many of the riots that took place had a strong economic angle; they were to put down Muslim entrepreneurs who had become moderately successful in their business such as leather, brass, and glass works. The riots helped in the transfer of ownership or at least control over business, a good example being the Ferozabad glass industry.[4] In eastern UP the capacity of Muslims to challenge the position of Hindus is not as strong. The Muslims are not landlords or Ashrafs (upper caste/class) most do not own land and are largely artisans in industry predominantly owned today by Hindus. Poverty levels among them are much higher and they are viewed as local converts. Consequently, they do not have the capacity and the potential to challenge the position of the Hindus and the communal mobilization by Hindutva forces. In the west riots have been orchestrated to 'put down' Muslims who in post-independence India gradually began to improve their socio-economic position. In the east in contrast, they have conceded the position of ownership to Muslim entrepreneurs unlike in the west where it was wrested from them. This is due to their smaller numbers as well as high poverty levels. The relations between Hindus and Muslims in the east are not as antagonistic and conflictual. The capacity of Muslims to respond is lower; they do not fight back most of the time.

[4] See Chapter 1, Chopra and Singh, 1972.

Middle Castes and Dalits in Eastern UP

In the eastern region there was conflict during the communal riots between the Dalits and the Muslims in which the OBCs also played a role. The Ahirs and the Kurmis, clean cultivating castes roughly equivalent to the Jats in the West, now form the dominant caste in the east UP plains. They are very conscious of their status as OBCs; landownership gives them power and ritual status as middle castes. A study by Jens Lerche in the late 1990s, argues that a number of 'different agrarian transitions', that is, trajectories of capitalist development can be identified within UP agriculture—western, central, and eastern (Lerche 1998: A-29). From each a 'different balance of power' emerges between the Hindu landowning middle castes and landless labour, most of whom are Dalits, from which we can extrapolate their relations with the Muslims today. In western UP, due to early commercialization of agriculture, the green revolution, and backward caste mobilization under Charan Singh from the mid-1960s leading to prosperity made the Jats a strong agricultural caste. In the east, Lerche argues that land reform after independence created a class of small farmers mainly from the middle-ranking castes—Yadavs, Ahirs, and Kurmis belonging to the OBC category—who pursue highly productive agriculture and later prospered with the spread of the Green Revolution to parts of this region. Srivastava's study also points to these middle-caste groups as mainly responsible for the higher yields during the 1980s (R. Srivastava 1994: 168, 170; 1995: 230).

The Dalits in the region consist mainly of Chamars, Pasis, Musahars, and other smaller sub-castes. During the colonial period their socio-economic condition was much worse than in western UP. Due to low wages and lack of employment they were *harwahas*, literally ploughmen bonded to the zamindars (M. Singh 1947). The Chamars collectively held a large amount of land in the colonial period, but their individual holdings were small and today they are dwarf-holders and agricultural labourers. As leather workers they could pursue their traditional occupation whereas the Musahars, Balmikis, etc., with nothing to fall back upon, were thrown upon land. The Dalits experienced two rounds of anti-feudal and anti-caste movements, which politicized them. During the 1920s, this region was the scene of an anti-landlord peasant agitation on issues concerning land, indebtedness, and wages, leading to the *kisan sabha* (farmers' association) and *eka* (unity) movements from Pratapgarh eastwards. The agitation was led by socialist leaders such as Narendra Dev and at times by low-caste leaders such as Baba Ramchand and Pasi Madari, who became very popular with the rural masses (Dev 1946; M.H. Siddiqui 1978). Second, in 1946 the same region experienced a spontaneous rural agitation by Dalits against landlords using the exploitative practice of *begar* (unpaid labour) which is performed not by cultivating peasants but by landless untouchable labourers (R.N. Rawat 1996). However, neither of these succeeded in improving the conditions of the Dalits, leaving them dissatisfied with the left forces as both land and social power remained in the hands of the landowning upper-caste elite. Most important, the left movements did not enable them to question the power of the landowning Bhumihars, a strong upper caste in the region.

A number of developments have helped make the Dalits more assertive by the 2000s. The spread of the green revolution into eastern UP in the 1980s helped improve the condition of agricultural labourers who are largely from the SC (Kripa Shankar 1993). However, much of this change has taken place in the northern districts of Gorakhpur, Basti, and Deoria, the districts lying in the southern part have undergone less change, the pace of change here has been slow and poverty remains. The green revolution increased investment in agriculture, while urbanization increased employment opportunities on farms, brick kilns, construction activities, and rickshaw pulling in the cities (Pai 2002: 83). The 1990s also witnessed a rise in literacy rate in the population, specially the Dalits, and a shift towards non-agricultural employment making use of affirmative action policies. Equally important is the rise of the BSP, leading to pride in identity and the spread of the power of the vote under its protection which has made Dalits more independent (Pai 2002: 84). Consequently, Lieten and Srivastava's study indicates that in the eastern region the hold of the Thakurs in the late 1990s was no longer as secure although they still dominated over the poorer sections that were dependent on them for employment, fodder, and loans. However, there was less pressure on the lower castes to perform menial jobs or refusal to pay minimum wages. They report strikes in central and eastern UP districts by agricultural labourers for higher pay since the 1980s (Lieten and Srivastava 1999: 135). The absolute dependence on landowners and old patron–client relationships disappeared. In addition, Dalits have given up demeaning occupations and are less prepared to suffer indignities (Ahmad and Saxena 1994). However, the large population, slow economic growth, agricultural mechanization, and the closure of sugar mills have led to increased unemployment, social and political discontent, and some unrest in the region in the 2000s.

Pasmanda Politics, Political Economy, and Criminalization of Politics in Eastern UP

Pasmanda Politics

The rise of the Pasmanda movement in the 1990s coincided with the decline of the artisanal weaving economy which provided the lower caste/class Muslims their livelihood as Ansari weavers in the eastern region. These developments coincided with the publication of the Rajender Sachar Committee report in 2007, which revealed in detail the educational and economic backwardness of the minority community for the first time. It was also the time when cases against alleged 'Muslim terrorists' began to come up such as the Batla House encounter and, on a daily basis, a number of cases that led to arrests of Muslim youth in eastern UP, creating a feeling of victimization. Equally important was the reaction of the BJP and its affiliates to the Sachar Committee report that such views were responsible for 'appeasement' of the minorities by the so-called secular parties—the Congress and the SP. The RSS in fact described the report as an attempt to divide the nation. Thus, the early 2000s was a period of disillusionment with lack of employment, distress in the weaving industry, and a feeling of unhappiness with the Indian state and the government in UP. For the Muslim youth the visible state is the local *thana* (police station) or police constable who is often hostile and whom they view with fear and suspicion. Consequently, Pasmanda politics has taken two forms in eastern UP in the 2000s, which affects the communal politics of the region: building new identities to demand social justice through redistributive politics and moving away from mainstream parties to autonomous politics through forming separate Muslim political parties, three of which arose in eastern UP.

Building a New Identity

In eastern UP, the Ansaris were affected by the creation of the new identity of Pasmanda to which they could relate and the organizations built to sustain it. The Pasmanda Muslim Mahaz argued that 80 per cent of all Indian Muslims are backward and fall into the Pasmanda category. Anwar Ali in his book *Masawat ki Jung* (Struggle for Equality), refers to the cultural traditions of lesser known Muslim castes of Gaddi, Bakhho, Nut, etc., such as having their own caste panchayats where Islam contends with customary traditions of these castes for loyalty (Ali 2005). The movement has been an internal critique of the Muslim leadership, which treats them as backward and presages a new kind of Muslim politics (A. Alam 2009: 171). Anwar Alam explains that the word 'pasmanda' should be understood more in class rather than in caste terms and the Mahaz represents a class of people in the lower Muslim castes, who experience discrimination based on their caste status. The Mahaz sees its present preliminary phase as one of struggle for equality in which questions of caste-based discrimination and providing self-respect will be the most important. It is only after this phase that questions of class would make sense within the politics of the Mahaz (A. Alam 2009).

Following Mandal, the Mahaz participated in the 'Save Reservation Rally' held in Delhi in December 1998 and published the 'Muslim Agenda 99' with a group of Muslim organizations such as the All India Muslim Personal Law Board and the All India Muslim Majlis-e-Mashawarat. However, the Mahaz published its own booklet titled 'Pasmanda Agenda 99' which categorically rejected the 'Muslim Agenda 99'. Arguing that since the majority of Muslims were already beneficiaries of reservation through the Mandal Commission recommendation, its real purpose seemed to be to bring the upper-caste Muslims within the fold of reservations which would enable them to corner all the benefits of reservation (A. Alam 2009).

Alam argues that the Mahaz vision of Muslim politics is radically different from that of the dominant Ashrafs of whom it is very critical. The Mahaz has raised issues such secularism and representation, and view the question of the Babri Masjid or Urdu not as a Muslim but as a 'national' question to be tackled at that level and not through negotiation between leaders of communities. Other important issues on the agenda of the Mahaz include reform of Personal Law, reservation for poorer Muslims in the Muslim Aligarh Muslim University, tackling poverty, internal reform, providing quality education, business skills, and employment for Ansari weavers, and adequate protection of their handlooms. The Mahaz in fact, charges the religio-political Muslim leadership to be in league with the Indian political parties such as the BJP to keep these emotive religious issues alive to preserve its own relevance. In exposing the unrepresentative character of most Muslim bodies and bringing out the issue of everyday needs of the average Indian Muslim, the Mahaz has the potential of changing the metaphors of the Indian Muslim political agenda (A. Alam 2009).

A problem among the Pasmanda Muslims in Mau and surrounding towns which affects their relationship with the Hindu community is the nature of education available, which has given them a narrow world view. On the one hand, from the early 1980s a number of the Ahl-i-Hadith madrassa students from Mau and elsewhere began getting scholarships for higher Islamic studies in Saudi Arabia, which provided them a narrow fundamental Islamic worldview. On the other, many prosperous Muslims prefer to educate their children until the secondary level and then put them into the family business. They send them to Madrassas in Mau, which teach basic English and mathematics, but their overwhelming focus is on religious issues. Mau has only one college and more than 10 major Madrassas and other smaller *maktabs* (elementary schools), and in the absence of any leadership, it is the Ulema and the products of these Madrassas who claim to be the leaders of the Muslims. The Madrassas run by Islamic sects teach a sectarian form of Islam which adds to the narrow-mindedness of the Muslim community.

In this situation, Arshad Alam argues that the Mahaz has not yet developed a strategy to put its agenda of helping the Ansaris in eastern UP into action. Rather, it is concentrating on politics and has lost the character of a 'movement' and compromised with its original agenda of democratization and equitable justice within Muslim society. Ali Anwar is no longer part of the Mahaz, which now looks like any other Muslim political party, satisfied with raising symbolic issues, not attempting to change the status quo. The only difference being that in the Mahaz, the political is being articulated by low-caste Muslims, something which was unthinkable a decade ago. This in itself constitutes an important social change, something for which the politics of Pasmanda Mahaz cannot be denied due recognition (A. Alam 2009).

The Mahaz supports the demands of the Dalit Muslims to be included in the Scheduled Caste category, and given the same benefits as Dalits of other religions. However, the issue of who constitutes the Dalit Muslims differentiates the Mahaz from the Backward Muslim Morcha. Whereas the Mahaz categorically posits that only certain castes are qualified to be called Dalits among Muslims, the Morcha uses the term Dalit Muslim in a much more broad sense, including even dominant middle castes like Ansaris and at times even the Sheikhs among the beneficiaries of reservation (A. Alam 2009).

The rise of the lower caste/class Muslims in the towns of eastern UP such as Mau, which has a large population of Muslims, has affected the relationship of the Hindu and Muslim subaltern. The Hindu subaltern groups, not only the Dalits, but the non-Yadav OBC and most particularly the MBCs mobilized by the BSP in the eastern region, also feel abandoned in recent years by the BSP, SP, and the Congress, which has failed to recover its former position in the region. The BJP under the leadership of Mahant Adityanath has been quick to exploit these feelings among both the Hindu and the Muslim subaltern groups. In the eastern region, both caste and communal feelings often interact and play a seminal role in the construction of everyday communalism. It enables Adityanath to gain the support of the Dalits and lower backwards and turn them against the Muslims. In fact, the rise of this section is part of the rise of the non-Brahmin, Hindutva groups in many states such as Maharashtra and Gujarat. This is because for almost a decade the BJP has attempted to mobilize and gain the support of the OBCs and Dalits in many states. This has affected the social space in which interaction between the Hindu and Muslim subaltern groups in towns such as Mau, Azamgarh, and Gorakhpur takes place. It is the small daily mundane tensions between the two groups, which could normally be solved through negotiations by their leaders or elders, which the HYV takes advantage of, creating day-to-day anxieties and small clashes between the two.

Muslim Autonomous Politics: Political Parties

These identity-based changes were responsible for the emergence of a desire for an autonomous Muslim politics removed from the mainstream which led to the formation of three parties by Muslim leaders in eastern UP: the Rashtriya Ulema Council (RUC) and the Peace Party of India (PPI) in 2008, and the Quami Ekta Dal (QED) in 2010 (Verma 2006). While the RUC was formed by clerics and educated leaders of the community, the PPI formed by Dr Mohammad Ayub Ansari, a surgeon and philanthropist, was an attempt to repeat the BSP experiment of building an alliance of the BCs, Dalits, and Muslims and thereby provide these groups a fresh alternative (A. Srivastava 2011). Most important is the Quami Ekta Dal (National Unity Party) formed in 2010, by its president Afzal Ansari, a party of well-known mafia dons such as the brothers Mukhtar Ansari, MLA from Mau Sadar, and Sigbatullaha Ansari, MLA from the Mohammadabad Yusufpur seat, both situated in eastern UP (*PTI*, 28 June 2016).

Two features of this development are of relevance to our study. First, the move to form independent parties was taken forward by the modern, educated younger sections of the Muslim community. Second, their action has triggered a debate within the community which is continuing and is important for the future direction of politics in eastern UP (S. Kumar 2017: 211). The Muslim intelligentsia, sections of the clerics, and the younger educated groups, were angry and disappointed with mainstream national and state parties such as the Congress and the BSP in the early 2000s. Most particularly they were angry and disappointed with the SP and Mulayam Singh—the leader viewed by Muslims since the late 1980s as their 'protector'—for not preventing the build-up of communal tension in the early 2000s that eventually led to the Mau and Gorakhpur riots of 2005 and 2007, respectively. The younger generation particularly, was unhappy over lack of action following the Batla House encounter in Delhi leading to the arrest of Muslim youth from Azamgarh. In contrast, many, upper-caste conservative Muslims have argued that the formation of independent Muslim parties might lead to a division in secular votes that could enable the BJP to win. The leaders of the new parties tried to allay these fears by pointing out that the 'so called secular parties' were no better than the BJP and the community would be secure only if it raises 'a genuine political alternative' from its ranks, giving up the 'anti-BJP vote bank tag' (S. Kumar 2017: 212). A brief look at the formation and performance of these parties helps us understand their impact on Muslim politics in eastern UP.

The immediate reasons for the formation of Muslim parties were two important developments: the Mau riots of 2005 and the strong reaction of the BJP to its unexpected defeat in the 2004 national elections. Smita Gupta's study shows that BJP leaders believing they had lost due to the moderate policies of Atal Behari Vajpayee, did their best using 'every weapon in its armoury' to renew its strategy of communal mobilization and gain as many seats as possible in the 2007 UP assembly elections (S. Gupta 2007: 2142). In eastern UP the party permitted its 'saffron storm troopers' to foment communal violence, erect billboards with communal messages, distribute CDs with anti-Muslim propaganda, and its leaders described Muslims in bad language. Gupta mentions strong anti-Muslim sentiments expressed while she was doing field-work prior to the 2007 assembly elections in the eastern region. She argues that it was not some fringe elements but the top leadership of the BJP that was supportive of the communal activities of the BJP–RSS. She points to the statements at the BJP National Council meeting at Lucknow where intemperate speeches were made describing Muslims as 'terrorists' and against the appeasement vote-bank politics of the UPA which supported them (S. Gupta 2007: 2145). During the election there were CDs circulated that put forward a number of stereotype images of Muslims—their loyalty to Pakistan, their large families, that they kill cows, and proselytize and abduct Hindu girls. L.K. Advani did not criticize these CDs when journalists spoke to him about them.

In the midst of the highly communal electioneering, on 5 April 2007, the Allahabad High Court gave a provocative judgment that the Muslims could no longer be considered a minority in UP. Although the ruling was stayed by a two-member bench of the same court the next day, it created a sense of insecurity among the Muslims in eastern UP particularly due to the activities of the VHP in Allahabad and Varanasi where they tried to stir communal passions. Ashok Singhal visited Varanasi on 11–13 February and at a VHP conference announced the decision to install an idol of Ram in every village in the state and launch a state-wide yatra to obtain support for candidates who accepted their agenda (S. Gupta 2007: 2143). Gupta describes many other attempts to create friction between the two communities in Varanasi including attempts to destroy the city's *sadbhavna* (communal harmony) commit-tee. In fact, across eastern UP attempts were made to create problems which were helped by Mulayam Singh Yadav's support to high-profile

Muslims such as Mukhtar Ansari or Atiq Ahmed of Allahabad which further vitiated the atmosphere (S. Gupta 2007: 2143). It was due to the strict control by the Election Commission that apart from one minor communal clash in Kanpur a few days before polling rioting did not take place (S. Gupta 2007).

Despite these provocations the Muslims of UP remained calm through the 2007 assembly elections, which Gupta argues was remarkable as they were now confronting a more potent campaign issue than that of the Ram temple—that of the 'ugly Muslim predator, terrorist and traitor' (S. Gupta 2007: 2142). In fact, she argues that the Muslims played a critical role in preventing the BJP from creating the kind of communal polarization the party needed so desperately to retain the 89 seats it had won in 2002. The result was that in 2007 the BJP won just 51 seats, its lowest score in 18 years (S. Gupta 2007). The 2007 assembly elections were held in the backdrop of simmering communal tension in all parts of UP including Gorakhpur. Zafaryab Jilani, Member of the BMAC and Muslim Personal Law Board in Lucknow, Abdul Batin Nomani the Mufti of Varanasi, and Adnan Farrukh Shah, the Mia sahib of Gorakhpur, the Mutwali of the waqf properties in the area, all sent out messages that peace was to be maintained. This peace was to be maintained either during the Friday prayers or other forums, especially after the Allahabad judgment (S. Gupta 2007: 2144).[5] Despite the vandalism by Yogi Adityanath's HYV, the leaders advocated calm as they argued that communal riots actually helped the BJP. Many leaders held that Muslims needed to forget about politics and be busy educating their children, getting jobs, and working towards creating brotherhood with the Hindus. However, Gupta quotes some other leaders who felt it was a matter of life or death. It can be argued that it was fear that kept Muslims from being provoked. Perhaps, the example of the Gujarat riots of 2002 was fresh in their minds.

In this situation, Muslim leaders decided to form independent parties of their own. Only the Uttar Pradesh United Democratic Front (UPUDF), a Muslim front made up of smaller groups was formed prior

[5] For details of the stand taken by the various leaders, see the interviews by Smita Gupta (2007: 2144).

to the 2007 UP assembly elections, the rest were formed prior to the 2009 Lok Sabha elections. The UPUDF failed to gain the confidence of the community, which decided to remain with mainstream parties selecting a candidate—not always a Muslim—but one who had genuine concern for them. After the elections Khalid Rashid Firangimahal, the Naib Imam of the Idgah Mosque of Lucknow, in an interview to Smita Gupta, held that he and others had opposed the UPUDF as it was felt India was a secular country and a religious party had no place in it and they would be criticized by the BJP and the Sangh Parivar. More important, he argued that, 'Muslims are the most secular section of the population in this state' (S. Gupta 2007: 2145). Thus, in the 2007 election despite their disillusionment with Mulayam, the Muslims voted for the SP which explains its second position despite facing strong anti-incumbency; the second choice was the BSP which helped it gain a majority. Many commentators described this as tactical voting but it kept the BJP out. In the election, the number of Muslim members of the UP assembly reached a new high of 56, almost 14 per cent in the 403-strong assembly: 29 won on a BSP ticket, 21 on an SP ticket, 3 on an RLD, and 1 on a UPUDF ticket while there were two were independents. Nine of these seats had been held by the BJP in the past (S. Gupta 2007: 2145).

Nevertheless, the Muslim parties have not performed well as they did not attract the large majority of Muslims who preferred to remain with the mainstream parties. Only the Ittehad E-Millait Council gained one seat, the Quami Ekta Dal (QED) two, and the PPI got two seats in elections in the 2000s. The greatest disappointment was the PPI, which was expected to perform well in its stronghold, eastern UP; Muslim voters preferred not to divide their votes and supported the SP. They could not bring themselves to vote for the party at the risk of the BJP's victory, which was leading a charged campaign in Poorvanchal under the leadership of hard-line Hindutva leader Yogi Adityanath. The QED managed to gain 354,578 votes in the 2014 national election. In a meeting held in Ghazipur in early June, QED held that like-minded parties should come on a common platform to deal with communal forces. Yet the party merged with the SP on 21 June 2016. Shivpal Yadav, brother of Mulayam Singh held that this would strengthen the SP (*PTI*, Lucknow, 21 June 2016). However, Chief Minister Akhilesh Yadav opposed the merger and called it off. Afzal Ansari of the party criticized this, saying he felt 'humiliated' and Akhilesh had done it due to his ego and 'branding'. However, by end October, Shivpal Yadav the president of the state unit of the party decided once again to merge the QED with the SP. The senior leaders of the party feel that in the coming 2017 assembly elections, the QED would help win seats in eastern UP where a tough competition was expected between the SP and BSP over Muslim votes. Eventually Akhilesh kept the party out and the QED decided to support the BSP.

At the same time the rise of these parties upset the SP which has always tried to portray itself as the party supported by Muslims in UP. In 2006, sensing the unhappiness of the Muslims the SP leadership had accelerated its attempts to appease Muslims. It decided to nominate an additional resident commissioner in New Delhi to establish better coordination with the National Commissioner for Minorities' Educational Institutions (NCMEI). It took steps to fill vacant posts in minority institutions, and decided to increase the representation of the minorities in government jobs, etc. However, the educated Muslims were not impressed as seen from the formation of independent Muslim parties.

The debate within the community over the future direction of Muslim politics in eastern UP has continued. More recently, Dr Ayub the leader of the PPI described the SP as the 'biggest communal party in the country' which failed to prevent the Muzaffarnagar riots and to provide decent camps to rehabilitate Muslims afterwards (Arunava Sinha, *Times News Network*, 11 January 2014). This attracted the wrath of the upper-caste leadership who alleged that the PPI was working for the BJP by dividing the 'secular votes' (Sinha 2014). Responding to these allegations, the leaders of the RUC and PPI argued that parties like SP, Congress, and BSP were only secular in name, using Muslims as vote banks and doing nothing for them. In an interview, Dr Ayub said that his aim was to 'break' the Muslims from the SP and bring them to the PPI, which was a truer representative of the community. Consequently, a division has arisen between the modern and the conservative leaders over the question of forming separate Muslim parties. A second division is the presence of Muslim clerics within parties such as the RUC whose attitude towards questions of discrimination and absence of justice within the community remains questionable.

Political Economy of the Mau–Gorakhpur Area

The economy of eastern UP has undergone a number of changes which underlies the growing communal divide in the region: the decline of the handloom sector of the weaving industry, globalization, fall in prices and loss of markets for products and conflicting commercial interests of the Muslim and Hindu weavers. A quick appraisal of the artisanal economy of eastern UP will help us understand how these changes have impacted communal politics in Mau and Gorakhpur.

The weaving and carpet making industry is spread across eastern UP, the major centres being Ballia, Mau, Mubarakpur, Deoria, Gorakhpur, Bahraich, Varanasi, Tanda, and Bhadohi. Many of these are facing problems. Besides agriculture, Mau about 90 km from Varanasi has long been famous as the powerhouse of textile weavers in Eastern UP particularly for the manufacture of silk sarees (Verma, Rai, and Khan 2005). After the decline of the textile industry in Varanasi and Mubarakpur, Mau stands as one of the last bastions of textile hubs of UP. A 1998–99 survey of the Ministry of Small and Medium Enterprises (MSME) put the number of power looms at 58,381 (Government of India, Ministry of MSME: District Industrial Profile of Mau District 2012). In 2005, there were approximately 75,000 power looms, about 60,000 were in the city. On an average, almost 1.5–2 lakh sarees are weaved on a daily basis. Several members of one family work on one loom and a full day's labour produces on an average two sarees (Government of India, Ministry of MSME).

In the era of handlooms most of the workers producing sarees were Muslim, and among them it was mainly the Ansaris who worked in sari manufacture. There was a time when sarees, 'lungis', 'dhotis', sheets, etc., made in Mau had their own distinct identity throughout the country; but now the economic condition of the weavers is steadily deteriorating. The saree trade has suffered economic losses repeatedly; both internal and external factors have been responsible. Political instability and communal tension has greatly harmed this industry (*Milli Gazette* 2002). In Mau, Muslims are in sizeable number and they have political control over the Mau township and normally one of them is elected Chairman of the municipal corporation, but this has not helped the poorer Muslims or helped the community when it comes to riots. Despite the number of Muslims, they have not been able to pressurize the government to help them. Today the textile and cloth industry is facing problems. These problems are affecting the livelihood of those associated with it due to the exorbitant increase in electricity charges, very limited supply of power, non-supply of raw material, excessive increase in the price of cotton, terry cot, and nylon thread, which have pushed the weavers to look toward other jobs.

When power looms were introduced here in 1960 people felt extremely happy. Swadeshi Cotton Mills, Swadeshi Mills and others were set up, but shortly after that the financial condition of small weavers working on hand looms gradually started deteriorating. As power looms required more money the character of this trade altered. Earlier the Ansaris used to make sarees by buying thread from Hindu Bania businessmen and selling their finished product to them. Over the last three decades, especially after the devastating riots of 1984, some Ansaris began to sell their sarees directly without going through middlemen. This led to social and economic mobility, but it also led to increased competition and often conflict with Hindu businessmen. Gradually, Hindus also entered the trade and a substantial number of them are said to work in this trade now. In addition, the number of big Hindu retailers has also greatly increased (*Milli Gazette* 2002).

Currently, the troubled saree trade in Mau is undergoing a period of economic crisis (Government of India, Ministry of MSME). In the 2000s, the local saree trade underwent an economic slump due to competition from cheaper sarees from Surat which have replaced sarees in the local market where the Mau weavers had a monopoly and elsewhere. This has led to a sharp decline in the weavers' wages in Mau. Earlier, work on one saree fetched Rs 80, but the wages have now been reduced to Rs 40. Similarly, embroidery fetched Rs 150 earlier, but now has gone down to Rs 80–85. The wages after a full day's work is not of one worker only; it is the combined labour of many members of a family working on one loom. Consequently, weaver's wages have drastically fallen and family income reduced as more than one person was involved in the trade. Other problems are sourcing the required materials, which have become more expensive and lack of electricity as small weavers cannot afford generators. Also after power looms, new Chinese machines, which can do embroidery earlier done by hand, have entered and are being used by big traders and weavers which has created a crisis of existence for small traders. At the same time, many other smaller weavers in parts of eastern UP were faced with unprecedented economic crises, being thrown out of employment due to dumping of foreign goods and 'open' market policies. All these structural changes and crises have expressed themselves in a violent form.

Banaras or Varanasi faces a different kind of problem. According to the report of the Entrepreneur Institute of India which helps develop skills among weavers, there are about one lakh handloom weavers at Varanasi, but presently only 40,000 are active.[6] In addition, there are hundreds of traders, dyers, designers, card-makers, and ancillary support providers. The annual turnover (at Varanasi prices) is estimated at around Rs 400 crores. While being concentrated in Varanasi city, the activity has spread to surrounding villages. About 70 per cent of the weaver force is in the city, of which 90 per cent are Muslim, while 30 per cent of the weaver force in villages is Muslim. The main product of the Banaras Handloom Cluster is the saree whose estimated share in the total value of output varies from 90 per cent to 95 per cent. The other products are dress materials, furnishing fabric, fashion accessories, such as, stoles and scarves. The saree segment typically consists of two kinds: satin-based work (largely Karnataka yarn) and organza type work (largely Chinese yarn). The former is concentrated in North Varansi–Badi Bazar, Alaypura, Pilikothi; the latter is visible in South Varnasi mainly in Madanpura. Most of the output (90 per cent) gets sold in Varanasi. However, a major problem is that the incidence of contractor weavers and co-op societies selling directly to traders/others outside Varanasi is very limited.

There are two developments which are exerting pressure on the Banaras saree, which affect the hand weaving segment, which is undertaken by Muslim weavers (Government of India, Ministry of MSME). The first is exclusivity; it is possible to make each heavily worked or embroidered ornamental saree exclusive because it is easy to make variations on a machine. This is not so in case of hand weaving and currently, there is an emphasis on exclusiveness. A basic, heavy saree may cost Rs 2,000 and work on it gets priced at, say, Rs 8,000, leading to a price of Rs 10,000. Unlike weaving, work pricing is somewhat

---

[6] Varanasi Handloom Cluster under Integrated Handloom, Cluster Development Scheme; Enterprise Development Institute of India, Gandhi Nagar, Gujarat, 2007.

discretionary and offers scope to the retail outlets for larger margins. The heavy work trend according to market observers is undermining the significance of exquisite weaves in the traditional aesthetic consciousness. This shift from woven to non-woven ornamentation, weavers apprehend, may not be temporary and poses a serious, long-term threat to the prospects of the higher-end Varanasi saree. In the lower-end segment, the Varanasi saree does not possess long-established or traditional brand equity. It has grown quantitatively in this segment as a result of expansion of the weaver force and market conditions and is fighting the entry of power-loom sarees. It manages to secure some volumes but mainly at the cost of the helpless weaver. Second, the brand equity of high-profile retail outlets now, in a certain context, matches or exceeds that of Banarasi high-end sarees. This has affected the value-chain; such retail outlets securing a larger share of the price cake; squeezing the share of Varanasi-based players. In both price segments, the saree has been facing problems and these problems do not appear temporary; notwithstanding occasional spurts in demand. The dress material, furnishing fabric, and accessories are selling on the strength of their own aesthetic/economic strength; without drawing strength from Varanasi brand equity. The non-saree product line, rather small in relation to the total Varanasi output, thus, is not showing any signs of noticeable growth (Government of India, Ministry of MSME 2012).

The estimated of share of export in handloom output at Varanasi is meagre and varies from 2 per cent to 3 per cent. Besides sarees for the ethnic population abroad, the other products exported are furnishing fabrics and accessories. The exports, in most cases, entail large volumes (for a given trader); the industry does not have networking systems. The orders are time-bound. The exporter, many times, convert it into a power-loom order. The products in the overseas market are largely positioned in purpose terms—sarees, table runners, curtains, stoles and its handloom identity remains either undeclared or low key. There are few countries, for example, Australia and New Zealand which offer incentives for handmade products and so importers ask for an appropriate certification from the Export Council; hopefully bringing the fact of handmade product into focus. However, most of the world does not require such evidence at all. The export products move largely on the strength of intrinsic aesthetics and workmanship;

bereft of Varanasi brand equity. The foreign buyers remain fairly removed from Varanasi in terms of reaching down directly to local traders and societies, leave alone weavers or asking explicitly for Varanasi weave and design. Under the quota system, handlooms were not within the purview of quota. Now that quotas are phased out, the advantage is wiped out. The industry has not been able to explore demand in neighbouring countries for saree/lahenga (Government of India, Ministry of MSME).

A study in 2009 points out that globalization, technical advancement, and particularly the inflow of Chinese fabrics has virtually destroyed the power loom and handloom leading to about two lakh Muslim weavers in UP becoming unemployed (Falahi 2009). The government had no plan ready to rehabilitate the traditional weavers and artisans when technological advancement took place affecting them. The study shows that in Varanasi, 70 per cent of Muslims were part of the weaving industry and a large number of them have shifted to rickshaw pulling based on loans from banks. In Varanasi, 40 per cent of such loanees from Punjab National Bank were weavers; many could not repay and committed suicide. While the government has waived electricity due from power looms, this has not been extended to handlooms. Consequently, they have been pushed into poverty; the areas in which they live in the city are devoid of basic amenities and their children who are dying of malnutrition (Falahi 2009).

These changes in the handloom weaving industry are closely related to the riots in the Mau region. The decline of the Mau economy, as the next chapter will show, has a direct impact on Hindu–Muslim relations in the city and the region. The antagonism surfaces in the cultural and religious field as riots take place due to clashes on religious events such as the annual Bharat Milap ceremony of the Hindus and Muharram of the Muslims. These clashes encouraged by the Hindutva forces on these occasions, described in detail in the next chapter, then translate into the economic arena. Mau shops and looms are occasionally targeted and burnt, sometimes along with those who work on them, when organized communal frenzy is orchestrated. Those familiar with the intermittent riots at Madanpura in Varanasi would testify that it unfailingly springs from the contradictions of the trade, whereby Hindu traders resort to non-economic means to oust Muslim traders who have graduated from the ranks of loom workers and offer better terms to the wholesale urban traders. As our fieldwork in the next chapter shows, during the Mau riots the Muslim establishments were marked out and burnt with the police not helping. There is also a strong feeling that the government—the riots happened during the regime of Mulayam Singh Yadav—did not intervene as Yadavs and backward castes were also involved, leading to disillusionment and support for the Muslim political parties, discussed earlier.

Another lesser-known component of the Mau economy is the fruit and vegetable market and competition between communities within it. In the Mau township, Muslims are owners of looms, but they are also fruit and vegetable vendors and are in the meat market (Rawat 2016). The commercial interest of Muslim vegetable vendors collides straight with the Khatiks, a Dalit community involved in the meat-selling business, including pork. The Hindutva forces cleverly use this contradiction in fermenting riots and involving Khatiks in it. Rawat argues that this is the 'modus operandi' of the communal forces who know it would be difficult to fight the Muslims directly; they therefore involve the Dalits. Over the years the Dalits and backwards have got highly politicized and gradually antagonistic towards the Muslims, due to economic differences and sustained Hindutva mobilization (Rawat 2016). The attraction of Hindutva in backward communities is not new. Except for Yadavas, who have been aligning with SP and the oppressed backward communities with the BSP, powerful Kurmi and Lodhs have found their ally in the Hindutva forces. Dalits, by and large, had remained outside the Hindutva fold, but in the 2000s the power elite is playing a dubious role trying to make a dent in this relationship and cultural norms come handy for them. This intra-subaltern conflict is visible in the Mau riots of 2005 described in the next chapter.

From Left Politics, Caste-centric Mafiadom to Religious Criminalization

There is a close interface between the decline in the artisanal and slow growth of the agricultural economy, economic backwardness, and the politics of criminalization in eastern UP which harks back to the 1980s, but has become more entrenched and today developed links with communal elements. In the first three decades of independence both the Communist and Socialist parties had a strong base in the eastern districts, the former having its strongest unit in the country in this region.[7] The support base of the left parties was in eight eastern districts with high population density and smallholdings, the most important being Azamgarh, Ghazipur, and Ghosi which returned MLAs in the 1962, 1967, and 1971 parliamentary and assembly elections (Brass 1968). The left organized the agricultural labourers, most of them SCs into labour unions against bonded labour and supported land re-distribution to poor peasants, lower land ceilings, and abolition of land revenue on smallholdings in the 1960s (Brass 1968). Land-grab movements were organized but proved a short-lived phenomenon and failed to help the peasants (R. Singh 1974: 45).

Between the mid-1960s and late 1990s the socialists were active in the region. Most important being Kalpanath Rai, a socialist and Bhumihar leader, who played an important role in the local politics of Azamgarh, Mau, at times Gorakhpur, and represented Ghosi in parliament for over two decades.[8] The period in which he was active is described as the 'Kalpanath Rai period' that brought development to the region making it an election issue (Agrawal 2016). He is credited with transforming the one-time small tehsil of Mau into a full-fledged district headquarter, providing a well-equipped hospital, DD relay

[7] The Communists did not secure any seats in the first UP assembly election in 1952, but in the second and third election, they captured 9 and 14 seats and 3.83 per cent and 5.1 per cent of the vote, respectively (Srivastava 1967: 328). In 1967, after the split, the CPI emerged stronger gaining 14 seats and 3.41 per cent while the CPM gained only one seat and a little over 1 per cent of the vote (Brass 1968).

[8] Beginning his career in 1963 as general secretary of the Samajwadi Yuvjan Sabha of UP, he held important positions in the Samyukta Socialist party during the 1960s before joining the Congress in 1974. In the Congress he was made General Secretary of the All India Congress Committee (AICC), was member of the Rajya Sabha for three terms from 1974 to 1992, of the Lok Sabha from 1989 to 1998 and deputy minister Parliamentary Affairs and Industry and later minister of state for power. Under the Narasimha Rao government, Rai held various cabinet portfolios such as Food and Power and during the late 1990s, he remained an important leader in parliamentary committees until his death in 1999. In 1993–4 he was minister of state for food and became controversial due to the sugar scam involving his ministry. He was jailed in connection with the scam, but was later acquitted free of charge (Agha 1996).

kendra, network of pucca roads with streetlamps, an elegant district collectorate building, two new spinning mills, and a thread-processing plant for the Muslim weaver population. He intensified development procedures in the district bringing technology, industry, prosperity, trade, and modern infrastructure to a part of UP known to be one of the most backward and poor. Also during his tenure as MP, the district was attributed to be very peaceful with no communal violence. Some have argued that after Rai, 'development paused' in Mau and nearby districts; not a single brick in the name of development has been placed after his death; rather criminalization of politics found space in the region (Agrawal 2016).

The decline of the left and socialist parties provided ground for the rise of criminalization of politics in Poorvanchal, but more particularly in the districts north of the Ghaghra river: Maharajganj, Deoria, Kushinagar, Siddharthnagar, Basti, and Bahraich. The 1980s witnessed serious upper-caste based criminalization of politics due to rivalry between two Mafia groups, Harishankar Tiwari, a Brahmin, and Virendra Pratap Shahi, a Rajput, both of whom were elected as MLAs from different constituencies. Joined by others such as Shriprakash Shukla, a Brahmin, they gained considerable political patronage and dominance in the region. Their dominance stemmed from the high stakes they had in the government corporations, railway contracts, timber market, coal mining, sand mining, petrol pumps, sugar factories, and many more areas.

Two factors promoted the rising criminalization in the 1990s: the slow pace of development encouraged competition, corruption, and crime on a large scale and second, it coincided with the decline of the SP and BSP by the late 1990s from being parties of 'social justice' for Dalits, lower castes, and Muslims, to parties interested in merely capture of power that pushed both of them towards criminal politics. It created heightened competition between these two parties as the BJP and Congress were in decline in the state and encouraged the links between politics, crime, and communalism as it pushed these parties to select candidates on the basis of 'winnability' which meant the use of muscle power and money to win elections. The result was the creation of an elaborate structure of criminalization of politics in which both caste and communalism interacted with politics, which helped the interests of mafia dons who moved from party to party depending on who they thought would win and provide them a share in the economic spoils of the region.[9]

Moreover, while the rise of lower-caste parties in east UP challenged the dominance of the upper caste in electoral politics, the NGOs, civil society, bureaucracy, business, and trade unions, continued to be in the powerful grip of the Bhumihars, Brahmins, and Thakurs (Rawat 2016). Consequently, a Mafia class arose within the upper castes as well as the Muslim community who were also respected leaders of their communities, and were keen to continue their hold over politics and the economy, which allowed them unrestrained freedom over the natural resources of the region. While the former did not get any threat from the Dalits and backwards whose leaders were not in a position to oppose them, for the latter the Dalit–backward–Muslim connection worked for them as they stood for 'secular politics' and gained support from leaders such as Mulayam Singh Yadav. When unhappy with Mulayam some of them moved to the BSP for help, which was equally willing to provide support.

While the BSP has given tickets to many criminals, since the late 1990s, the SP became the party of the new business, political, and criminal elements in the region. This was witnessed in the attempt to bring D. P. Yadav in prior to the 2014 elections and the close association with Muktar Ansari and his party the Qaumi Ekta Dal since the 1990s. Polarization of votes between the SP and the BSP threatened the very base of the upper-caste leadership in eastern UP, who began to join the BJP. Once in the BJP, blending of the communal angle helped them create a social constituency to win votes. As caste polarization and gang wars increased, it got converted into bigger units of religious polarization, which suited both the Hindutva gangsters and the dons

---

[9] A good example is Ramakant Yadav a leader from Azamgarh powerful in this area ever since 1999 (Manjul 2009). Around 17 criminal cases are still pending against him, including those under the Gangster Act and Goonda Act. He was with the SP in the early 2000s, but joined the BSP in 2004 and the BJP in 2008. In 2009, he won on a BJP ticket from Azamgarh to the Lok Sabha. In the 2014 Lok Sabha elections, Mulayam Singh Yadav defeated him. In June 2016, Ramakant Yadav invited Balram Yadav who was removed from the SP to join the BJP along with his son as he argued that Akhilesh Yadav by removing him had humiliated all Yadav leaders of eastern UP (Dainikbhaskar.com 2016).

espousing secularism in eastern UP. The killing of Krishnanand Rai in Mohammdabad, for example, gave the BJP a big opportunity to present him as a Hindu leader; BJP president Raj Nath Singh started a Nyaya Yatra and sat on dharna in Varanasi (Rawat 2016). Paradoxically in the 1996 national elections Rai, who had won twice from Ghosi as a socialist, stood an independent—as the Congress did not give him a ticket—supported by the upper-caste mafia which had emerged. The SP and the BSP fielded Noorani and Mukhtar Ansari two local dons against him hoping to gain the Muslim votes against the upper caste mafia. Rai won the fight against the dons in 1996, once again in 1998 as a Samata party candidate. However, after his death, neither his wife nor son, who took the help of the local dons of the constituency, could win against the BSP in the 2004 national elections.

From Caste-centric Mafiadom to Religious Criminalization

The late 1990s witnessed a number of gang wars in the state which led to the decline of the upper-caste mafia in eastern UP. In 1997, Virendra Pratap Shahi was killed by Shriprakash Shukla in Lucknow over mafia rivalry, thus bringing an end to the prominent Rajput mafia face dominating the region.[10] In 1998 Shriprakash Shukla was gunned down by the Special Task Force (STF) over reports that the former had taken Rs 6 crore in the early 1990s to kill the then BJP Chief Minister, Kalyan Singh (Rawat 2016). The weakening of the upper-caste mafia in the late 1990s provided space for the rise of Yogi Adityanath, Hindutva politics, and the emergence of everyday communalism in the area. As everyday communalism required the availability of unemployed youth driven by political aspirations and looking for a patron to acquire a sense of identity and purpose, the waning of the upper-caste mafia led the youth associated with them to shift their activities into the ambit of Hindutva politics. This structural shift in the nature of politics of the region provided space for change in the 'agency' of the leading figures dominating in the region; it also signified the shift from supremacy of caste-centric

---

[10] In 1996 Lok Sabha election Virendra Pratap Shahi contested from Gorakhpur on an SP ticket against Mahannt Avaidyanath, who happened to be the sitting BJP MP; the latter secured 236,369 (or 42 per cent) votes, the former secured 179,189 (or 32 per cent) votes.

mafiadom to categorical religious criminalization. Yogi Adityanath, then 26, was fielded as the BJP Lok Sabha candidate from Gorakhpur, on the behest of Mahant Avaidyanath who was not keeping well. The young Yogi won the election. However, unlike his predecessors from the Gorakshnath Peeth temple, Mahant Digvijaynath and Mahant Avaidyanath, who despite participating in active politics, refrained from actively intervening in the day-to-day activities of the region, he plunged into the active day-to-day activities of the region immediately, making him emerge as the new firebrand icon of Hindutva in the region.

An important factor that has helped in the rise of Yogi Adityanath is that the Gorakshnath *peeth* belongs to a non-Brahmin tradition and its Mahant is a Rajput rather than a Brahmin. This enabled the emergence of a distinct form of 'Non-Brahmin-Hindutva' in the hitherto Brahmin-dominated region with efforts to bring in the lower OBCs and Dalits into the ambit of the Hindutva forces. However, the shadow of the old Brahmin–Rajput mafia rivalry over resources and public space continued under the leadership of Yogi Adityanath, who had to tackle two challenges to his dominance. Being a Rajput whose stature in the region is considerably lower than the Brahmins, he had to forge an alliance with lower castes to maintain his electoral edge over rivals in general and Brahmins in particular. Second, his desire to dominate the everyday life of the region was possible only after completely marginalizing the old mafia, especially Brahmins like Harishankar Tiwari, who, though weakened were still active and reluctant to retire.

One particular incident reveals how Adityanath gained control over the older mafia and emerged dominant in the region. After he became the MP from Gorakhpur in 1999, goons allegedly acting on the behest of mafia-politician Harishankar Tiwari, tried to capture a palatial property in the Gorakhpur city belonging to a leading businessman, hailing from the Bania (trading) caste, Purushottam Das. Saurabh Vishvakarma, the vice president of Hindu Yuva Vahini, who is from the carpenter caste recounted what unfolded in detail:

> In 1999, when the goons of Harishankar Tiwari, tried to capture the property of Purushottam Das, the latter called the D.M. and S.P. but none of them responded. Finally, seeing no way out he called Yogiji, who immediately reached at the spot along with his supporters and started

protesting against the goons trying to capture the property. Immediately, the local people felt empowered and came in support of Yogiji and the goons had to make a hasty retreat. That was the last incident when some mafia has tried to have his sway in the city. Thereafter, they have been ousted as no one would dare to face the wrath of Yogiji. We at HYV are ready to go to any extent to implement his wishes. (Interview with Saurabh Vishwakarma, November 2016)

Saurabh Vishvakarma hence claimed that the 'reign of the erstwhile Brahmin mafia' and the 'Muslim lechery' were the twin evils that have been crushed under Yogi's leadership. Regarding the former, a dominant upper-caste group oppressive of the lower OBCs to which Saurabh belongs, he explained how under the leadership of Yogi Adityanath the Brahmin mafia lost their erstwhile dominant position:

Under the leadership of Yogiji, we have ousted the erstwhile Brahmin Mafia not only from the city but also from the region and they couldn't dare to come back again. Before Yogiji's ascendance and the formation of HYV, the city and the region was notorious for mafiadom and law and order problem. The business community was living under the reign of their terror. Yogiji and HYV under his leadership have ensured that no Mafia would ever dare to touch any businessmen in the area. Now, thanks to Yogiji, there is peace and law and order wherein everyone is doing their business peacefully. No business community has to live under the shadow of fear. The likes of Harishankar Tiwaris have been ousted from the town forever. (Interview with Saurabh Vishwakarma, November 2016)

Nor did Yogi Adityanath find entering the political arena in eastern UP easy in the late 1990s due to strong opposition from the mafia in the region. In the 1998 Lok Sabha election, which was his first, he won with a margin of 26,000 votes. However, in the 1999 Lok Sabha election, he contested against Yamuna Nishadh, a lower OBC who had the support of his numerically large community in the Gorakhpur Lok Sabha constituency (around 300,000). Empowered by the Mandal aspiration, Nisadh, the SP candidate, a former associate of the Gorakshnath Temple and a person with a criminal image, almost defeated the Yogi who managed to retain his seat by the bleak margin of just 7,322 votes (For details see, Election Commission of India 2017; also see, Manoj Singh 2016). It was his own non-Brahminical background but also the struggle against the entrenched upper castes and the local mafia that led

Adityanath to adopt non-Brahmin Hindutva and emerge as a dominant communalizing force in eastern UP in the 2000s, as discussed below.

Institutionalization of Everyday Communalism in Eastern UP in the 2000s

The rise of Pasmanda consciousness among the Ansari Muslims, their unhappiness at the steep decline of their handloom business—which has made them vulnerable to communal mobilization—the backwardness of the region, and the rise of criminalization of politics linked to caste and communalism, has provided fertile ground for the rise of Yogi Adityanath. These factors have contributed to the gradual institutionalization of everyday communalism in eastern UP. At the same time, the emergence of a Hindu consciousness in eastern UP is much older and dates back to the 1920s, which the more contemporary attempts at mobilization based on Hindutva have found useful.

History of the Hindu Right in Eastern UP

A recent study by Akshaya Mukul provides a history of the Gita Press in Gorakhpur established in 1923, by two Marwari businessmen turned spiritualists, Mahavir Prasad Poddar and Jaydayal Goyandka (Mukul 2015: 2). Meant originally for printing the Gita and a popular magazine, the *Kalyan*, it created over time an empire that speaks even today in a militant, Hindu nationalist voice. The ideas articulated by the Press played a critical role in the formation of a Hindu public sphere in the colonial period and the rise to political pre-eminence of the Hindu Right, which has continued into the post-independence period. It intervened and shaped the acrimonious debate between reformists and conservatives in the larger Hindu world. On issues such as cow slaughter, Hindi as the national language and the rejection of Hindustani, the Hindu Code Bill, the creation of Pakistan, India's secular constitution, the Press became the spokesperson of the Hindu position (Mukul 2015). Almost every notable leader and prominent voice including Mahatma Gandhi was used by the Press to support the Hindu cause.

Three developments helped the Press. First, the consolidation of Hindi at the beginning of the twentieth century as the language of the Hindus, and the rapid growth of a public sphere in which journals, newspapers, and publishing houses emerged. Second, the Gita Press was an enterprise where profit was not important, the aim being to spread the ideas of Sanatan Hindu dharma—an obscurantist version of it. Third, the 1920s were a period of competing political communalism between Hindus and Muslims (Mukul 2015: 4). The entire nationalism debate was vitiated by religious schisms, exacerbated by a series of communal riots on the issue of cow protection throughout the United Provinces. Congress leaders like Madan Mohan Malviya, Purshottamdas Tandon, K.M. Munshi, Seth Govind Das, and others who were not enthused with Congress politics, lent support to the Gita Press enterprise. The coming together of Sanatan Dharma leaders like Madan Mohan Malviya and the Arya Samaj in 1923 at Benares and the decision to make common cause on cow protection and reconversion to Hinduism (*shuddhi*) bolstered the conservative Hindu group (Mukul 2015: 4). This movement also led to the separation of two languages—Hindi for Hindus and Urdu for Muslims in 1900—which was endorsed by the British authorities (Mukul 2015: 5). The press had a rigid stance on the validity of the caste system and attacked both Gandhi and Ambedkar for their views on caste. In addition, though they claim to speak for all, even today it publishes material only for the three twice-born castes.

The Gita Press remains relevant today and is respected in eastern UP (Mukul 2015: 33). *Kalyan* has a circulation of over 20,000 copies while the English version has a circulation of over 100,000. It prints the Gita, Ramcharitmanas, Puranas, Upanishads, and monographs on the duties of the ideal Hindu family and role of women in all Indian languages. Reaching into middle-class homes, it has influenced UP politics by supporting various movements, ideologies, and organizations that promote Hindu identity and culture and opposing those it deems a threat to Sanatan Dharma (Mukul 2015: 289). The Press has influenced politics in eastern UP by steadfastly opposing communism and secularism in its writings (Mukul 2015: 328). Rather, it has supported the Hindu right by promoting a homogeneous, popular, bhakti-oriented brahamanical Hinduism to which spiritual aspirants of many theological and sectarian persuasions can relate (Mukul 2015: 23). It has supported cow protection and pressed the government to pass a law against cow slaughter. The Press has provided a platform for disseminating the ideas of the Hindu Right and communal organizations like the RSS and VHP. In 1964, when the VHP was created, Poddar was made its founding trustee (Mukul 2015: 317).

The Press has supported the Ram Janma Bhoomi movement since the 1940s when it helped Baba Raghav Das win the Faizabad assembly seat in 1948, defeating Acharya Narayan Dev. The Muslims of Faizabad who voted for Dev were threatened by the local Sadhus to vote for the Baba and not offer namaz at the Babri Mosque (Mukul 2015: 319). In the 1990s many articles supporting the RJBBM movement were published that upheld the idea that there was enough evidence that it was the birthplace of Ram and on the need to build a temple on the site. Many contemporary articles in *Kalyan* have an anti-Muslim tenor, such as pointing to the increase in Muslim population, which it is held is causing a major crisis (Mukul 2015: 426). Mukul Akshay points out that in times of crisis, *Kalyan* has exchanged the 'sobriety of a religious journal for the language of hate and religious identity' (Mukul 2015: 430). It has added to the polarization of society that is taking place including in eastern UP where the Ram Temple issue is located. Today, the Gita Press is no longer the only voice of the Hindu Right and to that extent, it has lost the importance it had. However, it still caters to a large number especially during elections. This was evident during the 2014 elections when it took up issues that the BJP was also propagating: removal of corruption, cleansing of Hindu society, need for a strong moral leader, a law banning cow slaughter, among others (Mukul 2015: 416).

The Yogi and Communal Mobilization in Eastern UP

In more recent times, Yogi Adityanath, the present Mahant of the Gorakhnath Math close to Gorakhpur town, has emerged in the 2000s as an independent, right-wing, prominent, Hindutva leader. The temple is a religious institution that runs two Gorakhnath temples, one in Nepal and the other a little south of Gorakhpur town. It is said to contain the *samadhi* shrine (tomb) and *gaddi* (prayer seat) of Gorakshanath. Adityanath's political influence is felt in the entire state as he has established himself as a hero of Hindu renaissance, but his rise has created a separate powerbase of the Hindu right in eastern UP (*The Times of India* 2014). He has had strained relations with the BJP for more than a decade as he has been seeking greater power in eastern UP causing at times conflict with the BJP leadership, though the party has found in him a useful base in the east (Jaffrelot 2014).

The Gorakhnath Math, an important institution of the Nath sect, is believed to have been founded by the Hindu God, Lord Shiva. Matsyendranath, a disciple of Shiva, passed this knowledge to his disciple Gorakhnath. The sect with twelve branches promoted by Gorakhnath later came to be known as the Nath sect. The followers of this sect suffix Nath to their names and are called *kanphata* because of the tradition of cutting ears, and *gorakhnathi* because they are devotees of Gorakhnath. These features of the syncretic tradition of the Math are provided in the literature published by the Gorakhnath Mandir (for details, refer to श्रीवास्तव सम्वत २०७१; बनर्जी सम्वत २०१६; गोरखनाथ-मंदिर सम्वत २०२९).

The Gorakhnath Math is over a hundred years old. Figure 2.1 provides a view of the math in 1962; it is much larger today. The Math has been involved in political matters for decades. An earlier head, Mahant Digvijaynath joined the Congress in 1921 and was arrested for taking

Figure 2.1   Photo of the old building of the Gorakhnath Math when Digvijaynath was the mahanth, 1962. It was much smaller than it is today.

Source: Old newspaper archives of Gorakhpur town.

an 'active part' in the Chauri Chaura incident, thereby putting a brake on Gandhi's non-violent, non-cooperation movement to which he was strongly opposed. He joined the Hindu Mahasabha in 1937 and soon became the head of the party's unit in the United Provinces. Shortly after independence, he was arrested for inflaming passions against Gandhi that contributed to his assassination and was imprisoned for nine months. After his release, he spearheaded the Ram Janmabhoomi movement of 1949, organizing a nine-day long recitation of Ramcharit Manas, at the end of which the idols of Rama and Sita were placed inside the Babri Masjid (for details, see Jha and Jha 2012). The Babri Masjid was locked down as a result, but it led to Digvijaynath's rise in the Hindu Mahasabha. Appointed the General Secretary at the national level, he won the election as MP of Gorakhpur in 1967. His successor, Mahant Avaidyanath who was also a member of the Hindu Mahasabha, was elected as MLA from Maniram as an independent in 1962, 1967, 1969, 1974, and 1977 and also as an MP from Gorakhpur in 1970 and 1989. Soon after, when the Sangh Parivar started its own Ram Janmabhoomi movement, he left the Hindu Mahasabha and joined the BJP and was elected as MP of Gorakhpur on a BJP ticket in 1991 and 1996 (Jaffrelot 2014).

His successor Yogi Adityanath, born Ajay Singh (5 June 1972) in a Rajput family in Uttarakhand holds a University degree and has been Member of Parliament from the Gorakhpur Lok Sabha Constituency five times since 1998, including most recently in 2014. He succeeded Avaidyanath at the young age of 22 and was appointed as Mahant on 14 September 2014 after the death of his Guru on 12 September 2014. Mahant Avaidyanath passed away on 12 September 2014. Yogi Adityanath has been active in the BJP and has moulded the Hindu forces in the region by a combination of alliances cutting across caste lines, and raising demands for better economic livelihood (Jaffrelot 2014).

Yogi Adityanath's influence has been strongest in the seven districts of Gorakhpur division (Gorakhpur, Deoria, Kushinagar, Maharajganj) and Basti division (Basti, Sant Kabir Nagar, Siddharthanagar). He is now spreading his wings in the Azamgarh division, of which Mau is a part. This is because in Poorvanchal, the region south of the Ghaghra particularly Varanasi and districts surrounding it, follow orthodox Hindu traditions. However, north of the Ghaghra a more open, eclectic, and radical atmosphere has prevailed historically as the *Gorakshak peeth* has a monastic order which according to the principles of Gorakhnath does not follow Brahminical or caste traditions so non-Brahmins (like Adityanath) may serve as priests. A second reason is that this region, except Gorakhpur district, has a large Muslim population. After the 1857 mutiny, many Muslims moved to the terai area (foothills) and the emergence of a large number of Madrassas has created intensive media attention on the Muslims of the region leading the BJP–RSS to join hands with the VHP to fight 'these anti-national' elements; which the Yogi has labelled as the 'hub of terrorism'. The region from Bahraich to Gorakhpur is also the focus of attention of Hindutva forces because it is the hotbed of Naxalite activities and the CPI(ML) and therefore expected to be the breeding ground of Muslim insurgents. Consequently, Hindutva politics is more intense here and the RSS has many workers in this region.

The strength and the reach of the Gorakhnath Temple Trust in the eastern region can be gauged from the fact that the Trust and its affiliates have at least 44 institutions linked to them, located in Gorakhpur, adjoining districts, and in Varanasi (Seth 2017: 13). No persons involved in these institutions is willing to talk about their finances, earnings, or income except to say that the 800 acres over which the Trust's institutions are spread are worth upwards of Rs 500 crore (Seth 2017). The main campus is spread over 55 acres, and apart from the temple includes a hospital, an Ayurvedic centre, a Sanskrit school with a hostel, a nursing institute, a *gaushala* with about 500 cows and a vermi-compost plant, a *dharmashala*, and an auditorium. The trust also owns 500 acres of both agricultural and forest land in Chowk Bajar area, which holds another *gaushala* and farms. A temple in Balrampur district is spread over 125 acres. The Math kitchen makes food for about 450 persons daily. Meals are also provided to some of the schools and colleges run by the trust at subsidized rates. Adityanath solely decides the menu. The Trust also runs five colleges, a polytechnic, a tailoring college, and a nursing college. Most of the students of the area go to these institutions as fees are low and facilities are good. The most successful of the Trust's ventures though are its three hospitals; Adityanath set up the main one in 2003. It has 350 beds, 22 departments, 440 staff members, a blood bank with facilities to handle dengue cases, and low patient charges. Patients come from Nepal and many parts of eastern UP (Seth 2017). More details pertaining to the institutions under the Math are available in its own literature published in commemoration of Mahant Digvijaynath who is credited with having created most of the educational and health institutions. Parlimentarians across party lines commended his institutional contribution in eastern UP (गोरखनाथ-मंदिर सम्वत २०२९).

In a region which is very backward, with poor educational facilities and institutions run by the government, hardly any employment and poor governance, the Gorakhnath trust stands out as a well-organized philanthropic organization and is very popular among the inhabitants. However, the trust and all the institutions under it are under the tight control of Yogi Adityanath; locals allege that they have CCTVs directly linked to his mobile so that he can closely monitor their working. In every institution of the Math there is a 'Peethadhishwar' chair covered with a saffron cloth reserved exclusively for Yogi Adityanath, on which no one else can sit. Muslim localities and small teashops lie on all four sides of the Math, which have come up over the years to cater to visitors. A significant change in the area is that since Adityanath became an MP, localities such as Alinagar and Urdu Bazaar near the Math have acquired new names visible on many shops and homes—Aryanagar and Hindu Bazaar (Seth 2017). Yogi Adityanath holds *janata durbars* at his office in the Math at which local and family disputes are resolved, the Yogi writes letters to government departments seeking favours to the supplicant and even to the railways to ensure that those with wait-listed tickets travel the same day. In sum, the Math seems to run a Robin Hood parallel government.

Yogi Adityanath and Non-Brahminical Hindutva

Yogi Adityanath has made Poorvanchal his Hindutva experimental laboratory. The attempt has been to communalize everyday lives in the region, using petty incidents on a regular basis, giving a communal colour to mundane events that are otherwise not even worthy of being called a serious crime, invoking issues from imagined Muslim fear, to terrorism to rising threat of Naxalism. An aggressive Hindutva unlike that of the BJP–RSS, it has no institutional sense except making best use of the syncretic, inclusive, and progressive tradition of the Gorakshnath Temple that he heads. His attempt to dominate the entire political and cultural space is seen from the fact that when he first emerged on the political scene, his supporters chanted, '*Gorakhpur mein rahna hai toh, yogi yogi kahna hoga!'* (To live in Gorakhpur one has to chant, Yogi, Yogi). As his area of influence has expanded, this slogan is also taking new forms: *'Poorvanchal mein rahna hai toh yogi yogi kahna hai!'* (To live in Poorvanchal one has to chant, Yogi, Yogi).

Two features characterize Adityanath's non-Brahmin Hindutva which makes it different from that espoused by the BJP–RSS. First, is the anti-Brahmin position, which is clearly seen in his successful fight against the Brahmin mafia in the late 1990s described earlier by Vishwakarma, which removed them from positions of power in the region leaving him dominant in the region. Second, is the pro-lower caste strategy and attempt to pitch them against the Muslims, which is visible in the statement made by Saurabh Vishwakarma:

> In the Muslim majority localities in the town (Gorakhpur) like, Unchwa, Tiwaripur, Jafra Bazar, Ilahibaad, Purana Gorakhnath, Turkman Pur, Naseerabad, Narshinghpur, Bahram Pur, Rajghat, Basantput Saray and villages in Gorakhpur and other districts, like Laxmipur in Sidhdharthnagar, the cohabitants hailing from lower OBCs and Dalits, face day to day harassment by the Muslims who target our sisters and religious occasions. The other Hindutva outfits have simply failed to protect the Hindus, especially the lower sections against the evil acts of the Muslims, making HYV under Yogiji, as the only hope for them. (Interview with Saurabh Vishwakarma in Gorakhpur, November 2016)

During the 2000s, Yogi Adityanath has attempted to bring the lower OBCs, most particularly the Dalits, into the Hindu fold and make the Muslim the 'other' with the aim of creating a unified Hindu cultural nation. As Badri Narayan points out, the strategy is not totally new as 'politically motivated communal forces' since the mid-1990s have been silently and ingenuously working among the Dalits and backwards (Narayan 2009: ix). However, it assumed importance in the 2000s because the poorer and smaller sub-castes situated in eastern UP began to enter the democratic arena. In eastern UP, the method followed by Yogi Adityanath and the RSS has been to promote and gain the support of Dalit sub-castes. As Dalits are highly fragmented with competitive and conflicting relations along regional and sub-caste lines, an approach of wooing the individual sub-castes was viewed as useful as each had its own ideas, heroes and stories which could be used for the purpose of mobilization (Narayan 2009:10). Narayan argues that while reinterpretation of the past serves as a powerful cultural capital for Dalit communities, the process of modernization makes Dalit sub-castes less confident and leads them to draw smaller and smaller boundaries for themselves vis-à-vis other sub-castes: from national to regional, to caste boundary, and eventually to sub-caste boundaries. Among Dalits it is their past suffering and humiliation that creates this unity against others and creates both individual and collective memories and their sense of identity (Narayan 2009: 4).

During the 2000s local Hindutva leaders, including those belonging to organizations headed by Adityanath, have been unearthing local histories and myths by which they could link Dalits to Hindutva and gradually building walls between them and others who had formed the composite culture of the villages. The attempt is to communalize the identity of different communities, their feeling of pride being slowly converted into a feeling of hatred for other communities (Narayan 2009). They are finding folk traditions of Dalit communities, which are against Muslims, and portraying them as enemies although they had lived in harmonious interdependence with each other for the last many centuries, thus creating a 'politics of hate' (Narayan 2009: xii).

This strategy is visible in three examples provided by Badri Narayan of linking of three Dalit communities, who are numerous in eastern UP, with the Ramayana: the Pasis, Musahars, and Nishads. The symbol of Lord Ram is being stretched at the local level by either linking him, or finding similarities between him and a local Dalit hero through which local myths are being 'Ramaized' (Narayan 2009: 21). The idea that the Pasis helped Ram throughout his period in the forest is propagated and thereby symbols of unity built between them and the upper castes (Narayan 2009: 30). Two brothers Dina and Bhadri, popular heroes of the Musahars, who are remembered as having fought against injustice and exploitation, have been re-interpreted as the reincarnations of Rama and Laxman, while Savari, a minor character in the Ramayana, is described as belonging to the Musahar caste. These stories represent the aspiration of the Musahars to rise and gain education and respectability (Narayan 2009: 21). Similarly, Guhya, the king of the Nishads, a caste of boatmen, is being projected in Allahabad and the surrounding regions, as the person who helped Ram cross the river in the forest. During the Rath Yatra, the Nishads transported large numbers of Kar Sewaks over water, and a temple to Nishadraj was built in Shringverpur (Narayan 2009: 313). A special issue of Panchjanya in 2004 titled *Samajik Nyay* with a wide circulation in eastern UP, attempts to show that Dalits and backwards have historically supported and died for Hindus in all riots and stood their ground against the Muslims (Narayan 2009: 30). The idea is to inspire Dalits to be part of the Hindu fold as they are shown as the saviours of Hinduism when it is in danger, true guardians of the faith (Narayan 2009: 31).

Another example shows how in the Bahraich region, the BJP has attempted to create anxiety among Hindus against the Muslims by counterposing the myth of local hero Suhaldev to that of Ghazi Mian and using it to bring Dalits into the Hindu fold by creating a new collective memory through a selective past (Narayan 2009: 26–7). The story of inter-communal harmony, of Hindus and Muslims visiting the dargah of Sayyad Salar Ghazi Mian specially during the month of May, has been woven by the Hindutva forces into a new story. This story denounces Ghazi Mian as a foreign intruder and establishes Suhaldev as a Pasi Hindu, a Dalit king, and hero who protected the Hindus from the intruders evil designs (Narayan 2009: 61). Aggressive hatred against Muslims is projected which has already led to a small riot over this issue in 2003 (Narayan 2009: 94). These strategies are used by the BJP in many parts of UP. However, in the eastern region they have become a part of the everyday communalism that Yogi Adityanath and his followers, described below, have attempted to institutionalize.

The Hindu Yuva Vahini and Everyday Communalism

Yogi Adityanath functions through different organizations, which he controls and calls cultural organizations. Included among these are the Hindu Yuva Vahini, Hindu Jagran Manch, Sri Ram Shakti Prakoshtha, Gorakhnath, Purvanchal Vikas Manch, Vishwa Hindu Mahasabha, and Hindu Mahasabha. But for Yogi Adityanath the most vital organization is the Hindu Yuva Vahini (HYV) that comprises mostly unemployed youth, petty criminals, and youth striving for an identity (Apoorvanand 2007). It was formed in April 2002 on the eve of the Ramnavami festival under his patronage at Gorakhpur. Organizationally, it has branches in all the 72 districts of UP.[11] Also the organization has a dedicated Media

[11]   http://www.hinduyuvavahini.in/sangthan.aspx.

and IT cell.[12] As per its constitution, the stated aim of the organization is to protest against cow slaughter, have faith in rebirth, and to unite Hindus of all castes and creeds.[13] On its formation, Yogi Adityanath had held that the Vahini was formed to control 'religious conversions', cow slaughter, and 'crimes against Hindu women' (Seth 2017: 13). The locals describe the HVY as 'Yogi ke sena'. Sunil Singh 42, the President of the UP Vahini and one of its founders says many names were considered when it was being formed such as 'Gau Rakshak Dal' and 'Yuva Vahini' and it was Adityanath who added Hindu to it giving it a definite cultural orientation. Singh says the Vahini was formed as there was *arajakta* (anarchy) in Poorvanchal. Madrasas were coming up in large numbers, there was human as well as drug trafficking on the India–Nepal border, and the government was not taking action. He says,

> Poorvanchal ke dushashan se nipatne ke liye, Hinduon, Daliton, Mahilaon ke samman ke liye, yuvaon ki sena sakriya hui (To rid Poorvanchal of misrule, to protect the honour of Hindu, Dalits and women, an army of youth was created). (Seth 2017)

The HYV sees itself as a cultural organization but it is known more for spearheading campaigns on issues such as Love Jihad, cow slaughter, conversions, crimes against Hindus, etc. (Seth 2017). Its members face many cases of rioting, violating prohibitory orders, causing hurt to public servants, and criminal intimidation under the Gangster Act. Sunil Singh proudly admits that there are 70-odd cases registered against him at Hapur Budhat Police Station in Gorakhpur including rioting and under the Gangster Act, which he says are inevitable if the fight is against misrule. As the protector of Hindus, for the HYV any small incident involving Muslims takes on vital importance and they reach the spot to create trouble. Most of their acts are destructive, such as arson, destruction of property, and beating. In eastern UP, Love Jihad, cow protection, beef, etc., have long been issues leading to conflict. A vivid example is the Mohanmundera episode in Kushinagar. Here, a Muslim boy raped a Hindu girl and the girl died during treatment. Three days later, after Yogi Adityanath heard of this incident, he arrived there with his Vahini workers. The property of all 72 Muslim families

---

[12] http://www.hinduyuvavahini.in/sangthan.aspx.
[13] http://www.hinduyuvavahini.in/samvidhan_1.aspx.

was looted, their houses were set ablaze, and the Masjid damaged. The police remained a neutral witness. There are several such examples of the Vahini's activities. If for any reason 'revenge' cannot be taken then they hold a meeting at the same spot that the event took place. They call such meetings 'Hindu Sangam' or 'Hindu Chetna Sangam'. An inhabitant of Gorakhpur points out that the Vahini is sustained by only one thing: fear—fear of public humiliation or of being beaten up—which is what makes people afraid of the Vahini (Seth 2017: 13).

The HYV has been involved in lots of communally sensitive activity. This includes the Mau riots of October 2005 and the Gorakhpur riots in January 2007, particularly the bomb blasts that took place in the Golghar area of Mau city and spread to Padrauna. This led to the burning of trains and buses in the vicinity and reports of arson in Mau, Basti, Kushinagar, Deoria, and Maharajganj (Engineer 2006). The slogan of the HYV was *'UP Gujarat banaenge/Padrauna shuruat Karenge'* (UP will become Gujarat, with Padrauna making a start).[14] During the Mau riots when Yogi Adityanath and his workers were not allowed to enter the town, he held a meeting at Dohri Ghat itself, where he was stopped. This polarized Hindus there and also affected the district panchayat elections, which emboldened his supporters in Mau and misinformation about the mass massacre of Hindus was communicated to places outside the district. When Yogi Adityanath visited Lucknow after the riots, he not only repeated the falsehood that Hindus were being massacred in Mau but also warned of revenge. The riots in Mau and Gorakhpur and communal incidents in adjoining areas created a rift between Hindus and Muslims in the region. Some analysts contend that the spread of Yogi Adityanath's work is really the result of administrative inaction.

In the UP assembly elections of 2007, the Hindu Yuva Vahini demanded that it would organize the elections in the eastern region on its own, but finally a compromise was reached with the BJP leadership (Engineer 2006). Adityanath demanded more than hundred seats in the eastern region for candidates selected by him, but the party leadership would not agree; after a negotiated compromise, possibly with the intervention of the RSS, eight of his candidates were fielded. With the approach of the 2017 assembly elections in UP the followers

[14] http://www.hinduyuvavahini.in/samvidhan_1.aspx.

of Adityanath have demanded not only seats, but that he should be declared the Chief Ministerial candidate of the BJP. While he has denied this, perhaps this is why the party leadership did not announce a Chief Ministerial candidate during the campaign.

During the 2000s, Adityanath has been involved in a number of controversies which have resulted in communal incidents. In 2005, he allegedly led a 'purification drive' which involved the conversion of Christians to Hinduism. In one such instance, 1,800 Christians were reportedly converted to Hinduism in the town of Etah. On 22–24 December 2006, Adityanath organized a three-day Virat Hindu Mahasammelan at Gorakhpur, during the same period when the BJP was holding its National Executive Meet in Lucknow. In January 2007, an altercation between Hindus and Muslims in a Muharram procession in Gorakhpur, led to the hospitalization of a young Hindu, Raj Kumar Agrahari. The District Magistrate issued orders banning Adityanath from visiting the site as it could inflame passions, but when Agrahari died, he disobeyed the magistrate and with his followers started a dharna on the site. They made inflammatory speeches and some of his followers set fire to a nearby *Mazar* (Muslim mausoleum) leading to imposition of curfew. Adityanath was arrested for breaking the curfew and jailed for a fortnight, on charges of destroying a Muslim tomb. His arrest led to further unrest and several coaches of the Mumbai-bound Mumbai–Gorakhpur Godan Express were burnt, allegedly by protesting HYV activists. However, the day after the arrest, the District Magistrate along with local police chief were transferred and replaced, which was widely perceived as a result of Adityanath's clout with Mulayam Singh Yadav. The tensions soon escalated to riots across Gorakhpur leading to the burning of mosques, homes, buses, and trains. After his release, Adityanath protested his jailing in the Parliament.[15]

In March 2011, the documentary film *Saffron War—Radicalization of Hinduism* accused Adityanath of promoting communal disharmony through a Virat Hindustan rally in rural UP. In another controversial incident in 2015, Adityanath shared the stage during a hate speech in which an unidentified speaker urged the Hindu audience to dig up the graves of Muslim women; recording of this event went viral on social

---

[15] Compiled from interviews during fieldwork in November 2016, details are given in Chapter 3.

media in March 2015. In August 2014, political activist Shehzaad Poonawala wrote to the National Commission of Minorities demanding that a police First Information Report be filed against Adityanath. Despite his dubious record, the BJP finds him useful in the east and is wary of trying to control him. Yogi Adityanath has also taken full advantage of the fact that political parties have abandoned the struggle for development in eastern UP leaving the field clear for him.

However, while the Yogi has been successful in socio-religious and cultural everyday mobilization using his position as the Mahant, the BJP until recently could not achieve electoral success in the region. In the 1990s and early 2000s, the SP and BSP continued to gain more seats in the UP assembly and parliament. It was only in 2014 that the BJP was able to win all seats except one in Azamgarh, won by Mulayam Singh Yadav. However, this may change with the continuous grass roots mobilization by the Mahant to create a larger and more inclusive Hindu support structure, which would be useful during elections. Moreover, the Mahant though a religious and social head has also become politically ambitious as viewed in the demand by his followers that he should be made the Chief Ministerial candidate for the 2017 assembly elections.

* * *

Our narrative of socio-economic and political change in Poorvanchal in the 2000s, shows that the region has specific characteristics that differentiate it from other regions within the state of UP. While institutionalization of everyday communalism is the aim of the BJP-RSS in both eastern and western UP, the context in which this takes place and the strategies used in the former are different. The number of Muslims is much less than in western UP and traditionally Hindu–Muslim relations have been more harmonious, evident from the much smaller number of major riots in the region. Social and economic change has historically been slow in the districts of eastern UP making it a backward region. It still remains a poor and backward agricultural economy and feudal society dominated by the upper castes of the region that form a small elite, though in more recent decades their position has been challenged by the backwards and the Dalits.

It was only in the 1980s that dynamism appeared in the economy of the eastern districts arising out of the second round of the Green

Revolution which was rice-driven and brought change in the region. Urbanization, non-agricultural occupations such as work in brick kilns, rickshaw pulling in the towns, construction, etc., provided some relief to the large number of landless labour in the rural areas. Literacy rates also improved and the rise of the backward castes including the Pasmanda Muslims and Dalits brought change; the SP and the BSP representing these groups have traditionally had a strong base in the region. Even then there remains a substantial gap in the economy of the western and the eastern region, which has affected socio-economic relations.

Despite the strong presence after independence of the left and socialist forces in this region, including Mau and Gorakhpur, the eastern districts have experienced the rise of right-wing Hindu forces beginning from the colonial period. This is evident from the role played by the Gita Press Gorakhpur, which was originally established to publish low-cost editions of the Gita, but which has emerged as a strong centre advocating Sanatan Dharma, upholding caste and majoritarianism, evident from its recent publications. It also supported the RJBBM movement and continues to support the efforts of the BJP and the RSS to establish the Hindutva ideology in the region.

Today, it is the Gorakhpur Math that has emerged as the centre of Hindutva activities in the region. The Gorakhpur Math has existed as an institution over a long period of time and earlier Mahants have also entered into politics, but its character has undergone change under Yogi Adityanath. He has tried to establish the Math as a strong, autonomous institution while keeping within the ambit of the BJP–RSS, which has led to the troubled relationship with the latter. Moreover, Yogi Adityanath belongs to a non-Brahminical tradition different from the Brahminical outlook of the RSS, which enables him to include in his followers the backward castes and more lately even the Dalits. While this orientation is in keeping with the 'non-brahminical' Hindutva ideology and social engineering strategy of the BJP since the late 1990s and is encouraged by it for political gain, the Yogi has become an independent power centre, trying to control the pattern of communal mobilization and thereby politics of the region, increasingly outside the control of the BJP. He has formed his own cultural organizations such as the HYV and attempted to put up his own candidates during elections, though he wants to continue his relationship with the BJP.

As our chapter indicates, two developments underlie the emergence of communalism in the region. The first is the rise of sociopolitical consciousness among all social groups, most particularly the Ansari Muslims of the region—particularly the younger generation—making them more aware and aspirational in terms of their future. The second is globalization which has led to a decline of the weaving industry throwing large numbers of artisans out of work. This has frustrated them and made them antagonistic to the Hindu trading community witnessed in the targeting and burning of Muslim establishments during the Mau riots as the next chapter will describe. These developments have made them vulnerable to communal mobilization by Yogi Adityanath and his HYV in this region. While economic factors are important, as the next chapter will show, inter-communal tension surfaces during cultural and religious events causing conflict, which has increased in recent years. A third factor has been the rise of Mafia dons who promote communalism at times and control the economy which indicates the lack of development, governance, and maintenance of law and order by the state government.

At the same time, there are differences in the nature of communal discourse and tension between the two districts of Mau and Gorakhpur. In the former, the political economy of communalism is more important due to the artisanal handloom industry in which both Muslim weavers and Hindu traders are involved in day-to-day business competition, affecting their relationship. This does not mean that Yogi Adityanath and his HYV do not play a role; they make full use of the day-to-day petty and mundane conflicts between the two communities to sustain communal tension. In Gorakhpur, where the number of Muslims is fewer and the presence of the artisanal industry is much less, the Yogi and his followers play a more central role institutionalizing everyday communalism in the town and the district.

Thus, communal forces and the forms that communalism takes in eastern UP, is complex and continually evolving and changing. It is against this backdrop that we move to examining the Mau and Gorakhpur riots based on extensive fieldwork in these two districts in the next chapter. Both the cultural and political economy aspects that everyday communalism portrays in eastern UP are evident in our fieldwork.

3 Communal Mobilization and Riots in Eastern Uttar Pradesh
Mau and Gorakhpur Districts

Against the backdrop of our narrative of significant socio-economic and political changes in the eastern region of UP over the last two decades, which underlie the emergence of communal mobilization in the 2000s, we now move to an analysis of the riots in our selected districts of Mau in 2005 and Gorakhpur in 2007. We argue, based on the field data, that while communal riots have taken place earlier in eastern UP, new patterns of communal mobilization by the BJP–RSS over a long period of time in the form of everyday communalism are visible in the 2000s and have become well established in our selected region and the sample towns in it. Large riots rarely take place; there have been none after the Gorakhpur riot of 2007. However, the Mau and Gorakhpur riots have been used to put into place new conflictual patterns of everyday relationships between different communities which create constant tension and small incidents that have become endemic in this region, with daily reports of such incidents being reported in the media.

The two districts of Mau and Gorakhpur were selected because these new patterns are clearly seen here and have worsened the relations between Hindus and Muslims, more importantly including the lower castes. In addition, communal politics in eastern UP in recent years can be broadly conceived as composed of two subregional blocs located on the north and south of the Ghaghra river, an aspect mentioned in the previous chapter. The districts falling north of the Ghaghra, namely, Gorakhpur, Deoria, Kushinagar, Maharajganj, Sant

Kabir Nagar, Sidharth Nagar, and Basti are considered the stronghold of Mahanth Adityanath and his organization the HYV. While the districts falling south of the river, namely, Azamgarh, Mau, Ballia, Ghazipur, and Varanasi are considered to be largely the stronghold of Mafia-politician, Mukhtar Ansari, though Adityanath has been able to extend his influence in more recent years into the southern region as well. It is the attempt by both to expand their respective spheres of influence in these sub-regions that gives rise to a complex phenomenon of Hindutva and the communal-mafia interface characterizing the region. Thus, in contrast to western UP where agrarian and caste politics interspersed with communal mobilization forms the backdrop in most of the region, in the eastern districts, the field work reveals differences between the two selected districts, which shows how the context in which communalism occurs is different in different districts and even neighbouring towns.

Our fieldwork show that in Mau, there is a clear interplay between business, religio-cultural practices, and the role of Mafia dons that the BJP–RSS take advantage of, which is largely undertaken by Mahanth Adityanath of the Gorakhnath Math. The impact of the decline of the handloom industry has led to pauperization of the Ansari Muslims involved in it, their unhappiness over lack of help from the government, and attempts by Hindu traders to take over this sector. It is a well-documented fact that most of the communal riots in India have taken place in areas where Muslims have a sizeable population and well-developed businesses such as Kanpur, Bhiwandi, Malegaon, Bhagalpur, Meerut, Moradabad, and Ahmadabad. However, in Mau, what is new in the 2000s is the manner in which Hindutva forces—under new leaders such as Yogi Adityanath who has become an independent power in the region—make use of this political economy divide to constantly, almost on a daily basis, drive a wedge between the two communities. Though there has not been a major riot since 2005, Hindutva forces create constant communal tension and small incidents to keep the Hindu–Muslim divide alive. Second, is the rise of mafia dons within both the Hindu and Muslim community, who it can be argued are perhaps not inherently communal, but who use the riots to their economic advantage as it increases their control over the local economy and polity. This has introduced change in the relationship between Hindus and Muslims in Mau, a town where the two communities lived in considerable harmony throughout the 1990s.

In contrast, the phenomenon of everyday communalism in Gorakhpur is more clearly visible as the 2007 riot was short, though violent, and can be described as an extension of the highly communal grass roots mobilizational style of Mahanth Adityanath. While Gorakhpur town has a weaving industry, the number of Muslims and looms is much less. The town is located in a largely agricultural district, which has in recent years suffered due to decline in agriculture and lack of alternative livelihoods, which has created much unhappiness. This and the presence of Muslims and Madrassas in the terai area, as explained in the previous chapter, has made it part of an area that has become an experimental laboratory of Hindutva in the eastern region. The town derives its name from the important Goraknath Temple under the Gorakhnath Math, involved in communal politics under its present head Mahant Adityanath. He together with his organization the HYV has been involved in much communal activity as we shall see, including the Mau riots of October 2005 and the Gorakhpur riots of January 2007. His work points to the love–hate relationship among various Hindutva outfits that while sharing the prejudice against the Muslim as the 'other' also endeavour to outdo each other as a better claimant of the Hindutva cause by accusing each other of betrayal and opportunism.[1] Thus, while the region has a distinct cultural component in its communal mobilization, the two selected districts display different features of the phenomenon of everyday communalism.

The fieldwork was carried out in Mau and Gorkhapur from 16–28 August 2016 and from 7–18 November 2016, respectively. Within these districts, Gorakhpur and Mau towns were selected for the fieldwork as the two main players—Mahanth Adityanath and Mukhtar Ansari—are located here and the impact of their work could be analyzed.

Mau and Gorakhpur Districts: A Profile

Mau is a small industrial town on the banks of the river Ghaghara (Saryu). The total area of Mau district is 1,715 sq km. and its

---

[1] For instance, Hindu Mahasabha accused VHP of usurping the Ayodhya movement and indulging in massive corruption. For detail see, http://indian-express.com/article/cities/lucknow/ram-temple-in-ayodhyahindu-mahasabha-claims-vhp-pocketed-rs-1400-cr-singhal-rubbishes-charge/.

population is 1,853,997, the urban population constituting 360,369 and the rural 1,493,628. Urbanization is lower in eastern UP—90 per cent of the population of Mau is rural and approximately 10 per cent is urban. Within this population, around 80.5 per cent are Hindus; the Muslim population is less than 20 per cent of the total. In 2011, Mau town had population of 2,205,968 of which male and female were 1,114,709 and 1,091,259, respectively (records of the district administration). However, what is important is that Muslims are primarily concentrated in the city where they account for 56.76 per cent of the total population.[2] The main industry in Mau is cloth weaving due to the presence of a large number of weavers in the district. At present, there are 2,641 power looms and 1,800 hand looms in Mau, which are the major source of employment for Muslim weavers (सूचना एवं जनसंपर्क विभाग, मऊ 2016: 57). People in rural areas are dependent on agriculture. The district has a parliamentary seat Ghosi and four assembly constituencies: Madhuban, Ghosi, Muhammadabad Gohana, Mau, and Rasra.

Jiyaudeen Barni's historical book gives a short description of Mughal emperor Akbar passing through Mau on his way to Allahabad. During his reign, Sher Shah Suri, who had defeated the Mughals, visited Kolhuvavan (Madhuban) to meet the great Sufi saint Syed Ahmad Wadva. Sher Shah undertook various developmental works for the development of the Mau region. During the construction of a military base and the Shahi Mosque, a large number of labourers and artisans came with the Mughal army. The labour force included skilled artisans and weavers, who originally belonged to Iran, Afghanistan, and Turkey, and settled here permanently, which gave birth to the unique Mau loom skill. The people attached to the thread used in the hand woven loom business came from Gorakhpur and settled here. It is also held that Mau and the area surrounding it came under the supervision of the Mughal Princess Jahan Ara, the elder daughter of Shah Jahan in 1629, where she built her residence and the royal mosque (Shahi Mosque) at a place called Katara. Two colonies were built for the settlement of the handloom and thread-making artisans, besides a colony named after her brother Aurangzeb called Aurangabad that exists today (सूचना एवं

[2] http://www.census2011.co.in/data/town/801200-maunath-bhanjan-uttar-pradesh.html.

जनसंपर्क विभाग, मऊ 2016: 3–4). Thereafter, for security considerations the area was converted into an army cantonment.

In Gorakhpur district Hindus constitute 78 per cent of the population while Muslims are 21 per cent. It is part of the Gorakhpur *Janapad* (cultural region) made up of the districts of Kushinagar, Basti, Deoria, Azamgarh, and parts of the Nepal terai (foothills) which was an important centre of Hindu Vedic culture. The size of the town is 5,484 sq km. while its population is 673,446 of which males constitute 353,907 and females 319,539 and the average literacy rate is 83.91 per cent (Census 2011). While Gorakhpur has a weaving industry, it is on a much smaller scale than in Mau. It is largely an agricultural district, located along the banks of the Rapti River, one of the most flood-prone districts of eastern UP. Agriculture is the main activity in the district. It lies in a backward region—in 2006, the Ministry of Panchayati Raj named Gorakhpur one of the country's most backward districts (out of a total of 640). It is one of the 34 districts in UP receiving funds from September 2009 onwards from the Backward Regions Grant Fund (BRGF) Programme (Ministry of Panchayati Raj National Institute of Rural Development 2008). Communal politics in the town as well as the district are influenced, as discussed in the earlier chapter, by the presence of the Gorakhnath Math and its head Mahanth Adityanath.

Despite the presence of everyday communalism in both western and eastern UP, the latter has some distinct features that are evident in the description of the fieldwork provided in this chapter. Despite the low level of urbanization in the region and most of the population residing in the rural areas, the riots in the 2000s have taken place in the towns and not the villages as in western UP, though there is some spread into the semi-urban areas as well. The reason is that most of the Muslim population resides in the towns and surrounding semi-urban areas and has shops and business establishments, which are the target during riots or, in everyday small conflicts. Second, it is the poorer level of communication and development in the rural areas, which isolate the villages from the communal events in the towns. Third, the handloom industry in Mau, and the Gorakhnath temple and its Mahanth, which are an important causative factor, are located in the towns.

Interface of Political Economy, Culture, the Mafia, and Communal Mobilization: Mau and Gorakhpur Riots

The Mau Riots

The aim of the fieldwork in Mau was to capture the interplay between political economy, cultural–religious practices and the role of the Mafia dons underlying the 2005 communal riots, their aftermath, and subsequent Hindu–Muslim relations in Mau town. A sample of respondents, both Hindu and Muslim, was drawn consisting of respected, well-known and long-standing, residents of Mau. The respondents were: Tayyab Palki, ex-Chairman of Mau Municipality; Jay Prakash Dhumketu, All India President of 'Progressive Writers Association'; Sushil Pandey, who claimed that his grandfather Pundit Bindeshwari Pandey constructed the Sanskrit Pathshala, an important landmark in the town demarcating the Hindu localities; Gulab Sonkar, a lawyer and senior Khatik (SC) community leader in the locality near the Sanskrit Pathshala; Ashish Kumar Chaudhary, a Dalit government employee, BSP supporter, and part-time LIC agent; and Anil Yadav, President of Rihayi Manch—an organization working for communal harmony in the state. From conversations with them and group discussions in the town, a historical narrative of communal riots including the 2005 riots was obtained.

Mau is not new to communal tensions and there have been a series of communal incidents in the past also. Figure 3.1 shows the road near the Sanskrit Pathshala, a communally sensitive area which has been the scene of many riots in Mau town as described a little later. There was overwhelming consensus among the respondents that the 2005 communal riots were an exception to the trend on both scale and intensity from the previous riots. The previous riots in Mau were localized and followed a set pattern: some petty incident, especially on some festive occasion, in a part of the town would happen, rumours would spread and there would be an immediate imposition of curfew by the district administration and the situation would immediately come under control. Muslims would accuse the riot-control police, the PAC as selectively being harsh and biased against them, that is, police rather than the Hindus would be the main villain in the Muslim perspective in the previous riots.

Figure 3.1   Muslims passing through the communally sensitive road near the Sanskrit Pathshala, the scene of many riots in Mau town.

Source: Photograph by Sajjan Kumar during fieldwork, 21 August 2016.

Respondents argued that understanding the nature of the previous communal tensions/riots at Mau was needed to make this aspect clear. It also enabled us to understand the trajectory of communalism in the town in the realm of political economy and society. In the 1969 riots as per eyewitnesses and particularly our respondents Tayyab Palki and Dhumketu, the first significant communal incident took place when Mau was still a part of Azamgarh district. Dhumketu vividly recalled the incident that happened when he was in his BA final year, it was the season of sugarcane cropping and the riot started in the urban area. Tayyab Palki, points out that it was the day of Taziya Muharram when the clash between Hindus and Muslims took place and tension escalated. Respondents from both communities alleged that their members were first beaten up by the other, leading to processions by Hindus as well as Muslims. As per Dhumketu, the rumour that a Hindu boy was beaten by the Muslims, resulted in a procession by the Hindus that was led by an important personality, Banarasilal Khandelval, then President of the Mau Vyapar Mandal, who used to control 80 per cent of loom thread in the town and whose clients were the Muslim weavers. From the Muslim side, the then ex-Rajya Sabha member Habib-ur-Rahman Noorani was a prominent participant, who was injured as he was hit on the head. As per Tayyab Palki, this angered the Muslims and they reacted, leading to escalation of the communal tension. Dhumketu recounts that curfew was imposed in the town, but it was the rumour of Muslims killing the Hindus that spread in Kopaganj and a few nearby villages leading to Hindus retaliating against Muslims in the village areas. He further narrates that until evening everything was peaceful on account of curfew, but in the night one could see the fire of burning crops in the farms that belonged to Muslims.

Dhumketu added that the main participant in the riots from the Hindu community were lower castes like, Yadavs, Rajbhars, and Nooniyas (Chauhans) who were instigated by the upper castes, besides their greed for the crops belonging to Muslims. On the other hand, Tayyab Palki recounts the extremely partisan role of the riot police, the PAC, during the curfew wherein they beat the Muslims by forcibly entering into their houses. He also recounts and corroborates Dhumketu's account of massive incidents of arson in the Muslim areas on the outskirts of the city. For instance, in Rampur Chakiya, a new settlement of Muslims, belonging to barber (Nai) castes, 10 households were burnt and a person named Ramzan died in that fire by the arsonists. However, features which characterize riots today were already present, the economic and business angle, participation of the lower caste Hindus and the biased role of the police.

Political Economy of the 1969 Riots

According to Dhumketu, the 1969 riot had primarily an economic angle for two reasons. First, both Hindu and Muslim rivals of Banarasilal Khandelval were eyeing to break his monopoly in the loom thread market. The moment he led the Hindu procession against the alleged beating of Hindus by Muslims on Taziya Muharram, the business elites from both the communities sensed an opportunity and that became a turning point in the already tense communal situation. As Dhumketu recounts, the participation of Khandelval made the Muslim loom weavers conscious of their economic interests, and they decided not to do business with him leading to a loss of 20–30 lakhs. The communal outlook seeped into the business domain that, in turn, witnessed the entry of Muslims into areas like loom thread and others that hitherto was under Hindu monopoly. Thus, by 1975, business relations were under a communal divide as the Muslim weavers entered the business and decided to purchase the raw materials and other things used in the loom sector, from their own community members. On the other hand, as already stated, the participation of lower Hindu castes in the riots, as per Dhumketu and Tayyab Palki, was driven primarily, not by their hatred of Muslims, but rather the incentive of loot and material gain. However, the 1969 communal riot in Mau was the turning point in setting the dynamics of Hindu–Muslim relations in the region.

Another significant communal incident in 1983 followed the old trend of communal tension related to the occasion of religious festivals. On the eve of Dussehra, a Hindu religious procession was passing near the Aurangabad Idgaah. They insisted on passing through the Muslim graveyard (*kabristan*), leading to a clash between the two communities. In that clash an ex-member of Mau Municipality, Md. Ibrahim (belonging to the family of Tayyab Palki) was hit on the head and died of brain haemorrhage, leading to further escalation of communal tension. Thereafter, the district administration imposed curfew to quell the situation. However, according to Tayyab Palki and other old Muslim respondents, the riot police, the PAC played a very hostile and prejudiced role during the curfew by picking and targeting the Muslims.

Similarly, in 1984 the communal clash started with the petty issue of a dispute between the two communities related to a contest over the place of a religious fest. The contention was over an open place near Sadar Chowk, at Ghasbazar chowk wherein traditionally Taziya is celebrated, but the Hindus decided to organize an Akhara (wrestling match) at the same place leading to police using mild force against the mobs to diffuse the brewing tension. Since, it was the market area and traditionally mutton is purchased in the morning in Mau, as per Tayyab Palki, there were many Muslim onlookers carrying mutton who also started running away the moment police started using force. In the chaos the mutton got scattered and splashed and the rumour was spread that the Muslims threw mutton upon the Hindus who were demanding the organizing of the Akhara at the place. However, Tayyab Palki points out, the police also supported the same version with the intention to shift the blame upon the Muslims for the violence and to justify their use of force upon the mob. As usual, this rumour helped escalate the tension, curfew was imposed, and Muslims allege that the PAC acted in an utterly partisan manner. In addition, in this riot, a government official, the SDM Indradev Singh, was also killed. It is against this backdrop that we now move to the 2005 riots which, it was argued, was a break from the previous communal incidents.

The 2005 Riots

The communal riot in Mau in 2005 should be viewed against the backdrop of the new emerging communal environment due to the orchestrated and calibrated attempts by respective organizations with vested interests of which the HYV of Yogi Adityanath was at the forefront, and second the organized strength of the Mafia dons. A brief account of the riots as given by the respondents is provided below which enables us to understand the role of both these organizations and individuals involved.[3]

The starting point of the 2005 Mau riots is rooted in the peculiar tradition that is followed in the two religious festivals, Bharat Milap (played during Dussehra) and Muharram by Hindus and Muslims, respectively. The Bharat Milap religious ceremony is held in the field that is adjacent to the Shahi Katra Mosque, a Muslim-majority area. Besides, the Sanskrit Pathshala is situated near the Shahi Katra Mosque and the Bharat Milap venue that is on the path taken by the Muslim Muharram procession. The problem started after the Shahi Katra Mosque built a gate that the Hindus claimed was encroaching on the field traditionally used for the Bharat Milap ceremony and the matter went to the court. However, at the behest of elders of both the communities, especially Maulana Mauli Latif, a school Principal, both the communities decided to resolve the issue amicably. It was decided that the chariot carrying Bharat on Bharat Milap would hit the mosque gate three times and in return, as a reciprocal gesture, on the eve of Muharram, the Taziya-carrying Muslim procession would step up on the three stairs of the Sanskrit Pathshala. A photograph of the Sanskrit Pathshala, an important landmark in the town, where this peculiar ritual takes place is given (Figure 3.2).

[3] At least two other descriptions of the 2005 riots are provided by Verma, Rai, and Khan (2005) and Rawat (2016) in which details of the various incidents and role of the police and local administration are provided, as these are well known they are used only selectively here. The emphasis is on the version provided by the interviewed respondents. Another book, which provides an understanding of the nature of the riots and their impact on the local population particularly the Muslims, is Rai 2014 (Hindi).

Figure 3.2 The Sanskrit Pathshala at Mau, the three stairs on which the persons carrying the Taziya during Moharram are allowed to climb are visible.

Source: Photograph by Sajjan Kumar during fieldwork, 21 August 2016.

The original intention behind the Tazia-procession climbing only three steps of the Pathshala, many respondents like Anil Yadav opined, was to provide a harmonious gesture, while Dhumketu argued that it was meant to satisfy the communal ego of both communities. Whatever may be the original intention it was meant to be a show of strength that created an air of tension in the area.

It was in this prevailing communally charged ambience that on 13 October 2005 the Bharat Milap ceremony was going on in the field adjacent to the Shahi Katra mosque. However, this time it coincided with the month of Ramzan and therefore on the fateful day, around 8:30 pm, the Muslims were offering 'Pesha Ki Namaaz', when as part of the Bharat Milap ceremony the local folk song called *Biraha* was being played on the loudspeaker. Thereafter, some Muslims came to the Bharat Milap venue and asked the organizer to turn off the loudspeaker as it was creating disturbance in their Namaz/prayer. Initially, the organizer turned the loudspeaker off. However, after sometime they started playing the *Biraha* again on the loudspeaker. Then, some Muslim youth came from the mosque, mounted the stage, and snatched the electric wires of the loudspeaker causing anger among the Hindus present there. Subsequently, the police came and the accused Muslim youths were arrested and taken to the police station. However, after some time they were released by the police, which did not go well with the Hindus at the Bharat Milap venue in general and the organizers in particular, who saw it as an act of rowdy behaviour of Muslims against the Hindus and partisan behaviour of administration. In protest, they decided not to celebrate the Bharat Milap that night and to postpone it for a further date.[4]

Tayyab Palki held that there were two factions among the organizers: one being in favour of continuing the ceremony of Bharat Milap while the majority was against the same, leading to the ceremony being postponed causing rise of communal tension. However, this version of the incident was negated by most of the Hindu respondents representing various castes and categories. They predominantly argued that the decision to postpone the Bharat Milap ceremony was unanimous on account

---

[4] Based on detailed discussions with respondents, especially Tayyab Palki, Jay Prakash Dhumketu, Sushil Pandey, Gulab Sonkar, and others on 16–18 August 2016 at Mau town.

of the twin issues of feelings of insecurity among the Hindus after the release of the accused Muslim youth, and as a protest against the rowdy behaviour of Muslims and the partisan role of the local police.[5] In fact, two Muslim respondents from Shahi Katra area also opined that the organizers of the Ramlila committee were unanimous in postponing the Bharat Milap ceremony and were in an agitated and protesting mood.

Conflicting Accounts

The incidents on the morning of 14 October 2005 are most contentious in terms of varying narratives about the beginning of the communal riot. The moot questions as to who started it, whether it started in a spontaneous manner or was organized, what was the role of political leaders and various organizations, are marred in contested narratives by Hindu and Muslim respondents.

The Dominant Hindu Respondents' Narrative

For instance, the majority of the Hindu respondents opined that the following morning on 14 October 2005, the Hindus were agitated upon hearing the news of the postponement of the Bharat Milap ceremony by the organizers of the Ram Lila Committee. Some of them went to agitate in front of the house of the President of the Ram Lila Committee, Madan Singh whose house was near the Sanskrit Pathshala. In their version,[6] the Hindus were agitated against the docile attitude of the organizers and consequently went on to protest against the president of the organizing committee. However, they held that the Muslims began gathering at the same spot leading to provocative sloganeering, stone pelting, and consequent clash. As per the account of the Hindu respondents, the Muslims started moving towards the Hindu localities in large number and in reaction and upon seeing the approaching Muslim mob, the HYV activists Ajit Singh Chandel and Sujeet Singh Chandel, whose house was adjacent to the Sanskrit Pathshala, opened fire in which five Muslims were injured. They claim that it was a defensive

[5] Sushil Pandey, Gulab Sonkar, Ashish Kumar Chaudhary, and others gave this version more emphatically.

[6] As told by respondents Sushil Pandey, Gulab Sonkar, Ashish Kumar Chaudhary, and others.

action as there was no police personnel and had they not fired upon the coming Muslim mob, their house that was in the front and the remaining Hindu locality adjacent to the Sanskrit Pathshala, would have come under Muslim attack. Further, they allege that the injured Muslims were deliberately taken in an open rickshaw (*thela*), toured the Muslim localities, and then went to the police station rather than to the hospital. From there Mukhtar Ansari carried them in his open jeep to the hospital for the treatment. They allege that this was meant to provoke the Muslims and exhort them to attack the Hindus.

The Dominant Muslim Respondents' Narrative

A completely different story of how the actual riot started on 14 October 2005 was provided by a majority of the Muslim respondents. For instance, Mumtaz Ahmed Ansari and Md. Alamgir, both residents of Shahi Katra and power loom-owning weavers by occupation, had this to say. They stated that in the morning of 14 October 2005, an agitated Hindu mob had gathered near the Sanskrit Pathshala and some of them started taking down the board at the beginning of Shahi Katra locality which had its name written on it. This led to heated exchanges between both communities leading to incidents of stone and brick pelting that further escalated, culminating in the firing by Ajay Chandel and Sujeet Chandel, activists of HYV. However, they agreed that it was the incident of taking the injured Muslims in an open rickshaw, after the firing, which triggered the anger of Muslims against the Hindus in the city area. Even Dhumketu emphasizes this point, even though he disagrees with the dominant Hindu narrative on the exact reason why they had gathered near the Sanskrit Pathshala on 14 October 2005.

In fact, a closer reading of the conflicting narratives by different sets of respondents indicates that the real reason for gathering nearby the Sanskrit Pathshala on 14 October was due to the organizational rivalries between the various members of the Ram Lila Committee as well as the BJP and HYV. In fact, we can reasonably infer that the president of the Ram Lila Committee, Madan Singh, affiliated to BJP, had unsuccessfully tried to continue the Bharat Milap ceremony despite police letting off the accused Muslim youth and that had not gone down well with the others. Therefore, in the morning the Hindu protesters led by the Chandel brothers affiliated to HYV had gathered near the Sanskrit Pathshala where Madan Singh's house is situated, to protest against him. However, the Hindu mob started blocking the road, had an altercation with Muslims, beginning with stone and brick pelting that culminated in the Chandel brothers firing and injuring five Muslims.

Unfolding of the Communal Riots

For the next 72 hours, rioting continued with hundreds of shops, homes, looms, factories, even schools and hospitals ransacked and gutted, while 11 people were killed. Both communities suffered equally, and terribly. For the first time, the riots spread to the rural areas.[7] Our respondents pointed out that the communal riot that started with the incident of firing upon the Muslims by Ajit Singh Chandel and Sujeet Singh Chandel, the activists of the HYV near the Sanskrit Pathshala, spread to the areas of Harkeshpura, Salahabad, and some others in a quick span of time, that is, almost simultaneously. Both the community members in their respective areas started indulging in the act of arson, loot and attack upon the shops and properties belonging to the other. The riot quickly became an act of destroying each other's property. In particular, at the Salahabad turn, the Hindu mob attacked a saree factory, known as the Shimla factory belonging to a Muslim, Haji Mukhtar. The rioters indulged in loot and arson when the owner of the factory came along with some Muslims and opened fire upon the fleeing rioters with looted goods. In that firing, a Dalit was killed. Thereafter, the Muslims indulged in loot and arson of the nearby Hindu shops. Similarly, when the riot started, some Hindus belonging to Yadav castes were beaten and roughed up as they were caught up in Muslim localities where they had gone to sell milk. Panicked they left their cycles and milk pots and rushed out of the city. However, the rumour spread that the Yadavs had been killed by the Muslims and this rumour had a detrimental effect upon the Muslims living in the villages. Similarly, a factory near the TCI turn area belonging to Muslim Md. Khurseed where the 'Zari designing machine' was installed was burnt and some workers killed.[8] In addition, there were many cases of

[7] Details of the areas in Mau town affected by rioting are provided in Verma, Rai, and Khan 2005.

[8] The respondent Tayyab Palki claimed that all workers were killed and thrown in the nearby river, an account that seems grossly exaggerated. However, the factory was burnt and looted.

Figure 3.3   Muslim power loom weaver in Mau; the community was badly
affected by the 2005 Mau riots.

Source: Photograph by Sajjan Kumar during fieldwork, 21 August 2016.

killing and injuring, loot, and arson reported despite the curfew. The
riot was at its peak for three days from 14 October 2005 till 16 October
2005. In terms of scale and intensity, the 2005 riots were exceptional
and different from the previous riots. Figure 3.3 shows a power loom
weaver in Mau whose business was badly affected by the riots.

It is therefore pertinent to assess as to how and in what way the
2005 Mau riot was different.[9] The Mau riots reflect the changing
trend in communal riots in the 2000s of low-caste Hindus particularly sections of the Dalits, emerging as important participants. The
overwhelming participation of Dalit castes like the Khatiks and Pasis,
backward castes like, Rajbhars, Nooniyas, (Chauhan) and even Yadavs,
signify the coming together of many lower castes under the Hindutva
fold, making the Muslim as a common 'other'. While in previous riots
the lower castes also participated, what demarcates the Mau riots is
that their participation had the prior support of the BJP and organizations like the HYV. The knowledge that they would be taken care

[9] For more details of the riots and the loss of both communities, see Verma,
Rai, and Khan 2005.

of in post-riot legal cases indicates an institutional entrenchment of this phenomena of participation by subaltern castes in anti-Muslim violence.[10]

The main community that bore the brunt of the riots in Mau were the low-caste Ansari Muslims who overwhelmingly belong to the weaving community. In fact, the rioters and arsonists specifically targeted the power looms and Bunkar colonies pointing to the emerging aspect of intra-subaltern conflict across religion. The sharing of the physical space between low Hindu castes and Muslims in urban localities, especially the Khatiks and Muslims, wherein the former are primarily vegetable sellers and put their stalls next to or in front of the shops of Muslims in the market area, generate day-to-day mundane tensions. In the event of a communal event, the Hindu low-caste participants not only link their mundane tension to the communal incident, but rather, they also factor in their perception of the pampered minority in those moments. For instance, the majority of the Khatik respondents remarked that the Rs 72 per month electricity bill scheme to the power loom owners was unfair, leading to 'tax theft' on the part of the Muslims. Thus, the precarious economic condition of Khatiks is also measured in relation to the Muslim weavers, with whom they share their immediate social space, and thus perceive them as pampered in relation to their own condition, even though in absolute terms the condition of the weaver community was intensely precarious.

Mafia Interface in the Mau Riots

Criminalization of politics does not always translate into communalism, but it has strong links and feeds upon it thereby further encouraging and supporting it. In this game, criminals use communal riots for their own purpose to improve their political and economic position. The mafia angle in the 2005 Mau riots is visible in the manner in which various players responded and invested in the riots and betrayed the interface between the two. The Mau riots started on 14 October and

[10] Rawat's study reports that a large number of shops owned by Muslims in the city are rented out to Dalits and backwards who pay a meagre rent for these prime location areas. Therefore, resentment against the Muslim and Dalit tenants, respectively, was reflected in many areas where shops had been burnt (Rawat 2016).

continued until 16 October. However, smaller incidences of arson and looting continued for a longer time. The politics in the immediate aftermath of the Mau riots showed the mafia dimension when on 29 October the BJP MLA from the Muhammadabad Assembly constituency, Krishnanad Rai was shot dead along with seven supporters, allegedly by the Mukhtar Ansari gang.[11] This killing, primarily on account of mafia rivalry was given a communal angle when on 30 November the then ex-chief minister of UP, Rajnath Singh, sat on strike at the Varanasi district headquarters. On 6 December, BJP senior leader L.K. Advani also came in support of Rajnath Singh and subsequently the BJP embarked on a 'Nyaay Yatra' against the criminalization of politics and communalization of crimes.[12] Similarly, the role of Yogi Adityanath and his predecessor Mahant Adwaitnath, in supporting one set of Mafia against the other, especially related to the Gorakhpur railway tender, is indicative of the easy fit of Mafia politics with communal politics.

The vilification of mafia politician Mukhtar Ansari and the portrayal of him as the main orchestrator of the Mau riots by the BJP and HYV activists in collaboration with can be understood against this background. In Mau, according to our respondents he is the best known 'criminal' with political links; he began as an independent MLA from Mau Sadar but his base is Ghazipur. The general perception is that Mukhtar Ansari is a murderer and an extortionist; he is accused in several cases of murder, kidnapping, and ransom and has been to jail several times. However, in the town he is well known and popular with a Robin Hood image. He has almost always allied with the ruling party in UP moving constantly between the SP and the BSP. In the 2002

[11] Rawat's study also argues that the real reason for the riots was the clash of interests in the town between SP leader Arshad Jamal, who controls the municipality of Mau, and Mukhtar Ansari, who is originally from Mohammadabad. Further, the Muslim mafia is allowed to exist by the administration and it strengthens the hands of the Hindutva rioters who, in turn, blame the Muslims. The Muslims of Mau support Muktar Ansari. He is their hero, but most of the Dalits and Hindus blamed Mukhtar Ansari for the 2005 riots. The administration cannot remain mute without the connivance of higher ups—in this case the SP government—and due to their support the champions of Hindutva and Islam remain totally out of bound for the administration (Rawat 2016).

[12] The CPI(ML) documents this in a report on the Mau Riots (Report by CPI(ML) 2006).

assembly elections when the SP allied with the CPI, the Mau Sadar seat was allotted to the CPI. Despite this agreement, SP workers worked for Mukhtar Ansari instead of the CPI candidate. Ansari also campaigned for several SP candidates in neighbouring areas. He finally supported the BSP government formed in 2002, but during the 2005 riots he was a supporter of the SP. The media's constant focus on Mukhtar Ansari has created the impression that the assaults on Hindus during the 2005 Mau riots were carried out at Mukhtar Ansari's behest. This does not seem true; Mukhtar Ansari's army has both Hindus and Muslims. Rather, he is viewed as someone who can 'fix' things that help both communities. For example, Mohammdabad has 24-hour electricity whenever Mukhtar Ansari is in town. It is beyond the imagination for the people of UP particularly those living in rural areas, to have even an eight-hour supply.

Barring a few Hindu respondents, the majority of our respondents held that Mukhtar Ansari did not play a negative role in the escalation of Mau riots. In fact, all the Muslim respondents held that he was wrongfully portrayed by the media, that ran his video of moving in an open jeep with arms on 14 October 2005 with the voice clip in the video muted. This gave the impression that he was exhorting the Muslims to attack Hindus, while later, the finding of the tapes with voice clips proved otherwise. In fact, he was appealing to the crowds to calm down and not to escalate the violence. It was recounted that he helped many injured, both Hindus and Muslims, taking them to hospital in his personal vehicle.

However, there was a second narrative that highlighted the unintended impact of Mukhtar Ansari's visit upon the Muslim mob. Respondents like Dhumketu, Sushil Pandey, Gulab Sonkar, and others argued that given the domineering image Mukhtar Ansari evokes, his very presence on that fateful day, that too in an open jeep with arms in full display, in full violation of curfew, contributed to further aggression of Muslims against Hindus. Especially in the city area, as they thought that they had the support of Mukhtar Ansari. In fact, Gulab Sonkar opined that in Mau every Muslim 'considers himself as Mukhtar Ansari' and had he not moved around the city on 14 October 2015, the Muslims would not have gone berserk as they did. In the final analysis, it can be inferred that despite his mafia-centric and dominant image, Mukhtar Ansari is not a communal personality as was portrayed by the media and organizations like the BJP, the HYV, etc. This is indicative of the linkages between the mafia gang centric politics in Poorvanchal as reflected in the Mau riots.

Role of Hindu Yuva Vahini: Emerging Intra-Hindutva Rivalry-I

The HYV, as described in Chapter 2, was formed in Gorakhpur in 2002 by Yogi Adityanath. Poorvanchal came under the intense influence of the HYV, so much so that it outshone other right-wing organizations like the BJP, the VHP, and other older Hindutva-driven organizations on the question of Hindu–Muslim issues. Be it the issue of cow slaughter, perceived victimhood of Hindus, the issue of over-population of Muslims including the malicious campaign against the higher birth rate of the minorities, and last but not the least the issue of Love Jihad. Besides, at the same time the arrest of many Muslims at the India–Nepal border by the security personnel on the charges of terror activities also suited their aggressive anti-Muslim propaganda. The modus operandi of the HYV is simple, communalize the mundane day-to-day petty issue if that involves a Hindu versus Muslim factor. Two incidents in which the HYV was involved in the Mau riots are given subsequently.

After the fateful night of 13 October 2005 when the Ram Lila Committee headed by BJP leader Madan Singh decided to postpone the celebration of Bharat Milap ceremony, the protest against the decision of the committee was led by head of the Mau HYV Ajit Singh Chandel and his brother Sujit Singh Chandel. It was under their leadership that protesting Hindu crowds gathered near the Sanskrit Pathshala, where Madan Singh resides. However, as the site of Sanskrit Pathshala is communally sensitive, being surrounded by Muslim and Hindu localities from two different sides, the gathering and sloganeering by the Hindu protesters brought Muslims into the scene who gathered against them. In that scenario, tension escalated, leading to stone and brick pelting by both communities against each other. The acrimony culminated in the Chandel brothers, whose house is on one end of the trisection near the Sanskrit Pathshala, climbing to the top of their house and firing on the Muslims, injuring two of them.[13] Thereafter, respondents representing

---

[13] This is based on interviews of Anil Yadav, Jay Prakash Dhumketu, Sushil Pandey, Gulab Sonkar, Tayyab Palki, and others from 16–18 August 2016. That the Chandel Brothers fired on the Muslims was corroborated by all the respondents even though they attributed different reason for the same.

both the dominant Muslim and Hindu section endorsed the fact that after the firing, when the house of the Chandel brothers were surrounded by the Muslim mob, they fled and Sushil Singh Chandel hid somewhere under the shelter of Yogi Adityanath.

Thus, the role of the HYV was crucial and central in the escalation of the already communalized scenario in Mau. It was driven by two reasons. First, it was used to demonstrate the leadership of HYV over matters concerning religious affairs. Second, to outshine the other right-wing leaders and outfits as happened on the morning of 14 October 2005, when the Chandel brothers led the Hindu mob and started protesting against the Ram Lila Committee president, a member of BJP, and ultimately fired upon the Muslim mob that had gathered there, leading to outbreak of massive communal riots.

Moreover, it was reported by the Muslim respondents, in particular by Tayyab Palki and Md. Alamgir aka Sheru Bhai, a Mau-based Muslim businessman, that the members of HYV spread false rumours in villages that Hindus were being massacred in the Muslim locality leading to retaliation by Hindus against the Muslims in the adjoining villages. In addition, Yogi Adityanath tried to come to Mau during the riots but he was stopped at Dorighat by the administration and could not enter the city.[14] In fact, Tayyab Palki asserted that in the run-up to the 2017 state assembly elections the activists of HYV are frequenting villages and communalizing the general ambience by talking about Hindutva, the Muzaffarnagar Riots, and Love Jihad. However, he could not give any tangible document or concrete witness in that regard. Finally, it has to be noted that the core of the social base of Yogi Adityanath's HYV is composed of the unemployed and frustrated youth, primarily hailing from lower Hindu castes like, Khatiks, Pasis, Rajbhars, Noonias (Chauhan), and some Yadavs who act as the foot soldiers of the organization on communal occasions.

Role of District BJP Leaders: Intra-Hindutva Rivalry-II

Despite the fact that the mentor of HYV, Yogi Adityanath has been a BJP MP, there has been intense rivalry between the Vahini and the BJP, wherein both the organizations have tried to claim themselves as the

---

[14] Interview of Gulab Sonkar on 16 August 2016.

better custodian of the Hindutva agenda. In this competitive intra-Hindutva context, we can assess the incident at Mau and the role of local BJP and HYV leaders. In the aftermath of the postponement of Bharat Milap ceremony by the organizing committee on 14 October 2005, the role of the BJP and HYV leaders and activists, at one level was similar, that is, to protest against the postponement by demonstrating in front of the house of the president of Ram Lila Committee, Madan Singh. However, at another level, driven by competitive rivalry each attempted to outdo the rival Hindutva organization by indulging in more communal action. In particular, the role of three BJP leaders, Prof. Ramji Singh (then MLC BJP), Bharatlal Rahi (BJP leader), and Nandlal Shahni (BJP leader) was utterly negative. All the three spread the propaganda that Muslims did not allow the Bharat Milap ceremony to take place by snatching the wire from the loudspeaker and roaming scot-free thereafter.[15] Strategically, they projected the local Sadar MLA and mafia don Mukhtar Ansari as the symbol of Muslim aggression thereby highlighting the underlying interplay of Mafia and communal politics in the region.

At the state level, BJP leaders like Kalyan Singh, Lalji Tandon, Keshri Nath Tripathi, and Rajnath Singh portrayed the riots as a result of the policy of minorytism in which the Hindus, their life, dignity, and property were being targeted. They blamed the don-politician Mukhtar Ansari for instigating and causing the riots against Hindus. Many of them constantly used the word 'massacre' for Hindus while in terms of actual loss of life, estimates vary from 7–12 people. Thus, the competitive intra-Hindutva rivalry between the BJP, RSS, and its outfits on the one hand, and HYV on the other, provided incentive to each group and their leaders to act in a manner that further escalated the communal riots.

The narratives and opinion of eminent respondents from both the communities suggest that the 2005 riots was exceptional from earlier riots on a number of grounds. In terms of scale and intensity they were broader than the previous ones. The rioters organized themselves and carried out the violence in a systematic manner on a large scale; it was the first time that incidences of loot and arson took place in broad daylight. It was also for the first time that schools and hospitals

---

[15] Interviews of Tayyab Palki and Dhumketu on 16–18 August.

belonging to the minority community were vandalized and large-scale attacks on mosques were made. The power loom is a lifeline for weavers; the imposition of curfew unlike earlier contributed to further spread of rumours as people were confined to their areas and could not move, giving rumour mongers freedom to spread provocative and false rumours. Earlier in the Muslim narrative, the main villain of the communal riot used to be the riot police, that is, the PAC rather than the Hindus. However, in 2005, the role of PAC was relatively praised to be neutral by the Muslims, with Hindus emerging as the main villain of the riot narrative. The 2005 Mau riots exposed the Mafia underpinning of communal incidents in a big way. Finally, for first time, the riots did not remain localized but were catapulted to the regional and state level by the effective organizational network of the HYV. Immediately after the riots in Mau, swift attempts were also made to incite communal violence in Ballia, Ghazipur, Azamgarh, Deoria, Meerut, and Agra.

However, the parliamentary elections of 2009 held after the Mau riots, were quite different with residents of the area wanting to put it behind them and move on.[16] 'That was just a nightmare for us and nobody today wants to talk about those troublesome days,' said Arvind Kumar Baranwal, a local trader of Mau town in an interview. 'Woh ek bura waqt tha jo guzar gaya, yehan par sabhi log miljul kar rahate hain (That was a bad time which passed away, people of both communities live in harmony here),' said Munnawar, a resident of Rouza locality, one of the worst affected areas during the communal violence. Prior to the 2009 elections both Baranwal and Munnawar held that there would be no shadow of the 2005 riots on the parliamentary elections. The overcrowded markets of Sadar Chowk, Aurangabad Rouza, and other areas and intermingling of people of both communities seemed to be testimony of their claim. However, tension continued as the Mau municipal area had a population of over 2.5 lakh with the ratio of Muslims and Hindus at 55:45 in the town; the figure was held as 65:35 in midtown areas including Harkeshpura, Sadar Chowk, and Rouza.[17] In 2009 instead of fielding its sitting MP Chandradev Rajbhar, the SP fielded Arshad Zamal, the Congress party Sudha Rai, the BSP Dara Singh Chauhan, and the BJP Ram Iqbal Singh, a former student leader

---

[16] An interview Binay Singh 2009.
[17] Binay Singh 2009.

of Banaras Hindu University (BHU). Besides, the Muslims are watchful of the OBCs who constitute 43 per cent of the total electorate—with the Yadavs alone accounting for nearly a lakh voters. With the close presence of Adityanath petty differences can become small low-key incidents which have become endemic.

The Gorakhpur Riots

The constitution of everyday communalism and riots in Gorakhpur is closely tied up with the Gorakhnath Temple and its activities described in the previous chapter. However, respondents in Gorakhpur gave us information based on local folklore, which is useful in understanding its role in everyday communalism in the city and the district. The Math was historically known for its radical, inclusive, and progressive approach to the caste question and in particular had an assimilative approach to questions of idol worship, Dalits, and lower-caste Hindus.[18] Also signifying the confluence of an inter-community past, the temple got a grant from the Mughal King Aurangzeb as well as Asif-Uddaulah along with the Imambara of the city.[19]

However, the colonial period witnessed a number of developments that changed the character of the Math bringing it gradually into the ambit of Hindu right-wing politics which has made it easier for the BJP–RSS and Adityanath to use it for their own purpose. In the last decade of the nineteenth century, the Math underwent a legal dispute on the question of its successor and by 1936, when the decision came, the communal ambience in UP was already vicious on account of competitive communal politics of the Hindu Mahasabha and the Muslim League. Digvijaynath, a person with a radical communal outlook, who hailed from Udaipur, Rajasthan and claimed to be a descendent of Maharana Pratap, was appointed the new Mahant of the temple, which in turn, witnessed a paradigmatic shift in its progressive character. Mahant Digvijaynath is also credited with involving the Gorakshnath Temple with active day-to-day politics. By 1935, under the influence of

[18] Interview with Dr Aziz Ahmad on 12 November 2016 in Gorakhpur town.

[19] Interview with Dr Aziz Ahmad on 12 November 2016 in Gorakhpur town.

Hindu Mahasabha leader Vinayak Damodar Savarkar, he parted ways with the INC and joined the Hindu Mahasabha, primarily on account of his differences with the Congress on the question of 'Nationalism and Communalism'. Not only did he imbibe a radical Hindutva outlook, but actively participated in the activities of the Hindu Mahasabha of which he went on to become the national president in 1961.

Demographically, Gorakhpur town which has less than 10 per cent of a Muslim population with no strong communal character is not a conducive place for the practice of communal discourse. However, our respondent held that it was the outlook of Mahant Digvijaynath and his hatred of the Congress and its stand of secularism, aided by his institutional position of being the Mahant of Gorakshnath Temple, which gave him the stature to attempt a radical Hindutva agenda by taking up communal issues. In fact, he was named as one of the accused in Gandhi's assassination based on the allegation that the pistol with which Gandhi was killed belonged to him.[20] However, for the lack of credible evidence, he was acquitted. Before that, he organized a huge meeting in the premises of the temple-run Maharana Pratap College[21] in 1946, where he called for revenge against the killings of Hindus in Noakhali. Further, in pursuance of his communal agenda, he emerged as one of the main conspirators in the 1949 Ram Temple dispute in Ayodhya. There the plan was to take advantage of the post-Partition communal atmosphere wherein the Muslims, on account of the legacy of the 'Muslim League', were not only suffering from a deep sense of insecurity, but were also seen as the 'suspect community' threatening the integrity of the nascent nation. In his attempt to communalize the general ambience of the town, he entered into active politics and started contesting elections as the Hindu Mahasabha candidate. Initially, in the elections, there used to be separate boxes for dropping the ballets for candidates belonging to different political parties and Mahant Digvijaynath used to candidly say that no Muslim should put his/her vote in his box as he would have to purify the same with 'gangajal'.[22]

---

[20] Interview with Dr Aziz Ahmad on 12 November 2016 in Gorakhpur town.

[21] Now a part of Gorakhpur University.

[22] Interview with Dr Aziz Ahmad on 12 November 2016.

Before his death on 28 September 1969, as the lone sitting Hindu Mahasabha MP representing the Gorakhpur seat, Digvijaynath had contributed immensely to the building of a number of educational institutions like Maharana Pratap Inter College, Maharana Pratap Shishu-Vihar, Gorakshnath Sanskrit Vidyapeeth, and ultimately the establishment of Gorakhpur University by merging the temple-run colleges into it. This propelled him as the leading sociopolitical figure against both the Congress leadership and policies in the region, where he had sowed the seeds of Hindutva by involving the temple and himself in politics (*Mahant Digvijaynath Smriti Granth* Samvat 2029, 1).

His successor, Mahant Avaidhyanath, who presided over the affairs of temple from 1969 until 1998, before his health started declining, was a relatively moderate figure, even though he was actively associated with the Ram Temple movement and was elected as MP from Gorakhpur four times. His approach, though located in the Hindutva worldview, lacked the aggressive and virile temperament of his predecessor Mahant Digvijaynath. Therefore, despite the Ram temple movement and Avaidyanath's active participation in the same, Gorakhpur remained largely peaceful in the 1990s. It was with the appointment of Yogi Adityanath as the successor of Mahant Avaidyanath in 1998 that the communal atmosphere in Gorakhpur underwent a marked change.

The impact of the mobilization by Yogi Adityanath and his HYV can be gauged from understanding the changes it has brought on society in eastern UP. Our respondents pointed out that in its own literature, the Math claims to have many Muslim disciples as well as followers. These followers include the famous Ranjha, a Muslim, who according to the sect official literature, after becoming the disciple of saint Gorakhnath went on to seek spiritual union with Heer, his beloved, after she was forcibly married to someone else by her family.[23] The Mandir's own literature, *Nathsiddhcharitamrit* provides thick examples of Muslim Yogis including Ranjha and others. This book is endorsed by past Mahants of the temple including Yogi Adityanath (Ramlal Srivastava Samvat 2017).

A recent study by Manoj Singh (2017) holds that the Nath sect had Muslim Yogis as well. He points out that in the region many villages even today are inhabited by Muslim yogis who wear saffron *gudri* or *kantha* (saffron clothes or rags) and wander through villages singing

[23] Interview with Dr Aziz Ahmad on 12 November 2016.

folklore on their *sarangi* (stringed musical instrument). They narrate through songs how Gopichandra son of Bengal's Raja Manikchandra, and Raja Bharthari the son of Raja Chandrasen and grandson of Raja Indrasen of Ujjain after meeting Gorakhnath became sanyasis under his influence. It is believed that the sarangi the Muslim yogis play was invented by Gopichand. The *Bharthari Charitra*, which the Muslim yogis sing, was first published by Dudhnath Press, Howrah. Some of them also sing about Shankar–Parvati's wedding and events from the Rama Katha, particularly the banishment of Bharat the brother of Ram to the forest.[24]

Singh's study based on extensive fieldwork in the region, reports that even today there are Muslim yogis who call themselves devotees of Gorakhnath and Bharthari, and associate themselves with the Nath sect. They live in villages of Gorakhpur, Kushinagar, Deoria, Sant Kabir Nagar, Azamgarh, and Balrampur. However, under growing pressure from within as well as outside the community, they are now leaving their traditions. Amidst rising communal violence and sectarianism, the yogis feel uneasy donning saffron. The younger generation looks down upon the practice and views it only as a form of begging. On the other hand, the Hindutva brigade looks at them as a threat because these Muslim yogis practice the philosophy and ideals against which they have based their politics of hate (Manoj Singh 2017).

In Badgo village, 75 households belong to Muslims with almost 24 belonging to yogis. A yogi named Qasim says

---

[24] Hazari Prasad Dwivedi in his writings says that during the time of Gorakhnath there were several upheavals in society. The arrival of Muslims had started; the Buddhist practices were inclining towards magic and witch-craft. Although the primacy of the Brahmin religion had been established, there was a large community of Buddhists and Shaivas who did not accept it. Gorakhnath organized all such groups and led them on the path of yoga. Several Muslims joined him too. Gorakhnath revolted against the distortions in Brahminism and Buddhism in terms of polytheism and extremism. He laid the foundation of Hindu–Muslim unity and opposed caste discrimination and other evils. As a result members of untouchable castes isolated by the Sanatan dharma joined the Nath sect in large numbers. Many of the followers were opposed to the varna system. Dr Pitambar Dutt Barthwal discovered 40 books written by Gorakhnath, most of them in Sanskrit, some in Hindi. Barthwal has compiled the sayings of Gorkhanath in *Gorakhbani*. For more details see, Dwivedi (1952: 28–34).

These are bad times. We are Muslims but we keep the *Ramayana* in our homes alongside the *Quran*. We narrate the tales of Baba Gorakhnath and his disciples Gopichand and Bharthari. Earlier, we were only jogis. Nobody asked us whether we were Hindus or Muslims. But nowadays, there is a lot of fear. Wherever we go, we are asked about our religion.

The village head, Mukhtar Ahmed held that the yogis should end the tradition of singing bhajans and look for other work. He said that he was issuing them job cards so that they leave their sarangis and pick up tools instead (Manoj Singh 2017). It is against this rich tradition of Hindu–Muslim harmony that Yogi Adityanath and his HYV are attempting the communalization of everyday life in the region.

Yogi Adityanath and Communalization of Everyday Life

Yogi Adityanath has not only emerged as the new aggressive Hindutva icon in the region in the 2000s. He has changed the shared discourse by communalizing the everydayness of the region through his highly active approach. The Yogi's employment of a calculated communal propaganda against the Muslim community has witnessed a new high in the region. Religion has emerged as the political prism for dealing with issues ranging from petty disputes over instances of eve teasing, land related clashes, and personal fights, to issues like disputes over religious lands, terrorism, drugs, smuggling, cow slaughter, and the vortex of 'Love Jihad' leading to communalization of everyday life in the city and the adjoining region. A list of communal incidents in Gorakhpur and adjoining areas since 1999 in which Adityanath was involved in are given in Table A3.1 in the Appendix. Also 29 FIRs Filed in the wake of the 2007 Gorakhpur riots accusing Yogi Adityanath and HYV members are given in Table A3.2 in the Appendix.[25]

In fact, this trend of communalizing the petty mundane incidents of everyday life in the region was also mentioned in the letter written to the then BJP Prime Minister Atal Behari Vajpayee by BSP leader

---

[25] Compiled from local media reports and personal interviews with Anand Pandey, a lawyer based in Gorakhpur; Mithilesh Mishra, a journalist at Rajasthan Patrika , who hails from Gorakhpur; Dr Aziz Ahmad; and Parvej Parvaz, editor of online blog, encountersindia.com, Talaz Aziz, now a Congress leader, all held between 8 November and 20 November 2016 at Gorakhpur town.) Also 29 FIRs Filed in the wake of the 2007 Gorakhpur riots accusing Yogi Adityanath and HYV members are given in Table A3.2 in the Appendix.

Mayawati in her capacity as the chief minister of the state. Her letter is quite revealing. She states that the activities of Yogi Adityanath were not in the national interest. She alleged that the Yogi was always eager to communalize petty incidents and thereby target Muslims by using propaganda against them and attempting to create communal polarization. Further highlighting the organizational modus operandi of Yogi Adityanath, she states that many new organizations had come up under his leadership where he created teams of unemployed youths to constantly communalize petty incidents on a regular basis by invoking issues like cow slaughter and cow cartels across Poorvanchal, making the area extremely sensitive.[26]

It is against this background that the 2007 Gorakhpur communal riots that affected the entire Poorvanchal region needs to be examined to deconstruct the nature of communal discourse in Gorakhpur and Poorvanchal under the leadership of Yogi Adityanath and the HYV.

The Making of the 2007 Gorakhpur Riots: 27–29 January

There is tangible and credible evidence that the 2007 Gorakhpur riot was not an exceptional event, but rather a part of the series of the 'everyday communalism' witnessed in Poorvanchal with the political advent of Yogi Adityanath and more intensely following the formation of the HYV. The riot was a part of a larger pre-planned and ongoing pattern-based communal agenda of Yogi Adityanath and HYV as mentioned in the 10 January 2007 dated report of Ramnayan Yadav, Station House Officer (SHO) Padrauna, District Kushinagar, sent to the Sub-Divisional Magistrate (SDM), Kushinagar. In this report, he forthrightly mentions a meeting of the HYV calling upon the members to follow the instructions of Yogi Adityanath to strengthen the Hindu community in the entire Poorvanchal by 'showing' Muslims their place. Allegedly a declaration was made in the meeting that no religious or public function of the Muslims would be allowed to be completed as that led to their assertiveness in the public domain.[27] However, no action was

---

[26] For details see, Mayawati's letter to then PM, Atal Bihari Vajpayee, as mentioned in her book, *Mere Sangharshmay Jeevan Evam Bahujan Movement ka Safarnama* (2006: 756–8).

[27] A copy of the original report is attached in the Appendix.

taken on the report by the district administration. Thereafter, barely after 15 days, the incident on the night of 26 January 2007 emerged as an opportunity to implement the pre-planned communal programme of communalizing the region.

On the night of 26 January 2007, on the occasion of the Shia Muslim festival of Muharram, a procession was proceeding towards the Imambara located in the city. On its way the procession passed through the DAV College where a marriage function was taking place. An orchestra programme was on in which girls were dancing, when some drunken youth started misbehaving with them, which led to a scuffle between the inebriated youths and members of the orchestra. Thereafter, the intimidated female members of the orchestra, who were chased by the drunken youth waving country made pistols, ran towards the main gate of the college and merged with the passing Muharram procession. A brawl broke out between the members of the Muharram procession and one of the inebriated youth, in which the latter fired from his pistol, leading to the injury of four Muslims who were part of the procession. The police personnel accompanying the procession arrested the accused. However, the enraged Muslim crowd, as per the police report, tried to enter the college premises, which the police attempted to prevent with some difficulty. Taking advantage of this diversion the arrested youth, who had fired and injured four Muslims, tried to escape but was caught by the procession mob and was beaten brutally, leading to his death during treatment.[28]

The police acted promptly and arrested the Muslims youths responsible for the same under the Crime No. 40/2007, charging them under articles 147, 148, 149, 298, and 302 of the Indian Penal Code (IPC). However, Yogi Adityanath intervened and gave the entire issue a blatant

[28] Report of SHO Tiwaripur police station who was accompanying the Muharram procession and was a witness to the incident is provided in the Appendix. In addition, the same incident was corroborated by interviewee Anand Pandey, a lawyer; Mithilesh Mishra, a journalist at *Rajasthan Patrika*, who hails from Gorakhpur; Dr Aziz Ahmad; and Parvej Parvaz, editor of online blog, *encountersindia.com*, at interviews held between 8 November and 20 November 2016 at Gorakhpur. However, the narrative was rejected by Saurav Vishvkarma, the Vice President of the Gorakhpur unit of HYV, who is an accused in the riots that followed the said incident along with his brother Chandan Vishvakarma during an interview on 12 November 2016.

communal colour. As the deceased Hindu youth, Rajkumar Agrahari, who had fired upon the Muslim procession, happened to belong to the Hindu Bania caste, that is, the business community, Yogi branded the incident as arising out of habitual oppression of Hindus by Muslims. Thereafter, he led a procession to the Naseerabad locality near the tomb (Mazaar) of a saint and began a protest. The crowd entered the tomb and ignited the property including religious texts. The Senior Superintendent of police (SSP) and District Magistrate (DM) could not prevent the mob from ransacking the place.

At 8 pm, prior to embarking on the above-mentioned protest, Adityanath gave a provocative speech in front of the Gorakhpur railway station against the killing of Rajkumar Agrahari.[29]

Consequently, there were a series of retaliatory incidents in Gorakhpur district. Yogi Adityanath, and HYV are not only continuing on their strategy of communalizing everyday life of the region, but have been rewarded by the BJP many times, for example, by being made campaign in-charge of UP for the 2009 Lok Sabha election and being given a decisive say in the candidate selection of the region. This has made Gorakhpur, which has a Muslim population below 10 per cent, primarily poor Pasmanda, with no visible public presence, become an experiment in new modes of communalism.

Role of the Local Administration and State Government

Role of the District Administration

In Mau, most of the respondents from both the Hindu and Muslim communities, though they pointed to the failure of the district admin-istration to contain the riots, surprisingly, did not treat it as the prime

[29] As the case against Yogi Adityanath is sub-judice it is not given here, but it definitely contributed to the Gorakhpur riots. The complete text of the speech in Hindi can be found in the FIR No. 2776/2008 under IPC Sections 153/153A/1 53B/295/295B/147/143/395/436/ 435/302/427/452 at Cantt Police Station, Gorakhpur, by Parvez Parvaz against Yogi Adityanath as the prime accused. The FIR was lodged only after the complainant moved the Allahabad High Court upon whose instruction the case against Yogi Adityanath was subsequently reg-istered on 2 November 2002, almost 23 months after the alleged incident and the speech.

villain of the communal narrative. In a major departure from the narratives pertaining to all the previous riots in Mau, in which the anti-riot police, namely, the PAC was perceived as the main villain, particularly by the Muslims, this time, barring a few incidents, the role of the PAC was reported to be almost neutral and fair by a majority of the Muslim respondents.

However, from an analysis of the narratives of the respondents and insights of some eminent people, it became clear that there were serious lapses on the part of the local administration that helped escalate the riots.[30] Some important examples can be cited. The immediate release of the accused Muslim youth, under political pressure, who had snatched the wire from loudspeaker on 13 October 2005; the failure to control and disperse the crowd that had gathered on the morning of 14 October 2005 in protest against the postponement of the Bharat Milap ceremony. Also, allowing the five injured Muslims to be taken in an open rickshaw trolley (*thela*) that deliberately passed through the Muslim localities further charging the communal atmosphere; allowing the Muslim protesters to take the injured to the local police station. In addition, allowing Mukhtar Ansari the local MLA, to take the injured to hospital in his vehicle thereby letting the don-politician emerge as the messiah and saviour of the Muslims. Most importantly, allowing Mukhtar Ansari, to roam freely in an open jeep with arms, throughout the city, despite the imposition of curfew, undermined the sanctity of the administration at a time when it was needed the most. Hindus and Muslims read and perceived the movement of Mukhtar Ansari differently: while the Hindus took him as a symbol of Muslim aggression, the Muslims read his act as an encouragement to defy the administration even though the mafia-politician himself wanted to act as 'Robin Hood' for both the communities.

---

[30] On 15 October, three additional companies of the PAC, 12 DSPs and 20 inspectors were sent to Mau; two more companies of the PAC were made available on 16 October which is sufficient for a small place like Mau. Yet on 14 October, both Hindus and Muslims suffered in terms of life and property. However, the violence on 15 and 16 October mainly affected the life and property of Muslims. It is not that the administration did not have a sufficient police force; in fact, it is a patent example of lack of will on the part of the state (Verma, Rai, and Khan 2005).

In Gorakhpur, the local administration was more alert and attempted to put down the riot. There is little doubt that the arrest of Yogi Adityanath stopped the riot from taking a bigger form. However, when the district administration led by the then DM Hari Om, arrested Yogi Adityanath following his violent communal action with the help of the HYV-led mob, the Mulayam Singh government transferred the DM, thereby emboldening the Yogi and the HYV. In an interview Hari Om, lucidly pointed out that the long-term and meticulously planned strategy of the saffron leader and his outfit was to 'communalize petty mundane incidents of everyday life'.[31] In fact, he stated,

> Yogi and HYV attempt to fetch benefit out of all issues—small and large. He acts as a communal provocateur even where there are no issues for the same, and colours them in a Hindu–Muslim framework. For instance, a Hindu girl is teased by a Muslim boy or the water coming out of drainage from Muslim house passes through a Hindu house, and similar insignificant incidents, they are communalized intensely. The HYV is spreading fast in the rural areas of Gorakhpur, Kushinagar and other districts.

Further, commenting upon the incident of 2007 he refused to call it a communal riot as by definition a riot involves both the communities in the clash, what happened after the incident of 26 January, he held, was the one-sided planned attack upon the other community ('Interview of Hari Om', *Outlook* 2007).

Similarly, the SSP Gorakhpur in his report to the District Magistrate pointed out that,

> As a result of the incident (near the mazaar) curfew had to be imposed in four police station areas in Gorakhpur city and there was communal tension in Gorakhpur district and the adjoining areas. At many places the incidents of ransom, loot and destruction of public property and transport took place. The state property was destroyed. As a result, the movement of public transport, like bus and train were affected.[32]

However, they received little support from the state government.

---

[31] Interview of Hari Om, the DM during the 2007 communal incident at Gorakhpur, given to *Outlook* magazine dated 19 February 2007, pp. 12–13.

[32] The report of SSP to DM under NSA/07 dated 8 February 2007 is attached in the Appendix.

Role of the State Government

Both the Mau and Gorakhpur riots took place during the regime of the SP with Mulayam Singh Yadav—described as the protector of the Muslims—as the Chief Minister. The Gorakhpur riots were just prior to the 2007 elections when the BJP, as discussed in the previous chapter, was keen to foster riots following its defeat in the 2004 national elections and with the approaching 2007 assembly and 2009 national elections. There were no riots once the Mayawati government was formed in mid-2007.

In Mau the riots were bigger, lasted longer, and there was greater loss of life and property. Hence the role of the state government was important. There is little doubt that the apathy of the state government was responsible for the riots continuing for three days. On 14 October, both Hindus and Muslims suffered in terms of life and property. However, the violence on 15 and 16 October, mainly affected the life and property of Muslims. The administration, as mentioned above, had sufficient police force but there was little pressure from the state to put down the riot, evident from the fact that it continued for three days and there was considerable loss of life and property (Verma, Rai, and Khan 2005). According to official information, eight persons died in the Mau riots over three days: two persons died on 14 October, two on 15 October, and four on 16 October. Among the dead were five Hindus and four Muslims. As per official information, 37 persons were injured between 14 October and 29 October. However, according to public information, there were many other injured persons who were not taken to hospital and were not included in the list. As of 30 October, the number of those who were arrested on charges of violence or only on suspicion was 442. Of these, 205 were Hindus and 237 Muslims. A large number of people complained of police excesses. In the weavers' colony, Muslim women and men complained that the police-PAC arrested people after breaking open their doors late at night; among the arrested, they alleged, were minors (Verma, Rai, and Khan 2005).

According to one estimate (Verma, Rai, and Khan 2005) more than 300 houses suffered arson, loot, and damage and about 300 small and big business establishments, shops, and kiosks were looted or burnt. The biggest losers were the Muslim weavers, many of whom were facing starvation. According to the report approximately 150–200 power looms—owned mainly by Muslims—were destroyed in the riots. The worst hit people were daily wagers with small earnings. Even 14 days after the outbreak of violence, Mau could not be linked via rail services. Even a fortnight after the riots began, the situation did not permit a simultaneous relaxation of curfew for a couple of hours in different parts of the city. The total losses suffered in Mau perhaps ran into crores. It is not possible to analyze the role of various persons, organizations, media, administration, and government as well as caste and communities in 2005 riots. On 18 October, many days after the riots began the police filed FIRs against about 250 persons including Mukhtar Ansari, BJP MLC Ramji Singh, Hindu Yuva Vahini leaders Ajit Singh Chandel and Sujit Kumar Singh and BSP ex-MLA Nasim Ahmad, on charges of inciting riots through speeches, murder, arson, and destruction (Verma, Rai, and Khan 2005).

Our discussion with the respondents, point to similarities in the role of the state government during and in the aftermath of 2005 Mau and 2013 Muzaffarnagar riots. In both cases, the state was ruled by the SP and there were charges of an implicit understanding between the SP and BJP even though the context of the riots was qualitatively different.[33] Most remarkable, was the absence of a visit by Chief Minister, Mulayam Singh Yadav during or after the Mau riots given their intensity and visits by many other leaders. The visit of the then Governor of UP, T.V. Rajeshwar to the curfew-bound town and his meeting with different groups and victims to take stock of the situation was criticized by the state government as political.[34]

One of the plausible reasons why Mulayam Singh Yadav did not visit the riot-affected at Mau, was the conscious attempt by the SP government not to be seen siding with any community when its core social base, Muslim and Yadavs, were at loggerheads. In fact, the most prominent rumour, though grossly inflated, that escalated the riots in rural area happened to be the killing of the Yadavs selling milk in the Muslim

[33] In fact, the report by *Sanjhi Duniya* on the Mau Riots highlights the instances of relative tolerance of HYV activities in the wake of the Mau riots, and the soft approach of the SP government towards the Hindutva leaders (Verma, Rai, and Khan 2005).

[34] Amar Singh the then General Secretary of the SP publically accused the Governor of playing politics by his tour of riot-affected Mau.

locality on 14 October 2005. In contrast, in the 2013 Muzaffarnagar riots the SP government was perceived to be clearly favouring the Muslims over the Jats. In Muzaffarnagar, the SP government did not need to appear neutral among the two contending communities as the party's core social base was not dented on account of non-existence of Yadavs in that region, and Jats not being SP voters. In Mau the approach of the state government was casual, besides the rhetoric of strict action and ignoring the popular demand for a CBI inquiry or a high-level inquiry by a retired high court judge, it appointed a probe under Neera Yadav, who herself was recently removed from the post of Principal Secretary on corruption charges. The role of the state government was limited to instructing the district administration to provide financial compensation of Rs 2 lakhs to the families whose properties had been gutted or looted.

Other parties like the Congress and BSP, sensing a conspiracy behind the riots, demanded a CBI or high-level probe besides accusing the SP and BJP of being hand-in-glove.[35] On the ground, there were also many instances of the involvement of local BSP and SP leaders in the riot. For instance, SP leader Amarnath Yadav who was later shot dead was a main accused in the riots, apart from BSP leader Manoj Rai who is currently the BSP candidate from the Sadar seat in the 2017 assembly elections.

Lack of Intervention by Civil Society

The reports on the riots by Verma, Rai, and Khan (2005) and Rawat (2016) point out that there was no effort by civil society to intervene and stop the Mau riots. As mentioned earlier, there was a time when Mau, Ghazipur, Azamgarh, and Ballia were places where left parties had strongholds and from where candidates of the Communist Party of India (CPI) were elected as MLAs and MPs. Today, while a CPI candidate loses his deposit, a person like Mukhtar Ansari gets elected. During the tense period after the demolition of the Babri Masjid, the intervention by CPI leader Imtiyaz Ahmad played a significant role in preventing violence. Even today, people remember his role and say

[35] This aspect appeared in various news reports, like http://www.milliga-zette.com/dailyupdate/2005/20051104-riots-politics.htm

that if he had been in the city during these riots, at least in Rauza and Chowk, Hindu shops would not have been looted. When a party with a people-oriented ideology and strong roots in the people's struggle loses its base, the forces that occupy its position inevitably flourish on riots and violence. 'Had Muslims not saved them, how have Hindus in the old city survived?' This comment from a political worker is very important. In Mau there are several persons who saved the lives of people and challenged the rioters like Haji Abdul Sattar, Abdul Samad, and Haji Wakil who challenged the rioters in Sindhi Colony, or like Salim Ansari, Qamruzzaman, and Haji Irfan who stopped the fanatics. On the other hand, there are people like Ashok Singh, who saved the Grihasth Plaza at Ghazipur trisection from arson, Anil Rai, who defended a furniture shop against looters, Hindu landlords near Ali building who saved Noorkamal, Dr Udai Narain Singh, who saved two lives, and Ashok Gupta, who gave shelter to nine Muslims (Verma, Rai, and Khan 2005).

In the case of Gorakhpur, the lack of intervention by civil society was due to the fact that Mahanth Adityanath had taken over and communalized the society of the town and surrounding areas. Institutions such as the Gita Press and the Gorakhnath temple have an important position in the lives of the people of the region and a wide network. Alternatively, civil society organizations do not seem to have a presence in the town.

Role of the Media

One of the reasons why the Mau 2005 riots were different from the previous riots, both on scale and intensity, could be attributed to the biased role played by the media. While the partisan role of local and vernacular media in the communal riots is known, it was the biased role of the national media, like *Hindustan, India Today, Times of India, India Express*, etc., along with the vernacular media that helped escalate the riots disproportionately. In fact, Dhumketu and Tayyab Palki alleged that they took the liberty in using the term *narsanhar* (massacre) of Hindus and similar other inflated and unverified accounts of the riots. A headline, 'मऊ में हिंदुओं का नरसंहार' (The Massacre of Hindu's in Mau) further intensified and polarized the communal atmosphere and caused the riots to spread in the village areas, where the Muslims were at the receiving end. The remarks by our respondents indicated that the media as a whole, barring *Amer Ujala*, went by popular rumours spread by vested elements, primarily the activists of HYV. The media showed little interest in the Gorakhpur riots and reported it as a local incident despite the violence and loss of lives. Only some websites maintained by Muslim organizations and local newspapers reported it.

***

Our narrative reveals the emergence of a new pattern of everyday communalism and riots in the 2000s in two important towns of eastern UP, Mau, and Gorakhpur. While communal tension is not new in these towns, large-scale riots have been rare. The 2005 and 2007 riots in Mau and Gorakhapur, respectively, have been the product of long-term, sustained, grass roots mobilization in order to institutionalize a new form of everyday conflict to create polarization between the Hindu and Muslim communities. A number of new features are visible in the manner in which communalism in Mau and Gorakhpur and adjoining districts is created and operates.

In the 2000s, the location of riots has shifted to new regions, where Hindu and Muslim communities have lived side by side for long sharing both sociocultural space and economic livelihoods. These are not the big urban areas as in western UP where Muslims have owned large businesses since the colonial period that Hindu merchants are now attempting to control or take over. Rather, in Mau the Muslim Ansari weavers have traditionally owned and worked on hand-operated looms in their homes producing cloth that has been marketed by Hindu traders who have a large presence in the town. The establishment of mechanical looms, globalization, and competition from Chinese products has affected the small Ansari weavers who do not have the funds to invest in large looms and in marketing their products abroad. This has provided space to Hindu traders to control the making and selling of the products giving them an edge over the Muslim weavers. This has created new relationships between the two, leaving them vulnerable to daily, mundane differences and small conflicts, which the Hindutva forces led by Yogi Adityanath are adept in using to create polarization over time. Consequently, the new form of communal mobilization is not large-scale, district-wide or state-wide mobilization, but rather attempts to institutionalize conflict on a daily basis by working on the evolving lines of cleavages between communities. These changes are visible in the town as Muslims are concentrated here and ply their trade; also, roads and communications are not as well developed as in western UP. Hence, small incidents and riots take place in the towns and do not spread deep into the rural areas, a feature increasingly happening in the more developed western region.

In Mau, public memory among leading citizens and intellectuals who formed our respondents in the town is strong regarding the trajectory that Hindu–Muslim relations have taken in the town since the late 1960s when the first signs of Hindu–Muslim conflict was witnessed in the post-independence period. Their narrative also indicates that the shift is due to economic change in the artisanal industry since the 1990s leading to a change in sociocultural relationships and more recently the rise of Yogi Adityanath and his attempt to foment communal tension. They were clear that the 2005 riots were the result of these long-term developments.

These new conflictual relationships have the potential of creating conflicts during festivals in which the two communities need to share cultural space in the city. The Bharat Milap ceremony is very old and earlier elders in the community sorted out differences, but the presence of right-wing elements that take advantage and create communal tension is a new phenomenon in Mau. This has created a trust deficit and created boundaries between the two communities due to which any false rumour of a particular community being attacked, or small deviation from agreed practices as, for example, moving too close to a Masjid during a Hindu procession or vice versa, can spark off conflict. This is visible in the difference in the narratives provided by leaders of both communities regarding the events that sparked off the Mau riots. The mobilization by the HYV has also created intra-Hindutva rivalry, which leads to suspicion and divisions within the Hindu community that further fuels conflict with the Muslim community. The presence of Mafia dons, such as Mukhtar Ansari, during riots also adds to the communal tension as he is viewed as siding with and encouraging the Muslim community, though this may not be true.

In Gorakhpur the social and economic context in which communalism is manufactured and deployed is different, the central feature being the presence of Yogi Adityanath and his HYV. Gorakhpur district and town has fewer Muslims than Mau and traditionally was not an area prone to communal conflict. The Gorakhnath Math, according to the respondents of the town, though involved in right-wing politics since the late colonial period, did not attempt to communalize the citizens of the town and region. The *peeth* has had Muslim followers and yogis who even today can be seen in the countryside singing in praise of Gorakhnath and his disciples. However, our fieldwork reveals that since the late 1990s the emergence of Yogi Adityanath, his HYV, and the presence of the BJP–RSS cadres, has led to attempts to institutionalize a new form of everyday communalism among the common people. The attempt is to communalize small, mundane, daily events, and features such as renaming Muslim areas and establishments, creating conflict over graveyards and Masjids and other common spaces thereby creating deep-seated prejudice against Muslims and fear in their minds.

Yogi Adityanath and his followers espouse a non-Brahminical, non-orthodox Hindutva, which has managed to successfully mobilize and incorporate in Gorakhpur and Mau and increasingly the surrounding areas, the OBCs, and Dalits along with the upper castes to create a united Hindu community against the Muslim 'other' who are then forced to adhere to Hindu values and customs. In spite of the Yogi's differences with the BJP and his attempt to create a separate Hindutva power centre in eastern UP, the leadership has supported him as his activities have enabled them to win elections in recent years, displacing the SP and BSP who traditionally had a strong base in the region. Our fieldwork shows clearly the highly successful, two-fold image of Yogi Adityanath in the region—a tough, Robin Hood figure due to provision of educational, health, and other daily necessities and facilities in a region ignored by the government and second, a feared but popular, Hindutva icon who has managed to institutionalize Hindutva ideology at the grass roots in the region.

Thus, our study shows how sustained mobilization over a period of time by Hindutva forces has been able to introduce substantial political and cultural change in eastern UP. A region where once left and socialist forces and later the social justice parties were dominant has become the experimental communal laboratory of leaders such as Yogi Adityanath and his religious organizations. He has deftly been able to make use of the general economic backwardness of the region, the crisis in agriculture, and the artisanal industry, lack of livelihood, the rise of criminals and criminalization of politics witnessed within all political parties, which has rendered the area as poorly governed. With this picture of everyday Hindutva and communalization of life in the region, we move now to western UP where communal tension and riots have increased in recent years, but operate in a different context though the methods used are very similar.

Appendix

Table A3.1 List of Communal Incidents Involving Yogi Adityanath and the HYV in Eastern UP since 1999

Year	District	Place	Incident
1999	Maharajganj	Panchrukhiya	This is the first incident when Yogi Adityanath was formally charged as an accused in the FIR for instigating the communal clash in the village Panchrukhiya in Maharajganj district, adjacent to Gorakhpur, on 10 February 1999. There was a dispute over the graveyard land in the village wherein a bell was attached to a banyan tree located in the land leading to the dispute. The matter was brought to the notice of district administration and PSC forces were employed there. However, Yogi Adityanath went to the site along with his supporters and reportedly gave a provocative speech accusing Muslims of being terrorists and advocating establishing a bomb factory in the village for the protection of the Hindus. Nearby, the then Samajvadi Party leader Talat Aziz was addressing a meeting over the issue when they

Year	District	Place	Incident
			were attacked by Yogi Adityanath's men, and Aziz's official bodyguard, constable Satyaprakash was shot dead. In the FIR, Yogi Adityanath was named as the prime accused.
2002	Kushinagar	Mohan-Mundera	On 16 June 2002, in Mohan-Mundera village in Kushinagar district adjoining Gorakhpur, a Hindu girl died after being raped by a Muslim youth from the same village. After two days, Yogi Adityanath and his HYV held a meeting in the village and spoke about revenging the incident like Godhara and consequently the crowd set fire to 47 Muslim houses.
2002	Gorakhpur	Nanthua	In Gorakhpur, on 23 June in a dispute between two youths—Indal, a Hindu and Alam, a Muslim—over an eve teasing incident, Alam attacked Indal with a knife. After two days, Yogi Adityanath along with his supporters held a meeting at the village and the crowd set fire to Alam's house.
2002	Maharajganj	Narkataha	On 20 August 2002, the dead body of a Hindu boy named Sanjay was found, upon which a crowd led by members of HYV attacked and killed two Muslim youths, Raseed and Anwar. Yogi Adityanath held a meeting in the village on 24 August and justified the killings.

(Cont'd)

Table A3.1   (*Cont'd*)

Year	District	Place	Incident
2002	Maharajganj	Badhepurva	In August 2002, on a dispute related to the location of the house of a Muslim in Badhepurva village in Maharajganj district, the house was demolished and the location was declared a 'dev-sthan' (god's place) by Yogi Adityanath.
2003	Gorakhpur	Ghasikatara	On 16 August 2003, a fight broke out between two groups of youths, Hindu and Muslim, in Ghasikatra colony in Gorakhpur city. The FIR named many Hindu youths, including HYV vice president Saurabh Vishvakarma as the prime accused, which in turn led to a tussle between Yogi Adityanath and DIG Jagmohan Yadav. However, the Mulayam Singh Yadav-led government ultimately transferred the DIG.
2003	Gorakhpur	City	On the eve of Holi on 19 March 2003, the Imam of Gazi-Rauja mosque in Gorakhpur city was killed by some unknown people. Following this the Muslims killed another person named Chandan Srivastav within 10 minutes of the earlier incident. In the retaliatory action, two Muslims were killed where the main accused were Chandan Vishwakarma and Saurabh Vishvakarma, the HYV officials who are close to Yogi Adityanath.

Year	District	Place	Incident
2003	Dewaria	Thawai	On 3 November 2003, in a place called Thawai in Dewaria city, a Hindu youth was killed by a Muslim over some personal dispute. In retaliatory action, the houses of as many as 48 Muslims were set ablaze by the mob led by HYV wherein the arrested persons were later released, allegedly, under Yogi Adityanath's political pressure.

Table A3.2   List of 29 FIRs Filed in the Wake of 2007 Gorakhpur Riots Accusing Yogi Adityanath and HYV Members

S. No. 1	Police Station 2	FIR No. 3	IPC ACT Invoked 4	Complainant 5
1	Cantt	141/2007	147/307/427	Tufail Ahmed
2	Cantt	2776/2008	153A/153B/295b/ 147/143/395/ 436/435/302/427/ 452	Parvez Parvaz
3	Kotvali	40/2007	147/148/199/298/ 302	Rajendra Prasad Agrahari
4	Kotvali	43/2007	147/153/297/435/ 506/379/295	Raseed Khan
5	Rajghat	49/2007	302/34/504/506	Rasheed Ahmed
6	Tiwaripur	57/2007	436/147/336	Ramesh Chandra Gupta
7	Tiwaripur	58/2007	436	Abad Hussain

(Cont'd)

Table A3.2 *(Cont'd)*

S. No. 1	Police Station 2	FIR No. 3	IPC ACT Invoked 4	Complainant 5
8	Gorakhnath	99/2007	436/143/427	Sweet House Ansar Road
9	Khajani	15/2007	147/148/149/332/ 353/153A/295/ 336/427/433/ 456/380/188/186	S.H.O- Khajani, Shyamnarayan Yadav
10	Gagaha	36/2007	143/295/436/361	DSP-Gagaha, Ramanuj Singh
11	Cantt	144/2007	427/295A/2/3(1) Gangster Act	Saheed Ahmed
12	Gorakhnath	99A/2007	435/423 and 3/4 Prevention of Damage to Property Act	SHO- Gorakhnath, Sunil Kumar Rai
13	Gorakhnath	99C/2007	427	Ali Hasan
14	Gorakhnath	99D/2007	436/427	Nabi Munawwar
15	Gorakhnath	99E/2007	436/427	Munivar Ali
16	Gorakhnath	99F/2007	436	Md. Shahid
17	Gorakhnath	435/428/ 427		Shamsher Ahmed
18	Kotwali	37/2007	147/323/504/ 506/336	Biral Ahmed
19	Kotwali	37A/2007	147/323/504/ 506/336	Sunil Kumar
20	Kotwali	40A/2007	147/148/149/ 323/307/504/ 506	Md. Samim

S. No. 1	Police Station 2	FIR No. 3	IPC ACT Invoked 4	Complainant 5
21	Khajani	16/2007	147/153A/295/ 435/188/504/506	DSP-Khajani, Deenanath Singh
22	Sahjanawa	41/2007	147/332/353/ 427/426	SHO- Sahjanawa, Rakesh Yadav
23	Sahjanawa	47/2007	295/147/153A	Md. Hasan
24	Sahjanawa	59/2007	153A/295/436	Wahid
25	Gagaha	37/2007	143/295/436/427	Baqreevan
26	Cantt	9/2007	143/153A/295/ 427/436/188	Md. Saheed
27	Gagaha	65/2007	147/153A/295/ 427/506	Zalim
28	Uruwa	20/2007	147/145/153A/ 295A/336/323/ 504/506	Naseeruddin

PART II

Western Uttar Pradesh

Political Economy of Agrarian Crisis and the Construction of Everyday Communalism

4

Agrarian Crisis, Changing Jat–Muslim Relations, and Everyday Communalism in Western Uttar Pradesh

Following the appearance of communal riots in eastern UP in 2005 and 2007, communal tension and small incidents emerged in some districts of western UP from 2011 onwards culminating in the major riot in Muzaffarnagar and adjoining districts in September 2013. The riots were surprising as our selected districts of Muzaffarnagar and Shamli, unlike other western UP districts such as Meerut, Agra, or Moradabad are not prone to communal disturbances. Even during the RJBBM riots, these districts remained calm except for a small riot in Muzaffarnagar in 1988. In fact, at Independence western UP emerged as a region with the least polarized class structures with a strong class of independent agricultural producers. The Jats, the major agrarian community together with other Hindu groups in the past have shared a harmonious relationship with the Muslim community.

Comprising 19 districts, during the colonial period the western region was one of the most dynamic regions in the erstwhile United Provinces. It had a high growth rate and commercial crops under a moderate *khudkhast* (self-owned and self-cultivated land by the peasant) rather than a zamindari or jagirdari system (Metcalfe 1979). There was no overwhelming poverty or large zamindars and at Independence as Mohinder Singh points out, even the Dalits were better fed and resembled their Punjabi neighbours unlike those in the eastern region where an oppressive, feudal landlord system continued (M. Singh 1947). In contrast to the eastern region, commercialization of agriculture began during the colonial period itself with the introduction of cash crops such as wheat, tobacco, and sugarcane. The British constructed two big canals—the Eastern Yamuna Canal in 1830 and sections of the Ganga Canal in 1855 and 1860—and the area watered by these, consisting of parts of western UP and Haryana, became very prosperous (Clift 1977: A83–A90). These features, as we shall see, make the form of everyday communalism different from the eastern districts.

As in the case of eastern UP, it was the defeat of the BJP in 2004 and more importantly in 2009 and the feeling of marginalization of right-wing forces at the centre and in UP, which led many members of the BJP to advocate a return to the core agenda of Hindutva of the party. While the communal tension and small incidents from 2011 onwards and the Muzaffarnagar riot of 2013 are described based on field studies in the next chapter, the focus here is on the reasons underlying the revival of communalism and riots in western UP in the 2000s. A central argument is that two significant underlying, long-term developments, both operating over a period of time played a key role in the resurgence of communal riots in the western districts. First, the planned and sustained everyday communal mobilization on the ground by the BJP–RSS in the region from the early 2000s onwards, followed by the long and highly divisive electoral campaign for the 2014 national elections under the leadership of Narendra Modi that further increased communal polarization. Second, agrarian decline, which began in the post-Green Revolution period, and the deepening of the crisis in the 2000s, which made the Hindus, primarily the Jats, and the Muslims highly vulnerable to communal mobilization, tension, and riots. While the former constitutes the political and aggressively visible form of the construction of communalism, the latter constitutes the underlying political economy aspect, which rendered it possible and effective.

Our study reveals that much before the rise of communal tension culminating in the Muzaffarnagar riots of 2013, the BJP–RSS had begun an intensive programme of grass roots, everyday mobilization in districts of western UP. The construction of communalism was attempted in carefully selected new social and economic contexts with a large Hindu and Muslim community, where the party did not have much presence and which had not experienced large-scale and violent riots earlier. Most important, rather than large riots as during the RJBBM period, the aim in the early 2000s was to create a number of small, low-key incidents, so as to establish a permanent system of oppression of Muslims. These small incidents were responsible for making western UP a 'tinder box' and eventually sparked off severe riots in Muzaffarnagar and neighbouring districts. The mobilization was undertaken by a new generation of young and local leaders selected by the BJP–RSS, who together with the cadres undertook quiet mobilization in the towns, but more importantly, for the first time in the villages of the region. The strategy proved useful as the villages where Hindu and Muslim communities live in close proximity experienced the most violent riots leading to an exodus of Muslims in 2013. A major goal was to break the Jat–Muslim alliance in the region and gain the support of the former who had supported the party in the early 1990s. As a consequence, the confrontation during the riots was mainly between the Jats and the Muslims due to a breakdown of the earlier harmonious relationship between them.

Another marked feature of communalism in western UP in the 2000s is that it has been intertwined with a long and divisive electoral campaign. The 2014 Lok Sabha elections provided an opportunity to build on the earlier mobilization, further polarize communities, create a Hindu vote bank, and perform well in UP contributing to a majority at the centre. This was possible due to the redefinition of Hindutva and methods of mobilization by the new BJP leadership of Narendra Modi and Amit Shah. The shift of power from the hands of the founders of the BJP—Atal Behari Vajpayee and L.K. Advani—to a new generation under the leadership of Narendra Modi led to the inclusion of the notion of development within the ideology of Hindutva taking it beyond older issues such as the Ram Temple or the Uniform Civil Code. The BJP under Amit Shah pursued an aggressive style of communal mobilization taking the long electoral campaign into smaller towns and villages using social media, which helped deepen the communal divide and win the 2014 elections. Both in the grass roots mobilization and electoral campaign, a more inclusive Hindutva platform was used to gain the support of the OBCs and Dalits to create a single Hindu identity and vote bank to obtain victory.

Equally important is the underlying, long-term decline in the agrarian economy of western UP that the BJP–RSS took full advantage of and which made communal mobilization leading to deep-seated communal polarization between the Hindu and Muslim community possible. In the mid-1960s, the Green Revolution contributed to the emergence of a surplus-producing, rich peasant class in western UP particularly among the landowning Jats making them a dominant political class in the countryside. The agrarian prosperity also helped the Muslims who constituted largely the landless labour. However, from the late 1980s, the western region entered a post-Green Revolution phase in which it has experienced long-term agricultural decline, no longer making agriculture a profitable enterprise. It led to the weakening of the Jat–Muslim sociopolitical alliance formed by Charan Singh. In the early 1990s during the RJBBM movement, the former moved towards the BJP while the latter preferred the newly formed SP and BSP. These shifts signalled the beginnings of communal divisions between the two communities in western UP.

The deepening of the agrarian crisis in the 2000s resulted in the breakdown of the already worsening relations between the Jats and the Muslims. In this situation, mobilization of the Jats was possible as they remained largely dependent on agriculture and the absence of alternative employment led to despondency among them and a growing perception that the Muslims, who traditionally did not own land, by taking up new non-agricultural employment and small businesses, had moved ahead. This created economic anxieties and cultural aspirations in the minds of the younger generation of both communities who felt left behind compared to other regions in the country. These changes were exploited by the BJP through well-organized and sustained mobilization to deepen the social and political divide between the Jats and Muslims, leading to rising communal tension and eventually the terrible Muzaffarnagar riots. Our narrative of communal mobilization by the BJP–RSS, the agrarian crisis, and changing relations among the Jat and Muslim community, provided below, will provide a background to the fieldwork on the riots in the selected districts of Muzaffarnagar and Shamli presented in the next chapter.

Castes and Communities in Western UP: A Profile

Certain historical and sociological features of western UP make it different from other parts of the state, which makes the socio-economic context in which communalism occurs, somewhat different. The 1931 Census enumerates the numerous castes and communities found in the western districts: upper-caste Brahmins and Rajputs, middle-caste

Jats, Gujjars, and others today described as OBCs and a number of castes today described as most backward classes (MBCs) such as Sainis, Kahars, Nais, Kumhars, and Gadarias (Turner 1933). Among Muslims upper castes/classes were Ashrafs such as Pathans, Saiyads, and Sheikhs, middle castes/classes such as Muley Jats and many lower castes today described as Pasmanda or backward such as Dhobis, Faquirs, Nais, Tellis, and so forth. However, in the agrarian society of the region, the Jats and the Muslims constitute two important communities that have lived side-by-side with close historical links between them. A brief look at these two communities and their interrelationship until the 1980s in western UP is attempted subsequently.

Jats in Western UP

The Jats, estimated to be around 17 per cent in western UP, are predominantly a rural community with a robust self-identity and sense of community. They occupy a strong position in the agrarian economy and politics of 17 districts, stretching from Baghpat to Agra, containing about 17 parliamentary and 36 assembly constituencies—notably, Muzaffarnagar, Meerut, and Shamli. They make up 6 per cent of the voters in western UP but can affect political fortunes in at least 10 Lok Sabha constituencies.

The formation of a Jat identity in north India is itself of fairly recent vintage as they possessed a rather fragile and inchoate sense of identity in pre-colonial India (Datta 1999: 1). Part of a system of migrating clans and tribes rather than a strict caste system, Jats came together in the colonial period to form a larger identity. This explains the fact that they do not fit neatly into the caste system, often keeping them socially apart from other castes standing at the middle level of the caste hierarchy. Today they consist of exogamous clans with affiliated villages forming a *Khap* or clan territory and living members of a *gotra* (blood relationship) forming a *biradari* or *bhaichara* (brotherhood). Jat identity can therefore be identified on several levels: varna, caste, and clan, and they can be Hindu, Sikh, or Muslim which suggests that religious identity is not always central nor are they noted for their religious devotion. Far more important for the Jat is the virile, hardworking, good agriculturalist and high rural status image (Bentall and Corbridge 1996: 39). According to Dwivedi's (1970: 385) account, 'They [Jats] … worship their ancestors and lineal gods, and believe in the potency of curses and the positive aspects of Karma. But they take all these on their merit, which consists in social expediency and utility. In short, their approach to religion is practical.' Nonica Datta describes the historical formation of a 'localized' Jat identity mainly in present-day Haryana but also adjoining western UP (Datta 1999: 2). The Jats consider themselves as well as Rajputs, Gujjars, Ahirs, and Sainis to compose a category of castes as belonging to the same varna category of 'Kshatriya' or as sharing hereditary 'martial proclivities or leadership qualities' (Datta 1999). The British however denied them the status of a Kshatriya caste. Rather the core of Jat identity is probably 'home-made' (Madsen 1991: 352). A number of peasant castes such the Muley Jat, Rajput Muslim, Tyagi, and Ranghar, converted to Islam, many of whom kept their pre-Islamic customs such as clan exogamy (Madsen 1991).

Originally placed within the large Shudra group, the definition of Jat in terms of varna and caste was largely moulded by the Arya Samaj between 1880 and 1930 under the leadership of Dayanand Saraswati who carved out a moral order consistent with Vedic principles and role for themselves in rural society (Madsen 1991: 52). Being part of the Arya Samaj meant that they accepted *Shuddhi* and cow protection (Datta 1999: 3172). However, Jats do not suffer from the social discrimination associated with some OBCs. As a group that owned substantial amounts of land and with a good knowledge of agriculture, they fought persistently for status as an agricultural caste in the colonial period and were able to make good use of the economic opportunities that colonial rule provided. The formation of the All-India Jat Mahasabha in 1905 put forward these demands vociferously. The leader who put forward the demands in the colonial period was Sir Chotu Ram in the 1920s and the 1930s. Another reason that helped the Jats was that the British identified them as a martial race and took them into the army, a tradition that continues and provides them employment. These developments made them a strong, locally dominant, and prosperous landowning caste in western UP (Pradhan 1966). The fact that they have only recently emerged from being considered Shudra to a clean agricultural caste also matters and is often the reason they distance themselves from the Backward Castes in UP. The attraction of the BJP in more recent years has been that this enhances the fact of being 'Hindu' during a period when the lower backwards and Dalits are questioning the position of all castes above them.

Two developments in the post-independence period further helped the landowning Jats to emerge as a strong, peasant class: the abolition of zamindari and later the Green Revolution. The former, by removing the absentee landlords, made them the dominant caste/class in the country-side in the western districts (Neale 1962). The latter in the mid-1960s helped in making Jats with medium-to-large holdings a locally domi-nant, surplus-producing rich peasant class (Z. Hasan 1989; Pai 1993; Patnaik 1988; Stokes 1978). In western UP on the eve of the Green Revolution, rich peasants with over 7.5 acres of land represented about one-fourth of the rural households and operated roughly three-fourths of the land (Z. Hasan 1989: 54–5). This differentiation is visible among Jats based on landholdings, but also between Jats and other groups par-ticularly Muslims and Dalits. By the late 1990s, the Green Revolution had a major impact on the wealth and lifestyle of Jat farmers with larger farms; they invested in tractors, electric tube wells, chemical fertilizers, high-yielding varieties of wheat and sugarcane, took to dairying and poultry and were able to hire a number of casual and farm servants who were largely SC (Jeffrey 1997; 2001). They were also able to educate their children who got off-farm jobs, especially salaried employment with the government. Muslims and Dalits were far less successful in entering into skilled non-agricultural employment and the majority remained as landless labour that could not get jobs outside. However, in more recent years these two groups have also moved to non-agricultural jobs.

Muslims in Western UP

The Muslims, largely an urban community consisting of about 18 per cent of the state population, form the largest religious minority though they are not a majority in any district. However, in as many as 13 Lok Sabha constituencies they account for more than 15 per cent of the electorate. The Muslims in western UP as in other parts of the state do not form a homogenous community. They are divided in the state into the Ashraf and Ajlaf groups, 68 castes and sub-castes and by dialect and geographical distribution. However, they do possess a sense of group identity based on cultural and historical factors, which enables them to come together in times of crisis. The Muslim popula-tion of UP in 1881 was 13.74 per cent of the population and had risen to 19.26 per cent by 2011 (Census 2011). Due to the mutiny of 1857 both the Hindu and Muslim landowners suffered as both lost lands which were confiscated by the British (Hardy 1972). Once the wounds of the Mutiny healed, many lands were returned to zamindars, *Patidars* (co-sharers) and taluqdars (land-owning aristocrats). The last were the most influential and numbered 272 of which 76 or roughly 28 per cent were Muslims (Robinson 1975: 20). At the beginning of the twentieth century, the Muslims held approximately one-fifth of the land in the United Provinces, in large amounts mainly around erstwhile centres of power such as Jaunpur, Allahabad, Fatehpur, Bareilly, Moradabad, Lucknow, Agra, and Bara Banki. In western UP where Muslims were more numerous and Muslim influence had been greater in districts such as Aligarh and Bulandshahr, there was a very powerful concentration of Muslim landlords (Robinson 1975).

Due to partition, a large number of the better-off, landowning, and educated Muslims from western UP including from Shamli and Muzaffarnagar, migrated to Pakistan leaving behind the poorer landless sections who were employed as agricultural labour by the Jats, a system that continues. According to official statistics, Muslims left behind as much as 14,221 bighas of land leading to large-scale hardship, much of which was again in western UP (Khalidi 1997: 79). A large number of big Muslim landlords who remained, lost land due to the Land Reform Act passed in 1951. They had to adjust to a new way of life in which they could no longer depend on agricultural income which caused them tremendous problems and 'many retired to the anonymity of their villages' (Hossain 1989: 278–9; Mustafa 1996: 14–15). The big absentee landlords suffered the most despite the compensation given as they had no experience of earning their living. The landowners particularly in western UP were also faced with the stigma of having supported the creation of Pakistan, as many had been members of the Muslim League (Khalidi 1997: 80). As a study points out, the abolition of zamindari was a signal for another transfer of property from the old elite to the neo-rich which prompted the real exodus of Avadhi Muslims to Pakistan. The Muslim landowners lost not merely land in the process but also their standing with the Hindu landowners and peasants who were seen as patriotic. As a result, many could not stand for election a good example being the Raja of Kotwara who lost the 1952 election and could not stand again though his family was a trustee of the ancient Hindu shrine of Gola Gokaran Nath in Lakhimpur Kheri (Misra 1998: 248).

The middle-sized landowners, most of them in western UP, were able to more successfully adapt to the new circumstances as they were in most cases educated and therefore able to evade certain provisions of the Land Reform Act. Some even began shifting cultivated land to mango groves and orchards and converted tenant holdings to *sir/* Khudkhast cultivated land with hired labour. Others were able to invest their savings into profitable businesses through access to the political leadership of the Congress party (Khalidi 1997: 81). Another group was those who had both land and who, through jobs, began to participate in the urban economy while remaining rooted in the rural areas. Active in the freedom movement as members of the Congress party they were able to retain lands, enter into well-paying jobs and business through political contacts and thus attempt economic diversification. A good example in east UP in the Avadh region, are the Kidwais (Bhatty 1973). Compared to the taluqdars of Avadh, the zamindars of western UP fared better over time because the area as a whole came under the Green Revolution technology, a good example being the Nawab of Chattari. However, the general Muslim peasantry in Badayun, Bulandshahr, Mathura, Moradabad, and Muzaffarnagar did not fare as well as other sections of the landowning farmers (Jafri 2004). Khalidi also points out that from various studies it does not seem that the condition of the Muslim agriculturist, particularly the small farmer/landless labourer practising subsistence agriculture, has substantially improved and is similar to that of his Hindu counterpart.

It is noteworthy for our study that not all Muslims in the rural areas have traditionally been agriculturalists in UP. In the 1921 statistics of the colonial government, only 3.35 per cent of 'Ordinary Cultivators' were Muslims.[1] A large number even today are artisans who participate in agriculture in the busy season but whose main occupation is not agriculture. The vast majority of landless Muslims until recently have been engaged in various forms of manual, skilled, or semi-skilled labour or as artisans: Julaha, duniya, Nai, Teli, Kumhar, or cleaners (Khalidi 1997: 86). In commerce, they did not lag behind and produced many items such as clothing, hides, perfumes, etc. A high percentage of workers and owners of small-scale industries such as locks and glass are located in Aligarh and Firozabad,

[1] Census of 1921 Part II: 296–307, reproduced in Brass (1974: 152).

respectively, either as owners or workers (Wright 1997: 32–50). After Mandal, many occupational groups in the 1990s Mandal have been demanding inclusion in the OBC category which would give them reservations in education and government jobs (Akbar 1990; Jayaram 1995; Kishwar Khan 1991; Roy 1996).

However, apart from a few big Muslim businesses in western UP in Moradabad, Saharanpur, and Khurja, the ownership of almost all the big businesses was in the hands of Hindu merchant castes who dominated commerce. In his study of the early colonial period, Bayly points to the prosperity of the Hindu *gunj* or market compared to the qasbahs of the Muslim gentry (Bayly 1992: 449). While there is much skill among the Muslims, studies show that they are unable to become the merchants or owners of such businesses and remain largely workers or at most retailers. In large parts of western UP such as Agra, Moradabad, Meerut, Lucknow, and Firozabad, Hindu merchants are able to dominate due to caste or the ability to join hands and push out Muslim, or by building a communal atmosphere.[2] Prior to the British annexation Muslim participation in the administration of the region later called United Provinces, was fairly high but fell later and Muslims did not take to education or government jobs in large numbers. In the immediate post-independence period, it is alleged that the UP government did not give jobs to Muslims and their numbers fell even more (Khalidi 1997: 96–7). The literacy rate and educational attainments have also remained lower than those of Hindus.

Political Economy of Communalism: Jat–Muslim Relations 1960s–2000s

An analysis of the changes taking place over time in the agrarian economy of western UP since the mid-1960s to the 2000s enables us to understand changing Jat–Muslim relations in the region over time and why the former became susceptible to communal mobilization by the BJP first during the RJBBM period in the early 1990s and once again much more forcefully in the 2000s.

---

[2] For a detailed description and list of studies of such shifts in western UP and eastern UP; see Khalidi (1997: 88–90).

Building an Alliance

In the mid-1960s, two developments happening almost simultaneously in western UP enabled the building of a sociopolitical alliance between the Jats and the Muslims: the Green Revolution and backward-caste mobilization. The new agrarian technology created considerable prosperity among the big and medium size landholding, middle peasants who were able to adopt it (Jeffrey 1997, 2001; Pai 1993). They were simultaneously attracted to and mobilized by the backward-caste movement which swept these districts during this period. It was Charan Singh, a peasant leader of the middle castes since the colonial period, who was able to harness these two developments and bring the Jats and the Muslims together in the districts of western UP by forming an agrarian party the Bharatiya Kranti Dal (BKD) in 1967 (Brass 2011). He was able to create a coalition of the Muslims, Ahirs, Jats, Gujjars, and Rajputs (MAJGAR) in western UP that gave centrality to agrarian politics from the mid-1960s to the late 1980s. Belonging to Baghpat district, which became the centre of this alliance, Singh was able to spread his influence over almost the entire region. The better-off Jats were the pivot of his MAJGAR; the Muslims actively participated while the Rajputs joined them in reaction to the Brahmin domination within the Congress. The Muslims of this MAJGAR were largely Muley Jats or those who had converted to Islam but shared with their Hindu counterparts economic interests. The MAJGAR was possible because the BKD and the later the Bharatiya Lok Dal (BLD) formed due to the merger with seven smaller parties, was able to build a base in the districts of western UP and a few in eastern UP—where the Green Revolution created a rich peasant class—and win elections (Pai 1993).

Consequently, upto the late 1980s the Jats and Muslims of western UP enjoyed a close and harmonious relationship in the region. During fieldwork in Muzaffarnagar in the late 1970s, Ravi Srivastava found that though the district had been affected by forcible sterilizations during the Emergency, the fabric of social relations among Hindus and Muslims had remained remarkably intact. Muslims and Hindus—Jats, Tyagis, Rajputs—had shared memories of common kinship relations in a distant past, they could be found sitting on a *charpai* (cot made of ropes) sharing a hookah. While anecdotes regarding a common shared past abounded and social differences were accepted as a matter of fact, there was little evidence of mutual recriminations and mistrust. Charan Singh built a successful political alliance on these grounds, making Jats vote together with the Muslims on many occasions (Pai and Srivastava 2013).

However, the MAJGAR has also been described as a 'marriage of convenience'[3] which lasted as long as all social groups within it benefitted economically and politically. In the post–Green Revolution period when agricultural decline set in and, after the death of Charan Singh, once the era of agrarian politics was over, it broke down. It is the breakdown of this alliance during the 1980s, described below, that led to communal tension and riots in western UP initially during the Babri Masjid period. Once again, more aggressively between 2011 and 2013, particularly in our selected districts of Muzaffarnagar and Shamli, between Jats and Muslims, though other Hindu castes and Dalits were also involved.

Agrarian Decline and Weakening of Jat–Muslim Relations

Agricultural decline began in the post-Green period during the 1980s when high-yielding varieties reached a plateau in terms of yields and prices in the districts of western UP. Agricultural decline worsened throughout the 1990s when, due to the economic crisis and liberalization of the economy, the attention of the government shifted towards business and industry. With globalization of the economy, there was a furtherance of the path of technological capitalist development inaugurated with the Green Revolution. Fiscal discipline and compression was applied to agriculture; subsidies to farmers on water, power, fertilizers, etc., were gradually phased out, controls on the internal market removed. At the same time private rather than government investment, agro-industry, and modern technology was to be encouraged in the agricultural sector. As surpluses from agriculture began to decline, industry made inroads into the western plains (For details see, Bhalla 1994: 1–22). Consequently, in western UP the landowning Jats, most of whom owned medium and small plots, suffered.

Another reason for the deepening of the agrarian distress particularly by the 2000s was the shrinking of landholdings, rendering agriculture

---

[3] Discussion with Shahid Siddiqui on UP politics, 4 July 2014 at New Delhi.

a losing proposition. A NABARD paper illustrates that landholdings in the marginal category (less than 1 hectare) constituted 67 per cent of all operational holdings in the country in 2010–11 (Ashraf 2015). The NSS survey data released in 2014 show that more than 60 per cent of the total rural households surveyed in 11 states were in deep debt. In the case of Muzaffarnagar, the agriculture census data shows that the number of marginal landholdings, excluding those held by SCs has increased. In Muzaffarnagar, the increase was from 1.64 lakh in 2000–1 to 2.03 lakh in 2010–11. These figures capture the depth of the social discontent in rural India, including a prosperous region like western UP (Ashraf 2015).

These changes in the agrarian economy of western UP adversely affected the Jats, creating despondency. Politically, following the death of Charan Singh in 1987, they had no strong peasant leader; Ajit Singh, his son, has not been able to play this role. As politics shifted towards identity-based mobilization the BLD became less important in UP politics; the Jats were no longer attracted by agrarian politics. As a result, the middle castes including the Jats were attracted by the BJP in 1991, and they shifted from the JD, which they had supported in large numbers in the 1989 elections. In western UP, the BJP was able to take over a number of prosperous districts from the JD: Muzaffarnagar,[4] Meerut, Bulandshahr, Aligarh, Mathura, Agra, Etah, Bareilly, Pilibhit, and Bijnor which have remained with it. In this way, the base built by the erstwhile BKD/BLD by Charan Singh was eroded. The JD could retain only eight seats in western UP in the 1991 assembly elections.

Filling the Vacuum: The Bhartiya Kisan Union

In the political vacuum created after the death of Charan Singh the mantle of providing leadership to the Jats was taken up by Mahendra Singh Tikait and the Bhartiya Kisan Union (BKU) formed by him in 1978.[5] Tikait was able to gain the support of the Jats because while

---

[4] In Muzaffarnagar there was a shift from the Congress to JD/SP and to the BJP in the early part of the 1990s.

[5] A recent study provides details of the formation and working of the BKU, the leadership of Mahender Singh Tikait, and its impact on politics in western UP (Joshi 2017).

the backward castes and Dalits formed parties of their own—the SP and BSP—the Jats after decline of the BLD could not find a new party to support their interests. The BKU was active in Muzaffarnagar and Shamli (Bentall and Corbridge 1996: 32); a good example was the large rally held against raising of electricity tariffs, which affects all farmers who use tube wells, in Shamli in January 1987. Tikait was the head of the second biggest Jat Hindu clan in western UP, the Balliana (D. Gupta 1988). He shunned electoral politics and concentrated on raising agrarian demands. Throughout the 1980s, Tikait was at pains to keep the BKU away from communal politics, Jat–Muslim unity remained under him, and he could rely on support from the Muslims of the region. He ensured that a Muslim Imam was visible on the podium beside him at most rallies, fully robed and bearded, and encouraged the voicing of Muslim as well as Hindu slogans.[6] He championed the cause of the Muslim minority, good examples being the rally at the Boat Club in Delhi in 1988 when he was able to unite five lakh farmers, both Hindu and Muslim. Another example is the Bhopa rally in 1989 when he agitated for the safe return of Nayeema, a Muslim girl who had been abducted (Bentall and Corbridge 1996: 33). It is important to note that Bhopa is located hardly 22 km from Muzaffarnagar, which has become a district prone to communal disharmony today.

However, in the late 1980s, the BKU began to decline and lose support in western UP. A factor often mentioned is strong opposition from the upwardly mobile Dalits who viewed the BKU as an exclusively Jat organization. Many SCs in western UP were members of the erstwhile Bharatiya Mazdoor Union (BMU) which was established by Jagpal Singh Mitharia in 1987 in western UP to challenge the employers cartel operated by many BKU members (Bentall and Corbridge 1996: 41). The BMU was concerned that the BKU was a vehicle for rich farmers and was trying to suppress farm wages in western UP (Bentall and Corbridge 1996: 42). However, the real reason was that instead of working with other farmer organizations in the country active at the time, Tikait and the BKU allied themselves with the BJP in 1991. His motives were not clear but the alliance damaged the relationship

[6] The slogans were both *Allah U Akbar* and *Har Har Mahadev* for the Muslims and the Hindus, respectively (Bentall and Corbridge 1996: 33).

of the BKU with the Muslim farmers of western UP, particularly in Muzaffarnagar and Meerut. The BKU lost credibility as it was seen as having moved towards the BJP just prior to the destruction of the Babri masjid in December 1992 (Bentall and Corbridge 1996: 34). It also alarmed the regions BC as constituting threat to their position within the BKU, because at that time the BJP was viewed as an upper-caste party they were not keen to support (Bentall and Corbridge 1996: 44). An inclusive political vocabulary used by Tikait, which had brought a large section of the landowning and agricultural community including Muslims, into the BKU was replaced by a more exclusive political grammar that threatened to prioritize caste and religion and the fight for the agrarian community lost importance.

Equally important, the explanation lies in the rapid and almost destabilizing social transformation taking place in western UP. Against the backdrop of the deepening agrarian crisis, three transitions took place in the late 1980s and early 1990s within a short period of time that disrupted the lives of the rural population. First, the conscious political mobilization by the BJP since the mid-1980s was responsible for the construction and reconstruction of identities and relationships based on them creating a big inter-community chasm in rural and urban areas. Second, the acceptance of the Mandal report by the V.P. Singh government in 1990 gave reservation to the 'other' backward castes, in which the Jats were not included. Consequently, the BCs/OBCs were able to gain reservations in government jobs creating among the Jats a strong perception of being left behind; while not opposed to affirmative action they felt it was unfair to be left out of the central OBC list, given their Shudra status. Tikait initiated a strong campaign against reservation, which had the effect of breaking the MAJGAR combine. The Gujjars and Ahirs left the alliance as they had benefitted from reservations, while the Rajputs joined the anti-reservationists whom the BJP supported in the early 1990s.

Third, the Jats faced the challenge 'from below' from the Dalits who, as landless workers in the countryside on their fields, began demanding higher wages and questioning their social status led by the BSP formed in 1985 (Pai 2002). They found the massive mobilization of the OBCs under the JD/SP and the Dalit upsurge from below under the BSP, threatening to their dominant position in the countryside. In this situation, the Hindutva ideology became a useful counterpoise to the Mandal issue and to Dalit assertion, as agrarian issues took a back seat.

Changing Jat–Muslim Relations in Villages: Beginnings of Communalization

Field studies in the early 1990s reflect the weakening of the relationship between the Jats and the Muslims. Jagpal Singh's study of two villages in Meerut district shows that the rural areas of western UP including villages for the first time, witnessed rise in the level of consciousness of a Hindu identity and belonging to a Hindu religion among the agrarian classes including the Jats and birth of communalism among a section of them (J. Singh 1992: 173). In an interview to Singh, M. S. Tikait points out that 'for the first time the Hindu and the Muslims got divided in the villages. And it has been because of the temple issue'.[7] The BJP attempted to mobilize the Jat peasantry in July 1990 when the Mulayam Singh Yadav-led JD government prevented BKU's supporters and leaders from holding a rally at Lucknow and jailed some of them (J. Singh 1992: 182). Already angry with the Congress, now with the JD, and with Ajit Singh also not supporting them, they decided on an alternative, the BJP. During his fieldwork, Singh found that these tendencies became more prominent once the Kar Seva, later the Rath Yatra of Advani, and the communal mobilization of the BJP–RSS started, and finally the destruction of the Babri Masjid. Singh's interviews of respondents shows that promises to build a temple and rumours and myths about the Muslims eating beef, etc., did influence the Jats (J. Singh 1992: 176). However, he argues this happened at a time when the Jats without a party of their own, were in search of an alternative party and decided to support the BJP.

A study by G.K. Lieten of about 149 villages in Shahpur block of Muzaffarnagar district during 1991, 1993, and 1994 provides a moving picture of social attitudes towards religion and political preferences in the district. Lieten found that most respondents felt that while their economic conditions had improved due to the Green Revolution, 'social quality of life had deteriorated'; earlier solidarity and bhaichara

[7] Interview with M.S. Tikait on 14 September 1994 quoted in J. Singh (1992: 186).

had broken down. There was a collective assessment of decreasing norms and values, cordiality and increasing *asuraksha* or insecurity in the immediate neighbourhood, the adjoining villages and the wider area (Lieten 1996: 1412). He points out that Jats, normally not religious, were affected by the Hindutva movement that swept the region; the village temples lying unused had been renovated and a loudspeaker played kirtans. However, Lieten's assessment is that the impact was not much; his interviews point to people grappling with the idea of religion and politics. Hindutva was an alien concept for most of the villagers; the discourse being on much more mundane issues such as jobs. Based on interviews with 149 respondents in 1993, Lieten argues that 'the form is religious, the content is political. It is aimed at awakening the Hindus' (Lieten 1996: 1414). There were few respondents who talked about Muslim domination or 'pseudo-secularism' and straightforward 'communal remarks' were rare. 'Close-range lived-in experience has taught them the overriding commonness of culture and interests.' Very few made remarks that Muslims should leave for Pakistan or that those who stayed must adhere to the rule of 'Hindu Rashtra' and family planning (Lieten 1996: 1414).

Regarding political preferences, with breakdown of the Congress and agrarian politics no longer important by the end of the 1980s, most social groups had begun to gradually shift towards the BJP. However, Lieten held that this did not imply an ideological alliance with Hindutva. The Jats in 1991 in this village had voted together as a *biradari* (community) for the JD as they viewed the BJP as a party still emerging. Even in 1992, some respondents saw the BJP as a party of capitalists and traders who wanted to divide the people by creating chaos and religious genocide. The Muslims were against both the Congress and the BJP, while the Brahmins supported the latter. By 1993, an alternative political formation the SP had emerged, and in the 1993 assembly elections it obtained 22.2 per cent of the votes and the JD an additional 28.1 per cent. However, in Muzaffarnagar in the assembly elections the BJP won gaining 39 per cent votes, the Congress could get only 2.2 per cent. The fieldwork at first suggests political polarization among the Jats in the 1993 elections following the demise of the Congress: the richer half supported the BJP and the poorer peasants the SP and JD. However, a closer look shows that the votes of the landless were fairly evenly spread over various parties. One-third of the poor peasants opted for the BJP and close to 50 per cent of the middle and rich peasants voted for the JD of Ajit Singh, the son of Charan Singh who soon after defected to the Congress (Lieten 1996: 1413). Thus the decision to vote, at least in 1991 was not linked to religious appeal. The BJP had initially a 'narrow electoral base' and its ideological base according to Lieten was 'even thinner'. The 1991 and 1993 BJP victory in Muzaffarnagar was possible due to upper class/caste support. While some of the Jats who voted for the BJP defended their choice in the language of religion, they were as conscious of the *labh* or material advantage that Hindu–Muslim conflict could deliver: their children would not have to face competition from the Muslims in jobs or in business.

Following the destruction of the Mosque during Lieten's final survey in 1994, 213 respondents who were questioned felt that both Hindus and Muslims were citizens of a multi-religious state, with equal rights and equal claims to citizenship (Lieten 1996: 1414). While there were differences on whether a Ram Temple should be built at Ayodhya or both a Temple and a Mosque, most did not approve of the destruction of the Mosque and stood for 'practical tolerance'. Rather, there was an understanding that the BJP was manipulating politics and using religion to gain power and had fooled the people into believing in the temple. For them the Indian nation continued to be conceived as secular; secularism and religious tolerance were distinctly considered as valuable and religion was viewed as having been misused for political purposes by the socio-economic elite (Lieten 1996: 1416). Thus, what we are witnessing is a gradual 'long term creeping communalism in western UP'; in the early 1990s, despite the destruction of the Babri Masjid, the Jats do not appear to be interested in further communalizing the situation.

However, these developments did lead to the gradual unravelling of the alliance with the Muslims who were afraid of the Ayodhya movement and the communal rhetoric and riots that followed it. The Muslims therefore decided to support the party opposed to the BJP the SP, which promised to be the saviour of the Muslims. This put the Jats and Muslims in opposing political camps in western UP. Following the destruction of the Mosque, the BJP began to refashion itself as a party of the OBCs and to bring the Jats into its fold. The move away from the older connections towards the BJP is clearly visible in the defeat of Ajit Singh in the 1998 Lok Sabha election from Baghpat, the seat long held by Charan Singh. The tenuous unity between the Jats and the Muslims finally broke down when Ajit Singh's Rashtriya Lok Dal (RLD) aligned with the BJP in the 2009 Lok Sabha election; it won five seats but the Muslims kept away from it. The 2009 alliance also provided legitimacy to the BJP even among those Jats, who considered it a party of the urban upper castes. Without Muslim support, the RLD could no longer counter the BJP as in the past.

While the Jats had no party of their own in the 1990s following the waning of agrarian politics and the decline of the BLD and the RLD, political changes are seen within the Muslim community in UP. Following the destruction of the Babri Masjid in 1992 the dispute lost importance, the BJP declined, and politics in UP underwent change. There was a shift from religion to caste-based identity politics as it was the SP and the BSP—two parties the Muslims supported—that became important. Consequently, by the end of the decade UP witnessed the rise of a post-Babri 'autonomous' Muslim politics. The community was now no longer afraid of the BJP with weakening of communal politics and the party under Atal Behari Vajpayee's government at the centre moving towards an agenda of development and reform. In this situation, three small parties—the Peace Party, the National Ulema Council, and the Uttar Pradesh United Democratic Party—emerged in 2008 as the Muslims felt they should form their own parties and not remain vote banks of others. However, these were largely eastern UP centred[8] with little presence in western UP, yet their formation points to rising political consciousness among the Muslims in the state.

Post-Babri Masjid demolition the relationship between the Jats and the Muslims remained ambivalent and uncertain. The two communities continued to live side by side in the villages of western UP but the earlier closeness and common political association was missing. It was not possible, given the changes in the economy and polity which had led to a decline of agrarian politics and the rise of caste and community based identity politics, to return to the close relationship of an earlier era, particularly that of Charan Singh. Rather, as Dipankar Gupta's study in the context of the Ahmedabad and Mumbai riots points out there was 'internalisation of strained conditions under which such communities

---

[8] See Chapter 1.

learn to live next to each other in a "new normal"' (D. Gupta 2011: 5). A new negotiated boundary emerged between the two communities that differed in significant ways from the earlier one already disrupted (D. Gupta 2011). Their economic relations continued; Jats continued to employ Muslims as agricultural labourers on their lands, but their social relations were no longer the same.

In this situation two developments were responsible for communal incidents in the 2000s. First, the deepening of the agrarian crisis in western UP which made the Jats dejected and aggressive, and second, the resurgence of communal mobilization by the BJP, which took full advantage of the unhappiness of the Jats and created a deep communal divide between them and the Muslims. It is these two aspects we now take up.

Everyday Communal Mobilization at the Grass Roots and a Divisive Electoral Campaign

It was on the rising unhappiness and despondency among the Jats that the BJP was able to build its communal mobilization at the grass roots and the divisive electoral campaign much before the 2014 national elections. The resurgence of communal mobilization by the BJP in the 2000s in western UP can be traced over two stages: after the defeat of the NDA government in 2004 when the BJP–RSS decided to revive the organization and base of the party in western UP through gradual but sustained everyday communal mobilization at the grass roots and second, prior to the 2014 national elections when under the leadership of Narendra Modi an attempt was made to build a strong, Hindu vote bank and win maximum seats in UP and thereby capture power at the centre.

Early Grass Roots Mobilization in the 2000s

Our discussions with local BJP–RSS leaders in Muzaffarnagar town suggests that the first round of mobilization in the early 2000s had two basic goals. First, to build a cadre and local leaders for the party and second to gain the support of the Jat community—which had supported them during the RJBBM period—and break their sociopolitical alliance with the Muslims of the region, which that had weakened but not broken down.

After two consecutive electoral defeats in the parliamentary elections of 2004 and 2009 and assembly elections in UP, the BJP leadership realized that it required within its fold strong leaders, preferably Jats, with a Hindutva outlook in the western districts. Two good examples of such leaders both of whom we met[9] are Umesh Malik and Sanjeev Baliyan both later connected with the Muzaffarnagar riots and the 2014 assembly elections. While Umesh Malik, an accused in the Muzaffarnagar riots, has been associated with ABVP since his student days in the late 1980s when he was also elected college president, has been actively associated ever since with the RSS and BJP, particularly in Muzaffarnagar. The rise of Sanjeev Baliyan, who was promoted despite not having an RSS or BJP background, signifies a well-calculated demographic and electoral strategy by the party. He represents the young, educated, and well-off section among the Jats that the party has endeavoured to bring within its fold as such leaders can influence the larger Jat community. Baliyan spent a major share of student days in Haryana at Hissar Agricultural University where he started working as Assistant Professor and thereafter joined the Haryana government as a veterinary surgeon. In 2012, he resigned from his government job and shifted to Muzaffarnagar to look after his real estate firm 'A2Z Builders and Developers', a leading real estate company in the region, and joined the BJP.[10] Thereafter, with great zeal he devoted himself in the service of Vijay Kashyap, an OBC and non-Jat BJP candidate from the Charthaval assembly constituency, which included his own native village of Kutba.[11] Even though Vijay Kashyap lost the election, the role of Baliyan in mobilizing the Jats for the BJP was much appreciated by the leadership.[12]

The selection of Muzaffarnagar district and villages within it for everyday communal mobilization at the grass roots by the regional

[9] While we had met them earlier in 2015, detailed discussions were held with both in Muzaffarnagar town on 16 and 17 December 2016.

[10] http://www.thehindubusinessline.com/news/national/muzaffarnagar-where-bjp-is-the-frontrunner/article5831673.ece.

[11] Kutba is one of our sample villages in Muzaffarnagar and formed the epicentre of the riots in the district.

[12] Interview with Prashant Tyagi, Muzaffarnagar BJYM leader and a close associate of Sanjeev Balyan, Ajmal-ur-Rahman, a businessman at Muzaffarnagar and old associate of Kanshi Ram in early 1990s, and Rajiv Sharma lawyer at Muzaffarnagar and member executive council Bharatiya Janata Yuva Morcha (BJYM) UP.

BJP–RSS leaders is evident from the active promotion of Baliyan by them. His success is evident from the fact that he was able to persuade both Nitin Gadkari, the then BJP president, and Rajnath Singh to participate in the Kisan rally that he convened at his village Kutba, on 5 February 2013.[13] A recent study also mentions an earlier public meeting in Kutba in November 2011, around six months before the 2012 UP Vidhan Sabha elections attended by Nitin Gadakari and Rajnath Singh, organized by Baliyan and Malik (J. Singh 2016). Following the Kutba meeting, both worked systematically in the villages dominated by their khaps (traditional caste panchayats) to popularize the Sangh Parivar. Indeed, it was from this meeting that Balyan came into the limelight, and later won a seat in the 2014 Lok Sabha elections (J. Singh 2016).

The attempt by the BJP to break the Jat–Muslim alliance in western UP began prior to the 2009 Lok Sabha election when the RLD led by Ajit Singh entered into an electoral alliance with the BJP. It was from the 2009 campaign onwards, in Muzaffarnagar particularly, that one could see the employment of communal issues, like the dignity of Hindu women, instances of eve teasing, alleged Hindu-victimhood, and ultimately charging Muslims with terrorism. It was during the campaign in May 2009 that Narendra Modi, then Gujarat Chief Minister with a hardcore Hindutva image, made his first visit to Muzaffarnagar to campaign for the RLD candidate Anuradha Chaudhary, a Jat. Modi gave a provocative speech to gain the support of the Jats, invoking the issue of Muslims eve teasing Hindu women and thereby claiming that Hindus were being reduced to second-class citizens.[14] In Modi's presence, Anuradha Chaudhary, who was contesting against BSP Muslim candidate, Kadir Rana, described the election as a 'battle' for the security of Hindu women and alleged that the victory of the BSP Muslim candidate would turn the district into a terror hub. An FIR was lodged against her for the statement.[15] However, Chaudhary lost the election despite

[13] Interview with Prashant Tyagi, Ajmal-ur-Rahman, and Rajiv Sharma at Muzaffarnagar.

[14] Interview with Prashant Tyagi, Ajmal-ur-Rahman, and Rajiv Sharma at Muzaffarnagar.

[15] http://www.hindustantimes.com/india/anti-muslim-quip-comes-back-to-haunt-anuradha-chaudhary/story-us2FI4E2rrvkY6mBxTR6PJ.html.

the communally charged campaign suggesting a clear rift among the Jats and the Muslims as the latter voted en bloc against the RLD causing heartburn among the former.

These developments made the BJP leadership realize the need for having a prominent Jat leader in its fold who could orchestrate a complete shift of Jats from peasant-based RLD-centric politics and their alliance with Muslims made by Charan Singh, to Hindu identity based BJP-centric politics, wherein the two communities would be pitted against each other.[16] This increased the importance of Sanjeev Baliyan as having a prominent Jat leader in the region in its fold was required to break the hold of the Ajit Singh-led RLD among the community.

Three factors worked in Baliyan's favour. First, being a Baliyan Jat, who command a majority in 84 villages of western UP, demographically he was well placed over Malik Jats, a majority of whom are found in Haryana. Second, his better economic profile gave an edge to his political ambition and third, his willingness to mobilize Jats into the folds of BJP by combining the Hindutva agenda of 'Love Jihad, security of Hindu women' with agrarian distress and pitting them against the Muslims. The Muzaffarnagar riot 2013 gave him an opportunity both to prove his Hindutva credentials in the eyes of the saffron outfits and canvass the Jats into a Hindutva discourse by actively roaming among the riot-affected villages and providing the legal and financial aid to all riot-accused Hindus, Jats and non-Jats. Therefore, he was the natural choice for Lok Sabha candidate in 2014 where the polarized campaign ensured his decisive victory against BSP's Kadir Rana who was also an accused in the 2013 riots. Thereafter his political elevation as a central minister in the Modi government, bypassing the stature of other prominent Jat MPs from the region like Satyapal Singh,[17] points to a well-calibrated BJP and RSS strategy of getting the Jats into its fold to further its communal mobilization more successfully.

The attempt to institutionalize everyday communalism at the grassroots is evident from Jagpal Singh's study (2016). The study shows that from 2013, the RSS tried to create a support base in the villages of

[16] Interview with Prashant Tyagi at Muzaffarnagar.

[17] Satyapal Singh, ex-commissioner of Mumbai Police, contested the 2014 election on a BJP ticket from Baghpat and defeated RLD president Ajit Singh.

western UP more consistently than before through its Mandal Yojna plan (a group of villages) similar to its Basti Yojna (colonies/slum) plan for cities (J. Singh 2016). During 2015–16 the RSS set up *shakhas* (branches) in all the 987 Mandals of Meerut division: Muzaffarnagar, Shamli, Ghaziabad, Meerut, Moradabad, and Bijnor. The RSS also planned to establish its shakhas in the villages situated along the roads under its 'Sadak Kinare Gaon' (roadside villages) plan. It sought to identify potential contact persons in these villages, who generally belong to the younger, new, non-agricultural, social classes/groups. This expansion was possible in collaboration with other member organizations of the Sangh Parivar already working in the area: VHP, Bajrang Dal, Durga Vahini, Samadhan Samiti, Gau Raksha Dal, Sanghe Shakti Kaliyuge, etc. Besides these, are the ephemeral organizations formed for specific purposes such as the protection of *izzat* of Hindu bahu–beti (protecting the honour of Hindu wives/daughters) stopping 'Love Jihad', *ghar wapsi* (preventing conversion from Hinduism), cow protection, etc. (J. Singh 2016). In the Muzaffarnagar riots, it was these organizations, which together with the new social classes that was responsible for violence and killing of Muslims.

Further, based on fieldwork interviews, Singh mentions meetings of these organizations in villages of Muzaffarnagar and Meerut districts (J. Singh 2016). Within a few years of the Kutba meeting in 2011 an organization—Sanghe Shakti Kaliyuge—was started by two youth of Kutba village, a Jat and Dhinwar (MBC), a mechanic. The units of the Sanghe Shakti Kaliyuge sprang up in several villages. Its members included youth (18–28 years) from different Hindu castes (Jats, MBCs, and Dalits) who played a leading role in attacking Muslims in the riot. An example Singh mentions is a 2013 meeting in Gotca village near Sardhana town in Meerut district organized by Sudarshan Chakra a VHP/Bajrang Dal leader that encouraged a large number of youth to join the Bajrang Dal. A Bajrang Dal activist mentioned to Singh that there were 70 Bajrang Dal activists in his village Baparsi, whose task was to protect cows, Hindu women, and Hindu culture from the attacks of Muslims. In the Muzffarnagar violence, Singh mentions that alleged incidents of molestation of Hindu women were used to campaign for protection of Hindu 'bahu beti ki izzat', which he argues were used to unite different Hindu castes (Jats, Gujjars, Rajputs, Brahmins, OBCs, MBCs, etc.) into a single community communally polarizing rural society, leading to communal riots (J. Singh 2016). Singh argues that the Sangh Parivar got emboldened to pursue its agenda after the formation of the NDA government at the centre in May 2014.

Singh's fieldwork shows, the communal divide also led a section of the Jatavs to shift from the BSP to the BJP (J. Singh 2016). Dalits in Shoron and Shahpur told Singh, that Muslim leaders help only Muslims over Dalits, even if these leaders belong to the BSP. One of them pointed out about Kadir Rana a Muslim, BSP leader: 'Party to hamari, Kadir Rana Muslmano ki madath karta hai. Hamne tho is baar Balyan ko vote di hai' (the party [the BSP] is ours but Kadir Rana [a Muslim BSP Member of Parliament] helps Muslims. This time [2014 Lok Sabha election], we have voted for Balyan [Sanjeev Kumar Balyan], the BJP candidate). However, Singh points out that this remark does not represent a general picture; his visits to villages—Khanauda, Maithana Inder Singh, Uldeypur, and Jalalpur—of Meerut district showed that rarely have the Jatavs voted for any other candidate than of the BSP. Elections he holds are not a good indicator of social relations. Within a few months of the 2014 Lok Sabha elections, the BJP lost the by-election in Kairana Vidhan Sabha constituency to the SP. However, in the Vidhan Sabha by-elections held in February 2016, the BJP won the Muzaffarnagar seat, and the Congress won the Deoband seat (J. Singh 2016).

Electoral Campaign 2014

Based on its earlier groundwork in the western districts, the BJP mounted a long, well-planned, competitive, and communally aggressive campaign. While officially it began in May 2013, when Amit Shah a close aide of Modi with a public, Hindu nationalist record in Gujarat was shifted to UP, efforts had begun much earlier. The success of the party was due to the grass roots mobilization begun in the early 2000s, the new leadership, re-orientation of the Hindutva ideology, and revamping of its organization. In this campaign the Jats were pitted against the Muslims; the Muzaffarnagar riots in September 2013 were possible, because the BJP invoked the notion of communal pride and honour, which led to the Jats voting as 'Hindus' in 2014.

Generational Change

The BJP experienced generational change prior to the 2014 elections when a new leader, Narendra Modi with his aides, replaced the older leaders/founders of the party Atal Behari Vajpayee and L. K. Advani with important implications for UP and the national elections in the state (Pai and Kumar 2015). Although Modi formally became the leader of the BJP in 2013, informally he was already in charge from 2009 onwards and promoted the mobilization at the grass roots as mentioned above. Among the new generation leaders in the BJP, Modi was able to take control of the party due to his three successive victories in the Gujarat assembly elections and his close association with the RSS which supported his bid to control the party. Modi represented the more hardline section of the party in contrast to the moderate section under Vajpayee and was able to centralize decision-making in his hands. Infighting among senior party leaders after the defeat in the 2004 and 2009 Lok Sabha elections enabled Modi to take over and reshape the party, its organizational structure, and Hindutva ideology. Consequently, Modi was able to control the UP electoral campaign and party unit just as he had in Gujarat (Pai and Kumar 2015).

Ideological Underpinnings: Hindutva Redefined

In the early 1990s, during the Babri Masjid/Ram Janma Bhoomi dispute, Hindutva was conceived as a largely religious ideology used for political mobilization and identified with mainly upper-caste Hindus. But during the 2014 electoral campaign, Modi redefined this ideology by including rapid economic development to create a strong and stable nation, and greater inclusiveness as it could appeal to a larger section of the electorate in UP, the upper castes/classes and the growing, upwardly mobile, aspirational, lower classes/castes (Pai and Kumar 2015). The campaign was based on a two-pronged strategy of both Hindutva and development. While under Vajpayee, development and economic reforms was prioritized over religious mobilization, as evident during 1999 and 2004 national elections. Modi promised rapid economic development in the state based on the 'Gujarat Model'. From being identified as the 'Hindu Hriday Samrat' in Gujarat, Modi tried to portrary himself as 'Vikas Purush'. Most of his speeches at rallies dealt with issues of corruption, slow growth, and poor governance, both nationally by the Congress-led UPA-II and the SP in UP. While speaking about the latter, he pointed out that availability of jobs in Gujarat attracted large number of migration workers from UP. Modi was able to address the frustration and unhappiness of the unemployed youth including the Jats who felt that UP had remained behind compared to many other states (Pai and Kumar 2015).

But the BJP did not abandon or, keep aside its strategy of communal mobilization to secure the Hindu vote. At the RSS–BJP meeting held on 9 September 2013, to decide on campaign strategies, it was decided that the core agenda of Hindutva—the Ram Temple, Common Civil Code and Article 370—would be used. The slogan *Jai Shri Ram* was used in most of Modi's rallies; the holy city of Varanasi was selected for him to contest, and his campaign in western UP was organized by the RSS-managed Vidya Bharati educational institutions.[18] The BJP manifesto released on 7 April 2014 was largely devoted to developmental issues and focused on economic growth, job creation, reducing corruption, keeping prices under control, and smart cities, etc (Pai and Kumar 2015: 49). However, the BJP under Modi's leadership combined communal mobilization with a discourse of development: while Modi stressed on development, party cadres specially in western UP employed highly communal and divisive strategies—used at times by Modi also—to create a broad Hindu votebank encompassing the upper castes, the backwards, and also the Dalits (Pai and Kumar 2015). Amit Shah's alleged outspoken Hindutva comments led the Election Commission of India on 11 April 2014 to ban his participation in election rallies, a ban lifted a few days later when Shah offered an apology and assured the Commission that it would not happen again (Anderson 2015: 53).

Revamping the Social Base and Organization

A number of steps were taken by Shah that considerably strengthened the organization in UP and improved the BJP's readiness for the election. He established a core team that analyzed the reasons for earlier electoral defeats; removed those who had lost elections, brought in new faces, and shifted veterans to new constituencies; this reshuffling

---

[18] See http://indianexpress.com/article/cities/mumbai/rss-takes-charge-of-modis-meerut-rally/

increased the party's chances of winning additional seats. Defunct district units were revived and committees were formed for over 80 per cent of the booths in the state (Pai and Kumar 2015).

Shah also tried to create a more inclusive social base for the BJP in UP to ensure that it gained large number of seats. The focus during the elections was not only on the upper castes—who constitute a small proportion of the population—but the OBCs and the Dalits and to create a more inclusive Hindu vote bank (Pai and Kumar 2015). The party gave 28 tickets to OBCs and importance to OBC leaders such as Kalyan Singh, Uma Bharti, Satyendra Kushwaha, Rameshwar Chaurasia, and Rajveer Singh. The party's decision to project Modi as a backward-caste 'chaiwala' (tea-seller) and the first OBC Prime Minister helped BJP obtain OBC votes. To obtain Dalit votes, especially that of non-Jatavs (Balmiki, Pasi, Dhobis, Koris, etc., who constitute 9 per cent of the total population of UP) the BJP decided to appropriate the legacies of B. R. Ambedkar and other Dalit icons. Shah organized meetings in several Dalit villages and promised Bharat Ratna for the BSP founder, Kanshiram. Modi addressed his second 3D rally, telecast live at several locations across India on 14 April 2014, with garlanding the statue of B. R. Ambedkar. Emphasis was also placed on obtaining the support of the MBCs, which led to the alliance with the Apna Dal, and provided a base for Modi in Varanasi and in some other Poorvanchal seats with high BC voters.

Accordingly, the BJP–RSS leaders fashioned a multipronged strategy which included a campaign called 'samajik samrasta' (social harmony) and established a 'samajik samrasta manch' or forum. Schools were set up in Dalit bastis, *samrasta bhoj* (inter-dining) were organized and sensitization campaigns to link Dalits with upper-caste Hindus. Organizations were established to work among Dalits: Dayanand Shiksha Kendra, Swami Vivekananda Shiksha Kendra, Jaya Baba Ramdeo Kendra, etc. Another strategy adopted as early as 1989 at the birth centenary of Hedgawar, was to search for similarities in the symbolic images of Hedgawar one of the founders of the RSS at his centenary and Dr B.R. Ambedkar to show the close affinity between their ideas. As Badri Narayan's work shows, the BJP used a number of strategies to bring together the upper castes and the Dalits. It propagated the idea of 'Ram Rajya' and Ram was propagated as a symbol of unity among the Dalits and upper castes. The idea was circulated that Dalits had played a monumental role in the entire life span of Ram, and Hanuman was described as a symbol of the deprived and underprivileged. This combined with the communal strategy of the party created on the one hand a deep Hindu–Muslim divide, and on the other it brought together the upper castes, backwards, and Dalits and underlay the excellent performance of the BJP particularly in western UP (Narayan 2009).

The Campaign, Communal Overtones Leading to Victory

During the campaign, unable to create state-wide communal polarization as in 1991 using the Ram Temple issue, the BJP–RSS cadres, which had started working on the ground much before 2014, attempted to orchestrate Hindu–Muslim tension by taking advantage of numerous, small, low-key communal incidents that began in 2011 itself but became more frequent and bigger by 2013. The long campaign had definite communal overtones. A good example in August 2013 is the stage-managed, confrontation over the Chaurasi Parikrama Yatra organized by the VHP, between the SP and the BJP with the former banning it and the latter supporting the efforts of the VHP (for details, see Pai 2013a). The Muzaffarnagar riots provided the BJP an opportunity to mobilize all Hindus, particularly the backward castes and Dalits, who had moved following decline of the BJP and the Congress, towards the SP and BSP. Amit Shah held small, quiet meetings in remote villages largely directed at Hindus to take 'revenge'. Addressing the Jats during his campaign on 4 April 2014 in Shamli village, the epicentre of the Muzaffarnagar riots, Shah reportedly said that the election, especially in western UP was 'one of honour … an opportunity to take revenge and to teach a lesson to people who have committed injustice'.

Certain features of the campaign in UP contributed to the BJP's excellent performance (Pai and Kumar 2015): it covered the state extensively under the tight control of Modi and Shah with excellent funding and good media coverage. More than 400 GPS-installed 'Modi-vans' with campaign material and speeches covered the dark areas beyond media's reach. In addition, extensive use was made of social media such as SMS, WhatsApp, e-mail, Facebook, and Twitter to create a 'Modi Brand' through a 'Social Media War Room' at the BJP's Lucknow headquarters manned by young volunteers from IT institutes under the RSS and ABVP. In sum, Modi ran a hi-tech, US presidential style, plebiscitary campaign, with extensive media coverage, in which the focus was mainly on him leaving out the party and other senior leaders.

The magnitude of the victory of the BJP was surprising as it had been in decline in UP in the 1990s. The BJP obtained 71 out of 80 seats with 42.3 per cent votes and its ally Apna Dal (AD) won two seats in eastern UP. Together, they swept nearly 84 per cent of the assembly segments of UP. It also stood second in all the seven constituencies that it lost (Pai and Kumar 2015). More important, an analysis of victory of the BJP indicates a sizeable shift towards the BJP by two key categories in UP—the OBCs and the Dalits—suggesting a change in the support base of the BJP from an upper-caste party to one which draws considerable support from the lower castes (Anderson 2015: 56). All BJP leaders who were implicated in the 2013 Muzaffarnagar riots and were given tickets won their seats with large margins. The riot-affected areas that went to poll in the first phase registered the highest polling and provided the highest victory margin for BJP in the state. For the first time in UP, no Muslim candidate was elected from the state. The BJP won all the seats where the Muslim population is more than 20 per cent and the victory margin of the party, although significant in all these seats, was the highest in constituencies with Muslim population between 20–30 per cent (Anderson 2015).

In western UP the election results in nine major districts—Saharanpur, Muzaffarnagar, Shamli, Baghpath, Meerut, Hapur, Ghaziabad, Noida, and Bulandshahr—which include 44 assembly seats, reflected the tremendous change. In the 2012 assembly elections, the BSP gained 15 seats, BJP 12, SP 10, Congress 4, and RLD won 3 seats. The BJP did not win in Muzaffarnagar, Baghpat, Hapur, and Ghaziabad in 2012. However, the situation changed totally after the 2013 communal riots, in the 2014 Lok Sabha polls the BJP swept the region by winning all the seats in these nine districts. In these districts, the emergence of communal fault lines between the Jats and Muslims affected the Congress–RLD alliance dependent on the support of these communities, and helped the BJP gain seats. The BJP definitely benefitted richly from the communal campaign it carried out in the region in the election and created a deep divide between the two communities.

Deepening Agrarian Distress in the 2000s and Breakdown of Relations

The BJP began its campaign for the 2014 national elections at least two years earlier and by this time the agrarian crisis had deepened, particularly affecting the smaller and medium Jat farmers in western UP. This enabled the party to take full advantage of the unhappiness of the Jats and their perception that the Muslims were doing better.

Two examples of the multifaceted agrarian crisis will suffice to make this clear: accessibility to water and the crisis of the sugar industry. An important feature that affected farmers in western UP was that unless they owned their own tubewells, the lack of public investment in irrigation affected them badly. A study of groundwater irrigation in 12 villages in western and eastern UP in 1981–2 and repeated again after a gap of twenty years in 2002 points to increasing problems (Pant 2004: 3468). The study shows that in the 1980s there was coincidence of caste and class and ownership of water extraction devices and a positive relationship with the size of landholdings, which meant it was largely the upper castes/classes who owned agricultural implements and tubewells. However, the more recent survey shows that backward castes/classes have surged ahead and are neck-to-neck with upper castes/classes. As public tubewells were not maintained and there were high power shortages, backward caste/class farmers have invested in private tubewells and generators. By the mid-1970s tubewell irrigation had overtaken canal irrigation as the main mode of irrigation (Pant 2004: 3466). A number of socio-economic reasons seem to be responsible: the BCs represent a sturdy group of hardworking cultivators who were the biggest beneficiaries of land reform and who have been able to improve their standing over the years. While this seems to be due to their numerical strength and sound agricultural base, their hold was further consolidated with the implementation of the Mandal Commission recommendations when they began to enter the bureaucratic corridors of power. Today with new political parties representing them, they have emerged as the 'new rural elites' affecting the position of the Jats (Pant 2004: 3468). At the same time public irrigation has diminished over the past 20 years, the deterioration being greater in the western region compared to the eastern region. There also seems to be greater dependency on canals in the former and on private tubewells in the latter. However, what is important is that dependency on their own resources is greater for obtaining water everywhere over last 20 years. Therefore, in both regions farmers have to buy water or make their own arrangements, which is expensive. In western UP the sample showed that 40.8 per cent of the respondents depend on it now compared to 28.3 per cent 20 years ago; in the east the proportion is 16 per cent in 1981 compared to 40.5 per cent today (Pant 2004).

More immediate is the crisis in the sugar industry in the western districts particularly in Muzaffarnagar and Shamli, which contributed to the communal tension and riots prior to the 2014 elections, as sugarcane is an important cash crop grown in the region over a long period of time. While the problem began around 2009, if not earlier, it is only after the riots that the crisis and its impact on the Jat farmers of the region has come to be recognized. Muzaffarnagar and Shamli districts are described as the sugar bowl of UP. Muzaffarnagar[19] is the second largest sugarcane producer in western UP. By the early 1990s about 191,644 hectares of cultivated land was under sugarcane and produced 11,472,645 metric tonnes of sugar (Baru 1990). In the colonial period, it was eastern UP beginning in 1874, which was a major producer of sugar. However, after independence UP lost its preeminent position in the 1960s to Maharashtra which developed a formidable sugar industry in the cooperative sector (Damodaran and Singh 2007: 3952). The mills in eastern UP which had operated on the landlord–moneylender nexus lost out and gradually the industry shifted to the western region where conditions were more conducive to growing cane. In the 1990s, with economic reform and the loosening of controls and de-licensing in 1998, there has been revival of the UP sugar industry with a decline of the cooperatives in Maharashtra. Starting from 2004–5 when the UP government introduced a number of incentives for mills, western UP has surpassed Maharashtra in terms of output of sugar and many new mills have come up. Sugar was a major crop during the Green Revolution and a differential impact on different classes of the peasantry created economic differences between the bigger and smaller Jat landowners, but also between the Jats and others in the agricultural economy.

[19] Shamli was a part of Muzaffarnagar district until recently.

During the Green Revolution period and even in the 1990s farmers found growing sugarcane a fairly lucrative business. A study of two villages in western UP in the late 1990s shows that as Jats owned most of the land and by growing sugarcane they became a prosperous community while the Muslims who had meagre or no land in many cases did not benefit as much; they largely constituted the labour (K. Siddiqui 1997). Wages did rise and so the labour did benefit, but not as much as the landowners. It was not merely landholding but access to credit, water, ownership of tractors, threshers, harrows, and other mechanized equipment was heavily concentrated in the hands of a minority of peasants. The bigger Jat landowners were also members of the cane federation which gave them better access to the market and sent most of their crop to the mills. Thus, the Green Revolution accentuated the process of differentiation. Another study of Meerut district in western UP in 2002—after the revival of the sugarcane industry in UP—where a number of sugar mills are located, points to how institutions responsible for purchasing of sugarcane are corrupt and perpetuate material inequalities among farmers (Jeffrey 2002). Mismanagement of sugarcane marketing and corruption allowed the rich farmers, almost all of them Jats, to obtain privileged access and higher prices to lucrative marketing opportunities. Jats were able to manage the cane societies, use corrupt practices, and political strategies such as support of the BKU.

However, since at least 2012–13, western UP farmers are unhappy over the economic losses they have faced in growing cane which has caused them much anguish. A study points out that the crisis is most acute in the Upper Doab region, also referred to as 'Jat belt' as the Jats make up roughly a tenth of its population and a third of those engaged in farming. The Muzaffarnagar riots, in which Jats played a central role, took place in this region. A major problem is that sugar mills have stopped crushing cane and delayed earlier payments to farmers leaving them with little or no income. The Upper Doab districts, account for more than 47 per cent of the overall cane dues and 80 per cent of first-instalment arrears owed by mills in UP (Harish Damodaran, 27 June 2016, *The Indian Express*, New Delhi). In fact, Shamli tops in sugarcane production, for 2015–16 the districts average cane yield of 807.76 quintals per hectare based on official figures was not just higher than the 665 quintals for the entire state, but even that of neighbouring districts such as Saharanpur, Baghpat, Muzafarnagar, and Meerut. However, there is nearly Rs 300 crore in dues for the districts farmers (Damodaran 2016a). In Shamli 765,000 odd farmers who delivered 193.11 lakh quintal of cane to the district's three mills—Bajaj Hindusthan's Thanabhawan, Rana Sugar's Ltd, and Shadi Lal Enterprises Ltd. This total sugarcane was worth Rs 538.46 crore at the official state advised price (SAP) whereas the mills have disbursed only Rs 240.70 crore, which makes it nearly Rs 300 crore dues for a single district (Damodaran 2016a).

The crisis has badly hit small Jat farmers as the average Upper Doab farmer owns 15 bighas (nearly one hectare or 2.5 acres) and not even 10 per cent has more than 30 bigha (five acres). Sugarcane cultivation was, in the past, remunerative for even small farmers, as they had access to irrigation, and mills made regular payments. However, with fragmentation of holdings and lack of cane payment Jat farmers are taking to selling milk and working in factories; something they would never have imagined earlier. The Jats are angry, as Rajvir Singh Mundet the Shamli-based convenor of the Bharatiya Kisan Mazdoor Sanyukta Morcha pointed out, it is assumed that they are a rich and powerful farming community. While in the past they had leaders such as Charan Singh and Mahendra Singh Tikait, today they are poor and their voice matters little in the region (Damodaran 2016a).

Damodaran gives the example of Mokam Singh who supplied 22 buffalo carts of cane each laden with 18 quintals to the sugar mill belonging to Shadi Lal Enterprises Ltd in the 2015–16 crushing season. These 400 quintals would have fetched him about Rs 1.12 lakh at the UP government's advised price of Rs 280 per quintal. However, all he got from the mill after it stopped crushing was Rs 44,000. This has upset the household economy of Singh and that of many others in the district as he is finding it difficult to pay the fees of the private school that his two grandchildren attend in Shamli town. He has not paid the fee of Rs 3,000 per month since March 2016. The farmers complain that the SAP has remained unchanged at Rs 280 per quintal and they are not getting even that (Damodaran 2016a).

With the mills both crushing cane and blocking their payments, farmers are borrowing to meet their needs. The problem of delayed cane payments has been going on since 2013–14 and initially farmers used their Kisan Credit Cards (KCC) meant to purchase seeds, fertilizers, and water to meet household expenses, but they have exhausted this option and are in deep trouble. The crisis in the primarily agrarian economy of Shamli is reflected in its banks—public sector, private, and cooperative—which had large outstanding advances of Rs 2,224.77 crore on 31 March 2016. Much of it is loans taken against the KCC, a facility allowed to meet short-term credit requirements for crop cultivation. The result is that farmers who earlier were quick to return the credit provided have not repaid most loans (Damodaran 2016b).

The crisis has impacted the education of the children, with farmers unable to pay fees to private schools to which they had begun to send them since the early 2000s. Shamli and surrounding towns witnessed a sudden rise in private English-medium schools from 8 to 24 during the period from 2007–8 to 2012–13, when the UP government raised its State Advised Price (SAP) for sugarcane from Rs 125 to Rs 280 per quintal. Of these 12 were in Shamli itself and the rest in smaller towns of the district. These schools charge monthly fees ranging from Rs 500 to Rs 2,000, apart from Rs 500–600 as conveyance charges, as they transport students from interior schools to the towns. Small farmers have been impacted the most as they sent their children to private schools with some difficulty as the government schools do not teach subjects such as English or Computers. These schools are now facing a financial crisis, with the cane SAP remaining unchanged since the 2012–13 sugar season and mills unable to pay even this to farmers. Every private school in the district now has outstanding fee dues, ranging from Rs 30 lakh to Rs 50 lakh and many children are returning to the government schools in their villages (Damodaran 2016b). Thus, the Jats of the western districts, particularly Muzaffarnagar and Shamli are an unhappy and disgruntled community, angry with the government—which underlies their anger with other communities that they perceive as doing better—and their demand for reservation.

Changes in the Muslim Community and Relations with Jats

At the same time, significant changes within the Muslim community in western UP added to the unhappiness of the Jats and to their declining relationship with the former. By the 2000s, due to economic changes such as more rapid urbanization and communication links between rural and urban areas and improved educational attainments, many persons particularly the younger groups in the region began to take to non-agricultural occupations. A new social class—stretching across the traditionally agricultural–non-agricultural divide—emerged in the villages of western UP which increased the interaction between town and village. The rural–urban divide became less, leading to the use of the term 'r-urban' to describe the increasing mobility of villagers. Many villagers in our sample villages travel daily to close by towns for work, including labourers. Villagers have learnt new skills such as plumbing, carpentry, masonry, cleaning buildings, and so forth which has made them service providers. This shift is witnessed in all caste groups but is examined in our fieldwork in the next chapter among Muslims as it brought a change in the relationship between them and the Jats.

By the 2000s these changes were marked among Muslims in western UP as they traditionally did not own land[20] and were agricultural labourers or artisans who gradually began to move to small-scale household business or trade or shops, that is, selling items of daily use, clothing, electronics, and utensils. While the men pursued these new occupations, working only during the busy season, the women continued to do agricultural labour in the fields. Many had traditional artisanal skills that could be honed and used. The field study in our sample villages points to the rise of a new class of entrepreneurial Muslims who had borrowed money from the Jat landowners in order to carry out their business. Their flight from their native villages to the refugee camps after the riots has made the problem worse. Social jealousy among the Jats at the new-found entrepreneurship of Muslims, some of whom until recently had worked on their fields, contributed to the worsening of relations between the two communities making both communities vulnerable to attempts to create communal tension and riots.[21] These feelings are particularly strong among the younger generation of both communities; it was a fight between them that was the immediate cause of the Muzaffarnagar riots.

Impact: Rising Aspirations, Despondency among Jats

These socio-economic shifts in the districts of western UP in the 2000s made the landowning middle castes, more particularly the Jats,

[20] See Chapter 1, p. 124.

[21] As the next chapter shows, it has continued to negatively affect relations as the Muslims who took loans from the Jats have fled from their villages and are not in a position to return the money taken.

unhappy, aggressive, and antagonistic to groups whom they perceive as having stolen a march over them. A study by Craig Jeffrey in 2010, illustrates the dilemma in which the younger generation of Jats found themselves and their attempts to deal with new threats and challenges such as Economic Liberalization, the rise of the OBCs, a small educated Dalit class, and improvement in the economic conditions of the Muslims (Jeffrey 2010). A development led some of these young people to believe in a particular vision of the future—the IT revolution in India—but they could not realize their aspirations. A large part of the problem is that UP is an economically backward state, no government has in recent years attempted to promote development and even in the better-off western districts finding professional jobs is not easy.

Based on fieldwork in the late 1990s in rural Meerut and again in 2004/2005 in Meerut City, Jeffrey's study focuses on two related forms of 'waiting' (Jeffrey 2010). 'Imagined waiting' among the rich farmers of the district who, finding agriculture no longer a paying occupation 'invested' the surplus they had gained from agriculture in the education of their sons and continue to hope that they will obtain employment in the new emerging sectors of the economy. Second, 'purposeless' timepass among the educated urban youth who, unable to obtain the desired employment commensurate with their education face considerable hardship and frustration in some cases, but can do no more than 'wait'. These young men have built a culture of timepass by hanging around street corners, joining local politics through the new panchayats, cane societies, befriending local officials, politicians, and police, exploring methods to keep the rising Dalits in their place, and diversification strategies as agriculture is no longer as paying. Many call themselves 'fixers' and protest against corruption, the mismanagement of educational institutions and local bodies, or the conduct of government officials. Some form the foot soldiers of political parties, taking part in the violence that often accompanies electoral campaigns. Their unhappiness arises out the realization that the richer, upper caste/class groups in the region have out-manoeuvred them due to better connections and better education. The study shows how modernization and development often reshape the social and political life of the middle and lower classes in postcolonial contexts such as the western districts of UP (Jeffrey 2010).

Thus, rapid social and economic change and young men on a short fuse, created an explosive combination of poor education, unemployment and politics, the sense of frustrated opportunity and empty time. There was also a perception that Muslims are pampered by the state, deliberately created by clever mobilization by right-wing groups that also underlay the communal incidents after 2011. Having lost their economic clout due to the agrarian crisis, fragmentation of land, loss of political relevance, and denied reservation, this generation of dominant agrarian castes—Jats, Gujjars—have taken recourse to cultural machismo; political appeals around cultural humiliation and assertion that catch fire. They find that their former Muslim sharecroppers and workers find new kinds of work. The younger generation of Muslims has taken to petty entrepreneurship such as mobile repairs or selling goods.[22] This resentment can erupt over any issue; the Muzaffarnagar riots began over a young man allegedly hitting a woman from another community. As the Jats began to find themselves politically marginalized and economically badly hit, going with a dominant force such as Hindutva gives them psychological empowerment. Earlier they may not have bothered about what was happening in Gujarat or Maharashtra, but now these abstract affiliations have become important and matter. The Muslims did not like the Jats joining hands with the BJP in 1991. By the 2000s the Jats did not like the Muslims doing better in non-agricultural jobs.

***

Our narrative of the trajectory of communalism in western UP has attempted to understand the reasons underlying the second wave of severe communal riots in the region in the 2000s. During the early 1990s communal mobilization around the RJBBM dispute did create communal tension divisions between the Jats and the Muslims, but the former did not take these tensions further; their concerns were more centred over the growing agrarian problems in western UP. The earlier harmonious relationship between the two communities definitely weakened, but did not completely break down. Consequently, the intervening period was one of comparative peace with caste-based

[22] See Chapter 4.

identity politics playing a central role. Two developments were responsible for the resurgence of communal tension and riots in the 2000s: communal mobilization undertaken by the BJP to achieve political and cultural ascendancy in western UP and to win the 2014 national elections, which created deep divides between the Hindus and the Muslims. Second, the deepening agrarian crisis in western UP and changes in the rural economy, which affected the rural populace particularly the landowning Jats, making them highly vulnerable to the Hindutva ideology and mobilization based on it.

Our analysis points to differences between the Hindutva ideology and methods espoused during the RJBBM movement and during the 2000s. Beginning in the early 2000s the BJP–RSS attempted grass roots, everyday mobilization among Hindus in western UP to build a base in a region where it had little presence. It built organizations, cadres, and a network of local leaders in the towns and villages of the region building on small, mundane, conflicts, and incidents to create deep-seated, communal polarization between the Hindus, particularly the Jats, and the Muslims over a period of time. The 2014 national elections provided an opportunity to take this mobilization further, which helps explain the high level of preparedness and the magnitude of the victory in UP. The extensive communal mobilization in western UP during the electoral campaign had a two-fold political aim: to help achieve a majority at the centre in the 2014 national elections and to mobilize not only the upper castes but also the middle and lower castes on the basis of Hindu nationalism. The BJP was keen to replace the caste-based identity politics pursued by the SP and BSP, which had made them strong in the 1990s, with communal politics which would which allow it to occupy a central position. This would enable it to fracture the Muslim vote banks that the SP and the BSP had built up and create fear in the minds of the minority community. Our analysis indicates that it is these ideas and actions of the BJP that underlay the Muzaffarnagar riots in 2013 which has created a Hindu vote bank and fear in the minds of Muslims, many of whom as the next chapter will show, are still living in relief camps in UP. Finally, once in power, the BJP hoped to introduce cultural change to make India a united, Hindu nation.

All this was possible with the advent from 2009 of a new, post-Vajpayee generation of BJP leaders—Narendra Modi and his close aide Amit Shah. The new leadership believed that the decline of the BJP in

UP and its defeat in the 2004 national elections was because the party had moved away from its ideology of Hindu nationalism. In keeping with the changed situation due to globalization and the rise of an educated, upwardly mobile, consumerist, middle and lower middle class, they reformulated the Hindutva ideology and the methods of mobilization employed. Modi decided to use the notion of development together with Hindu nationalism to put forward the idea of a strong, economically and culturally empowered Hindu nation in which the Muslim population would be the 'other' who would have to conform to majoritarian values. This they believed would appeal to the new aspirational Hindu middle class, both in the urban and rural areas.

Second, while in the 1980s/90s Hindutva was an ideology meant for the Hindu upper castes, by the 2000s the party had decided to mobilize the middle and lower castes in order to create a socially inclusive Hindu vote bank, which would bring it to power at the centre and give it a strong position in UP. This explains the mobilization, particularly of the Jats, who were unhappy over their economic and political position in western UP. However, while the notion of development was used in speeches by Modi, communal mobilization remained an important tool to create polarization between the majority and minority community carried out by the BJP cadres on the ground, and at times by Modi and Amit Shah. As our study shows, the BJP made rich gains; it swept almost all the seats in western UP in the 2014 elections, which were earlier usually won by the SP or the BSP.

At the same time, it was the longer term forces of the political economy of communalism that made it possible to pitch the Jats and other Hindu groups against the Muslims in western UP first during the Ram Mandir dispute but more forcefully from 2011 onwards, culminating in the 2013 Muzaffarnagar riots. The Green Revolution, which had created prosperity within the Jat landowning community in western UP, from the late 1980s entered a phase of decline as it failed to spread to smaller farmers, due to high cost of inputs and lack of public investment in agriculture. This was compounded after 1991 due to neglect of agriculture with both public and private attention being focussed on industry. Consequently, agrarian politics lost importance in western UP particularly after the death of Charan Singh; the BLD disappeared and by the early 1990s, identity politics based on caste and communalism became important with the rise of the SP, BSP, and the BJP. In this situation, the Jats and their new organization the BKU formed by Tikait after the death of Charan Singh became attracted towards the BJP and supported it in the 1991 assembly election in UP. The Jats were also attracted to a 'Hindu' party due to the challenge by the Dalits from below. Due to these developments the Jat–Muslim alliance formed by Charan Singh in western UP could not be sustained and the BJP found it possible through communal mobilization to create antagonism between the two communities which had close social and political relations earlier.

It was the deepening of the agrarian crisis in western UP, and the revival of the BJP using the Hindutva agenda together with promises of development by Narendra Modi in the 2000s, which made the landowning peasantry particularly the Jats, susceptible to the Sangh Parivar's divisive politics. The Jats became increasingly despondent and aggressive over neglect of agriculture, particularly the crisis in the sugar industry, which has impacted their daily lives. Simultaneously, changes in the rural economy, particularly among the younger generation of Muslims, enabled the rise of new social classes/groups who took to non-agricultural jobs and businesses, which made the Jats feel left behind. Added to this was the failure of successive governments to provide them reservation in education and employment, which they believed was responsible for unemployment among the educated younger generation and their perception that the Muslims had improved their economic position. These factors created an explosive situation that the BJP exploited and which underlies the violence by the Jats against the Muslims in western UP.

Our study suggests that a gradual communalization of society and polity in western UP has been taking place over a long period of time. The BJP has succeeded in making full use of the neglect of agriculture, the lack of development in Muzaffarnagar and adjoining districts, and the unhappiness of the people to create deep communal polarization in a region which remained until recently largely free of communal tension. Thus, the BJP–RSS leadership has used the method of incrementally building up its political and cultural presence in western UP over time which will ensure it is in power and can impose a majoritarian rule over the minority community. It is against this backdrop that we now move to an analysis, based on fieldwork, of the rise of communal tension in western UP from 2011 onwards culminating in the Muzaffarnagar riots in September 2013.

5 Communal Mobilization and Riots in Western Uttar Pradesh
Muzaffarnagar and Shamli Districts

Against the background of shifting Hindu, particularly Jat–Muslim, relations from the late 1980s to the 2000s and sustained and organized communal mobilization based on Hindutva by the BJP and its affiliates, we now move to examining communal riots in western UP. The focus will be on the period from 2012 onwards when a number of small, low-key incidents began, which culminated in the Muzaffaranagar riots of September 2013 and their aftermath. The riots of 2013 have been described as the worst riots since the Gujarat riots of 2002 and our fieldwork points to a Muslim pogrom in some of our selected villages of Muzaffarnagar and Shamli district. The longer-term underlying socio-economic factors, which made possible the construction of communalism by the BJP in the 2000s, after a period of relative calm in UP in the 1990s were discussed in Chapter 4. In this chapter, the focus is upon the more immediate political factors and events that precipitated the riots. Based on our field investigation we argue that the communal incidents from 2011 onwards and the Muzaffarnagar riots were 'political' in nature being a deliberate attempt to polarize communities and create vote banks prior to the 2014 national elections. At the same time, the longer-term agenda of the BJP–RSS was to gain 'political and cultural ascendancy' in order to transform the democratic polity into a Hindu nation. Political parties played a key role in fomenting the riots for political gains. While the BJP undertook communal mobilization there was competitive communalism between parties, most marked between the BJP and SP. Second, the growing antagonism and breakdown of the social and political alliance between Jats and Muslims since the late 1980s made them vulnerable to mobilization and consequently communal violence was primarily between these two communities in western UP.

A number of immediate changes in UP politics underlie this new wave of communal incidents in the western districts and elsewhere in the 2000s. The BSP credited with being a party during whose regime there have been no major communal riots was defeated in the 2012 assembly elections. Despite gaining a majority in the 2012 elections, a new stridency was visible on the part of the SP leadership which realized that its support base was not as strong as in the past due to rapid social change within UP. Although it had gained the support of a substantial section of the Muslim community, its social base among the backwards had weakened. The 1990s had witnessed unravelling of backward-caste identity, despite Mulayam Singh's best efforts to make use of the Mandal upsurge and create a homogenous, backward caste constituency for the SP, due to increasing class divisions among the various sections of the backwards. Consequently, the SP remained largely a Yadav-based party, with other sections moving towards other parties. Second, the fragile post-Mandal equilibrium came under intense pressure due to the rising demands for reservation by the Jats who had been left out in the original compromise that there would be a cap of 50 per cent on reservations. At that point it had been felt that fresh OBC groups would not be included and it was hoped that due to globalization jobs would become available in the private sector, which did not happen at least in UP.

Another significant development, already discussed in Chapter 4, was the generational shift within the BJP which brought a new leadership led by Narendra Modi that replaced the older leaders/founders of the party—Atal Behari Vajpayee and L.K. Advani. Having succeeded in winning three elections in Gujarat despite the 2002 riots, Modi was keen to revive the organization and social base of the party in UP, which was in decline, with the help of the RSS. This led to the shifting of Amit Shah from Gujarat to UP, and attempts to revive the Hindutva agenda of a Ram temple at the disputed site. Thus, both the BJP and SP were on a weak footing and as our fieldwork narrative shows, worked in tandem to create communal disharmony and strengthen their own position. Unable to engineer state-wide communal polarization as during the

Ram Temple movement, the BJP tried to orchestrate Hindu–Muslim tension and incidents wherever possible. The SP, as the ruling party, made little attempt to stop the small communal incidents, which built up, leading eventually to a major riot; nor did it attempt to punish the guilty and the camps set up to look after the displaced Muslims were of very poor quality. The communal tactics of the BJP worked in UP giving it a big victory because an aspirational younger generation was disturbed and the middle class angry as the promised benefits of post-liberalization economic growth had proved elusive (Pai 2015). Just when it seemed that there was a waning of identity politics and UP had emerged from the destabilizing turmoil of the 1990s, there was a slide back, as competitive, communal politics reared its head again.

The riots in western UP have been studied based on fieldwork in two districts: Muzaffarnagar and Shamli. They were selected as they formed the core region in which the riots were severe and the largest number of killings occurred. Both districts exhibited certain key features visible in the riots in western UP: first, the 'new' form of communalism consisting of a large number of low-intensity, small, but at times violent incidents and continuous tension between the Hindu and Muslim communities from 2011 onwards, leading to the severe Muzaffarnagar riots in September 2013. Second, sustained and planned communal mobilization to create polarization between communities by the BJP and its affiliates which, as our fieldwork shows, began much before the 2014 elections, from at least 2009 in order to build a broad Hindu vote bank inclusive of the OBCs and Dalits. Third, the riots in towns such as Muzaffarnagar, Moradabad, and Shamli spread into the rural areas, seriously affecting villages in our selected districts for the first time. The main aim of the fieldwork was to establish the proximate local factors that led to communal conflict and large-scale riots for the first time in rural areas, the communal mobilization prior to the riots, and the role of the state government during the riots and afterwards in helping the affected population. Most importantly, also to examine the impact of the riots on the relationship between Jats and Muslims but also the relationship of these two communities with the Dalits who constitute a major segment within our sample villages.

Three rounds of fieldwork covering urban and rural areas were undertaken during 2015. The attempt was to obtain contrasting narratives about the riots and their aftermath from the two major social groups involved in the riots—the Jats and the Muslims—in our samples.[1] Accordingly, the chapter is divided into three parts. The first part provides a narration of the smaller incidents and clashes from 2011 onwards and the events that culminated in the major Muzaffarnagar riots, fieldwork for which was carried out in Muzaffarnagar town through interviews with important local Muslim leaders and activists. The second part describes the intensive fieldwork based on interviews and group discussions in selected riot-affected villages in both the selected districts. The villages selected fall into two categories for which fieldwork was conducted separately. First, three Jat-dominated villages—Lisadh, Kutba, and Fugana—that were the epicentre of the riots where a large number of Muslims were either killed or they fled from these villages to refugee camps in which many still remain. Second, two Muslim-dominated villages—Loi and Khampur—to which Muslims fled from Fugana and other villages, in order to obtain the Muslim point of view, which was not possible in the first category. Some of these fall in Shamli district. The third section discusses the views of the two groups on the role of the local administration and state government during and after the riots. The concluding section of the chapter analyses the impact of the communal riots on the possible longer-term social relations between Hindus and Muslims and politics in western UP including the fortunes of political parties and electoral politics.

Communal Tension and Clashes: 2011 to 2014

The Selected Districts: Muzaffarnagar and Shamli

Muzaffarnagar was part of the Saharanpur district (west)-cum-Muzaffarnagar district (north) Lok Sabha seat in 1952. Until 2011 Shamli was a part of Muzaffarnagar district; it lies to the east of Muzaffarnagar town and has a similar history and geographical features. The larger district of Muzaffarnagar lies in western UP, 150 km north of Delhi. Muzaffarnagar town is quite old, founded in the reign of Shahjahan

---

[1] While a questionnaire was used to interview respondents in the sample in both urban and rural areas, discussion on specific issues proved useful and the narration of events by many respondents is provided in the chapter. In villages, group discussions were also held. Names of respondents have not been given to conceal their identity.

and was named after a minister of the Emperor who received it as a Jagir together with some surrounding villages. The British occupied the region in 1803 after which changes began and a sub-division was set up in 1824 under which much of the district was formed, but changes continued and the present-day district emerged in 1954 after independence (Uttar Pradesh District Gazetteer Muzaffarnagar, Government of Uttar Pradesh, 1980). The area covered by the present district of Muzaffarnagar lies in the upper Doab of the Ganga and the Yamuna and is a historic area which was part of the Hastinapur kingdom where the epic battle of the Mahabharata was fought. The Jats of western UP are divided into a number of Khaps and Muzaffarnagar is covered by the Khap Baliyan, which is active even today. The district gazetteer records that all sections of the population of the district took part in the 1857 uprising (Uttar Pradesh District Gazetteer Muzafarnagar 1980: 37). It also witnessed much action during the national movement with a branch of the INC and the Gandhi Seva Sangh set up there; a branch of the Muslim League was also formed. An annual session of the Congress was organized at Muzaffarnagar town on 27 October 1922 and was attended by eminent leaders such as Sarojini Naidu, Madan Mohan Malviya, and Motilal Nehru (Uttar Pradesh District Gazetteer Muzafarnagar 1980: 42). The district was also part of the national movement during the late colonial period when it gathered momentum and was visited by Gandhi ji and others. The INC got a majority in the district in the 1937 assembly elections (Uttar Pradesh District Gazetteer Muzafarnagar 1980: 45).

In the undivided district of Muzaffarnagar, Muslims constituted a sizeable minority, being slightly over one-fourth of the population, according to a study in 1999 (Lieten and Srivastava 1999). Despite the diverse religious groups, it has a secular tradition that goes back many decades. Atkinson, an officer in the colonial administration (1867: 77) reported that 'there is none of the religious bigotry which is so characteristic of the relations between Musalmans and Hindus in other districts'. Many of the Muslims were converts from the Hindu population, and carried with them many of the rituals and popular beliefs. Jats, Dhobis, Ranghads (ex-Rajputs), Julaha (weavers), and so forth, were some of the jatis which in the course of history had converted to Islam (Blunt 1931: 200–3) and who remained functionally integrated into the economic and cultural life of the villages. Partition also did not have much impact, Hindus and Muslims remained united under the INC umbrella

(District Gazetter Muzaffarnagar 1980: 80). During the communal violence the traditional village panchayats joined together to fight the fanatics (Pradhan 1966). According to Srivastava's study, the Hindus do not subscribe to the standard Brahminical religious practices; the Jats particularly depart a great deal from them in many respects (Lieten and Srivastava 1999: 93). According to one estimate, the community wise break up in (undivided) Muzaffarnagar was Muslim 27 per cent, SCs 21 per cent, Jats 12 per cent, and Brahmin and Kahars around 5 per cent each; Rajputs, Gujjars, Vaishyas, and Tagas are also present in sizeable numbers. Chamars who make up 16 per cent and Balmikis (4 per cent) are dominant among SCs (H.D. Singh 1996).

The area of the divided new district of Muzaffarnagar is 4008 sq. km. and has six tehsils, 14 Vikas Khands, 247 towns, and 1019 villages (Census of UP 2011, Administrative Atlas, vol. 1: 45). According to the Census of 2011, Muzaffarnagar had a total population of 4,143,512 of which 1,191,312 was urban with a total no of 676,642 households. Of this, the total literate population was 2,417,339 with a literacy rate of 60.67 per cent, literacy rate among males was 71.91 per cent and females only 47.81 per cent (Census 2001). The total SC population was 561,250, with Chamars constituting the largest section followed by Balmikis and Koris. While Hindus formed the majority with 2,151,009, the district had a substantial population of 1,349,629 Muslims. Between 1952 and 1962, the Congress party was able to win the assembly seat of Muzaffarnagar; in 1967 and 1971 it was captured by the CPI. From 1977, it has had a chequered history: the BLD won in 1977, the Janata Party in 1980, the INC in 1984, the JD in 1989, and the BJP in 1991(H. D. Singh 1996).

As per provisional reports of 2011 Census, the population of Shamli district was 107,266; of which male and female are 57,187 and 50,079, respectively. Hindus were 68.93 per cent and Muslims approximately 28.21 per cent (Census 2011). The average literacy was 80.32 per cent of which male literacy was 86.21 per cent while female literacy was 73.70 per cent, which is higher than in Muzaffaranagar district (H. D. Singh 1996).

The Political Economy of the Region

Muzaffarnagar has long been described as one of the richest districts in the country though there are sharp inequalities and polarization within the rural population. The district did not have any large zamindars renting out huge areas of land; instead peasants engaged in self-cultivation dominated the agrarian structure. Prior to the abolition of zamindari, 32.1 per cent of the land in the district was held as sir and khudkhast (Neale 1962). This meant that after the abolition of zamindari the basis for commercial expansion was far stronger here and evidence for this can be seen in the expansion of the agricultural labour force as a proportion of the total population engaged in agriculture. In Muzaffarnagar, the proportion rose between 1961 to 1971 by 18.3 per cent and in 1971–81 by 19per cent as compared to UP averages of 10.8 per cent and 6.4 per cent (Z. Hasan 1989). As described in Chapter 4, the western districts from the mid-1960s experienced commercialization of agriculture and prosperity together with a process of democratization leading to social movements among the lower castes who have questioned upper/middle caste dominance. These features are true of Shamli district also as it was a part of the larger district of Muzaffarnagar. As a result of the commercialization of agriculture in the region, we find both brick houses and mansions with tractors and motorcycles and other households who do not even possess a bicycle. In Lieten's study in the mid-1990s, while one-third of the families did not possess even a bicycle, more than 40 per cent of the total sample had a TV set and 12 per cent possessed a motorcycle. A TV set in the house of a landless labourer or small peasant was still an exception but in the houses of middle level peasants, it was a normal sight; for rich peasants a motorcycle and tractor were integral assets (Lieten 1996: 1412). However, he observes that the poverty of the agricultural labourers did not amount to destitution as wages were reasonably high and occasional migration for work helped many to overcome the lean season (Lieten 1996). However, in more recent years agrarian distress is visible due to agricultural decline even in the more prosperous districts of western UP, which has contributed to social divisions and conflicts.

Narratives on Communal Incidents Leading to the Muzaffarnagar Riots

Much before the Muzaffarnagar riots, low-intensity communal polarization and rising violence was witnessed in many parts of UP from 2012 onwards when the SP came to power defeating the BSP. In fact, violence began during the election campaign for the assembly elections itself. Consequently, media reports point out that in the first 10 months of the SP government, there were 104 incidents of communal violence that left 34 people dead and 456 injured. Communal riots began in Pratapgarh district in June 2012, spread to Mathura, Faizabad, and Bareilly, which did not experience such incidents even during the demolition of the Babri Masjid, and further across the state (Pai 2013a). These developments took place despite the absence of any Hindutva campaign as in the early 1990s. It is against this backdrop that the events prior to the Muzaffarnagar riots are examined below.

In order to understand the beginnings of communal tension and the low-intensity incidents, the forces involved, and how these finally led to a major riot in the district in September 2014, fieldwork was conducted in Muzaffarnagar town for four days from 24 to 27 July 2015. During the fieldwork, intensive discussions were held with three groups. First, community leaders from the Muslim community particularly the Jamiat-Ulema-Hind which organized the relief camps prior to those set up by the government and brought together all Muslim organizations keen to help. We interviewed Maulana Nazar Qasmi and Moosa Qasmi, the District Head of the Jamiat-Ulema-Hind and in-charge of the relief operations and media in-charge of the Jamiat, respectively, who narrated to us the events leading to the riots. Both are respected leaders in their own community and Qasmi due to his proximity to the SP is an important person who has been given security. Both are viewed as secular in outlook, are trusted in the district, and have long been involved in many Hindu–Muslim negotiations and conciliatory measures like organizing collective marriage ceremonies for the Hindu and the Muslim community. They were joined by two social activists: Mohammad Alamgir and Naushad Quraishi. Second, a number of NGOs run by Muslims who were involved in helping the riot-affected victims in the district: Paigham-e-Muhabbat led by its president Zia-ur-Rahman; All India Muttahida Mahaz led by Shahnawaz Aftab; Shaheed Ashfaqullah Khan Society led by Shabaz Aftab and Muslim Voice of India led by Ajmal Ur Rahman. Three, members of the media who covered the riots—such as Muhammad Gulfam editor, *Shah Times*, a local daily of Muzaffarnagar. Fourth, advocate Faizziayab Khan who is fighting cases for Muslims who are affected by the riots. Fifth, public representative Asad Zama, ward member, who is also accused of making inflammatory speeches along with Kadir Rana. Based on these interviews, a narration of events prior to and during the Muzaffarnagar riots is provided.

The interviews conducted in Muzaffarnagar town from 24 to 29 July 2014 as well media reports reveal that communal tension and small incidents were present in the district for more than a year before the outbreak of the riots. From the narrative of the respondents, it seems that local BJP leaders were active in the rural parts of the district on a day-to-day basis, politicized these incidents, and gave them a communal colour. The local police administration was also divided along communal lines, which made it difficult to check these incidents. Thus, the atmosphere was already communally charged much before the Muzaffarnagar riots and any small incident was given a communal colour. The social polarization these created was evident in the partisan and inflated manner in which these incidents were narrated by respondents even after two years.[2] Three examples provided by our respondents will suffice to show the situation in the district.

An incident in a Gujjar-dominated village, Buchakheri in Kairana block, Shamli district with 200–250 Gujjar and 15–20 Muslim households, a couple of days before Holi in March 2013 was given a communal angle by local BJP leaders. The wood stored for the Holi bonfire was set ablaze by someone. The Gujjars accused the Muslims for the incident leading to Hindu–Gujjars attacking Muslims and their mosques in the village. BJP MLAs Hukum Singh, a Gujjar, and Suresh Rana, a Rajput, came to the village in support of the Gujjars and condemned the firing by the police ordered to contain the situation. The firing was linked to the religion of the then SP of Shamli, Abdul Hameed—a Muslim officer—who was accused of being partisan towards the Muslims, thereby giving the police action a communal colour.

A second incident, according to respondents, that triggered communal tension in the area was the alleged rape of a Dalit girl from Haridwar district, by four Muslim men in Shamli in July 2013. While Muslim respondents held that the girl was of bad character and had willingly accompanied the Muslim youth, according to the media and some Hindu respondents it was a case of abduction and rape by the Muslim youth. The girl managed to flee and approached the police who

---

[2] According to one estimate approximately 140 villages in Muzaffarnagar, Shamli, and Baghpat district were affected by this riot (Rao et.al, Report 2014).

refused to take action, leading to anger among villagers. The local BJP leaders somehow got hold of the girl and made her file a case against the Muslim youth accusing him of rape. The police led by SP, Abdul Hameed it is alleged, took no action, acted in a partisan manner and lathi charged the protesters. In protest, BJP MLAs, Hukum Singh and Suresh Rana sat on hunger strike. However, Muslim respondents allege that when the demonstrators led by BJP MLA Hukum Singh turned violent, and the SP tried to bring the situation under control, the local SP leader, also a Gujjar and president of the Zila Panchayat, grabbed Hameed by his collar and Hukum Singh attacked him with a sharp weapon. It was in response to this behaviour that the SP ordered a lathi charge, and according to the Muslim respondent who claimed to be an eyewitness, only Dalit and Muslim constables complied. In fact, District Magistrate Surindra Singh, a Jat left the spot at that moment and Hammed was transferred, leading to celebration in police lines; finally the transfer order was withdrawn.

The third and better-known incident widely reported in the media that vitiated the communal atmosphere was the proposed Chaurasi Kos Yatra[3] by the VHP in UP was also mentioned by the respondents. The Yatra is a traditional religious practice in UP but it was never taken up by any political organization or party. However, in August 2013, the VHP not only gave a call for the Yatra but also sent invitations to many Hindu saints across the country to participate in the same. The 20-day yatra, involving a 252 km *parikrama*, was to start from Ayodhya on 25 August, pass through 600 villages with a sizeable Muslim population, across six districts, and culminate at Ayodhya on 13 September. To seek clearance for the proposed pad-yatra, Ashok Singhal met Mulayam Singh Yadav almost a week before the proposed date. This caused great unhappiness among SP Muslim leaders like Azam Khan who openly criticized Mulayam Singh Yadav for meeting Ashok Singhal. In response the state government decided to ban the proposed Yatra on 20 August, which was met by defiant VHP activists and leaders deciding to defy the ban and proceed with their yatra. The state administration blocked the way to Ayodhya, made tight security arrangements, and arrested many VHP activists, supporters, and saints across the state who were on their way to Ayodhya to go ahead with the yatra. Consequently, VHP

[3] Literally, an 84-mile pilgrimage.

and the BJP propagated the idea that the Yatra had been banned by the state government to appease the Muslims and described the government as anti-Hindu. The confrontation was in fact stage-managed by the BJP and the SP (Pai 2013a). Unable to create state-wide tension and communal polarization, the BJP tried to create a Hindu–Muslim divide wherever possible. Outwardly, the BJP described the ban as a move by the SP to appease Muslims, while the SP described the BJP as a Hindu communal party. The former hoped to revive itself by aggressively upholding the right of the Hindu community to hold a religious event in a secular democracy; while the latter hoped to bring more Muslims into its fold and benefit in 2014.

The Kanval Incident and the Outbreak of the Muzaffarnagar Riots

Many other small incidents were taking place across western UP around the same time that were given a communal angle; they caused small incidents but none of them escalated disproportionately. It was in this background that the Kanval incident at Muzaffarnagar on 27 August 2015 took place, which precipitated the Muzaffarnagar riots. What exactly triggered the unfortunate event at Kanval on 27 August 2013 has many versions. According to some Hindu respondents, the prime cause for the entire incident was eve-teasing by the deceased Muslim boy Shahnawaz. They also pointed out that these kinds of incidents are on the rise. However, the Muslim respondents stated that it was a minor incident wherein Gaurav's motorcycle collided with Shahnawaz's bicycle that culminated in three youths being killed.[4] The FIRs filed, by the fathers of Gaurav and Shahnawaz, on the same day of the incident and in the same police station Jansath, narrate the motorcycle

---

[4] Media reports point to the existence of communal fault lines. The Hindus held that, 'Shahnawaz was always a trouble maker. Two years back, he even ran away with a Muslim girl. He had also slapped a police officer few days back. One of the relatives was a history-sheeter at the local police station. He constantly passed comments on the Jat girl. Her brother objected and that is how the incident took place,' says Mahendra Singh, a resident of village. However, Muslims of the village do not mention any eve-teasing in their narration. They say Shahnawaz was just young and a little hot-blooded (*The Times of India*, New Delhi, 12 September 2013).

accident as the starting point of the incident. Nowhere does the FIR (FIR 190/13 on 27.8.2013, DOI 27.8.2013), filed by the father of the deceased boy, Gaurav mention the incident of eve teasing. Further, there is a difference in the date of the reported motorcycle accident. The FIR filed by Gaurav's father (FIR 190/13 on 27.8.2013, DOI 27.8.13 P.S. JANSATH), states that the accident happened a day before, that is, on 26 August 2015 and alleges that the attack on 27th was a pre-planned one by the Muslims. The FIR filed by Shahnawaz's father (FIR 191/13 on 27.8.2013, DOI 27.8.2013 P.S. JANSATH), on the other hand, states that the accident happened on 27th, that is, on the day of the incident. Therefore, it can be inferred that the dominant perception that the incident at Kanwal was the outcome of an incident of eve-teasing by a Muslin youth could not be substantiated.

The Kanwal incident culminated in major riots in Muzaffarnagar district due to a combination of mischievous use of technological and politico-communal factors. It also indicates poor policing and maintenance of law and order as it was a small incident and could have been nipped in the bud. Two days after the Kanwal incident, it probably could have remained a localized incident. On 29 August 2013, a person named Shiv Kumar uploaded a fake video of a Muslim mob lynching two youths under the title 'See What Happened in Kanwal' on Facebook; the video was instantly shared by BJP Jat leader and MLA Sangeet Som. Within a matter of hours, the video went viral vitiating the communal atmosphere and laying grounds for the escalation of communal tension throughout Muzaffarnagar and neighbouring areas. This fact has been verified by the FIR (FIR 596/13 P.S. Khatauli) filed by the Khatauli Police Station in-charge which mentions all the relevant details.

Following the Kanwal incident, the role of some political and religious leaders from both the Hindu and Muslim communities was crucial in escalating the communal tension. The commemoration of the deceased life by Hindus and Muslims in the area acquired the character of a competitive vengeance demonstration. Sanjeev Balian, a Jat and then BJP Vice-President of Uttar Pradesh announced a Jat Mahapanchayat at Bhartiya Inter College, Nangla Madaur on 31 August 2013. Though the police administration denied permission and imposed Code of Criminal Procedure (CrPC) 144 in the area, the Jats led by Sanjeev Balian attended the Mahapanchayat in thousands;

communally provocative speeches were made at the gathering. In the communally charged atmosphere, the crowd set a motorcycle on fire after the meeting as mentioned in the FIR (FIR 29/2013 on 31.08.2013).

Simultaneously, many Muslim leaders also called for and held a Panchayat at Shaheed Chowk in Muzaffarnagar on 30 August to express their anger over the Muslim youth killed at Kanval. Being Friday there was a large gathering of the Muslims in the adjoining mosque and consequently 15,000–20,000 Muslims attended the Panchayat at which prominent Muslim leaders made very provocative speeches. Interestingly, the Muslim respondents argued that the Shaheed Chowk gathering was in retaliation of the earlier announcement of the Jat Mahapanchayat, but in reality the Chowk meeting took place one day before the Jat Mahapanchayat. Moreover, Muslim respondents claimed that no communally provocative speech was made at the gathering and that some miscreants spread false propaganda in this regard. However, the FIR filed against the Muslim leaders by the administration (FIR 593/13 dated 31.08.2013 P.S. Kotwali Nagar) indicts and names 10 prominent Muslim leaders as accused: Kadir Rana (MP BSP),[5] Maulana Zameel (MLA Meerapur), Noor-Salim Rana (MLA Charthawal), Asad Zama (Ward Member), Said-ud-Zama (Ex-MP Congress), Salman Said (Congress Leader); and activists Naushad Qureshi, Ehsan Qureshi, Sultan Mushir Qureshi, and Musharra Qureshi.

Maulana Nazar Qasmi of the Jamiat pointed to another attempt to further polarize the Muslims made by Maulana Nazeer from Jansat in Muzaffarnagar district (see FIR) who decided to lead a march till Kanval comprising of more than 10,000 Muslims on 3 September 2015, despite imposition of CrPC 144 in the area. When the administration tried to stop the gathering from proceeding to Kanval, he incited his supporters to make phone calls to a large number of Muslims to announce in their areas via loudspeakers at mosques to gather there in large numbers. As a result, thousands of Muslims gathered, the situation became very tense, and the administration found it very difficult to prevent their March to Kanval and called for further reinforcements. Ultimately, Maulana Nazeer, on seeing the arrival of a large number of police personnel, made a sudden tactical retreat on the pretext of offering Namaz. This

[5] Kadir Rana had left the Samajwadi Party in 2007 to join the Rashtriya Lok Dal and then switched to BSP in 2009.

incident and the narration is corroborated by the FIR (FIR No. 195/13 dated 3 September 2013 P.S. Jansath).

In their narration, Muslim respondents pointed to another Mahapanchayat of Jats held on 5 September (two days before the well-known Mahapanchayat of 7 September) that was not reported anywhere. It was claimed that the former Mahapanchayat was headed by Baba Harkishan Singh Malik (70 years) the Mukhiya of the Malik Khap Panchayat. It was also claimed that the then SP Crime, Kalpana Saxena had videographed the proceedings of the Mahapanchayat at which more than 500 Jats were distributed arms. As per their version, the Mahapanchayat was followed by the call for a Muzaffarnagar Bandh (shut down) and another gathering on the 'terahvi' (13th day after death) of Gaurav and Sachin. Thus, the incident at Kanval became the rallying point for communal polarization throughout western UP in general and Muzaffarnagar in particular.

Communal mobilization reverberating around the Kanval incident on the part of the Jat community witnessed maximum mobilization on 7 September 2013 when the famous Mahapanchayat was held at the same venue at Bhartiya Inter College, Nangla Madaur. Two aspects are worth mentioning here: it was attended by all the prominent BJP leaders from the region, namely, Sangeet Som (Jat), Hukum Singh (Gujjar). Suresh Rana (Rajput/Thakur), Sanjeev Balian (Jat), etc. Second, as per the version of the Muslim respondents, the Jats coming from their respective villages to the site of Mahapanchayat, that is, Nangla Madaur, deliberately took the route passing via Muslim villages and ransacked the same while coming and going. It is difficult to establish the truth as the Jats and Hindus gave different versions. However, one thing that was corroborated by the copy of the FIR (FIR No- 103/2013 dated 7 September 2012) was that the Jats attending the Mahapanchayat were armed with non-lethal arms and provocative speeches were made in the presence of prominent BJP and BKU leaders from the region, leading to the Jats ransacking property and setting vehicles on fire.

It was the attack on Jats returning from the Mahapanchayat on 7 September 2013, by the Muslims when they were passing through Muslim-dominated villages like Jolly (Jauli in some reports) and others along the Ganga Naher (canal) which sparked off the retaliation by Jats in villages dominated by them. As far as the attack on Jats returning after attending the Mahapanchayat on 7 September 2013 is concerned, there are different narratives depending upon the religious identity of the narrator. For instance, all the Muslim respondents we talked to asserted that the Jats were the ones who started attacking the passers-by in the Muslim villages when they were returning from the Mahapanchayat. They recounted many incidents where some Muslims were killed or injured by the returning Jats armed with firearms and other weapons. In fact, it was strongly asserted by some Muslim respondents that at Jolly, a Jat killed a person and tried to abduct a Muslim woman in his tractor and it was this killing and attempted abduction that led to the anger of Muslims in that village and neighbouring ones, due to which they gathered and clashed with the Jats. As per the version of the Muslims, it was the Jats who first opened fire on the Muslim crowd gathered there to set the abducted woman free. In fact, many FIRs that we possess provide different versions with regard to who initiated the clash at Jolly and other villages on the evening of 7 September 2013.

Police reports (FIR No- 236/19 dated 7 Spetember 2013 P.S. Shahpur; FIR No- 249/13 dated 8 September 2013 P.S. Bhopa) filed by the Police Inspectors present at the respective sites/villages establishes two facts. First, the Muslims attacked the Jats returning to their respective villages after attending the Mahapanchayat on 7 September; and second, the attack was pre-planned. Not only were the Jats fired upon, but also exchange of firing also took place between the Muslims and the police. At the same time, it should also be noted that many FIRs filed by the Muslims indicate that there were casualties in the Muslim community too on that particular day. The media has also reported that around 2,000 Jats returning from the Mahapanchayat held at Kawwal were ambushed by a Muslim mob armed with assault rifles and other sophisticated weapons near Jauli canal on 7 September (*DNA* 2013). The mobs set fire to 18 tractor trollies and three motorcycles. According to an eyewitness account, the bodies were dumped into the canal. Although six bodies were recovered, it was rumoured that hundreds were missing. Bodies of three Jats were found at the site of violence and three bodies belonging to Hindus were fished out from Jauli Canal. The District Magistrate agreed that many bodies were still missing, but doubted whether the missing people were killed or had migrated earlier from the village. Survivors of the Jauli Canal incident added that the policemen who were watching the assault did not help the victims, as they had said that 'they do not have orders to act'. This

Jauli Canal incident aroused Jats to go on a rampage against Muslims with the claim that the latter were responsible for the killings. What is clear is that on 7 September 2013 when the Jats proceeded to their Mahapanchayat via the Muslim villages and returned along the same route, while returning along the Jolly (Jauli) *nahar* (canal) clashes took place and riots started from the evening of 7 September.[6]

This violent clash started the riots, the Army was deployed and curfew was imposed in Muzaffarnagar and neighbouring Shamli district (*DNA* 2013). The clashes continued for the next three days, even with the curfew and use of the army with casualties increasing to 43 by 12 September 2013. An official of the state home department said that 38 people died in Muzaffarnagar, 3 in Baghpat, and one each in Saharanpur and Muzafarnagar (*Tehelka* 2013b). The magnitude of the riots can be understood from the fact that the army was deployed in the state for the first time in 20 years (*India Today* 2013). Approximately 1,000 army troops were deployed and curfew was imposed in the violence-hit areas. About 10,000 PAC personnel, 1,300 CRPF troopers, and 1,200 Rapid Action Force personnel were deployed to control the situation (*Tehelka* 2013a). The police made around 10,000 to 12,000 preventive arrests. They cancelled 2,300 arms licenses, seized 2,000 arms, and filed seven cases under the National Security Act (*The Times of India* 2013). The first case of gang rape was registered in the aftermath of the riots from village Fugana. Later two more cases of rape were registered in October. It was reported on 15 November 2013 that a total of 13 rape and sexual harassment cases were registered over the past two months of rioting and the report named 111 people in the incidents, but no arrests had been made till then (Furqan Ameen Siddiqui 2013).

From Communal Clash to Muslim Pogrom

It seems clear from the narratives of our respondents that till the incident at Jauli and other villages on the evening of 7 September

[6] Some accounts point out that a local mosque was attacked, provocative slogans like *Jao Pakistan, warna Kabristan* (Go to Pakistan or graveyard), *Hindu ekta zindabad* (Long live Hindu unity), and *Ek ke badle ek 100* (For one life, we will claim 100 lives) rent the air. Muslim shops and houses were looted and vandalized (Dhabade 2016).

2013, the earlier incidents were akin to minor communal clashes with sporadic incidents of both communities attacking each other following the Kanval incident. However, what followed was a shift from a Jat–Muslim clash to a one-sided killing of Muslims by the Jats. This shift took place when the Jats coming from the Mahapanchayat did not return to their respective villages by nightfall due to the attack upon them by Muslims at Jolly and other places; the rumour spread in the Jat villages that they had all been killed. Consequently, Jats in different villages held a Panchayat and decided to take revenge. On the same night, they started killing the Muslims in their villages. The killing of Muslims in large numbers continued on 8, 9, and 10 September. In fact, on 8 September 2013, the Jats also killed a journalist. To borrow the term used by a Muslim respondent, there was a *'Qatl-e-aam'*

Figure 5.1   A Jat stands in his sugarcane field in Fugana village which he claims was burnt by Muslims during the riot.

Source: Photograph by Ram Kumar, ex-Pradhan, 7 October 2013.[7]

---

[7] All the photos for Fugana village dating from 2013 were provided by ex-Pradhan Ram Kumar who had them taken just after the riots. The authors have the permission of the villagers to publish these photos.

Figure 5.2   Jat men in Fugana village against the backdrop of a destroyed Muslim house. The Jat sitting in front on the charpoy on the right has bought the property after the Muslim family fled the village. Many such properties were bought by the Jat villagers after the riots were over.

Source: Photograph by Ram Kumar, ex-Pradhan, 11 August 2015.

(pogrom) since the night of 7 September 2013 that continued until 10 September 2013.

The epicentre of violence against the Muslims is difficult to locate but was mainly three Jat-dominated villages, namely, Qutba, Lisadh, and Fugana that witnessed maximum violence against the Muslims. In Kutba 9 Muslims and in Fugana 11–12 Muslims were reported to be killed, while in Lisadh there was unparalleled violence and killing along with rape. There, as per the Muslim respondents versions, the Muslims were killed and cut into pieces in the village 'Ara Machine' (woodcutting machine) before their bodies were dumped in the canal. The narration may be exaggerated but the fact remains that the 'Ara machine' in Lisadh was owned by a Muslim who was the first one to be killed at the site. It is reported that apart from Lisadh, there were 7 cases of rape (6 in Fugana and 1 in Kutba) wherein 27 Jats are accused. Besides, there were many instances of Muslims being killed in other areas too.

The antagonism between the Jats and the Muslims in Fugana, one of the worst affected villages, is evident in Figures 5.1 and 5.2. The photos were provided by Ram Kumar, ex-Pradhan of the village; but both sides were keen to show they had suffered during the riots. The Jats pointed to the photos of their destroyed sugarcane crop which they alleged was burnt by Muslims; the Muslims were keen to provide evidence that their destroyed properties were bought by the Jats once they left the village leaving them little desire of returning to their native village.

Impact and Relocation of Muslims

Regarding impact of the riots on the Muslim community in Muzaffarnagar and Shamli districts the respondents held that the worst affected were those residing in villages traditionally dominated by Jats. Among them Kutba, Lisadh, and Fugana stand out as the worst affected as Muslims were not only killed and attacked but were forced to flee their villages. At the time of the interviews from 24 to 27 July 2015 not a single Muslim family had returned to these three villages as they feared for their life and safety. This is also true of many other Jat-dominated villages. However, it should also be borne in mind that another factor that prevented the return of Muslims to their respective villages after the riots is the conditional compensation of Rs 5 lakhs wherein the receiver of the compensation it was alleged, has to declare that s/he will not return to his/her respective village after getting the said compensation amount. In fact, the Samajvadi government ensured that after compensation was given no one was allowed to remain in the respective camps. It is alleged that Mulayam Singh went to the extent of stating that after compensation, those staying in the camps were criminals who wanted to grab government land. It is against the backdrop of the narration by prominent Muslim leaders and activists that we turn now to the narratives from the Jats in selected severely riots-affected villages.

Narratives from Jats in Selected Riot-affected Villages

As the communal riots were primarily between the Jats and Muslims in western UP, fieldwork was conducted in three villages of Muzaffarnagar district where the former are in a majority. The fieldwork was conducted during 10–11 November 2015 in three the Jat-dominated villages of Kutba, Fugana, and Lisadh. They were selected because they formed the epicentre of the 2014 Muzaffarnagar riots as mentioned above. In total

10–15 respondents were interviewed in each village who were from the age group of 17 to 85.[8] The average landholding of the Jat families interviewed ranged from 20–40 acres and their educational qualification ranged from matriculation to graduation with a few even having higher degrees. The respondents consisted of males[9] primarily from the Jat community, though in all the three villages some Dalit and upper-caste respondents were also interviewed. Besides, two Muslim families in village Fugana, who returned because unlike the large majority of Muslims who are labourers in the village, they own 20–25 bighas of land, were also interviewed.

The Sample Villages

All our three sample villages of Kutba,[10] Lisadh,[11] and Fugana[12] are large and well-populated villages. Kutba has an area of 416 hectares and population of 4,830 (2,603 male) and 781 households with a total SC population of 653 (Male—358, Female—295) (Census 2011). Only 2,904 persons, that is, a little more than half the population are literate and 1,926 are illiterate; as many as 1,147 females are illiterate. Lisadh village is spread over 1,770 hectares, with a population of 13,077 of which 7,128 are male, the total number of households are 2,029 (Census 2011). The total SC population is 1,258, of which 696 are male and 562 female. A little over 8,275 persons, which is a little more than half the population, are literate of which 5,075 are male with 4,802 illiterate persons. Fugama has an area of 1,159 hectares, the total number of households is 1,500 and the population 9,190 of

[8] Pradhans were also interviewed. Jat villages have two pradhans: the traditional community pradhan and the democratically elected pradhan of the panchayat. During the discussion in the village, it was the traditional pradhan who spoke most of the time. Their authority supersedes the authority of the democratically elected pradhan and is part of the Khap at the village level. Also, group discussions were held in every village.

[9] Although many females responded in places where people were sitting in groups or in a family, they simply endorsed the narration of the male members sitting there.

[10] Village code 111025 as per census 2011.

[11] Village code 110766 as per census 2011.

[12] Village code of Fugana village is 110580.

which SC population was 864 (Census 2011). Only 6,176 persons are literate despite there being three primary and two middle schools in the village and a college 3 km from the village.

Lying in the western region which is the most developed in the state, all the villages have good paved as well as mud roads and footpaths connecting them to the main road. They are hardly 3–4 kilometres away from bus and railway stations and are close to towns such as Sangli, Burdwan, and Shahpur. All of them have more than one primary and middle school, one secondary school and a college 3 km away. They also have amenities such as primary health care and maternity and child welfare centres just about 1–3 km away; in Kutba there are two and in Lisadh there are four registered medical practitioners; a hospital is situated very close to Fugana village. All the villages have a commercial bank, post office, and cooperative bank 3 km away. However, basic amenities are lacking: in all the villages the major source of drinking water is hand pumps; in Kutba there is only one for the whole village. Power is available only for irrigation but not for domestic use. In Kutba the total irrigated land area is 359 hectares; the total cultivable waste (including *gauchar* [pasture] and groves) is seven hectares and the area unavailable for cultivation is 50 hectares (Census 2001). In Lisadh, the total irrigated land area in the village is 1,378 hectares, total cultivable waste (including gauchar and groves) is 76 hectares and the area unavailable for cultivation is 176 hectares (Census 2001). In Fugana the total irrigated area is 1041 hectares of which the total cultivable waste (including gauchar and groves) is 33 hectares; the area unavailable for cultivation is 83 hectares with irrigation available through government canals and bore wells but without electricity (Census 2001). The main source for irrigation is canals with 197 government canals passing through the irrigated land in all the villages.

The main source of employment and income is agriculture, but small household industries have also become important. The largest manufactured item in Fugana and Kutba are jaggery followed by coarse sugar. In Fugana carpets and in Lisadh bricks are the main manufactured items, followed by jaggery. However, the Census of 2011 notes a large number of persons unemployed in the villages: in Kutba as many as 3,325 (Male—1,384, and Female—1,968) persons are unemployed; in Lisadh 8,692 (Male–3,512, Female–5,180) and in Fugana 6,316 are unemployed (Census 2011). Thus, despite the existence of schools and a college nearby in all the villages only 50 per cent are literate and there are few jobs available even for those educated, which is a source of much unhappiness.

In our selected villages most of the Jats are literate; the Muslims who are labourers along with Dalits mainly constitute the illiterate section. The three sample villages are dominated by two well-organized clans of Jats, namely, the Baliyan Jats and the Malik Jats, whose well-organized Khap structure, spreads through 84 and 52 villages in western Uttar Pradesh, respectively. However, if we add the villages falling in the trans-Yamuna region in the neighbouring state of Haryana, the number of Malik Jat villages account for a total of 104. Out of the three villages, Kutba is dominated by Baliyan Jats while Lisadh and Fugana are dominated by Malik Jats. The two deceased Jat boys, Gaurav and Sachin belonged to the Malik Jat community. Apart from Jats, the selected villages are inhabited by Dalits and upper castes along with a significant population of Muslims who have fled after the riots. At the time of the fieldwork no Muslim family was living in any of these villages, the only exception being Fugana village where two Muslim families owning around 20–22 bighas of land have returned.

The Jat and non-Jat respondents interviewed were unanimous that it was the first communal riot occurring in a rural area in their district and the first ever in their own village. In fact, all of them strongly claimed that there used to be complete harmony and a symbiotic relationship among Jats and Muslims. They all claimed that hitherto only urban areas experienced such riots. It is interesting that on being questioned, there was near agreement in the responses of all the respondents—both Jat and non-Jat Hindus—that the responsibility for starting the riots lay primarily with some Muslim culprits who are also local leaders, for vitiating the communal atmosphere by intervening in a completely partisan and provocative manner, apart from making inflammatory speeches. They held the following seven leaders/groups or parties responsible for creating communal tension and riots:

1. Shahnawaz and Muslim villagers of Kanval.
2. Amir Alam (ex-MP, Samajvadi Party).
3. Nawajish Alam (MLA, Budhana, Muzaffarnagar) who is Amir Alam's son.
4. Azam Khan.

5. Muslims who attacked Jats returning from Mahapanchayat on the evening of 7 September 2013.
6. Muslims who attacked Jats from other villages returning from the Mahapanchayat on the morning of 8 September 2013.
7. The Samajvadi Party government for not intervening.

However, Hindu political leaders were not blamed by even a single respondent. In fact, the majority of respondents praised them for helping the community in the wake of arrests, FIRs, and other legal actions. In particular, local BJP leaders like Sanjeev Baliyan, Sangeet Som, Nitin Malik, and Umesh Malik were commended for their prompt help to their community members, especially, the accused ones. These leaders were praised for arranging the lawyers, securing their bails, and providing them constant legal services. But there was anger and boycott of BJP leader Suresh Rana (MLA) a Thakur by caste, in Fugana village due to his refusal to carry a Brahmin youth wounded by a bullet in his car to the nearby hospital. Nevertheless, barring this incident, the general perception of majority of the respondents was along religious lines wherein local Hindu leaders were commended for their role in helping out the community in its allegedly difficult times, while local Muslim leaders were blamed for encouraging the riots. It was consistently narrated that when the DM and SSP of Muzaffarnagar, Surendra Singh and Manjil Saini, acted swiftly and arrested the accused from both the sides, the Muslim leaders listed above intervened and got the Muslim accused released, while the Jats remained arrested. In fact, many of the respondents claimed that after securing the release of the Muslim accused in the Kanval case, Nawajish Alam drove them back in his personal car. However, upon asking for any factual evidence for the same or as to why the said incident had not been reported in any of the media news, the respondents were clueless and silent. Further, it was alleged that senior Samajvadi party leader, Azam Khan got both the DM and SSP (Surendra Singh and Manjil Saini) transferred for arresting the accused from both sides in a swift and non-partisan manner. They claimed that had the DM and SSP not been transferred, the situation would not have taken such an ugly turn.

From the perspectives of Jats and non-Jat Hindus from these three villages, the role of the state government in letting the Muslims hold a Panchayat at Shaheed Chowk in Muzaffarnagar town on 30 August

2013, despite the prohibitory orders under Section 144 of CrPC wherein provocative speeches were made by leading Muslim political leaders from the Congress, BSP, and SP, was viewed as an attempt to give Muslims a free hand. This charge was further endorsed by emphasizing the fact that rather than dispersing the Muslim Panchayat, the newly appointed DM, Kaushal Raj Sharma, walked to the Panchayat and received petitions from them. In contrast to this leniency, the strict role of the district administration in preventing the Jats from reaching the place of their Mahapanchayat at Nangla Madaur, the very next day, 31 August, was claimed to be one of the primary reasons that angered the Jat and other Hindu communities, due to a perceived sense of injustice.

More importantly, it was claimed that the sense of anger of the Hindu community in general and Jats in particular, against the completely partisan approach of district administration and state government, deepened further in the aftermath of the allegedly pre-planned attacks on people returning from the Mahapanchayat on the evening of 7 September 2013. Hence, they explicitly blamed the Muslims as the harbinger of the riots by being the first to create communal tension by eve teasing the Jat girls, holding the Panchayat, and finally attacking the people returning from the Mahapanchayat.

However, upon being asked that who was responsible for the killings in their villages, the responses were surprisingly similar in all the three villages—'it was the Jats from *other* villages who were attacked the day before and had to hide throughout the night, who picked the fight with Muslims in their villages on account of simmering anger and feeling of vengeance for what Muslims had done to them and in the process killed some of them'. This claim of shifting the blame onto the outsider Jats, was contradicted by their narration, when they mentioned in passing that the outsider Jats were joined by a few miscreants from their villages too. Hence, there seems to be a strategy of shifting the blame upon outside Jats and exonerating majority of the villagers mentioned as accused in various FIRs.

Apart from the question of the persons responsible for killing the Muslims in the three villages, the biggest discrepancies between the narration of the Jats and Muslims, was on the question of the number of deceased Muslims in their villages. While there was a fair response in Kutba village, where the majority of the respondents claimed almost the exact number of Muslims that were killed, that is, 8 to 9, the respondents in Fugana and Lisadh were diplomatic in their response.

In Fugana and Lisadh where 12 and 15 persons, respectively, were reported to have been killed, the respondents claimed that the number of deceased happened to be just two in both cases, and the rest were simply missing as their dead bodies could not be found. An ex-Pradhan of Fugana village mentioned in passing that his brethren in Lisadh had the tactical advantage of having a sawmill that could have helped them in disposing of the dead bodies by cutting them into pieces. Finally, all the deceased in the three villages were Muslims, though two persons in Fugana village, one Jat and one Brahmin, were wounded in firing while returning from the Mahapanchayat on 7 September 2013.

Shifting Socio-economic Equations between Social Groups

An attempt was made to understand whether there were local, social, and economic jealousies underlying the riots and also the new socio-economic relations that have emerged after the violent conflicts that all groups faced in our sample villages. The responses of the Jat respondents in the three villages clearly indicate that prior to the riots, the Jats and Muslims had close social and economic relations. First, there was a mutuality of interests between the two communities because the Jats, being the landowning class, needed the Muslims of their villages as farm labourers and for other mundane work. This symbiotic relationship was traditional and had a created dependency of Jats over Muslims. Second, in recent years a significant number of Muslim men had set up petty garment businesses, and would ferry and sell garments in the locality while their wives and other womenfolk continued to work as farm labourers. This resulted in Muslims borrowing money frequently from the Jats on interest. Thus, Jats in their respective villages were not only the landowners but also moneylenders, leading to both communities developing close equations for their respective interests, reflected in their day-to-day interactions. In fact, many elderly Jat respondents proudly claimed that equations were so close that Muslims used to invite them to sort out their familial and other problems. Besides, they also stated that politically there was no divergence of views and Muslims always got along well with the Jats in their respective villages.

Against this backdrop, whether social and economic jealousies of Jats against improvements in the conditions of Muslims in their villages constituted one of the reasons for the outbreak of communal riots, invited a complex response. Proud of their position as a locally dominant community, the Jat respondents summarily rejected this argument pointing to the poor conditions of the Muslims who were dependent on them for their day-to-day livelihood. However, a closer look at their responses points to Jat unhappiness at the implicit but growing existence of social and economic assertion by the Muslims in the district in recent years. First, the establishment of petty garment businesses indicated a shift in the dependence of Muslims from working on Jat farms to small entrepreneurships. In this backdrop, the claim by Jats in all the three villages that the Muslims who have fled the villages owe them a minimum of Rs 2–3 crores taken as loan on interest, itself points out the shifting financial clout of Muslims as compared to their earlier subdued position. Second, Jat respondents provided many stories of young Muslim men, particularly Quraishi's, having all the resources to present themselves as fashionable youth by wearing good clothes and carrying mobiles in order to entrap Hindu girls. Describing the Muslim youth as having a pernicious agenda, these examples betrayed the jealousies that Jat youth have developed against the former. However, since the explicit mention of these issues would be a stigma and against the self-perceived dominant image of Jats, they try their best to reject any such suggestion even though it is implicit in their responses why the Muslims constitute a problem for them.

The Jats held that Hindutva as an ideology was in no way responsible for the communal riots, but rather it was Islamism that is at the roots of such phenomena, endorsing their viewpoint by pointing to issues from cow slaughter, Love Jihad, and the rising population among the Muslims. While no Jat respondent mentioned the issue of Love Jihad, when questioned, all of them asserted there was a conspiracy by the Muslims to target Hindu girls. They even cited detailed methods employed by the Muslims youth, like wearing red thread on their wrist and standing in front of Hindu temples, pretending to be Hindus; Muslim youth being given money and funds in Madrassas to act impressively, etc. Interestingly, upon being asked about the existence and occurrence of any such incident in their own villages, they pointed to such incidences happening in many towns. The mismatch between perception and reality over the issue of Love Jihad, especially among the Jats, was colossal. Nevertheless, most of them were strongly convinced about the existence of such a conspiracy and hardly cared for the factual corroboration. The rumours and unconfirmed media reports had entrenched their perception over the issue. Against this backdrop, it was the general opinion that with both communities being engaged in a legal and perceptual conflict and located at the opposite ends of the political continuum, the possibility of any improvement in the relationship between Jats and Muslims seemed almost impossible in the near future.

However, things changed completely in the aftermath of the communal riots. First, displaced from their villages, Muslims are no longer available as farm labourers or for borrowing money. Second, the political symbiosis between the two communities has completely broken as they are now located at opposite ends of the political spectrum. Muslims are now being appropriated by non-BJP parties in general and SP in particular, the Jats are, as of now, completely in the fold of the BJP. Most importantly, the equations between the two communities have completely changed not only on account of Jats killing the Muslims, but also due to hundreds of on-going legal cases, involving crimes such as rape, murder, and loot against each other. Moreover, it seems that community elites, leaders, and political parties, supporting both the communities, respectively, will not allow a reconciliation to take place in the near future. The mere amount of legal cases coupled with on-going politically charged ambience in the wake of the impending state elections of 2017, it seems, has ensured that the tenuous equations between the two would remain bitter.

The three sample villages have a meagre population of upper castes, mainly Brahmins, Banias, and a few Thakurs. In general, the upper castes showed their solidarity with the Jat community and actively participated in both the Panchayats. But, barring some exceptions, they were not part of the attack on Muslims in their respective villages which was led by Jats and other lower castes. Their support to Jats was reflected through gestures like narrating their perspective to the press, assisting them in legal matters, and making a common political ground. It is another fact that now the solidarity between Jats and other upper castes has somewhat waned on account of Jats putting forward the impression that they did not get adequate support from them and had to bear the burden alone, and upper castes accusing Jats of not forgetting the centrality of caste centricism. Interestingly, the only exception to this trend were found to be a few Tyagis from neighbouring villages, whom we could interview, and found that they were more inclined towards Muslims due to their close relations with them and their dislike for the Jats. However, their distant spatial location from Jat-dominated areas made their responses qualitatively different from other upper castes who were more sympathetic to Jats.

One of the most significant changes in social equations in the aftermath of the riots has taken place in the relationship between the Dalits, Muslims, and Jats. Going by the majority of the responses from the three villages, including that of a few Dalit respondents, the Dalits did not try to protect or help Muslims, but rather, in many cases they actively participated in the riots starting with attending the Mahapanchayats, to attacking the Muslims in the respective villages. This fact also gets corroborated by the FIRs filed by the Muslims in which Dalits are also accused as the culprits along with Jats. In fact, in all the three villages, there are still some people in jail in connection with their role in the riots which include Dalits. Nevertheless, it is not clear whether the participation of Dalits in the riots was of their own accord, or a result of the dominant power equation in the respective villages wherein they could not afford to be seen either siding with Muslims or remaining neutral. Interestingly, many Jat respondents in Kutba village alleged that it was Kashyaps (Dalits) in their villages that started attacking Muslims along with outside Jats. The Dalits on their part corroborated the narration of Jats on the reasons for the outbreak of riots in Muzaffarnagar district and their villages, but were silent about their political orientation.

These changes are reflected in the response of Dalit respondents in all three villages, which suggest that equations between Dalits and Muslims are bitter, though the latter dislike the Jats, even more. As a corollary, the relationship between Jats and Dalits has significantly improved, though the change is instrumental and circumstantial. After the complete desertion of Muslims, Jats are facing an acute shortage of labour and the Dalits are now in constant demand. Besides, the legal cases in which both communities are accused as culprits by Muslim complainants, has created a sense of relative solidarity among them. Thus, the communal riots have impacted on the relationship between Dalit with Muslims and Jats differently; their equation with Jats has improved while in the case of Muslims, there is animosity.

On the question whether the riots were an attempt to segregate and ghettoize Muslims, the majority of the responses suggested that prima facie the riots were not started with this objective. However, there was definitely an element of revenge and imagined community pride against the Muslims. However, the hard fact remains that once riots took place, segregation and ghettoization of Muslims is the logical result of politics from both the quarters. The majority of Jat respondents opined that there is a possibility that some of the Muslims may return to their respective villages in the future. The state government had provided a sum of Rs 5 lakhs per family for reconstruction of their ancestral homes and many Jat respondents did state that after the riots they were in touch with the Muslims from their villages who were willing to come back to the village but were allegedly waiting for the money to be allotted to them. However, on further discussion, they did admit that the majority of the Muslims would never return back to their respective villages for a number of reasons.

First, there was a strong rumour that there was a conditionality attached that the Muslims who received the compensation would not return to their own villages. This rumour it was alleged was put forward by the Muslim community elites and leaders who have a vested interest in not letting the Muslims get back to their villages as in the relocated places they have emerged as a strong vote bank that can be consolidated and communally mobilized from Panchayat to national elections. Muslim leaders are also pointing out that if they returned to their ancestral villages the Jats would persuade/pressurize them to take back the cases filed against them. Second, a majority of the Muslims who have fled their villages happen to be either labourers or petty entrepreneurs who have no land left behind in their ancestral villages. Hence they have no strong incentive to come back to their villages as after getting the money they have got a house and some money to start their business afresh. In fact, almost two-thirds of Muslims have already sold their houses in their respective ancestral villages to the Jats which means they have little incentive to return. Finally, most of the Muslims who had fled their villages and got resettled in neighbouring Muslim-dominated villages, have started coming to their ancestral villages and could be seen as working as labourers in several capabilities. Thus, while the old interdependent relationship has been somewhat restored, the spatial separation has got entrenched.

In all the three villages no significant measure/effort was taken by the government to mediate peace between the Jats and Muslims. There have been many efforts by the community elders of the Jats to persuade and bring the Muslims back to their village and ensure peace. But all such efforts have been frustrated as the Muslims suspect that all these reconciliatory efforts are nothing but a ploy to convince them to take back cases against the Jats. This seems true as most Jat respondents held that they are ready to forgo the money that the Muslims had borrowed and to assure them of their safety in case they decide to return, except for the implicit conditionality of their taking back all the cases. As far as hostility against Muslims is concerned, it is in the air, in their opinion, in their articulation, and had it not been for the harsh legal measures by the government, they would not have bothered much about the situation of Muslims who have fled their respective villages. The efforts to buy peace are just an instrumental measure, part of a cold calculation rather than any change of heart or remorse on their part.

The strong feelings among the Jats that they have suffered during the riots while the SP government favoured the Muslims is visible in the

Figure 5.3 Angry Jat women in village Fugana armed with sticks and knives holding a protest demanding 'justice' from the government and the police who they held had wrongly arrested their menfolk for participating in the riots.

Source: Photograph by Ram Kumar, ex-Pradhan, 28 September 2013.

angry procession by Jat women against FIRs being registered and their menfolk being arrested and taken away from the village in Figure 5.3.

These feelings are visible in the overarching consensus among all the Hindu respondents that the financial compensation for the Muslims was disproportionately high, and the majority of them got 3 to 4 times more compensation than the actual number of members per family affected by employing fraudulent methods. The popular sentiment among the Jats, which was shared by the Dalits and upper castes, was that the state government has been disbursing the money among Muslims 'like water' with the avowed aim of appeasing them and garnering their votes. It was constantly pointed out that apart from the 5 lakhs compensation for displacement, money was generously disbursed for occasions like marriages. Also that the Muslims had received so much of relief material like pottery, blankets, and clothes that they roamed around the villages to sell them. Finally, when asked what should be done to ensure that riots do not take place again, the majority of Jats held that there should not be any political intervention and the police and local administration should be allowed to work on its own. Second, the government should treat all its citizens equally; a jibe at the alleged partisan role of the SP-led state government.

Questions regarding impact of the riots on political equations prior to the 2017 Assembly elections, received multi-layered and open-ended responses. Many respondents pointed to a strong anti-SP sentiment not only among the Jats but also Dalits and upper castes in the region. But while the younger Jats were inclined towards the BJP, some of the older Jats did not deny the possibility of considering the Lok Dal. Dalit respondents gave a double-layered response stating that they would choose between supporting the BJP and BSP, but one thing that they are clear about is 'not voting for Muslim candidates'. Hence, the BJP may not be the natural choice of Hindu voters in the region but the dominant fault-line would be on religious lines wherein the religion of candidate would matter more than caste in case one of the candidates happens to be a Muslim.

Thus, the challenge for a party like BSP would be to address the determination of its Dalit voters not to vote for a Muslim candidate. The dilemma would be either to field non-Muslim candidates and get the Dalit votes wherein it may lose support of willing Muslim voters, or field Muslim candidates and let a significant section of Dalit voters, otherwise supportive of the BSP on caste considerations, shift to the BJP. In short, the crux of the 2017 Assembly elections in western UP seems to be the twin possibility of 'caste' or 'religion' becoming the main pattern of mobilization at the constituency level. 'Caste' may emerge as a stronger factor if there is no Muslim candidate and BSP would have an edge, however, if either of the candidates happens to be a Muslim, irrespective of the party, it is more likely that support would be mobilized on religious lines and the BJP will have an edge in those constituencies. Thus, the challenge for the BSP would be to devise a strategy wherein it can secure maximum Muslim votes by fielding minimum Muslim candidates; a tough task by all measures.

Narratives from the Displaced Muslims in their New Villages

The third round of fieldwork in Muzaffarnagar was held between 6 February and 14 February 2016 with the aim to capture the narratives of the Muslims who have been displaced from Fugana village in district Muzaffarnagar and have settled in two villages, namely, Loi and Khampur. An attempt was made to capture the response of the riot-affected Muslims concerning the genesis of riots in their village, the role of Jats and other Hindus, the local administration, the state government, and most importantly its consequences on their relationship with Hindus, politically as well socially. Also, the political economy of the post-riot scenarios on their lives and a comparison of the same with the Jats was the main focus of the fieldwork. In sum, the contrast of narratives of the Muslims from the same village with that of Jats were intended to capture the changing Hindu–Muslim dynamics in Muzaffarnagar district in the aftermath of the 2013 riots.

The Muslims who fled from the Jat majority villages have settled in a newly constructed colony, Jamiat colony, in the Muslim-dominated village of Khampur. The colony was built by the Jamiat Ulema-e-Hind (Arshad Madni) with the cooperation of villagers led by the village head Saeed Ud Zama (ex-Village Pradhan and a member of District Panchayat) who gave land free, or at a very reasonable price. Our respondent, Firoz Sheikh (45) and his mother (Munni 75) narrated the unexpected and horrifying experience they went through on the morning of 8 September 2013. They recounted that they heard about the disturbances in the neighbouring areas due to the clashes between the Jats and Muslims, while the former were going and returning from the Mahapanchayat on 7 September. They also started getting calls from their relatives in other areas advising them to leave the village as a safety measure. While they were trying to decide whether to leave, some Jat villagers led by the former village Pradhan Harpal (around 50 years), an influential person in the village came and appealed to them not to leave as it would dent the village reputation and assured them of their safety. However, within about twenty minutes of the assurance, the Jats started attacking the Muslims; 7–8 were killed leading to panic as the Muslims tried to save themselves by locking doors and fleeing to the fields. The Jats killed all the Muslims they could lay their hands on and destroyed some of their property. Figure 5.4 shows that the mosque in the village was also vandalized.

In fact, Firoz alleges that the Jats in an internal meeting the previous night itself had decided to kill the Muslims. This means that the narrative by Firoz and Munni, which other respondents supported, contradicts statements made by the Jat respondents during the fieldwork

Figure 5.4 A mosque vandalized in Fugana village during the riots.

Source: Photograph by Ram Kumar, ex-Pradhan, 25 September 2013.

earlier in their villages. First, the claim by the Jats in Fugana village, that it was the Jats returning from 'other' villages who on the morning of 8 September, angry with Muslims attacking them on their way home, were the ones who killed the Muslims in their village. It indicated that it was Jats from the village itself that attacked, and also it was a pre-planned rather than spontaneous attack on the Muslims.

The respondents pointed out that what was even more disturbing was the lack of response when the Muslims called the local police station. It was only after Firoz and other villagers called Nahid Hasan, MLA Kairana in Shamli district and recounted their terrible experiences, that he gave them the mobile number of the DM, Muzaffarnagar who on being informed about their precarious situation intervened, and sent the police to the village. However, it is alleged that by the time police came it was 4pm and during the day many Muslim villagers had been killed or injured, all they could do was to take the dead bodies and injured out of the village. As the Jats grouped together and were agitated on the arrival of the police, the Muslims requested the DM once again, who realizing the hostile atmosphere in the village had them escorted the same night to Loi, the nearest Muslim village

Figure 5.5 Muslims leaving Fugana village with their belongings with the help of the police for the resettlement camps.

Source: Photograph by Ram Kumar, ex-Pradhan, 4 October 2013.

in the neighbourhood. Figure 5.5 shows Muslims leaving Fugana village with their belongings with the help of the police for the resettlement camps.

The respondents who were shifted to Loi and Khampur pointed out that for the first 4–5 days they were in a precarious condition as they did not receive any government help. They were dependent on the support of the Muslim villagers and community leaders whose support was very commendable, but whose capacity to help was limited. As more Muslim refugees began arriving in Loi village there was a serious crisis of food and shelter. Figure 5.6 shows the Muslim resettlement colony in Khampur established by the Jamiat leader Syed Arshad Madani in which even today living conditions remain very poor. It was only after the media started highlighting their plight that the administration came forward and in coordination with the community leaders and organizations like Jamiat Ulema-e-Hind (JUH) started sending help. But the overall situation, due to the poor response of the district administration and state government, remained precarious. Moreover, the Muslim respondents argued that the allegation by the Jats that they

Figure 5.6 The Muslim resettlement colony in Khampur established by the Jamiat leader, Syed Arshad Madani. Living conditions remain very poor but the Muslims do not want to return to their native villages.

Source: Photograph by Sajjan Kumar during fieldwork, 2 December 2016.

got sumptuous help from the government of Rs 5 lakhs per family along with other emoluments like money for marriages was not true as there was a strict background check by the administration with community leaders and organizations like JuH helping them. In addition, allegations of corruption were denied as the money was not paid in cash but was transferred to the recipients accounts. But respondents conceded that in some cases they paid back to villagers who had helped them in getting the compensation and had come to their rescue in the initial days. But it was completely voluntary and the number of such cases was few.

Social and Economic Impact of the Riots

The economic impact of the riots has been devastating on the families of the Muslim respondents and their livelihood. At the time of the fieldwork, they pointed out that the compensation money they received was over; the riot had brought many members under one roof, leaving the responsibility of earning mostly upon one person, making their day-to-day situation precarious. They held that rather than compensation, a job to each riot-affected family would have been better as it would allow them to take care of themselves. Community leaders and organizations like JuH are no longer concerned about their economic situation as they are resettled in a colony; though the rehabilitation is according to them, more like a makeshift arrangement. The respondents immediately began to look for new jobs and many had to resume their old farm work in the Jat villages, which is difficult and unpleasant. But they were very clear that this economic interaction with the Jats does not have the potential to translate into the social and political harmony of the old days. Further, the respondents pointed out that they had learnt to accept the fact that now their new Muslim neighbours are their 'new family' and they are learning to treat each other as their companions in any function or activity. On a negative note, it is resulting in ghettoization of the communities as the Muslims are now into a separate, demarcated space with no sharing of the same with the Hindus. Politically, the control of the Muslim leaders and organizations they realize is now complete. For instance, in Khampur, in the Jamiat Colony, visits by Jamiat Ulema-e-Hind leader, Arshad Madni and sermons about their victimhood and the help provided, was frequently recounted. Besides, local leaders like Saeed-Ud-Jama who has undoubtedly done extremely positive work will use them politically to further his political career against his old political rivals from the village.

Views on Role of Political Parties in Starting and Fanning the Riots

Both Jat and Muslim respondents in all the fieldwork sites, pointed to the BJP and the SP as the parties responsible for the deterioration of the communal situation, culminating in riots. There was a popular perception that along with the BJP which had political incentives in communalizing the region, the SP too wanted communal polarization and low-intensity incidents before the May 2014 elections with the aim of polarizing the Muslims and then emerging as their saviour. The SP also hoped to marginalize rivals like the BSP through this strategy, who were attempting to gain the Muslim vote. The SP strategy it was alleged was that such incidents should be administratively controlled and calibrated, but the orchestrated riots went out of proportion.

But apart from this stand on the role of parties in fomenting riots, predictably there were differences between the views of the Muslim and Jat respondents on the specific role played by the BJP and the SP. For the Muslims, the indifferent attitude of the state government when small but violent communal incidents took place and its decision not to prevent the 7 September Jat Mahapanchayat from taking place, despite the area being under CrPC 144, made the intention of the SP suspect. Many Muslim respondents suspected the involvement of SP leaders in the killing of Muslims during the riots such as, Mukesh Chaudhary, a Jat from Mukundpur 2 km from Qutba-Qutbi—whose own brother was allegedly involved in the murder of eight Muslims. The role of BJP leaders and other Hindutva outfits like the VHP in western UP and particularly in Muzaffarnagar–Shamli was also quite clear to the Muslim respondents. The issue of the so-called 'Love Jihad' had been vitiating the communal atmosphere in the region and BJP leaders had made this a major propaganda issue to mobilize people on their side. However, in the context of Muzaffarnagar riots, the BJP leaders, Hukum Singh (MLA and a Gujjar), Sangeet Som (MLA, a Jat), Sanjeev Balian (Vice President of the state BJP, a Jat), and Suresh Rana (MLA, a Thakur/Rajput) played an active role in communally polarizing the Jats by providing all kinds of support to them. In fact, it was the fake video of a Muslim mob lynching two youths shared by BJP leader Sangeet Som that went viral escalating communal polarization throughout the region. Besides, BJP leaders not only supported the Jats but actively participated in their Mahapanchayats and made provocative speeches. It was also reported that Nitin Gadkari had visited Kutba village (which happens to be the village of Sanjeev Balian, BJP leader) and a Panchayat was held.

The Jat respondents in the Jat-dominated villages, were categorical in blaming the SP as the party responsible for starting and fanning the riots. It was alleged that in its quest to secure the Muslim vote, the ruling party had given a free hand to the Muslims even before the Kanval incident. They blamed the SP of not only being openly partisan, but of deliberately vitiating the atmosphere by provocative steps like forcing the district administration to act in a prejudiced manner and not punishing the Muslim miscreants/accused during the riots, with the intention of getting their votes in the impending elections. The respondents argued that had the administration acted promptly and fairly in the aftermath of Kanval incident, the riots would not have taken place. They alleged it was a deliberate ploy on the part of SP leaders like Azam Khan that angered the Hindus in general and the Jats in particular. Some Hindu respondents accused SP leader Azam Khan of pressurizing the administration into arresting nine family members of Gaurav and Sachin for the murder of Shahnawaz at Kanval, while none were arrested initially from the Muslim side for the murder of the two Jat youth. The BSP and Ajit Singh's Lok Dal were criticized for not coming to the rescue of the Jat community and blamed for being mute spectators due to their desire for Muslim votes. Finally, during the discussion it became clear that as of now, there is a sense of disappointment and anger among the Jats against both the BJP and the SP. But it was much greater against the latter; their response to the former was multi-layered as all the respondents summarily rejected the charge that the BJP prepared the ground for the riots, even though, the majority of them accepted that the saffron party emerged as the natural beneficiary of the riots. The crux of their response was that the electoral benefit of the riots to the BJP was incidental and unintended, rather than the result of a well-orchestrated strategy.

On being asked whether they felt the BJP and the SP were working in tandem with each other, the Muslim respondents agreed. During the riots and even during the fieldwork, there were conspiracy theories and rumours circulating among our Muslim respondents that pointed to a mutual understanding between the BJP and SP. Many Muslim respondents held that there was a meeting in Delhi, somewhere in the Lodhi road area, between Amit Shah and Mulayam Singh Yadav's brothers Shivpal Yadav, Dharmendra Yadav, and Balram Yadav on 1 June 2013, regarding the 84 Kos Yatra planned by the VHP as well as one with Ashok Singhal. It is believed that some kind of understanding took place between them. On expected lines, all the Jat respondents answered in the negative. They singularly blamed the SP for spreading and fanning the communal riots. Nonetheless, a section of Jat youth in Lisadh and Fugana villages expressed their anger against the BJP for abandoning the community after winning the 2014 Lok Sabha elections and argued that all logistical and legal help came only from the Jat leaders belonging to the BJP, rather than from the BJP as a party. All respondents in the three villages did not think that the RSS was active during the riots. Almost all the respondents asserted that the Muzaffarnagar riots were orchestrated by political parties to gain either the Muslim or Hindu vote bank in the wake of the impending Lok Sabha elections. They supplemented this assertion by pointing out that had there been no election, the Kanval incident would have been handled much better and would have remained a local incident. In this respect, the responses of the Jat and Muslim community remain the same except for blaming different political parties and sets of leaders for the riots.

Role of the State Government, Local Administration, and the Police

The role of the state government, local administration, and the police has come under much criticism before, during and after the Muzaffarnagar riots from the media and reports by activists and scholars. The ruling SP leadership and administration failed to stop the small, low-intensity, but violent communal incidents which took place in UP from 2012 onwards, nor the major Muzaffarnagar riots in September 2013. The failure of the police and local administration to stem the rising communal tensions and the Muzaffarnagar riots has been attributed to the political leadership which did not allow the administrative machinery to perform their duties correctly. They were hampered and demoralized by the lack of support and clear direction from political leaders, making them at times spectators to violence; second, there were communal elements within the police and local administration. Additional director general of police Arun Kumar admitted to lapses: 'There may have been some administrative lapses and possibility of polarization behind communal incidents cannot be ruled out. But now we are more alert and taking all preventive measures,' he said (5 May 2013, *The Times of India*, web edition). The Kanval incident on 27 August 2013, a small incident between few youth, which finally precipitated the Muzaffarnagar riots, could have been better dealt with by the administration. The SP government allowed the Jats backed by the BJP to hold the Mahapanchayat on 31 August at the Bhartiya Inter College, Nangla Madaur which was attended by prominent BJP leaders from the region and created a communally charged atmosphere.

The local administration did not stop the Jats while coming and going back from the Mahapanchayat from deliberately passing through Muslim villages, leading to confrontation and killings. The riots eroded the moral authority of the state and its instruments—the police and local administration—among the minority community in UP. The report of a team in December, led by Mohan Rao and others which probed the riots and visited the camps set up in the aftermath of the riots, indicates that the Muslims lost confidence in the police and were disappointed that the SP, a party that which has traditionally enjoyed their support, failed to protect their life and property (Rao, Mishra, Singh, and Bajpai 2013). According to the report approximately 140 villages in Muzaffarnagar, Shamli, and Baghpat districts were affected by this riot (Rao et al. 2013). The report points out, 'The clashes reflect total breakdown of the governance. There is thorough communalization of the state machinery. The police and administration did little to prevent the violence ... The Administration talks of giving protection by RAF and PAC. PAC has historically been viewed as a communal force and it does not have any promising record of protecting Muslims during communal flare-ups' (Rao et al. 2013: 36, 38).

Nor did the state act immediately; the accused in the riots were issued a chargesheet by the Special Investigation Team (SIT) probing the riots almost two years later. BSP MP Kadir Rana, BSP MLA from Charthawal, Noor Saleem Rana, party MLA from Miranpur, Maulana Jamil, Congress leader Saeed-uz-Zama, his son Salman Saeed, city board member Asad Zama Ansari, ex-member of the city board Naushad Qureshi, trader Ahsan Qureshi, Sultan Mushir, and Naushad were ten persons chargesheeted by the SIT probing the Muzaffarnagar riots for provoking communal tension with inflammatory speeches during a Muslim community panchayat. The chargesheet was filed in the court of Chief Judicial Magistrate Narender Kumar by the SIT on 7 March 2014 in connection with the alleged hate speeches made in the Khalapar locality of the city on 30 August 2013 by the accused in defiance of prohibitory orders clamped following tension in Kanval village in the district (Web news, 8 March 2014, 'UP Riots: 10 Muslim Leaders Charge-sheeted by SIT'). In December 2014, Union Minister Sanjeev Baliyan, BJP MLA Sangeet Som, BJP MLA Suresh Rana, BJP MP Bhartendu Singh, and four others had surrendered in a court in UP in connection with the Muzaffarnagar riots. They and six other accused are facing charges for violating prohibitory orders, deterring public servants from discharging their duties, and also wrongful restraint. It is alleged that the accused participated in Nadala Mador Mahapanchayat meeting and incited violence through their speeches in the last week of August of 2013 (*The Times of India*, New Delhi, 10 December 2014).

The state administration has also failed to provide justice to those affected by the riots. Of the 6,400 persons accused of crimes in 534 FIRS, charges were pursued in only 1,540 (Mander 2016) Most of the cases of murder were closed without a chargesheet or trial claiming that the accused were 'unknown persons'. In the two episodes of killings in Kanval village that started the riots, the Muslim men accused of killing the Jat cousins Sachin and Gaurav were duly arrested and chargesheeted. In contrast, the police closed the case related to the murder of the Muslim boy Shahnawaz, claiming no one who had killed him was alive. The six accused Prahlad, Vishan, Devender, Jitendra, Yogender, and Ravinder were given a clean chit saying they were not found involved in the murder of Shahnawaz. However many eyewitnesses confirmed that the Jat cousins were accompanied by many other men who participated in the murder but escaped. Only three of the 25 accused in six gangrape cases have been held. In one rape case, all the accused men have been acquitted; in another, after three years no one has been arrested; and in the other rape cases, all the accused are out on bail (Mander 2016).

It was the Supreme Court that while hearing petitions in relation to the riots held the SP government in UP prima facie guilty of negligence in preventing the violence and ordered it to immediately arrest all those accused irrespective of their political affiliation. The court also blamed the central government for its failure to provide intelligence inputs to the Samajwadi Party-ruled state government in time to help sound alerts (Anand 2014). The court held that 'more effective and stringent measures are to be taken by the state administration' and issued several directions pertaining to compensation to victims, their rehabilitation, and a free and fair investigation. It reminded the state government of its responsibility 'to prevent such recurrence of communal violence in any part of the state' and held 'sincere efforts shall be made to apprehend all the accused irrespective of political affiliation and produce them before appropriate court'. Regarding the six rape cases reported from the camps, the court said the state government's special investigation cell should arrest the accused. It ordered an additional compensation of Rs 5 lakh to all rape victims, besides other rehabilitation assistance. To the relatives of those killed, the court asked the UP government to pay Rs 15 lakh each as compensation, beside adequate compensation to farmers who lost their source of livelihood such as tractors, cattle, and sugarcane crops. It also restrained the state government from recovering the amount given to people for settling in other places if they want to come back to where they lived before the riots (Anand 2014).

Regarding the role of the state during the riots, our sample respondents—both Jats and Muslims—in Muzaffarnagar town and in the sample villages, were critical and in some cases hostile to the local administration and the state government, though based on different perspectives. These views are significant as they reveal the poor opinion and complete lack of trust and confidence in the state and its instruments such as the police and local administration. What is particularly disturbing is that caste and religion played a role and the administration seemed to have taken sides in their actions during and after the riots. In fact, the respondents judged the actions of officers based on caste/religion and expected them to behave in a partisan manner if they belonged to the same community. Consequently both the Jats and Muslims felt they had been deprived of assistance, while the opposite side had been given the required attention and help at crucial times during the riots. The views of both groups also reflect the deep divide and antagonism towards each, which fuelled the riots.

The Muslim respondents interviewed in Muzaffarnagar town accused the local police personnel, that is, at the SHO level and the district administration particularly the DM of being partisan and biased towards the Hindus. The prime reason according to them was caste, as most police and administrative personnel are Jats. They point to many instances where it was the Jats involved in rioting who were allowed by the SHO to file an FIR in villages where they were dominant and many Muslims were killed. One example given was Samarpal Singh a Jat incharge of Bhopa police station in Muzaffarnagar. He is alleged to have refused to file many cases brought by Muslim victims and in fact, himself filed a FIR accusing the Muslims of attacking and killing the Jats on 7 September 2013 at Jolly village. In fact we have a copy of the FIR (FIR No- 249/13 dated 8.9.13 P.S. Bhopa) filed by Samarpal Singh, SHO, Bhopa Police Station in which he happens to be the complainant and has named many Muslims as the accused. At the district level, the Muslim respondents accused the then DM Surendra Singh, a Jat, of not only being partisan against the Muslims after the Kanval incident but also provoking the Jats: a claim that seemed slightly exaggerated. When asked to substantiate their claim they cited the instance that in 2013 out of a total of 35 'Gun-Licence[s]' that were allotted, 32 went to Jats. Singh was transferred in the aftermath of Kanval incident.

At another level, the Muslims allege the unfair arrest of many Muslims as they were named in the FIRs while the administration was lenient towards the Jats despite their violence many times on and around the occasion of Mahapanchayat. They also held that while the Muslims were prevented from holding their gathering to discuss the Kanval incident, the Jats were not prevented from organizing on the issue despite the imposition of curfew at that time. The Muslim respondents also expressed their unhappiness over the statement of the then DGP of UP, Devraj Nagar, when he was asked about the administration's response with regard to the proposed Mahapanchayat of Jats on 7 September 2013: 'Panchayat na Rokenge na Tokenge. Kanoon Haath me nahi lene denge.' (The administration will neither prevent nor intervene the happening of the Panchayat but won't let anyone take the law into his hands.)

However, he did not keep to his promise. Jats with arms were not prevented from attending the Mahapanchayat. Thus, there was a widespread feeling and some substance in the claim by the Muslims that the role of administration at local as well as district and state level, despite SP being in power, had been partisan.

A majority of the Jat interviewees in our three sample villages held that the local administration (DM) and local police (SSP) acted in a fair and prompt manner, while they described the role of the state government as being completely partisan and unfair. In the aftermath of the Kanval incident, the local authorities acted swiftly and took care of the persons involved. However, this non-partisan approach of the state, in their perspective, was shattered the moment the DM and SSP, Surinder Singh and Manjil Saini, were transferred within a day, allegedly at the behest of Azam Khan. Thereafter, in the narration of the Jats, the police, and local administration always played a partisan role at the behest of leaders of the SP and thereby ended up vitiating the communal atmosphere. To cite some of the examples narrated by the majority of the Jat respondents, while Muslims were given a free hand for any offence, the Jats were demonized by being falsely implicated in fake cases of rape, murder, and loot. To endorse their point, many of the Jat respondents claimed that being a proud community they can kill or get killed, but would never commit the act of rape in their own village as mentioned in various FIRs. Similarly, many logical anomalies were pointed out such as Muslim families with below poverty line (BPL) status filing cases of loot and arson against Jats and claiming loss of gold and silver jewellery. Similarly, it was alleged that Muslims were forcibly taken out of the villages in police control room (PCR) vans on the instructions of SP leaders. Thus, seen from the perspective of Jats, the state administration did not do much to put down the riot; rather they contributed in encouraging it by acting in a completely partisan manner.

In contrast, the Jats praised the role of some local political leaders (MLAs and MPs) who also happened to be Jats, such as Sanjeev Baliyan, Sangeet Som, Suresh Rana, and Hukum Singh for their support to community members. It is noteworthy that with regard to the role of these local leaders, the issue was not whether they took any measure to mitigate the communal tension, but whether they stood by the community the same way that Muslim leaders backed the Muslim cause. The openly provocative role of these leaders reflected by their speeches in Mahapanchayats, was described as a morale booster for the once-proud but now wounded Jat community. The role of these leaders was especially appreciated for providing logistic help to the community against the 'conspiracy' of the state government and Muslim politicians. The role of the local MP and MLA was highly provocative but from the vantage point of Jats they emerged as the saviours of the community.

The Camps

After the riots, thousands of Muslims were shifted to make-shift camps at various villages or areas dominated by Muslims in the district where the maintenance was pathetic and it was upto civil society organizations and Muslim religious organizations to take whatever care possible.[13] The Muslims also held that the Samajvadi government ensured that after compensation was given no one would be allowed to remain in the respective camps. It was alleged that Mulayam Singh went to the extent of stating that after compensation those staying in the camps would be criminals who wanted to grab government land. The National Human Rights Commission (NHRC), which did a survey, reported on 22 October 2013 that seven deaths had occurred in the Loi relief camp and organizers at Malakpur camp in Shamli district admitted that eight babies died. In Joula camp out of 30 deliveries in the camp three babies had died (*The Indian Express* 2013).

The Muslim respondents, both in Khampur and Loi village, ruled out any possibility of ever returning to their respective village, namely, Fugana. A major reason is deep distrust and fear of the Jats who—despite being their own villagers and neighbours—had fatally attacked them in a pre-planned manner. Hence, the alleged assurances by the Jats of guaranteeing their safety do not impress them. They see a ploy behind the appeal by the Jats that they may be pressurized to withdraw cases and upon refusal to do so, may be harassed again. They alleged that the Jat villagers looted their belongings and some photos that we showed them, of Muslim villagers taking away their belongings from their homes, were claimed to be true, but it was pointed out that the

[13] Some of the villages mentioned by the Muslim respondents who were running the relief camps were Bassi Kalan, Shikarpur, Jolly, Purwaliyan, Sher Nagar, Khampur, Roodkali, Bhandura, and Bhalwa.

articles were nothing but insignificant items such as straw for cooking. They held that whatever valuables they had were not in the photos, as the killers had already looted them.

Three years after the riots, the Aman Biradari and Afkar Foundation undertook a comprehensive survey of the persons displaced by the riots. Their report titled *Living Apart* found that even after three years the large majority of the refugees who fled their villages remain 'exiled permanently' from their native villages, painfully rebuilding their lives in small makeshift colonies (Mander et al. 2016; also see Mander 2016). The survey points out that at least 75,000 persons had fled and taken refuge in Muslim-dominated villages. Without any public remorse by their attackers, any official or community initiatives for reconciliation, and any attempt at justice these persons are unable to return to their native villages.

The survey reports that with small grants from the government or NGOs, but mainly with usurious loans from private moneylenders, they have bought house-plots in hastily laid out colonies in Muslim-majority villages in what were cultivated fields. Seizing the opportunity to make windfall profits, local large farmers and real estate developers sold these plots at exorbitant rates to the displaced persons (Mander et al. 2016). The indifference of the state government is also reflected in the fact that there is no official record of these mostly self-settled colonies and no effort to provide them access to basic public goods and citizenship entitlements. The survey discovered 65 refugee colonies, 28 in Muzaffarnagar and 37 in Shamli housing 29,328 residents. However, this does not cover countless refugees who bought houses, settled in already existing Muslim settlements, or migrated out of these districts, or even the state. The survey estimates that the mass communal violence led to at least 50,000 people permanently expelled from their villages, of which 30,000 were found living in the new refugee colonies (Mander et al. 2016).

The survey points to poor conditions and the almost complete absence of the state from these colonies apart from the initial compensation amount of Rs 5 lakhs. The displaced were forced to abandon or sell at throwaway prices their properties in their native villages, which makes the state compensation negligible. Much of the support came from Muslim organizations or from the Sadbhavna Trust which assisted 230 households to design their houses and choose their neighbours in

Apna Ghar colony; the CPI(M) gave one lakh to each displaced household in Ekta Nagar. Muslim charities collected money from overseas for a few colonies but often charged the refugees for their land and houses. Often the support came with strings attached such as adoption of more orthodox beliefs or refusing to give land titles to the buyers. In 41 of the 65 colonies, households are still unable to build houses and live in makeshift structures with plastic roofs and temporary walls. In the others with grants, personal labour but also loans from private moneylenders, they have been able to build all-weather brick houses though these are small and modest. The developers rarely invested in drinking water, sewerage, drainage, or electricity and the district administration at most installed a hand-pump. They lack basic amenities; in Muzaffarnagar 82 per cent colonies do not have clean drinking water, 93 per cent no street lighting, 61 per cent no drainage, and not a single colony has a public toilet. In Shamli, 97 per cent colonies lack drinking water, 76 per cent streetlights, 70 per cent drainage, and 97 per cent colonies have no public toilets. Education and childcare services are very poor. More than half the colonies in Muzaffarnagar and two-thirds in Shamli have no primary school within a kilometre of the colony. Less than a quarter have Integrated Child Development Services Scheme (ICDS) centres and none of the people have Mahatma Gandhi National Rural Employment Guarantee Act (MNREGA) job cards in any of the colonies. In Muzaffarnagar in 27 out of 29 colonies, no one has a ration card and in both districts virtually no one gets old age, widow, or disability pension (Mander et al. 2016).

Thus, what we are seeing is the emergence of a 'new-normal' (D. Gupta 2011) in inter-community relationships between the Jats and the Muslims after the riots. The precarious situation that the Muslim victims are located in at present and the lack of alternative employment available, has pushed them to re-establish 'economic relations' with the very people responsible for killing their brethren, but they have insulated themselves from social and political interaction with them. While it may seem normal that they are going to work in their erstwhile villages or among the Jat community, an important shift has occurred. The Muslims prefer their ghettoized social life separate from the Jats on account of the horrible memories of the riots. Hence, it is getting back to a normal that is qualitatively different from the one prior to the riots. The Jat perspective contains a completely different set of propositions and assumptions about the causality of the Muzaffarnagar riots and their implications for the future.

* * *

Our fieldwork narratives suggest that the Muzaffarnagar riots, one of the largest and extremely violent riots in recent decades in UP, was the result of three major elements. First, planned and sustained construction of communal divides based on the ideology of Hindutva through mobilization by the cadres of the BJP–RSS in the region over a period of time and more actively prior to the 2014 elections. Second, changing socio-economic relations between the Hindus particularly the Jats and the Muslims which made them vulnerable to attempts at communal polarization. Third, complicity on the part of the ruling party the SP and the negligence of instruments of the state under it to check the growing communal incidents leading to the horrendous riots in September 2013.

There is considerable evidence to indicate that the riots were organized and engineered by the BJP–RSS with their local leaders and cadres who were active on the ground in the region since the early 2000s. The entry of Narendra Modi and his aide Amit Shah laid the basis for a second stage in the communal polarization that was already being attempted in order to build a strong and inclusive Hindu vote bank and win the 2014 elections. As the BJP had no issue comparable to the RJBBM to create large communal riots throughout the state, it decided to create small incidents that kept communal tension simmering between the majority and minority community alive. This made the communal divide deeper, rendered the Muslim community the 'other', and eventually led to the Muzaffarnagar riots.

The SP leadership played a complicit role in that it made little or no effort to put down the growing communal tension and small incidents, which led to the more violent riots. As the 2014 elections were approaching the leadership believed that the prevailing communal atmosphere would enable them to gain the support of the frightened Muslim community and win seats, a ploy that proved wrong. The strategy of a calibrated and low-intensity, creeping communalism could not be maintained by the BJP or the SP and the latter failed to control the outbreak of a large-scale riot. Some of our respondents pointed out that there was an implicit understanding between the two parties and they worked in tandem with each other between 2011 and 2013.

Certain features of the Muzaffarnagar riots make them different from earlier ones in UP suggesting the use of new methods to create a permanent divide between the majority and minority community. Communal mobilization around small but divisive issues were fanned and kept alive to create a deep divide between two communities that had peacefully lived side-by-side for many decades. The idea was to create constant communal tension, so that over time at the appropriate moment a riot could be created. Western UP is a comparatively developed region in the state and the fast spread of urbanization has linked towns to villages enabling the easy spread of communal ideas and incidents into the villages. Rapid social change in the villages, namely, the rise of new social classes, increase in literacy, aspiration for professional employment, and better lifestyles particularly among the younger generation in both communities, has made them amenable to the spread of communal thinking and attitudes.

At the same time, the western districts provided a fertile area for the experiment by the BJP for a number of important reasons. The long-term decline in agriculture, including the sugar industry in the 2000s hurt the Jats who, as a landowning community, have not been quick to move to non-agricultural jobs for which there is considerable competition. Western UP, despite some progress compared to the rest of the state, remains a backward region with little industry or professional opportunities. In contrast, within the Muslim community, which traditionally held little land, a new social class had emerged that had taken to non-agricultural jobs including small-scale businesses. This created the strong perception among the Jats—fanned by the local BJP cadres—that the Muslims who until recently were agricultural labourers on their fields had become well off. As our fieldwork shows, many Muslim entrepreneurs had borrowed money from the big Jat landowners to finance their fledgling enterprises, which they now find difficult to return. This was accompanied by the notion—also encouraged by the BJP cadres—that Muslim youth had become successful, wore good clothes, and carried the latest mobiles to attract Hindu girls who then eloped with them. The riots, as we have seen, were precipitated by an incident of eve teasing, news of which spread on social media in the district causing tension.

Our fieldwork also suggests that major riots are not possible without the connivance of the state and the party in power. From 2012 onwards, a number of low-intensity communal incidents were happening which the ruling SP did little to stop. What is more disturbing is the role of the police both before and during the riots; under the control of the SP, they did little to maintain law and order and put down the riots with a firm hand. If the small incidents earlier had been controlled the Muzaffarnagar riots could have been prevented. Nor has the SP punished the guilty, which has created the feeling that rioters from the majority community can get away with wrongdoing which has spread distress among the Muslim community, a section of which has refused to return to their native villages. Finally the refugee camps set up by the government have made the Muslim community unhappy as they are of poor quality, the compensation low and the government has been putting pressure on them to return to their villages which they find difficult.

The Muzaffarnagar riots have impacted social relations between the Jats and Muslims and earlier political equations in western UP. While the clash during the RJBBM period affected the close ties that existed earlier between the two communities the alliance had not completely broken down. The Muzaffarnagar riots have created hostility, which is still evident during fieldwork in our sample villages almost three years after the riots. The 'new normal' (D. Gupta 2011) which has emerged is limited to the economic sphere with some Muslims returning to work on the fields of the Jats, but social intercourse is avoided. In the political arena, the riots signalled the end of Jat dominance in western UP. Their earlier prominence as a political force was contingent upon their alliance with the Muslims from the late 1960s under the leadership of Charan Singh. It was possible due to the symbiotic relationship that both the communities enjoyed in the region wherein both were part of the farming community with Jats being the landowning class and Muslims mainly the labourers. Today, a Jat–Muslim alliance seems impossible; nor can the Jats align with the Dalits due to social factors. This leaves them with no option but to support the BJP, which will accommodate them, but not give them the dominant position they used to enjoy earlier, which in turn could mean the end of Jat politics in this region.

Finally, the ground situation in our selected districts of Muzaffarnagar and Shamli is still tense despite the absence of communal riots for the last two years. The ongoing legal cases related to the Muzaffarnagar riots by the Jats and Muslims against each other, and the logistical support by political parties to the victims will ensure longevity of the communal voting pattern into the 2017 UP assembly elections. The success of the Hindutva experiment in changing the form of communal tension lies in making them dispersed rather than spectacular, extending them to rural areas rather than just urban spaces. It is done in such a stealthy manner that on the classical and old parameters of communal riots, it becomes difficult to point out whether, the low-intensity communal tensions whose spread is much larger, could actually be considered a communal phenomenon or not, especially, when the death toll may be comparatively low. What is more threatening are the phenomena of normalization of anti-Muslim prejudice and a sense of common justification of violence against them.

Conclusion

Uttar Pradesh, a politically important state within the Indian Union, has experienced communalism and many incidents of Hindu–Muslim riots in the colonial period and in post-Independence India. In the immediate post-Independence period, the state witnessed, despite Partition and the riots that accompanied it, relative communal harmony, the gradual emergence of a composite culture, and building of bridges between the Hindu and Muslim communities. This was possible due to the liberal legacy of the national movement, existence of a nationalist leadership, and the adoption of a democratic constitution that addressed the needs of a diverse social and religious society. However, this period proved short-lived, riots reappeared in the 1960s and 1970s and more important the RJBBM movement, the destruction of the Babri Masjid in 1992, and the riots that followed shook the country. Following the destruction of the Masjid the BJP entered into long-term decline for almost two decades.

The resurgence of communal tension and riots in the 2000s marks a new chapter in UP society. Our study has explored the reasons underlying the reappearance of communalism and riots in the state after a long period. It shows that communalism and riots in the 2000s are taking place in a post-Congress, post-Ayodhya polity in a different social and political setting; the ideology, methods, and strategies by which it is pursued has been substantially different from earlier episodes. The reasons lie in both the momentous developments that have taken place in UP society, and the changes that have taken place within a 'new' BJP in terms of its leadership, outlook, and manner of functioning.

Our study argues that there are fundamental differences in the two rounds of communalism and severe riots in UP in the post-independence period, which can be described as major turning points for its society and polity. The first was in the late 1980s to early 1990s around the RJBBM dispute, and second, major riots in the 2000s in some districts of eastern and western UP. The RJBBM mobilization was based on history, mythology, faith, and culture and was planned as a large-scale, highly visible, participative movement, using a Rath Yatra to appeal to mainly upper-caste Hindus across UP and the country. It delved into cultural reserves and historical memories to create militant Hindu assertion. The aim was to install Hindutva as a powerful, religious, and right-wing political ideology and tool for building a Hindu nation. In the debate that ensued on the RJBBM movement many scholars argued that communalism in India was the result of deep, communal fault lines from the past which could be awakened from time to time to create Hindu–Muslim riots. It led to heightened communal feelings, evoked a passionate response from large sections and created a Hindu vote bank across north India, which enabled the BJP to capture power in UP in the 1991 assembly elections and later at the centre in 1999.

However, the BJP leadership found that once the Masjid was destroyed, the emotional upheaval and fervour associated with the RJBBM movement weakened and there was peace in UP during the 1990s. Although the movement created deep polarization between the two communities and was socially a deeply disturbing episode, in terms of politics it proved to be a short-lived phenomenon, the issue reached electoral exhaustion very fast. By the early 2000s, particularly following the poor performance of the BJP in the 2002 UP assembly and the 2004 national elections, it was felt that Muslims had ceased to be afraid of the BJP and UP was witnessing the beginnings of an autonomous Muslim politics for the first time.

In contrast, our study has shown that from the early 2000s onwards the BJP—more aggressively since the emergence of a new generation leadership under Narendra Modi—has adopted a new Hindutva strategy of 'institutionalization of everyday communalism' that is qualitatively different from the earlier RJBBM period. It underlies the revival of the BJP and the political ascendancy of the party in UP and on the national scene. This model in our study forms a common thread that runs through both the selected regions of eastern and western UP, and provides a theoretical tool to analyse the rise of communalism and riots in the state. Based on our model and fieldwork data, we now try to draw some conclusions regarding the new form of communalism that we are witnessing in contemporary UP and its implications for our democracy.

I

Everyday communalism exhibits new features and employs innovative methods that has changed the practices through which communalism was traditionally manufactured and practised in UP. The sites in which this strategy has been used in UP in the 2000s are different from those in the immediate post-independence period or during the RJBBM movement. The earlier sites of communal disturbances were places where Muslims had established their artisanal and other businesses during the colonial period and in some cases managed to prosper in the post-independence period, such as Moradabad, Firozabad, Azamgarh, and Agra. The clash in such places was with Hindu traders who after independence were keen to take over these businesses or to control them. Some towns in UP were also traditional sites of communal clashes from the colonial period onwards such as Meerut, Kanpur, and Ayodhya.

In contrast, our study shows that in both eastern and western UP the districts of Mau, Gorakhpur, Muzaffarnagar, and Shamli where riots have taken place in the 2000s, are not areas where major communal clashes have occurred earlier; rather Hindus and Muslims have lived here side–by-side harmoniously over a long period. New sites have been consciously selected by the BJP leadership where it was felt that assertions, anxieties, and conflicts were emerging over issues such as a growing agrarian crisis and fall in income in a once-prosperous region, emergence of mafia dons, rise of a class of frustrated, educated but unemployed youth, increasing cultural conflict over religious practices, decline in local industry due to globalization, etc. Or, areas of visible incipient conflict between Hindu and Muslim communities as in western UP where conflicts could be engineered between the Jats and Muslims prior to the Muzaffarnagar riots, or Yadavs, Dalits, and Muslims in eastern UP in recent years. This strategy of moving to new areas has provided fertile ground required for the success of the experiment of everyday communalism. It has enabled the BJP to spread its social network at the grass roots and its electoral support into newer areas where it had earlier found penetration difficult. These areas are in regions where parties such as the Congress, SP, and BSP and smaller ones such as the RLD had a stronghold.

However, the defining feature of the institutionalization of everyday communalism in these new, selected areas is that the relationship between communalism and riots has undergone a fundamental shift in the contemporary period. The 2000s have witnessed a combination of quiet communalism and low-intensity incidents, a steady rise in 'communalism without communal riots'. Riots no longer promote communalism; rather it is the steady and long-term work at the grass roots among the common people by the right-wing forces that promotes the growth of constant, everyday, communal tensions and polarization, which only at times spills over into big and violent riots. The BJP has attempted a slow, but persistent, almost creeping communalization of society and polity and of Hindu–Muslim relations, over a long period. By recruiting local leaders in various regions of UP the party has created extensive networks in civil society for this purpose. The aim is to communalize small, trivial, daily incidents and based on them small, low-intensity, controlled, and calibrated incidents which promote the growth of a communal ideology of hatred and its spread within the population. It is a deliberately and carefully planned approach, a quiet revolution to bring fundamental change in the relations between the majority and minority community. Consequently, we are seeing a series of small communal incidents that have changed the nature of communal disturbances from being spectacular to low intensity, episodic to frequent, and from being urban-centric to rural. While in eastern UP this process is largely witnessed in the towns, in western UP, a more developed region with greater communication between urban and rural areas, villages have also been the location of such mobilization, witnessed in the fact that many were the epicentre of the Muzaffarnagar riots in 2013.

Consequently, certain regions in UP have become the experimental laboratories of Hindutva where it has introduced a successful social revolution in urban areas and villages. The attempt is to establish majoritarian rule and ascendancy of right-wing ideology and politics over the hearts and mind of the people particularly the Hindu community. A strategy by the BJP–RSS that has been highly successful is to identify local grievances or problems, whether real or alleged of the Hindus and use them to create a feeling of victimhood while portraying the Muslims as being 'appeased' by parties like the Congress, SP, and BSP. The aim is to assimilate the Muslims into Hindu cultural values and norms through banning of beef, cow protection, and use of nationalism as a unifying tool; to create suspicion, alienation, and antagonism and make the Muslim the 'other' in the eyes of the Hindu community. It is in keeping with the counter argument by some scholars that in post-independence India, communalism in UP and elsewhere in the country does not merely draw on past memories, but is the result of steady, hard work by the right-wing forces to introduce change in the 'public culture' to bring it in line with the Hindutva way of thinking. In this way, an incremental increase in social divides at the grass roots has been underway since the early 2000s that went unnoticed by most observers until recently, and which has proved highly successful.

The effort to institutionalize everyday communalism has left its mark in the 'new normal' that today defines the relationship between the Hindu and Muslim community. This is visible in our selected districts in eastern and western UP in everyday intercourse between the two communities and in the voting pattern in elections. In eastern UP, it has affected the relationship between the Muslim Ansari weavers and Hindu traders in Mau; both continue to ply their business but remain wary of each other. There is also less social interaction during Hindu and Muslim festivals compared to the past. In Gorakhpur over the years, there is a changed perception about the Math among the Muslims in the city. In both towns, the relationship between Dalits and Muslims has undergone much change; there is suspicion and antagonism compared to the past. In western UP, the relationship between Jats and Muslims has undergone much greater change; the scars of the 2013 riots remain. Most Muslims even four years after the riots have not returned to their native villages and remain in poorly built, ghettoized, resettlement colonies; some out of economic necessity have returned to work on the fields of the Jats. A section of the Jats has bought properties left behind by their Muslim neighbours, which has worsened the relationship. Everywhere painful memories remain, which makes a return to the past impossible and future relationships highly uncertain.

The new strategy has also harnessed changes in the political economy and related cultural realms in UP society and polity that have created social jealousies and economic anxieties due to factors such as agrarian decline, lack of development, emergence of a class of educated unemployed, globalization, and decline of the artisanal industry. Hence, the 2000s have experienced a political economy of communalism; the interface between the politics of unequal development and everyday communalism has made the populace vulnerable to mobilization and the spread of communal discourse and frequent clashes. This sustained communal polarization without needing a communal riot that UP has witnessed since the early 2000s, marks a new shift in the nature of communal praxis. It is evident in policies of communal surveillance, politicizing and normalizing the everyday lives of the people along implicit religious identitarian lines, bringing under purview their food, cultural preferences, mingling with other communities, gender relations, and so on.

Our fieldwork suggests that these efforts to institutionalize everyday communalism described above have been attempted over a number of stages. The first was an early experimental phase beginning around 2002 following the Gujarat riots, which picked up in 2004 after the defeat of the BJP in the national elections and in 2009 under a new BJP leadership. This witnessed quiet work on the ground by selected local leaders mostly belonging to the RSS, who were able to establish themselves and the ideology of Hindutva within the Hindu community. This low-key, silent strategy, proved to be politically more convenient and manageable and was carried out by the affiliates of the Sangh Parivar such as the HYV and various kinds of Senas set up in parts of UP, without the top leadership being involved.

The second stage, which was not so quiet, was the long and divisive electoral campaign beginning almost two years prior to the 2014 national elections that provided an opportunity to deepen social divides between the majority and minority community. The strategy of everyday communalism was deftly linked to electoral politics as the social networks established earlier, were used to create Hindu vote banks to capture state power and establish majoritarian rule. There was also use of social media on a large scale to spread the Hindutva message. The long-term strategy has provided rich electoral dividends to the BJP, which has been able to establish itself in many regions of UP, something that it could not achieve earlier.

The excellent performance of the BJP in UP in the 2014 national elections, which contributed to an absolute majority and the capture of power at the centre, has inaugurated a third phase of introducing cultural change through methods such as Love Jihad, cow vigilantism, the alleged Hindu exodus in Kairana, and the beef ban, etc. This has been carried out by the so-called 'fringe elements' of the Sangh Parivar such as the HYV, Bajrang Dal, cow vigilante groups, and others who in more recent years have moved gradually into mainstream politics becoming more powerful. Everyday communalism remains an ongoing exercise at the grass roots, though after the victory in the 2014 elections and a BJP government in power at the centre, it is now much more open and well known.

Leadership has played a central role in the success of the new strategy of constructing everyday communalism. The innovative strategies and tactics employed have been taken forward by the new generation leadership, which has emerged within the BJP in the 2000s replacing the original founders of the party—Atal Behari Vajpayee and Lal Krishna Advani. The new leaders, Narendra Modi and Amit Shah, his close aide from Gujarat who was appointed the President of the BJP, and their supporters in the party with the help of the RSS, have been the architects who have both revived the party organization on the ground and honed and sharpened this strategy. These leaders are the product of developments that the country has experienced in the 1990s such as globalization leading to the rise of a consumerist middle class and an aspirational subaltern class in UP and understands the need to introduce a change in the ideas, techniques, and strategies that need to be used today. Narendra Modi and his supporters in the party were convinced that the retreat from the principles of Hindutva during the Vajpayee regime was responsible for the decline of the party in UP and its defeat in the national elections of 2004 and 2009. They felt that without first mobilizing on the ground in urban and rural areas in UP to create a strong Hindu vote bank, it was not possible to capture power in UP, other states in the Hindi heartland, or at the centre. They were able to skilfully use the mobilization in the early 2000s begun by the RSS and its affiliates at the grass roots, for the electoral campaign of the 2014 national elections, creating an unprecedented victory; understanding the changes taking place in UP they shaped suitable strategies.

In sum, the aim of the BJP is both political and cultural. To capture state power, establish a majoritarian democracy, and introduce cultural change in society and thereby create a strong Hindu Rashtra. The goals remain the same as during the RJBBM phase, but the strategy in terms of both ideology and methods employed keeping in mind changes in UP society and polity, have undergone a manifest change.

II

Another key feature of everyday communalism that underlies its success and requires separate discussion, is the subalternization of Hindutva. In contrast to the RJBBM period, mobilization in the 2000s has not been limited to the upper castes, but attempts in various ways to reconstruct Hindu identity, making it more socially inclusive in order to draw the backward castes and Dalits into the Hindutva fold. First is the re-invention of the Hindutva ideology to include along with Hindu nationalism, an agenda of rapid economic development in UP and the country to create a proud and prosperous Hindu nation respected in the comity of nations. This has particularly appealed in a backward state like UP where aspirations and hopes of a newly educated, younger generation particularly among the poor and backward sections are not being met. Second, in its mobilization the BJP has employed a strategy of 'non-Brahmin Hindutva' which is more inclusive of all sections of the population particularly the lower castes/classes and is different from the upper-caste variety traditionally associated with the RSS. These carefully crafted strategies and tactics proved useful because of changes that were sweeping over UP by the late 1990s.

While identity politics espoused by the SP and BSP promising self-respect and dignity played a central role in the 1990s, the 2000s witnessed a waning of politics based on primordial identities creating space for a desire for development. Globalization and economic reform created a new consumerist and aspirational middle class initially in the early 1990s among the better off castes/classes who expected faster economic development. They felt that states such as Maharashtra and Gujarat had been able to make good use of the opportunities liberalization offered, while states such as UP were left behind. By the end of the decade these ideas spread to the lower castes/classes and there was a feeling that the social justice parties—the SP and BSP—who had enjoyed power for almost a decade in UP, had failed to meet the expectations of their constituencies, namely, the backward and lower castes.

The SP despite its roots in the socialist ideas of Ram Manohar Lohia was not able to use Mandal to create a homogeneous, united, backward caste community under its aegis. By the late 1990s, it came to be identified as a Yadav party with little apart from rhetoric to offer to the large number of OBCs in the state. The non-Yadav OBCs feel under-represented in the SP leading to jealousy, making them open to align with anyone who pampered them and made them feel represented. Further, poor governance, lack of an agenda of development, breakdown of law and order during the SP regime, and finally its failure to prevent the riots in Mau and Gorakhpur in eastern UP and Muzaffarnagar and Shamli in western UP in the 2000s led to unhappiness. Both the Hindus and sections of the Muslims who formed part of its core support base were unhappy. The BSP, which began as a radical anti-upper-caste party, attempted to join hands with the Brahmins prior to the 2007 elections in order to capture power. However, while in power it found it difficult to cater to the social and material aspirations and needs of both the Dalits and the Brahmins, angering the powerful Jatavs among the Dalits. Disappointment on the part of the lower castes with these parties provided space for the resurgence of the BJP in the 2000s. Consequently, in the new discourse of the BJP, Hindutva and development came to be seen as two sides of the same coin.

These ideological shifts were paralleled by a move to bring, as part of the non-Brahminical Hindutva strategy, the subaltern castes into the BJP fold in UP. The promotion of this variety of Hindutva is visible not only in UP but in states in the Hindi heartland and others such as Gujarat, Karnataka, and Andhra Pradesh. In states where the BJP is in power, the leadership has been from the non-Brahmin rising OBCs, the exception being Maharashtra. In UP even during the Ram Temple movement in the early 1990s the party promoted backward caste leaders such as Kalyan Singh and Rajnath Singh. However, during the 2000s a more concerted effort, as part of the strategy of everyday communalism, has been made to make the lower castes a part of the BJP. Politically this has brought them rich dividends as these leaders have been supported electorally by their communities, contributing to the victory of the BJP.

Despite the fact that the lower castes are attracted to the promises of economic development made by the new leadership, the shift towards the BJP cannot be explained as a purely instrumental move to improve their economic position. Mobilization of the lower castes based on the strategy of non-Brahminical Hindutva has been successful because affected by the process of modernity these groups are attracted by the idea of being associated with an upper-caste Hindu party. For many castes who until recently were counted among the Shudra such as the Jats, OBCs, and MBCs, the experience of being included in the 'Hindu' fold has been a powerful and 'fascinating' attraction. The process of grass roots everyday mobilization has specifically targeted these groups using a process of Hinduization by co-opting their past heroes, struggles and victories, good examples being the use of figures in the epic Ramayana to display their proximity to the upper-caste Hindus. A mix of history, mythology, culture, and politics has been part of the dissemination of the new Hindutva ideology.

Further, for many groups such as the Jats and OBCs experiencing the feeling of being 'Hindu' is needed during a period when their dominance is being questioned by an upsurge from below by the Dalits whom they have considered as standing below the line of pollution and therefore inferior. In western UP it is also driven by a perception among the Jats that the Muslims with whom in the past they had political ties, have taken to new non-agricultural occupations and their younger generation has stolen a march over them. The strident demand for reservation is also driven by such perceptions. This is witnessed in the shift of many Jat, OBC, and Dalit leaders towards the BJP prior to the 2014 elections. While earlier they identified and challenged the upper castes as the 'other' who were to be opposed, today the attempt by the BJP is to create a unified, single 'other' for all Hindus, the Muslim.

Thus, success of the new Hindutva strategy of everyday communalism among the subaltern groups lies partly in the desire for being 'Hindu' and partly in the desire for more rapid development which would improve their economic position, providing them opportunities to catch up with the better-off castes/classes. The new BJP leadership has been able to understand and harness the rising desire for cultural and economic upward mobility among the subalterns. The process of subalternization of Hindutva is primarily interplay of the active agency, cultural and political aspirations of the Hindu subalterns and the democratic compulsion of the Hindutva discourse. Thus, the new communalism that UP has witnessed since the early 2000s, cannot be understood by applying old analytical frameworks as the spatial flow, low-key intensity, frequency, and the social base of communal discourse has changed in accordance with the corresponding change in the society.

III

Analysis, based on extensive field study, of how construction of every-day communalism is taking place in our two selected regions of eastern and western UP teaches us that the prevailing socio-economic and political context determines to a great extent the manner in which com-munalism is constructed and operates. It provides an understanding of the strategies of mobilization used in different regions of the state with varying degrees of success. Field studies in various parts of UP and the country could provide a rich understanding of how communal forces are working and their impact.

Eastern and western UP, which have emerged as new sites for con-structing everyday communalism, are different in terms of their history, social composition, landowning patterns, past patterns of mobiliza-tion, and levels of economic development. Beginning in the early 2000s it was first in eastern UP that an attempt was made to begin a sustained effort at everyday communalism at the grass roots among the Hindu communities to gain their support and to create deep-seated polarization between them and the Muslim community. Our fieldwork shows that eastern UP being a poor and backward region, with few amenities, opportunities, and absence of governance has been more vulnerable and was more easily mobilized by the BJP. The failure by political parties that have dominated this region—the left parties in the immediate post-independence period, the Congress party during its heyday of dominance upto the late 1980s, and in the 1990s the SP and the BSP—to provide social and economic upliftment to the poorer lower castes has left them unhappy and dissatisfied. Globalization and the decline of the handloom weaving industry across eastern UP further created despondency, leaving them highly vulnerable to cultural mobi-lization. In Mau, this is visible in the celebration of religious festivals of the Hindus and Muslims, which have become sites for communal conflict, though it is the underlying economic relations that are the driving factors. In Gorakhpur, the national BJP leadership, aware of the socio-economic changes in the city, has tolerated the creation of an autonomous political and cultural empire under Yogi Adityanath in the east since the late 1990s. Thus, though political economy is of vital importance for the local populace, cultural identification has gradually become significant due to constant overtures, suggestions, and everyday mobilization over time.

The popularity of the Gorakhnath Math and its Mahant Yogi Adityanath, stems from his success in removing the earlier oppressive Brahmin mafia and creating parallel, but authoritarian and tightly controlled governance structures to meet the urgent but daily needs of the people, which have been ignored by state governments, including in vital areas such as roads, education, and healthcare. At the same time, under him the Gorakhnath peeth has moved from a radical, non-upper caste, religious organization that provided space to Muslim yogis and Dalits, to a purely Hindu organization in which the lower castes/classes have been given much space and the Muslim made into the outsider. The HYV consists largely of the lower backwards, which has given them a voice, creating anxiety in the minds of the Muslims. Adityanath is feared due to his involvement in many communal conflicts including the Mau and Gorakhpur riots, but he has a Robin Hood, welfarist image, which has made him a popular Hindu icon in the region. This has enabled the BJP to penetrate into the region, creating communal divides, and taking over the electoral base of the SP and the BSP, which was strong in the 1990s.

In contrast, our field study in western UP, a historically more developed region with a prosperous, Hindu particularly Jat agricultural community, suggests that it has until recently been far less amenable to everyday communal mobilization. Traditionally Jats constituted a dominant, confident, self-conscious, and often oppressive community with landed assets, who considered themselves as standing much above the backwards and the Dalits. Good agriculturists, the colonial policy of introducing commercial agriculture and recruiting them in the army, forged a strong occupational and class-based identity among them as hardworking, honest farmers or army men; cultural identity took a secondary position. Moreover, their identity as 'Hindu' was forged by the Arya Samaj a non-Brahminical, reformist Hindu body, which provided them the ideals of a simple, rustic, and rational way of life.

It is the deepening agrarian crisis since the late 1980s, which has made agriculture no longer profitable that has destroyed their livelihood and way of life, making the Jats amenable to the communal overtures of the BJP first in the early 1990s, but to a much greater extent in the 2000s. The loss of their strong occupational identity and the self-assurance it provided them vis-à-vis other Hindu castes such as the OBC and Dalits and particularly the Muslims, provided space for the emergence of cultural identity. Due to the changed circumstances, everyday mobilization in targeted villages by local BJP cadres broke the Jat–Muslim social and political alliance, creating hostility between the two communities leading eventually to the violent riots in 2013. This also explains their demand for reservations, which they feel will help them obtain non-agricultural jobs, resume their earlier way of life, and recoup the losses arising out of the agrarian crisis. These shifts have particularly affected the younger generation of Jats making them hostile to the younger generation of Muslims who they perceive as doing better than them, an idea fanned by the BJP using the familiar rhetoric of appeasement. The BJP has successfully invoked among the Jats the notion of 'Hindu pride'; it is no longer the class identity but cultural identification with a larger Hindu upper-caste community that has become important for the Jats. In the 2000s, the BJP has been successful in prioritizing culture over class and the economy, despite growing economic distress in both regions.

IV

At the same time, an important reason for the success of the communal agenda of the BJP–RSS is the growing institutional and systemic weaknesses in the UP polity that have come to the fore in the 2000s. The decline and decay of political parties has meant that the state has suffered from the politics of 'competitive communalism'. The Congress party during the Nehruvian period propagated and supported secular politics, attempted to protect the life and liberty of the Muslim community, and prevent communal politics, though it was not always successful. However, under the leadership of Indira Gandhi, during the 1980s the party shifted to the right after the formation of the BJP. Both under Indira and Rajiv Gandhi the party began to practice 'soft Hindutva' to cater to the Muslim community and meet the challenge of the new right-wing forces. Rajiv Gandhi's actions on the Shah Bano judgement, allowing of the Kar Seva at Ayodhya, and most important opening of the locks of the Babri Masjid provided the BJP ample opportunity to mobilize the Hindus around the RJBBM dispute. In addition, the Congress party, which was in power at the centre when the Babri Masjid was destroyed by a mob on 6 December 1992, did not take any action.

Similarly, the SP and the BSP in the early 1990s were deemed to be secular parties who opposed the Ram Temple movement and were able to gain the support of the Muslims and lower castes. They joined hands to defeat and 'contain' the BJP in the 1993 assembly elections. Mulayam Singh Yadav opposed the Rath Yatra led by L.K. Advani and earned the title of 'Maulana' Mulayam. Observers argued that while the upper castes in UP supported the BJP, the backwards and the Dalits under the leadership of their respective parties were secular in their outlook. However, the collapse during the decade of the 1990s of the liberal ideology and political parties representing it such as the Congress, SP, and the BSP; the decay and hollowing out of these parties and the resulting inability to address the needs of the people, have made them irrelevant in the present scenario, which has weakened the democratic system.

While the BJP has been blamed for the communal disturbances in UP, the SP cannot be fully absolved. It was in power during all the major riots in UP during the 2000s and indulged in competitive communalism for narrow political gains. A large number of small communal incidents took place between 2011 and 2013 prior to the Muzaffarnagar riots when it was in power in UP. The SP government led by Akhilesh Yadav did not take action as it hoped that due to the rising communal tension the Muslim community would support it in the 2014 national elections. Nor did it prevent the Muzaffarnagar riots or provide adequate shelter and help to the Muslims who fled their villages. Few of the accused in the riots have been punished.

The BSP has been the only party in UP during whose regime there have been no communal riots. However, it has been out of power since 2012 and performed poorly in the 2014 national elections losing some of its support base to the BJP. This means opposition to the BJP during the 2000s has been very weak allowing it to pursue its communal agenda without much hindrance. It has been quick to occupy the vacuum arising out of the lack of a credible opposition party, group, or leader. Civil society too in UP has not thrown up forces that could counter the slow inroads of communal ideas among the populace; in fact, the cadres of the BJP–RSS have come to occupy the civil society space through penetration at the grass roots.

The complicity of the state in UP in the 2000s and its instruments such as the police and the local administration, have allowed riots to happen and to persist over a number of days. Communal bias on the part of the police and political control over its actions by the party in power has made it ineffective in performing its basic task of protecting the citizenry. This was true in the Mau riots in which violence against Muslims and targeted looting of their shops and business establishments continued for three days without firm action by the police. In Gorakhpur, the police could not take action against Yogi Adityanath and his supporters during the 2009 riots due to the intervention of the SP government headed by Mulayam Singh Yadav. The Muzaffarnagar and Shamli riots would not have happened if the initial small incidents from 2011 onwards and the Kanval incident had been dealt with firmly. Politicians visit the site of the riots much later and make promises to the riot affected and of improving the police force, which are rarely followed up. During our fieldwork, many respondents pointed to bias on the part of the police in dealing with riots, siding with the majority community and not acting in time or protecting those against whom the pogrom was happening. Communal riots can be described as part of the larger breakdown of the law and order machinery of the state and the lack of political will on the part of the political class to control communal forces and not use them for political advantage. Thus, communalism is the product of the collapse of state institutions in UP; whichever party has been in power has used the instruments of the state for its own ends.

V

Our study suggests that the extensive grass roots mobilization carried out by the BJP–RSS in UP during the 2000s, based on the goal of institutionalizing everyday communalism has the potential of creating far deeper and more sustained divisions between the Hindu and Muslim communities compared to earlier rounds of communal mobilization since independence. While communal riots earlier disturbed equations between communities, they were episodic and it was possible to reach a new normal once peace had returned. The institutionalized riot system described by Paul Brass was used to create big riots, but once the conflict was over, it disappeared until the next time. In contrast, the new communal discourse is ever present, aimed at a slow, pervasive and gradual communalization of society and polity over a number of stages. First, institutionalization of everyday communalism using petty, banal incidents to create suspicion, divisions, and boundaries between communities. Second, these are used to gain support and capture state power and carry the process further by communalizing the institutions and the machinery of the state. Third, to introduce cultural change within society 'from above' employing state power to create a Hindu nation in which the minority community has to conform to the values and customs of the majority. The grass roots mobilization in the early 2000s in parts of UP and the communal campaign combined with promises of rapid development in UP prior to the 2014 national elections, helped provide the BJP a majority at the centre, making its goal of introduction of societal and cultural change possible.

A process of democratic secularization—though slow and halting— had begun in UP and in post-independence India, particularly during the Nehruvian period and was in place despite periodic communal disturbances. Under it, a process of slow integration of the Muslim community into the political mainstream had made some progress; this process is no longer visible today. The establishment of a majoritarian democracy has replaced it, where the Muslim minority is viewed as less equal to the Hindu majority, as second-class citizens; a 'we' and 'they' culture is developing. There has been a move from 'soft Hindutva' to 'hard' aggressive, muscular, and impatient Hindutva, which is narrow, dogmatic, and authoritarian in its worldview. Further, the attempt to subalternalize and put into place a non-Brahminical Hindutva means that a large section of society is under the influence of the right-wing forces. This is seen not only in the electoral support that this section has provided to the BJP, but also the lack of any critical response on their part when an attack is made on the minority community by cow vigilantes or other groups.

UP with its divisive communal past, economic backwardness, pervasive social inequalities, continuing conservative outlook, and entrenched caste and communal identities has produced a specific variant of, or type of, communalism that is different from that found in other states. It has a capacity of creating much greater and permanent divides than in the past because the BJP has obtained an absolute majority both at the centre and in UP. The new strategy of everyday mobilization has made UP into a perpetual, communal cauldron from which there seems little escape at present. Our analysis of everyday communalism and riots in the contemporary period points to a deep-seated crisis of liberalism in UP and the country that is not being addressed. While liberal parties have collapsed, the left parties are unable to understand the crisis emerging out of the cultural politics of our time as their worldview has always been fixed on material aspects and they are not able to understand or deal with the cultural ascendancy of the Hindutva forces. What we are witnessing is the spreading saffronization of both society and the state in UP. Under BJP rule, this process is gradually spreading to other parts of the country. It is not a passing phase but is going to continue affecting the democratic fabric of state and society not only in UP, but the country.

Epilogue

The long and often divisive electoral campaign for the UP assembly election 2017, and the continuation of many small, violent communal incidents, despite the massive victory and the formation of a majority government by the BJP, illustrates both the success and continuation of our model of 'institutionalization of everyday communalism' in the state. In this epilogue, we discuss the meaning of the electoral results and the formation of a government headed by Hindutva icon Yogi Adityanath as the chief minister, and the continuing role of communalism in the everyday politics of UP. We argue that the BJP leadership has been building a new 'Hindutva social coalition' consisting of the upper castes, but which importantly gives primacy to large sections of the OBC and Dalit since the early 2000s, evident in the results of the 2014 national elections and the recent 2017 UP assembly elections. Our epilogue is divided in two parts. The first will briefly describe the 2017 election results to understand the massive victory of the BJP. The second will examine the continuing trajectory of everyday communalism in UP since the Narendra Modi government took office in 2014, in the run up to the 2017 elections, and after the appointment of Yogi Adityanath as the chief minister of UP on 19 March 2017.

The 2017 Assembly Elections

In the UP assembly elections whose results were declared on 11 March 2017, the BJP gained an overwhelming three-quarter majority obtaining 315 seats out of 403 and 39.7 per cent of the votes cast; its allies winning another 13 seats. The massive sweep of the BJP is visible in the poor showing of the opposition: the SP gained 47 seats, the BSP 19, while the Congress was reduced to just seven, the RLD to one and independents to three seats. The SP and BSP retained 21.8 per cent and 22.2 per cent of votes, respectively, but could not translate them into seats. The share of Muslim seats was the lowest since 1991; only 11 sitting Muslim MLAs were re-elected. The BJP did not give a ticket to a single Muslim even though they constitute over 19 per cent of the population and over 30 per cent in quite a few districts of western UP. The SP and BSP gave a large number of tickets to Muslim candidates, but the votes cast for them were divided between candidates of these parties (Election Commission of India 2017).

A recent study of the elections results shows that the largest number of successful BJP candidates belong to the upper castes. The new assembly consists of 44.3 per cent upper-caste MLAs, 12 per cent more than in 2012. The share of BJP MLAs is 48.2 per cent of the upper castes, 23 per cent of the non-Yadav OBC and two-thirds of the non-Jatav MLAs. The return to power of the BJP it is argued, has been accompanied by a resurgence of support by the upper castes as the BJP gave 48.6 per cent of its tickets to upper caste candidates (Vernier 2017). However, the more important question, relevant for our study, is who voted for the upper-caste candidates? The upper castes constitute just 22 per cent of the population of UP and therefore require the support of other castes to be elected in large numbers. In contrast, the OBCs constitute 35–40 per cent of the population, the Yadavs are the largest, but are barely 8 per cent in the 200-odd non-Yadav OBCs;[1] the Dalits make up 21.2 per cent of the population (Census 2011) of which the Jatavs consist of 10.3 per cent.

An analysis of the profile of voters who voted for the BJP given in Table E.1 shows that in the 2017 assembly elections the BJP obtained as much as 66.1 per cent of the votes cast for upper castes. The party could gain only 9.7 per cent of the Yadav and 9.4 per cent of the Jatav Dalit votes. However, the party obtained 56.5 per cent of the Kurmi–Koeri, 59.7 per cent of the other OBCs and 38.9 per cent of the non-Jatav votes. In short, without the support of the subaltern castes the party could not have gained a massive victory.

[1] UP has the highest OBC population in all Indian states (*PTI* 2007).

Table E.1   Percentage of Votes Cast By Various Castes for BJP
in UP Election 2017 Post Poll

Caste/Community	Vote Percentage 2017
Upper Caste	66.1
Yadav	9.7
Kurmi + Koeri	56.5
Other OBCs	59.7
Jatav Dalits	9.4
Non-Jatav Dalits	38.9
Muslims	8.9
Others	41.7

Source: Centre for the Study of Developing Societies, National
Election Study, Uttar Pradesh Post Poll 2017.

Further, it is noteworthy that despite large number of upper caste BJP candidates winning elections since the 1990s in UP, the party has always appointed non-Brahmin Chief Ministers—Kalyan Singh, a Lodh, and Rajnath Singh and Yogi Adityanath, both Thakurs. Similarly, many of the top party office bearers have also been selected from the non-upper caste groups such as, Babu Singh Kushwaha, Om Prakash Rajbhar, Vijay Kumar Kashyap, and Sakshi Maharaj. By selecting Dinesh Sharma, a Brahmin and Keshav Prasad Maurya, an OBC as the two Deputy Chief Ministers, the party leadership has tried to balance the aspirations of different castes.

The success of the strategy to institutionalize everyday communalism and thereby create a broad-based Hindu vote bank is visible in the electoral results in our selected districts. In Muzaffarnagar district, the site of the 2013 riots, the BJP won handsomely in all the six assembly constituencies, in Shamli it won in two constituencies out of three in the district, the highly contested constituency of Kairana described a little later, was won by the SP. In Gorakhpur a large district, out of ten constituencies the BJP swept in nine, one by a narrow margin was won by the BSP. In Mau, out of four constituencies the BJP won in three,

---

[2] UP has the highest OBC population in all Indian states, *PTI*, 7 May 2007, as mentioned in ToI, http://timesofindia.indiatimes.com/india/UP-has-the-highest-OBC-population-in-all-Indian-states/articleshow/2012439.cms, Accessed on 18 May 2017.

Mukhtar Ansari won the fourth on a BSP ticket (*PTI* 2007). These are districts where in the 1990s the BJP did not have a strong base. In western UP, it was the RLD or SP, which won; eastern UP was the stronghold of the SP and BSP after the decline of the Congress.

The results of the 2017 assembly elections point to the massive support base that the BJP has been able to build among the lower castes in UP without whose support it could not win an election; it also enables the party to win an election with very little support from the Muslim community. We argue that two reasons underlie the resurgence of the party in UP of which the recent elections are a mirror reflection. The use of everyday communalism since the early 2000s which enabled it to create a strong Hindu, upper caste/class base, and second, the adoption of the strategy of non-Brahmin Hindutva to widen its social base to gain the support of the backwards and Dalits.

Widening of the Base: From Social Justice to Aspiration

The massive victory of the BJP in the 2017 elections can be understood as part of the larger shift in UP from the 'politics of social justice to aspiration' of the lower castes in the 2000s. The 1990s were a period when primordial identities based on caste and community were important. The decade witnessed the rise of political consciousness among the backwards and the Dalits who, as upwardly mobile groups, challenged the position of the upper castes in society, demanding social justice. They SP and the BSP, respectively, mobilized them, leading to these parties dominating the politics of the state, a period when the BJP was in decline. However, the 2000s witnessed two interrelated changes: the weakening of identity politics and return of the agenda of development based on hope and aspiration; second the decline of the SP and BSP, which provided space for the revival of the BJP and its strategy of mobilization of the lower castes.

The BJP has taken advantage of both these changes casting its net wide, beyond its upper-caste clientele to create a more socially inclusive, 'non-Brahminical Hindutva' to include those so far excluded. This inclusive strategy was used during the 2017 electoral campaign to attract the backwards using a two-fold campaign strategy of development and communal mobilization. UP is a backward state and Narendra Modi's campaign promise of bringing in development raised the hopes and aspirations of the backwards and Dalits. The failure of the SP and the BSP to provide development during their period of dominance in the 1990s has given tremendous space to the BJP. Modi packaged development for the lower castes as something denied by earlier governments. Added to this, Modi's ingenious twisting of demonetization into a class issue, which would extract black money from the rich, made him the supporter of the poor. Moreover, the BJP under Narendra Modi particularly targeted the non-Yadav OBCs and non-Jatav Dalit groups who the SP and the BSP neglected, it was felt, as against their core constituents. Thus, during the 2017 election campaign it was the promises of development made by Modi in speeches during numerous rallies across the state, prior to all the seven phases of the election, that greatly contributed to the massive victory of the BJP in UP.

The promise of development has particularly attracted the most backward groups whose expectations have been roused and who are today an upwardly mobile group frustrated with the lack of development. Among OBCs, it is the Kurmis whose representation has increased the most; they make up 29 per cent of the OBCs in the present UP assembly (*PTI* 2017). The lower OBCs—Nishads, Mallahs, Malis, Baghels, and so forth—still remain underrepresented. However, this is because they consist of many small groups, the votes get divided among them and each gains only a modest amount. The Suheldev Bharatiya Samaj party won on three reserved seats; on the fourth a Rajbhar (MBC) candidate was elected. The Apna Dal (Soneylal) won three reserved seats and on the other two seats, upper-caste candidates won, while a Brahmin candidate gained the lone seat won by the Nishad party (Vernier 2017).

At the same time, though the issue of development was given great importance initially, during the 2017 campaign, a communally divisive agenda was also used by Modi and Amit Shah. While the BJP did revive older issues such as the Ram Mandir, what created much more impact were Modi's controversial, communal remarks such as the references to both *Kabristan* (graveyards) and *Shamshan* (cremation grounds) being built in Muslim and Hindu villages, respectively, and of availability of power in areas populated by both communities to avoid discrimination (*The Indian Express* 2017a). These words were aimed not so much against Muslims, but to consolidate its upper caste but more particularly, the new, lower-caste, Hindutva vote bank. The strategy paid rich dividends: the Jats and non-Jatav Dalits in western UP, and the non-Yadav OBCs and non-Jatav Dalits in eastern UP voted for the BJP. The backwards and Dalits are also attracted by the idea of becoming a part of a 'Maha Hindu identity'. It is noteworthy that the backwards, including the Jats, have recently emerged from the ranks of Shudra. Both these groups who have been oppressed and discriminated against by the upper castes and feel marginalized, are happy at being included by the BJP, which they view as a Hindu party.

A Hindu Icon as Chief Minister

Having achieved a huge majority, the BJP appointed Yogi Adityanath, Hindu icon and Mahant of the Gorakhnath Math in eastern UP, as the Chief Minister on 19 March 2017. While observers were surprised, his selection is part of the Hindutva strategy of the BJP–RSS. Yogi Adityanath has successfully used two major strategies of the BJP in the 2000s. Institutionalizing everyday communalism at the grass roots and propagating subaltern Hindutva. These strategies aim not at creating large riots, but to make Hindutva gradually acceptable in the eyes of the common man and render the Muslim as the 'other', in which the Yogi has been successful through long-term mobilization, patronage, and work among the people in eastern UP. His Janata durbars—at which even Muslims make requests—to resolve everyday problems of the people, have given him a popular Robin Hood image as protector of the middle and lower castes, including the business community. Further, being a non-Brahmin, he has been able to carry out these tasks easily. The RSS has found him very successful in these ventures and making him Chief Minister sends a message to the people and the party workers about the goals of the BJP.

Further, the Yogi has a love–hate relationship with the BJP leadership as he established himself as an independent power centre in eastern UP with a distinct form of Hindutva, through which he has gained dominance over the region and increasingly party workers, many of whom also come from the subaltern castes. By making him Chief Minister the BJP hopes to 'contain and control' the Yogi and yet use him to consolidate its hold over the rising, upwardly mobile (Pai 2017), non-Brahmin elite which is visible today in UP and within the party. In addition, the party leadership has tried to show that the

agenda of economic development is not lost, by designating two deputy Chief Ministers who are expected to concentrate on developmental
programmes leaving the Chief Minister free to pursue the Hindutva
agenda. Moreover, it is expected that the PMO and senior bureaucrats
in Delhi will tightly control the government. Yogi Adityanath, in his
first interaction with the media, held that he will follow PM Modi's
'Sabka Saath, Sabka Vikas' agenda and work towards development and
'good governance'.

The Continuing Trajectory of Everyday Communalism

Following the formation of a majority government at the centre under
Narendra Modi in 2014 it was felt that the BJP would concentrate on
fulfilling its promises of development made during the campaign that
had contributed to its victory. But, a number of incidents showed that
having gained power an agenda of communal polarization and introducing cultural change assumed importance: 'Love Jihad', 'ghar wapsi',
cow vigilantism, the Rohit Vemula case, the Una incident, the attempt
to bring change in educational institutions, branding institutions and
individuals anti-national, and various attempts to show Muslims as the
'other' within Indian society, etc. A common feature in all these incidents since 2014 is the involvement of local BJP workers/leaders or so-
called 'fringe' groups of the Sangh Parivar, which is increasingly moving
into mainstream politics. The top leadership has remained quiet apart
from reiterating, from time to time, that such groups would be punished, which has not deterred them. This is a convenient arrangement
that leaves the former free to pursue the development policy agenda,
while the fringe groups perform their task of creating constant communal tension, antagonism against, and fear among Muslims in UP
(Daruwalla 2017).

Politics of Everyday Communalism Prior to the 2017 Elections

The strategy of everyday communalism to create communal divides
continued in the run-up to the 2017 assembly elections evident in a
growing number of incidents: the beef ban, *gau rakshak* groups, the
Dadri lynching incident, the alleged Kairana 'exodus', etc. Two incidents described below should suffice to illustrate this. The Kairana

incident is an example of an attempt to create communal tension over local issues to create a broad vote bank inclusive of all sections of the Hindus, to marginalize the Muslim community, and win the 2017 assembly election in the town. It also points to the involvement of local BJP leaders in the attempt to create communal divides in places where the two communities have lived peacefully. On the other hand, the Dadri lynching case involving the allegation of cow slaughter and beef being eaten demonstrates the attempt to create prejudice against Muslims and to push them to adhere to values and traditions of the majority community, in this case, not to slaughter cows or eat beef. Western UP was the region where such incidents were staged, as it was feared that the Jats who were unhappy over not being granted reservations would shift back their votes from the BJP to the RLD, SP, or BSP. The latter parties were also aggressively campaigning in order to take advantage of the frustration of the Jats.

In June 2016, BJP Lok Sabha Member of Parliament from Kairana, Hukum Singh, released a list of 346 members of Hindu families that, according to him, had allegedly fled this town in Shamli district of western UP, fearing persecution and atrocities at the hands of Muslim criminals and extortionists. It is noteworthy that Singh is an accused in the 2013 Muzaffarnagar violence (Pankul Sharma 2016). The issue of 'exodus of Hindus' from Kairana assumed importance in the media as it became linked to the 2013 Muzaffarnagar riots, as some Muslim families had fled from their native villages to the town. It became an important campaign issue for the BJP and was given prominence in its election manifesto in which the party promised to stem this migratory tide if voted to power. BJP President Amit Shah called the allegations of a Hindu exodus an 'eye opener' at a public rally in Allahabad, and later cautioned 'UP should not take Kairana lightly'. Aligarh's BJP MP Satish Gautam declared that there is a need to find out about 'other Kairanas'. Union Home Minister, Rajnath Singh held that the SP government was not taking action and Hindus were suffering (*PTI* 2016). The party also cleverly transformed the issue into a mission to save Hindu women's dignity.

The issue became highly divisive and communal when the complaint of 'forced exodus' was investigated by the National Human Rights Commission in response to a complaint filed by Monica Arora, a Supreme Court advocate and active member of the BJP. As a study argues, the report of the Commission on 21 September 2016, surprisingly claimed that the allegations were 'serious' and that several Hindu families had 'migrated' from Kairana because of the 'increase in crime' and 'deterioration' of the law-and-order situation after victims of the Muzaffarnagar riots settled there (Zoya Hasan 2016). Hasan points out that the report provided no substantive authentication of its controversial findings: no details of the time frame or total number of Muslim families that settled there, or Hindu families that left or reasons behind their decision to do so; or that the demography of the town had undergone change or of deterioration of law and order (Zoya Hasan 2016).

Based on an enquiry by the Shamli district administration, a UP Home Department spokesman said that 188 of 346 families mentioned in the list had left over five years ago. In addition, 66 families had left Kairana 10 years ago; 60 families were living elsewhere for reasons relating to education, employment, health, or others, and 28 families mentioned in the list were still residing in Kairana. Most people in the area said that the prevailing lawlessness in Kairana had misleadingly been painted in a religious light ahead of the 2017 assembly polls. In the light of these findings, Hukum Singh tried to retract and explain his position claiming that perhaps the number of those who left Kairana was less. In fact, his eldest daughter Mriganka Singh, a political novice, was contesting the assembly seat and it seemed the issue was created to gain Hindu votes for her. However, she lost the election against the sitting SP MLA, Nahid Hasan, which shows that the issue was manufactured to create communal polarization ahead of the elections (Ali 2016).

The Dadri incident is an instance of cow vigilantism which post-2014 has become common in UP. On 28 September 2015, in village Bisara near Dadri a small town in western UP, a mob of villagers attacked the home of a Muslim, Mohammed Ikhlaq at night with sticks and bricks. They accused him of stealing and slaughtering a cow calf that night (*The Indian Express* 2015a). The villagers seized some meat found in the refrigerator, though the family insisted it was mutton. The Ikhlaq family had lived in the village for several generations and not faced a problem. Their neighbours tried to stop the mob, but by the time the police arrived, Ikhlaq was dead and his son Danish seriously injured (*Deccan Herald* 2015).

The incident created deep divides within the village. The police registered FIRs and arrested eight persons on 1 October based on the testimony of the family members, of serious charges of rioting with deadly weapons and murder, among others. Chief Minister Akhilesh Yadav gave an ex-gratia of Rs 2,000,000 and police protection, but the family preferred to shift to Delhi on 6 October. The involvement of the local BJP was alleged when on 3 October, Vishal the son of BJP leader, Sanjay Rana, was arrested in connection to the case (*The Hindu* 2015). However, local villagers protested against the arrest, set fire to vehicles, and vandalized shops, one person was injured and the police had to fire in the air to disperse them (*The Indian Express* 2015b). While Union Home Minister Rajnath Singh promised strict action, another Minister Mahesh Sharma termed it 'an unfortunate accident' and BJP leader Sakshi Maharaj criticized the ex-gratia amount and said that if a Hindu had been killed his family would have received much less (*Zee News* 2015). The PM initially maintained silence; later during a speech on 15 October 2015 he termed the incident *dukhad* (saddening) but held that the centre could not be blamed.

Finally, feeling they would not get justice, in December 2015 the relatives of Mohammad Akhlaq met Chief Minister Akhilesh Yadav and expressing satisfaction on the monetary support, requested him to close all further inquiries into the case. Despite this, on 9 June 2016 a judicial magistrate at the Surajpur district court issued a direction on a petition filed by a Bisara resident against murdered Mohammad Ikhlaq and his kin for alleged cow slaughter. On the night of 28 September, police had collected a sample of the meat from Akhlaq's house in Bisara and sent it for laboratory testing and a top government official had claimed that it was mutton.[3] However, later the petitioner to the Surajpur district court based his plea on a report by a forensic lab in Mathura that a meat sample taken from the site of the attack belonged to 'a cow or its progeny'. The fact that the meat found in Akhlaq's home was mutton or beef has no bearing on the crime of lynching, but it has led to polarization in the village and trouble for the family from which they are finding little respite. They find it difficult to reside in Bisara their ancestral village any longer.

[3] http://timesofindia.indiatimes.com/india/Dadri-lynching-Meat-in-Akhlaqs-fridge-was-mutton-not beef/articleshow/49280525.cms.

Communal Polarization after Victory in 2017

Following the victory of the BJP in the UP assembly elections, the newly appointed Chief Minister Yogi Adityanath in a speech promised that 'development of all, appeasement of none' was his government's policy, adding that there would be no discrimination on the basis of caste, religion, and gender (*Hindustan Times* 2017). However, a perusal of the first three months of the working of the new government suggests it has not kept to his promise on these counts. The government has found it difficult to control gau rakshaks particularly the HYV often leading to violence, and its anti-Romeo squads proved counter-productive and had to be dispersed. Second, the attempt to polarize communities continues to be visible both in communal incidents that have taken place and in divisive policies pursued by the new government. Two incidents in Saharanpur provide a good example of the former, and the ban on 'illegal' slaughterhouses in UP, the latter.

Since the new government assumed office, the number of communal incidents, big and small, in which aggressive HYV workers wearing saffron scarves are involved have increased. The HYV, which describes itself as a social and cultural organization formed by Yogi Adityanath in 2002, was earlier confined to Gorakhpur and adjoining districts, but after the victory of the BJP in 2017, it has spread all over the state. When Yogi took over as CM there was a record surge in applications for joining the organization—from an average of 500–1,000 every month to about 5,000 per day (Lalmani Verma 2017). The Vahini has also become more independent and assertive, and it is alleged, is no longer under the control of the Yogi. Even during the campaign there were internal differences leading Yogi Adityanath to dismiss its State President Sunil Singh who wanted to put up candidates against the BJP. In March, a circular issued from HYV headquarters said that the background of those applying would be carefully checked and those joining would be given a post in the organization only after working as an ordinary worker for six months (Lalmani Verma 2017).

The growing number of incidents involving the HYV it is reported, has created differences between Yogi Adityanath and the RSS (Lalmani Verma 2017).The latter has conveyed to Yogi Adityanath its reservations regarding the HYV, cautioning that it has become a 'parallel' organization to the BJP–RSS cadres that signals rampant indiscipline. RSS leaders point to the growing criticism from opposition parties and the media and are worried about the impact this would have on the image of the government as the BJP has returned to power after 15 years. Consequently, in March Yogi held separate meetings in Gorakhpur with the HYV and the RSS and reportedly urged the former to maintain 'decency', not to misbehave with any officer, or misuse saffron the party colour, and instead concentrate on monitoring government work (Lalmani Verma 2017).

Similarly, the anti-Romeo squads consisting of police officials that were aimed at protecting women against eve teasing and stalking proved very unpopular with the younger generation. Disliked as a form of moral policing and harassment of young couples who wished to spend time together, the squads were criticized as working outside the law, had little impact on women's security, and had to be disbanded (*TNN* 2017).

A number of violent incidents in western UP show that the new government has not been able to effectively manage and handle the administration and the police, and proved unsuccessful in maintaining law and order. This is evident in the constant transfers of senior officers in the police and district administration in Saharanpur. Saharanpur district in western UP recently experienced two violent clashes both due to attempts to hold processions to honour caste/community icons: Dalit–Muslim conflict took place on 20 April 2017 at village Sadak Dudhali due to an Ambedkar Shobha Yatra taken out by a Dalit group; and second, a Rajput–Dalit clash on 5 May 2017 at village Shabbirpur arising out of a Maharana Pratap Shobha Yatra by Rajputs (Pai and Kumar 2017). These incidents need to be understood against the background of sociopolitical changes in recent years within communities in the district.

The Chamar Dalits in the two villages and in Jatav Nagar in Saharanpur city are divided into BJP-affiliated and pro-BSP Dalits (Pai and Kumar 2017). The former are largely the younger group attracted by the BJP; many Dalit organizations working separately, have further divided the community. In Sadak Dudhali the Gada (lower caste) Muslims who form roughly 80 per cent of the village have traditionally shared space with the Dalits leading to cooperation and confrontation. But the advent of non-Brahmin Hindutva, which pitched the latter against the former, has communalized the petty confrontations, which underlie the recent clashes. These divides are not new, having developed over time evident in an earlier Dalit–Muslim clash in 2006 when Dalits of the village were prevented by the Muslims from taking out a procession of Saint Ravidas, which triggered a protest across Saharanpur city. This tension did not completely die down, local BJP leaders are aware of this, and in April 2017 realized that the village and the city were amenable to caste and communal polarization. In contrast, in Shabbirpur, Rajputs are the dominant community, but their sociopolitical pride and authority has been challenged more recently by politically mobile castes like Jats and Gujjars and the advent of non-Brahmin Hindutva; there are also economic anxieties due to a deepening agrarian crisis depriving them of their occupational identity as prosperous farmers. In this situation, the Dalits provide a soft target particularly during a non-BSP regime (Pai and Kumar 2017).

In both villages the administration denied permission for the proposed Shobha Yatras, aware of the underlying tensions.[4] But the younger Dalits in Dudhali and the Rajputs in Shabbirpur went ahead, leading to violent clashes when the processions passed through the Muslim and Dalit quarters of these villages, respectively. In Dudhali the procession was led by the sitting BJP MP, Raghav Lakhan Pal an OBC himself, who threatened that the 'shobha yatra' would go through the city and Sadak Dudhli on 23 April, and that 'he would not allow Saharanpur to become Kashmir'. The police ordered an FIR against Lakhanpal and over 500 others for the violence, vandalism, and attack on the house of the Senior Superintendent of Police and the DM's office; order was restored only after the city of Saharanpur was turned into a fortress (Ali 2017). In Shabbirpur, during the clash, a stone hit a 25-year-old Thakur fatally. His death further enraged the community and Thakurs from neighbouring villages gathered at Shabbirpur and set at least 25 Dalit houses on fire. They allegedly attacked police and fire brigade personnel who had rushed to the village. A fire engine was damaged and several people, including a police inspector, were wounded in the attack. Caught between loyalty to party and community, BJP-affiliated senior Dalit leaders in the district, while showing solidarity with the Dalits of Shabbirpur, tried to keep out of the incident.

---

[4] For details of the two incidents, see Pai and Kumar (2017).

Dalits of Shabbirpur have received tremendous support from their brethren across UP and many other states; at least 50 thousand gathered at Jantar Mantar in New Delhi on 21 May to protest atrocities by upper castes (Angad 2017). On 20 May, 180 Dalit families in the village converted to Buddhism in protest against what they called unfair targeting of their community particularly the burning of their houses. The Yogi Adityanath government has not been able to stop the caste violence which is continuing unabated in Saharanpur. Following the two violent incidents in Sadak Dudhali and Shabbirpur, the UP government immediately transferred the SSP and the DM. But, on 23 May, a Dalit was killed while returning from a rally held by Mayawati in Saharanpur, and on 24 May a Thakur youth was shot and sustained injuries, leading to suspension of both the officials on 24 May (*The Indian Express* 2017b).

Politics over Slaughterhouses

The decision to ban all 'illegal' slaughterhouses and place curbs on mechanical abattoirs in the state by the Yogi Adityanath government, within a few days of assuming office, provides an example of divisive policies rather than attempts to help all communities improve their livelihood. The order is based on a promise in its Election Manifesto to look after UP's livestock that had suffered badly under previous governments (*IE Nation* 2017). While the ban is on 'illegal' units, since March 2017, media reports indicate, that the new government does not seem keen to allow slaughterhouses to function in UP. There are many complaints by abattoir owners both big and small, most of whom are Muslims, who allege the local administration is harassing even legal set-ups, and renewal of licenses is not taking place.

In a backward state like UP, the meat industry is one of the largest, and exports account for Rs 26,685 crore annually (Jeelani, Parashar, and Khan 2017). The industry ranges from government-owned slaughterhouses in cities such as Lucknow, big meat export companies like Al-Saqib Exports (P) Ltd and Al-Faheem Meatex Pvt Ltd, on the outskirts of Meerut, and Allanasons in Aligarh and Unnao, to small shops owned by individuals. The new policy has caused much economic loss and harassment to owners, most of whom are Muslims and loss of jobs to workers. Except for butchers specialized in 'halal' (Islamic) slaughter, a large number of workers in almost all the abattoirs are Hindus. According to the All India Meat and Livestock Exporters' Association, a ban on meat exports would mean a loss of at least Rs 11,350 crores of revenue for UP, which accounts for nearly 50 per cent of India's total meat exports and would affect the livelihood of 25 lakh people, directly or indirectly. Already the industry it is held has suffered losses due to demonetization and closure of mechanized slaughterhouses will add to its problems. Meat-exporters are considering legal options against the ban on mechanized slaughterhouses in UP (Jeelani, Parashar, and Khan 2017).

The subject of closing slaughterhouses is not new; the Yogi Adityanath government is merely taking forward a policy that the BJP has long supported. One of the reasons for the delay in renewal of licenses by local authorities in recent years has been the victory of the BJP in ward-level elections in various municipalities in western UP in 2015, following the party's victory in the 2014 national elections. Since then, Municipal officials have been under pressure to close slaughterhouses and start the process of issuing licenses all over again; in many areas no licenses have been renewed since 2014. A senior SP leader, who won one of the assembly seats in Muzaffarnagar in the 2017 assembly elections, has alleged that the BJP, after winning, is doing everything possible to deprive the Muslims of economic benefits and opportunities (Parashar 2017). The National Green Tribunal in 2015 had ordered that slaughterhouses would have to take permission from the UP Pollution Control Board (UPPCB) and/or environmental clearance from State Level Environment Impact Assessment Authority (SEIAA) besides permission from local authorities to run slaughterhouses. But owners of slaughterhouses allege that while in the past these authorities often delayed, they eventually gave permission, but they feel under the BJP government this will not happen (Parashar 2017).

Even Allanasons, one of the oldest and largest export units with many plants in the state, have complained of harassment. During an inspection at its Unnao plant which employs 2,100 persons, many of them Hindus, two local members of the Hindu Jagran Manch in saffron scarfs, though denied permission, managed to force their way into the factory to conduct their own check. No illegality or lapses were found. In Meerut, Bajrang Dal activists raided a meat packaging unit without informing the authorities and beat up a worker. FIRs have

been registered by the administration against a number of establishments, but none of the animal carcasses recovered has been proved to
be that of the cow. Many Hindus who voted for the BJP are workers in
Allanasons and other big factories across UP, are losing jobs and are
unhappy (Jeelani 2017).

A section of the Muslim community in UP blames the previous
government for deliberately delaying modernization of government
slaughterhouses across the state to keep the butcher community's vote
captive, yet allowing illegal slaughter, to gain the Muslim vote. Others
hold, they voted for the BJP in the hope that they would promote
development and are unhappy at losing their livelihood. Across the
state, the associations of meat traders—buffalo, goat, chicken—who are
keen to do business legally, announced an indefinite strike in March
2017, demanding renewal of licenses, due for renewal on 1 April, and
a temporary place to slaughter animals, until the modernization of the
slaughterhouses takes place (Masih 2017a).

The political fallout of the actions of the new BJP government shut-
ting down slaughterhouses and meat shops, is that the cow vigilante or
gau rakshak strand of Hindutva politics so far restricted to the fringes,
has since the 2017 elections become active. These groups spread half-
truths and rumours to gain support for their activities such as decrease
in livestock in UP due to slaughter, particularly cow slaughter. They
also accuse the previous SP government of having given a free rein to
cow slaughter and favouring of Muslims in this trade. However, the UP
livestock census and the National Dairy Board's figures for UP show a
consistent upswing in buffalo population and milk production (Masih
2017b).

Finally, the Central Environment Ministry has announced new,
strict rules on 26 May 2017 prohibiting sale of animals—cows, bulls,
bullocks, steers, heifers, calves, and camels—across the country, for
slaughter or religious sacrifice, at livestock rural markets and animal
fairs. The official reason given is that it will end the uncontrolled and
unregulated animal trade, prevent slaughter of healthy, milch cattle,
stop illegal slaughterhouses, ensure food safety standards, and weed
out middlemen as farmers can directly sell cattle to slaughterhouses,
increasing their income (Mohan 2017). However, the rules will make
it more difficult in UP and other states, for even legal slaughterhouses
to source cattle for meat as currently it is at the rural cattle markets that

most animals are traded for slaughter. Introducing new infrastructure to implement these rules will take much time and effort and it remains to be seen if the UP government will take active steps to do so. There seems little doubt that such a policy will definitely affect both small and big slaughterhouses, most of them run by Muslims, and the big meat exporters in UP.

***

Our analysis shows that the victory of the BJP at the centre in 2014 began the process of introducing cultural change, creating fear, and marginalizing the minority community, witnessed in the variety of incidents such as Love Jihad, the issue of nationalism, conversions, gau rakshaks, but more importantly the Kairana exodus and Dadri lynching. A similar story is now unfolding in UP witnessed in the handling of the seminal issues of law and order and development, promised by the new government. On both counts the new government faces serious challenges.

The Yogi Adityanath government has not been able to control the gau rakshaks from the HYV or other right-wing organizations functioning within the state. Most important, it has not been able to stop the violent incidents in Saharanpur district, which have continued for over a month. While it is true that the government has been in power for hardly three months and it can be argued that the previous SP government allowed law and order to deteriorate. These incidents are a result of mobilization over time by BJP leaders at the grass roots leading to creation of a broad, winning Hindutva social coalition, consisting of the upper castes and large sections of the backwards and Dalits, whose internal contradictions on the ground have now come to the fore. The collective and violent retaliation by Dalits in Shabbirpur, has exposed the existing faultlines within the Hindu community, and disrupted the political strategy of non-Brahmin Hindutva exposing its weakness, leaving the BJP leadership worried. On the other hand, the violent assertion by the upper castes, jealous of the rising clout of the lower castes, points to attempts to control them. Moreover, in both these incidents, the commonality of interests between the sociocultural agenda of various Hindutva organizations and the aspirations of Dalit groups, came together to clash with and make the Muslim the common 'other'. Similarly, in the developmental agenda, the policy to close down so-called 'illegal' slaughterhouses and new rules governing sale of cattle has created economic difficulties and unhappiness within the Muslim community, which is largely involved in the trade.

In sum, the results of the 2017 assembly elections and various incidents discussed show that our model of institutionalization of everyday communalism has continuing relevance with the BJP having achieved power both at the centre and in UP. The Hindutva strategy of creating religious divides will continue, as it seems that even if the BJP succeeds in bringing in development in UP as promised, the path for winning the 2019 elections will be through communal polarization.

Glossary

Ahir	Backward caste found mainly in north India
Ajlaf	Low-caste/class Muslim deemed equivalent to Hindu backward castes
akhara	Ground where wrestling matches are organized
Allah-U-Akbar	Islamic phrase meaning 'Allah is the greatest' used as part of the five daily prayers and an expression of joy after happy life events
Arjzal	Low-caste/class Muslim deemed equivalent to Hindu Scheduled Castes
Arya Samaj	Hindu organization that attempted to reform Hinduism
Ashraf	Upper-class/caste Muslims
avatar	New form
Bajrang Dal	Right-wing youth brigade named after the Hindu god Hanuman
Baliyan Jat	Jat belonging to the Baliyan Khap
bandh	Form of protest through shut down of all commercial establishments
Bania	Hindu trading caste
Bharat Milap	Hindu festival celebrating the meeting between the brothers Ram and Bharat in the Ramayana
Bhumihar	Powerful landowning upper caste in north India
biradari/ bhaichara	Brotherhood traditionally arising out of commonly held land and/or blood ties

Brahmin	Highest caste in the Hindu caste system
charpai	Cot made of wood and ropes
Chaurasi Parikrama Yatra	Ancient tradition of an 84-mile walking pilgrimage circumnavigating holy places in eastern UP, believed to provide salvation
Dalit	Name given to the former untouchables, meaning 'oppressed'
democratic pradhan	Elected headman of a village under the Panchayati Raj system
dharmashala	Free lodging place for pilgrims
dharna	To sit on protest
Dhobi	Washerman, a backward caste
duniya	Muslim backward caste
Faquir	Muslim or Hindu mendicant monk regarded as a holy man
gauchar	Village pasture used to graze cows
gaushala	Institution that cares for cows, particularly those too old to produce milk
ghar wapsi	Return to the Hindu fold after conversion
Gorakhbani	Sayings of Saint Gorakhnath after whom the temple in Gorakhpur is named Gorakshnath
gotra	Meaning 'clan'; families sharing a blood relationship/line are held to belong to the same gotra
Gujjar	Pastoral, agricultural ethnic group in north India
gunj	Marketplace largely of Hindu merchants
Hindi Pracharini Sabha	Organization for propagating the Hindi language
Hindu Yuva Vahini	Hindu youth brigade
bahu beti ki izzat	Protecting the respect of Hindu daughters and daughters-in-law against molestation by outsiders, usually Muslim men
Hindu Hriday Samrat	Leader who conquered the heart of the Hindus
Hindu Mahasabha	Right-wing organization of all Hindus
Hindutva	Right-wing Hindu nationalist ideology

hookah	Single- or multi-stemmed instrument for vaporizing and smoking flavoured tobacco used in north India
Imam	Muslim cleric usually in charge of a mosque
izzat	Respect
Jai Shri Ram	Hindu greeting invoking the name of the Hindu god Ram commonly used in north India
Jamaat-e-Islami	Islamic political organization and social conservative movement founded in 1941
Jamiat Ulema-i-Hind	Islamic organization in India founded in 1919
janapad	Traditional cultural regions in India
janata durbar	People's court to resolve problems
Jat Mahapanchayat	Community gathering made up of several Jat Khaps representing different clans held to discuss important community issues
Jatav	Sub-caste of the Scheduled Castes in north India
Jat	Dominant landowning community believed to be of Indo-Scythian origin
Julaha	Weaver caste belonging to the backward castes
Kabristan	Muslim burial ground
Kahar	Backward caste community traditionally water carriers
Kashyap	Sub-caste of Scheduled Castes
Khap	Community organization, assembly of elders representing a clan or a group of related clans found among the Jats in north India
khudkhast	Self-cultivated by the owner, not leased out
kirtan	Group-singing involving ancient Sanskrit chants of spiritual or religious ideas
Koeri	Backward caste in north India
Kshatriya	Warrior caste standing just below the Brahmins; traditionally Hindu kings belonged to this caste
Kumhar	Potter caste belonging to the backward castes
Kurmi	Backward caste in north India
labh	Economic advantage
Lodh	Backward caste in north India

Love Jihad	Term used to describe alleged attempts by Muslim boys to lure Hindu girls and marry them
Madrassa	School for Muslims where Islamic education is imparted
Mahanth	Head of Hindu temple
Mahasabha	Organization/gathering of the entire caste or clan group
Majlis-e-Mushawarat	Organization to unite all Muslims
maktab	Elementary school for Muslims where Islamic education is imparted
Malik Jat	Jat belonging to the Malik Khap
Mandir	Hindu temple
Masjid	Muslim place of worship
Math	Hindu religious organization
Most Backward Caste	Most backward caste among those officially identified as backward
Momin	Muslim sect also called Ansari in eastern UP
Muharram	Muslim festival; Shia Muslims observe and respect Muharram as the month that martyred Hussein ibn Ali, the grandson of Muhammad
Mukhiya	Traditional leader
Nai	Barber, a backward caste
non-Brahmin-Hindutva	Hindutva ideology modified to include Hindus who belong to the lower castes
Other Backward Class	Hindu caste/class officially identified as backward and provided reservation
panchayat	Assembly of wise and respected elders (*panch* or five) chosen and accepted by the local community to settle disputes between individuals and between villages
Pasis, Khatiks, Jatavs, Chamars, Pasis, Musahars	Sub-castes among the Scheduled Castes
Pasmanda	Backward class/caste of Muslims
Pathshala	School
Patidar	Co-sharer of the same plot or pati
peeth	Traditional seat/place of a Hindu spiritual leader

Peethadhishwar	Ceremonial chair reserved for the head of a spiritual institution
Pesha Ki Namaaz	Special namaz or Muslim prayer at a mosque
qasbah	Muslim living area or marketplace
Qatl-e-aam Mass-killing or pogrom	Quraishi Muslim caste in the Indian subcontinent
Rajbhar, Nooniya	Backward castes in eastern UP
Rajput	Patrilineal clans of western, central, and northern India who claim to be descendants of ruling Hindu warrior classes
Ramaized	Providing a role to the lower castes in the Ramayana, thereby creating a more inclusive Hindu epic
Ranghad	Rajput who converted to Islam found in UP
Rath Yatra	Procession in a vehicle made to look like a traditional chariot
Rashtriya Swayamsevak Sangh	Hindu right-wing, nationalist sociopolitical organization
Saini	Caste in north India, traditionally landowners and farmers
Samajik Nyay	Social justice
samajik samrasta	social harmony
samrasta bhoj	inter-dining by different castes to remove caste barriers
Sanatan Hindu dharma	Original name used in the Vedic period of what is now popularly called Hinduism or Hindu dharma; also use to connote a more orthodox variety
Sangh Parivar	Organizations associated with the RSS collectively referred to as a right-wing family
saree	Traditional dress worn by Indian women
Shahi Imam	Muslim cleric
Shakha	Branch of an organization
Shamshan	Hindu cremation ground
Shobha Yatra	Felicitation procession
shuddhi	Reconversion to Hinduism

Shudra	Fourth and lowest of the traditional varnas (social classes), traditionally artisans and labourers
sir	Per head (sir) for revenue purposes; self-cultivated by the owner, not leased out
Taga	Also referred to as Tyagi; as held, they were Brahmins who took to farming
Taluq	District or region from which land revenue was collected
taluqdar	Big feudal landlords of a region
Telli	Oil pressers, a backward caste
Thakur	Honorary title, meaning 'chief', used by landlords and people of royal families usually belonging to the upper caste
thela	Small pedal cart for carrying goods
traditional pradhan	Traditional headman of a village
Tyagi	Surname and historically a Brahmin caste, but now mostly engaged in farming and not offering priestly services
Ulema	Muslim clergy
Vaishnav	Hindu sect, followers of the Hindu god Vishnu
Vaishya	Business community
Vishva Hindu Parishad	World Hindu Organization
Vikas Purush	Man who undertakes development
Virat Hindu Mahasammelan	Grand gathering of Hindus
Yadav	Pastoral caste in north India, part of the backward castes
Yogi	Hindu spiritual leader
zamindar	Feudal landlord

Bibliography

Primary Sources

Census of India 2001, Report of the Technical Group on Population Projections Constituted by the National Commission on Population, available at http://www.jsk.gov.in/projection_report_december2006.pdf. accessed on 13 March 2016.

———, 2011, Uttar Pradesh Profile, available at http://censusindia.gov.in/2011census/censusinfodashboard/stock/profiles/en/IND009_Uttar%20Pradesh.pdf, accessed on 13 October 2016.

Department of Information and Public Relations, Mau, Uttar Pradesh- Department wise Description of Developmental Works in Mau District, 2016.

District Gazetter Department, U.P. District Gazetter, Muzaffarnagar, 1980, available at http://gazetteer.up.nic.in/ViewPdf.aspx?Dst=RQ%3d%3d-55VEGPf2brs%3d&DsName=TXV6YWZmYXJuYWdhcg%3d%3d-n7FVUA4vfu8%3d, accessed on 10 March 2016.

Government of India, Ministry of MSME, District Industrial Profile of Mau District Carried out by: Br. MSME-DI, Varanasi, available at http://dcmsme.gov.in/dips/Mau%2012..12.12.pdf, accessed on 7 April 2016.

Joshi, Siddharth. 2017. 'Resisting History? Agrarian Change and Farmer's Mobilization in Western Uttar Pradesh 1985–2015.' Unpublished PhD thesis, Indian Institute of Management, Bangalore.

Kumar, Sajjan. 2017. 'Hindutva, Mandal and State Security Discourses: Reconstitution of Muslim Identity in Uttar Pradesh and Bihar since the 1980s'. Unpublished PhD thesis, Centre for Political Studies, Jawaharlal Nehru University, New Delhi.

Mishra, Ranganath. 2007. *National Commission for Religious and Linguistic Minorities*, New: Ministry of Minority Affairs.

National Institute of Rural Development. 2008. *Note on the Backward Regions Grant Fund Programme, Gorakhpur.* 8 September, available at rural.nic.in/sites/downloads/committee/Background%20Note%20on%20NIRD.pdf, accessed on 2 September 2016.

Rawat, Ram Narayan. 1996. 'The Making of the Scheduled Caste Community: A Study of the Scheduled Castes Federation and Dalit Politics in Uttar Pradesh, 1946–48', MPhil Thesis, Department of History, New Delhi: University of Delhi.

Report of the Varanasi Handloom Cluster under Integrated Handloom, Cluster Development Scheme. 2007. Gujarat: Enterprise Development Institute of India, Gandhi Nagar.

Sachar, Rajindar, et al. 2006. *Report on Social, Economic and Educational Status of the Muslim Community of India.*

Reports on Riots

BJP. 1993. *White Paper on Ayodhya and the Ram Temple Movement.* New Delhi.

Economic and Political Weekly. 1978. 'Editorial: Aligarh Riots: Study Team's Findings', 13(46):1882–5.

Engineer, Asghar Ali. 2006. 'Communal Riots—2005 (Part II): Major Riot in Mau, U.P', Mumbai: Centre for Study of Society and Secularism.

Graff, Violette and Juliette Galonnier. 2013a. 'Hindu–Muslim Communal Riots in India I (1947–1986)', *Online Encyclopedia of Mass Violence.* Paris: Sciences PO, available at http://www.massviolence.org/Article?id_article=736.

———. 2013b. 'Hindu–Muslim Riots in India II (1986–2011)', *Online Encyclopaedia of Mass Violence.* Paris: Sciences PO, available at http://www.massviolence.org/Article?id_article=738.

Mander, Harsh, Akram Akhtar Chaudhury, Zafar Eqbal, and Rajanya Bose. 2016. *Living Apart: Communal Violence and Forced Displacement in Muzaffarnagar and Shamli.* New Delhi: DK Publishers.

Rao, Mohan, Ish Mishra, Pragya Singh, and Vikas Bajpai. 2013. 'Communalism and the Role of the State: An Investigation into the Communal Violence in Muzaffarnagar and its Aftermath', available at https://nbsdelhi.wordpress.com/2014/01/07/communalism-and-the-role-of-the-state-an-investigation-into-the-communal-violence-in-muzaffarnagar-and-its-aftermath/, accessed on 7 June 2016.

Report by CPI(ML) on Mau Riots. 2006. *Mau Dange Ka Sach: Gangwar kee Raajniti par ek Nazar* (Hindi). Allahabad: Sabad Prakashan.

Verma, Roop Rekha, Vibhuti Narain Rai, and Nasiruddin Haider Khan. 2005. *An Exclusive Citizens Report, Mau Riots a Report,* available at https://ideas.repec.org/p/ess/wpaper/id247.html, accessed on 4 February 2016.

Secondary Sources

Books and Articles in Hindi and Urdu

Ali, Anwar. 2005. *Masawat ki Jung* (Struggle for Equality, Urdu). New Delhi: Indian Social Institute.

Banerjee, Akshay Kumar. 2016. Ideal Yogi- Sri Sri Yogiraj Baba Gambhirnath, Gorakhpur Temple, Gorakhpur, Samvat.

Dainikbhaskar.com. 2016. Speech by Ex-Member of Parliament, 'If Balram Yadav joins BJP, We Will Elect Him As MLA Along with His Son', 23 June.

Dwivedi, Hazari Prasad. 1952. *Hindi Sahitya: Udbhav Aur Vikas*. New Delhi: Rajkamal Prakashan.

Mahant Digvijaynath Smriti Granth. Samvat 2029. Gorakshnath Temple, Ashwin, Krishna 3, Gorakhpur.

Mayawati. 2006. *Mere Sangharshmay Jeevan Evam Bahujan Movement ka Safarnama*. New Delhi: Book Centre.

Rai, Vibhuti Narain. 2014. *Shahar Mein Curfew Tatha Anya Chaar Upanyas* , Vani Publication, Delhi.

Srivastava, Ramlal. 2017. Nathsiddhcharitamrit, Gorakhpur Temple, Gorakhpur, Samvat.

Books and Articles

Agha, Zafar. 1996. 'Appealing for Sympathy', available at http://indiatoday. intoday.in/story/elections-1996-kalpnath-rai-earns-upper-caste support/1/281175.html, accessed on 15 January 2017.

Ahmad, Imtiaz. 1967. 'Indian Muslims and Electoral Politics', *Economic and Political Weekly*, 11 March: 521–3.

———. 1974. 'The Muslim Electorate and Election Alternative in UP', *Religion and Society*, 21(2): 1951–2.

———. 1982 *Sunday*, 7 September .

Ahmad, Imtiaz and N.C. Saxena. 1994. 'Caste Land and Power in UP', in K.L. Sharma (ed.), *Caste and Class in India*, pp. 171–208. New Delhi: Rawat Publications.

Akbar, M.J. 1978. 'Varanasi: How and Why Muslims and Hindu Kill Each Other', in Udayan Sharma (ed.), *Violence Erupts*, pp. 47–58. New Delhi: Radha Krishna.

———. 1988. *Riot after Riot: Report on Caste and Communal Violence in India*. New Delhi: Penguin Books.

———. 1990. *Entrepreneurship and Indian Muslims*. New Delhi: Manak.

Alam, Arshad. 2009. 'Challenging the Ashrafs: The Politics of Pasmanda Muslim Mahaz', *Journal of Muslim Minority Affairs*, 29(2): 171–81.

Alam, Javed. 1983. 'Dialectics of Capitalist Transformation and National Crystallization', *Economic and Political Weekly*, 18(5): 29–46.

Ali, Mohammad. 2016. 'BJP MP Backtracks on "Exodus" Claims', *The Hindu*, New Delhi, 14 June.

———. 2017. 'BJP MP's March Triggers Clashes in Saharanpur', *The Hindu*, Meerut, 21 April.

Amin, Shahid. 1982. 'Small Peasant Commodity Production and Rural Indebtedness: The Culture of Sugarcane in Eastern UP: 1880–1920', in R Guha (ed.), *Subaltern Studies*, Vol. I, pp. 39–87. New Delhi: Oxford University Press.

Anand, Utkarsh. 2014. 'SC Holds Akhilesh Govt Guilty of Negligence, Orders Arrest of All Muzaffarnagar Accused', *The Indian Express*, New Delhi, 26 March.

Anderson, Benedict. 1983. *Imagined Communities*. London: Verso.

Anderson, Walter. 1972. 'The Rashtriya Swayamsevak Sangh—III: Participation in Politics', *Economic and Political Weekly*, 7(13): 673–82.

———. 2015. 'The Bharatiya Janata Party: A Victory for Narendra Modi', in Paul Wallace (ed.), *India's 2014 Elections: A Modi-led BJP Sweep*, pp. 46–63. New Delhi: Sage.

Angad, Abhishek. 2017. 'On the Run, Bhim Army Founder at Jantar Mantar: Stage Set for Struggle', *The Indian Express*, New Delhi, 22 May.

Apoorvanand. 2007. 'Riot, Manufactured in Gorakhpur', *Tehelka*, 17 February.

Ashraf, Ajaz. 2015. 'Opinion: Why the BJP and the Rural Distress are to Blame for the Violence of the Jats', 19 October: 10, available at https://scroll.in/article/732464/why-bjp-and-the-rural-distress-are-to-blame-for-the-violence-of-jats, accessed in December 2015.

Aslam, Mohammad. 1990. 'The UP Muslim 1947, 1967, 1987', in Jim Masselos (ed.), *India Creating a Modern Nation*. New Delhi: Sterling Publishers.

Atkinson, Edward. 1867. *On the Collection of Revenue*. Boston: A. Williams.

Badhwar, Inderjit and Pankaj Pachauri. 1989. 'Communalism: Dangerous Dimensions', *India Today*, 31 October, available at http://indiatoday.intoday.in/story/with-ramshila-movement-militant-hindus-launches-offensive-to-counter-muslim-fundamentalists/1/324033.html, accessed on 5 September 2016.

Baru, Sanjay. 1990. *The Political Economy of Indian Sugar: State Intervention and Structural Change*. New Delhi: Oxford University Press.

Bayly, Christopher. 1992. *Rulers, Townsmen, and Bazaars: North Indian Society in the Age of British Expansion, 1770–1870*. Cambridge: Cambridge University Press.

Bentall, Jim and Stuart Corbridge. 1996. 'Urban–Rural Relations, Demand Politics and the New Agrarianism in Northwest India: The Bharatiya Kisan Union', *Transactions of the Institute of British Geographers*, 21(1): 27–48.

Bhalla, G.S. 1994. 'Introduction', in G.S. Bhalla (ed.), *Economic Liberalisation and Indian Agriculture*, pp. 1–22. New Delhi: Institute for Studies in Industrial Development.

Bhatty, Zarina. 1973. 'Status and Power in a Muslim-dominated Village of Uttar Pradesh', in Imtiaz Ahmad (ed.), *Caste and Social Stratification among the Muslims in India*, pp. 89–106, New Delhi: Manohar.

Blunt, E.A.H. 1931. *The Caste System of North India with Special Reference to the United Provinces of Agra and Oudh*. London: OUP.

Brass, Paul R. 1962. 'An Industrial Labour Constituency: Kanpur', *Economic Weekly* special number, July: 1111–18.

———. 1970. 'Muslim Separatism in United Provinces Social Context and Political Strategy before Partition', *Economic and Political Weekly* 5(3–5): 167–86, available at http://www.massviolence.org/PdfVersion?id_article=736.

———. 1974. *Language, Religion and Politics in North India*. Cambridge: Cambridge University Press.

———1980. 'The Politicization of the Peasantry in a North Indian State: I', *The Journal of Peasant Studies* 7(4): 395–426.

———. 1985. *Caste Faction and Party in Indian Politic*. New Delhi: Chankya Publications.

———. 1991. *Ethnicity and Nationalism: Theory and Comparison*. New Delhi: Sage.

———. 1997. *Theft of an Idol: Text and Context in the Representation of Collective Violence*. Princeton: Princeton University Press.

———. 2003. *The Production of Hindu–Muslim Violence in Contemporary India*. Seattle and London: University of Washington Press.

———. 2006. *Forms of Collective Violence, Riots, Pogroms and Genocide in Modern India*. Gurgaon: Three Essays Collective.

Burger, Angela S. 1969. *Opposition in a Dominant Party System: A Study of the Jan Sangh, Praja Socialist, and Socialist Parties in Uttar Pradesh, India*. Berkeley: University of California.

Chakravarti, Sudeep. 1993. 'Money Talks: Business Interests Could Act as a Unifying Force between Hindus and Muslims', *India Today*, 31 January: 40–1.

Chandra, Bipan. 2012 [1987]. *India's Struggle for Independence 1857–1947*. New Delhi: Penguin Books.

Chaturvedi, Swati. 2016. *I am a Troll*. New Delhi: Rupa Publications.

Chopra, Suneet and N.K. Singh. 1972. 'Ferozabad Anatomy of a Riot.' *Economic and Political Weekly*, 19 August: 1711–13.

Clift, Charles. 1977. 'Progress of Irrigation in Uttar Pradesh, East–West Differences', *Economic and Political Weekly*, 12(29): A83–A90.

Dalmia, Vasudha. 1997. *The Nationalization of Hindu Traditions: Bhartendu Harishchandra and Nineteenth Century Banaras*. New Delhi: Oxford University Press.

Damodaran, Harish. 2016a. 'The Bitter Tales of Shamli's Sugarcane Farmers: "Netas talk palayan (exodus), our issue is bhugtan (payment)"', *The Indian Express*, New Delhi, 20 June.

———. 2016b. 'UP Sugarcane belt crisis spills over to schools, spike in fee default', available at http://indianexpress.com/article/india/india-news-india/up-sugarcane-belt-crisis-spills-over-to-schools-spike-in-fee-default-2878132/, accessed on 10 September 2016.

Damodaran, Harish and Harvir Singh. 2007. 'Sugar Industry in Uttar Pradesh: Rise, Decline and Revival', *Economic and Political Weekly*, 29 September: 3952–7.

Daruwalla, Keki N. 2017. 'So What If There's Been No Riots.' *The Economic Times*, New Delhi, 30 May.

Dasgupta, Biplab. 1980. *Agrarian Change and the New Technology in India*. Geneva: Macmillan Co. Ltd.

Datta, Nonica. 1999. 'Jats: Trading Caste Status for Empowerment', *Economic and Political Weekly*, 6 November: 3172.

Dayal, John and Ajoy Bose. 1977. *Delhi Under Emergency*. Delhi: ESS Publications.

Deccan Herald. 2015. 'Bisara Faces Political Polarization', 3 October.

Deshpande, Satish. 2015. 'The "Restrained Riot" of Atali', *The Hindu*, 20 June.

Dev, Narendra. 1946. 'Kisan Movement in Uttar Pradesh, *Socialist and Nationalist Revolution*. Bombay: Padma Publications.

Dhabade, Neha. 2016, 'Truth is Still Unknown', available at http://frontier-weekly.com/articles/vol-49/49-1/49-1-Truth%20is%20Still%20Unknown.html, accessed on 12 October 2016.

Dhulipala, Venkat. 2015. *Creating a New Medina: State Power, Islam and the Quest for Pakistan in Late Colonial North India*. New Delhi: Cambridge University Press.

Dreze, Jean and Haris Gazdar. 1996. 'Uttar Pradesh: The Burden of Inertia', in Jean Dreze and Amartya Sen (eds), *Indian Development: Selected Regional Perspectives*. New York: Oxford University Press.

DNA. 2013. 'Jolly Canal Killings Triggered the Muzaffarnagar Riots', 14 September.

Dubashi, Jay. 1992. *The Road to Ayodhya*. New Delhi: Voice of India.

Dwivedi, Girish Chandra. 1970. 'The Origin of the Jats', *Journal of Indian History*, 48(2): 378.

Election Commission of India. 2017. 'General Election to Vidhan Sabha, Trends and Results 2017, Partywise; Constituencywise—All Candidates; Constituencywise Trends', available at http://eciresults.nic.in/PartyWise ResultS24.htm?st=S24, accessed on 20 May 2017.

Engineer, Asghar Ali. 1977. 'Do Muslims Vote as a Block?', *Economic and Political Weekly*, 12 March: 458–9.

Engineer, Asghar Ali. 1983. 'Socio-economic Basis of Communalism', *Mainstream*, 21(45): 54–64.

——— (ed.). 1990. *Babri-Masjid Ramjanmabhoomi Controversy*. Delhi: Ajanta Publications.

———. 1991a. 'Lok Sabha Elections and Communalisation of Politics', *Economic and Political Weekly*, 26(27–28): 1649–52.

———. 1991b. 'The Bloody Trail Ramjanmabhoomi and Communal Violence in UP', *Economic and Political Weekly*, 26(4): 155–9.

———. 1992. *Politics of Confrontation: The Babri-Masjid Ramjanmabhoomi Controversy Runs Riot*. New Delhi: Ajanta.

———.1994. 'Bangalore Violence: Linguistic or Communa', *Economic and Political Weekly*, XXIX, (44): 2854–8.

———. 1997. 'Communalism and Communal Violence, 1996', *Economic and Political Weekly*, 15 February: 323–6.

Falahi, Mumtaz Alam. 2009. 'People's Tribunal on Condition of UP Muslim Weavers in Varanasi Tomorrow', *TwoCircles.net*, 17 November, accessed on 8 July 2016.

Fernandes, Leela. 2007. *India's New Middle Class Democratic Politics in an Era of Economic Reform*. New Delhi: Oxford University Press.

Frankel, Francine. 1978. *India's Political Economy 1947–77*. New Jersey: Princeton University Press.

Freitag, Sandra. 1989. *Collective Action and Community, Public Arenas and the Emergence of Communalism in North India*. Berkeley: University of California Press.

Geetz, Clifford. 1973. *The Interpretation of Cultures*. New York: Basic Books.

Ghosh, S.K. 1987. *Communal Riots in India, Meet the Challenge Unitedly*. New Delhi: Ashish Publishing House.

Gooptu, Nandini. 1997. 'The Urban Poor and Militant Hinduism in Early Twentieth-century Uttar Pradesh', *Modern Asian Studies*, 31(4): 879–918.

Gopal, S. (ed.). 1991. *Anatomy of a Confrontation: The Babri Masjid–Ram Janmabhumi Issue*. New Delhi: Penguin Books.

Gupta, Dipankar. 1988. 'The Country Town Nexus and Agrarian Mobilization: The Bharatiya Kisan Union as an Instance', *Economic and Political Weekly*, 23(51): 2688–96.

———. 2011. *Justice before Reconciliation Negotiating a New Normal in Post-riot Mumbai and Ahmedabad*. New Delhi: Routledge.

Gupta, Sisir K. 1962. 'Moslems in Indian Politics 1947–60', *India Quarterly*, 28(4) (October–December): 380.

Gupta, S.K. 1985. *The Scheduled Castes in Modem Indian Politics: Their Emergence as a Political Power*. New Delhi: Munshiram Manoharlal.

Gupta, Smita. 2007. 'The Rise and Fall of Hindutva in Uttar Pradesh, 1989–2004', in Sudha Pai (ed.), *Political Process in Uttar Pradesh: Identity,*

Economic Reforms and Governance, pp. 110–36. New Delhi: Pearson Longman.

Hansen, Thomas Blom. 1999. *The Saffron Wave Democracy and Hindu Nationalism in Modern India*. New Delhi: OUP.

Hardy, Peter. 1972. *The Muslims in British India*. Cambridge: Cambridge University Press.

Hasan, Mushirul. 1988. 'Indian Muslims since Independence: In Search of Integration and Identity', *Third World Quarterly*, 10(2): 818–42.

———. 1997. *Legacy of Divided Nation: Indian Muslims since Independence*. Delhi: Oxford University Press.

Hasan, Zoya. 1989. 'Power and Mobilization Patterns of Resilience and Change Uttar Pradesh Politics', in Francine Frankel and M.S.A. Rao (eds), *Dominance and State Power in Modern India: Decline of a Social Order*, pp. 133–203. New Delhi: Oxford University Press.

———. 2016. 'Kairana and the Politics of Exclusion', *The Hindu*, New Delhi, 27 October 2016.

Hassnain, S.E. 1968. 'Failure of the Muslim Majlis Mushawarat', in *Indian Muslims Challenge and Opportunity*, pp. 69–96. Delhi: Lalvani Publishing House.

Haynes, Douglas E. 2012. *Small Town Capitalism in Western India: Artisans, Merchants and the Making of the Informal Economy, 1870–1960*. Cambridge: Cambridge Studies in Indian History and Society.

Hindustan Times. 2017. 'CM Adityanath Promises no Bias on Religion; No Harassment of Couples in UP', 15 May 2017.

Hobsbawm, Eric. 1983. *The Invention of Tradition*. Cambridge: Cambridge University Press.

Horowitz, Donald. 1985. *Ethnic Groups in Conflict*. Berkeley: University of California.

Hossain, Attia. 1989 (first published 1961). *Sunlight on a Broken Column*. New York: Penguin-Brooks Virago Press.

Imam, Zafar (ed.). 1975. *Muslims in India*. New Delhi: Orient Longman, pp. 81–8.

India Today. 2013. 'Army Deployed in Muzaffarnagar After 11 Killed in Clashes', 18 September.

IE Nation. 2017. 'In Its Pre-poll Manifesto, the BJP Had Said That if Voted to Power, It Would Shut all the Illegal Slaughterhouses and Impose a Blanket Ban on Mechanized Abattoirs.' 23 March.

Jaffrelot, Christophe. 1996. *The Hindu Nationalist Movement in Indian Politics*. New York: Columbia University Press.

———. 2014. 'The Other Saffron', *The Indian Express*, 6 October, New Delhi.

Jafri, S.A.A. 2004. *Socio-Economic Condition of Downtrodden Minorities in Lucknow Metropolis*. Lucknow: Giri Institute of Development Studies.

Jalal, Ayesha. 1994 [1985]. *The Sole Spokesman: Jinnah, the Muslim League, and the Demand for Pakistan*. Cambridge: Cambridge University Press.

Jayaram, Geetha. 1995. 'The Muslim Traditional Potters of Khurja: History, Identity and General Features', *Islam and the Modern Age* 26, nos ii–iii, May–August: 83–136.

Jeelani, Gulam. 2017. 'Job Loss Fear Looms over UP's Biggest Slaughterhouse where Hindus Outnumber Muslims', *Hindustan Times*, Aligarh, 3 April.

Jeelani, Gulam, Brajendra K. Parashar, and M. Tariq Khan. 2017. 'UP Slaughterhouses: All about the Rs 15,000-cr Industry that Employs 25 Lakh People', *Hindustan Times*, 30 April.

Jeffrey, Craig. 1997. 'Richer Farmers and Agrarian Change in Meerut District, Uttar Pradesh, India', *Environment and Planning*, 29(12): 2113–27.

———. 2002. 'Caste, Class and Clientelism: A Political Economy of Everyday Corruption in Rural North India.' *Economic Geography* 78, no. 1 (January): 21–41.

———. 2010. *Timepass Youth, Class, and the Politics of Waiting in India*. California: Stanford University.

Jha, Krishna and Dhirendra K. Jha. 2012. *Ayodhya The Dark Night: The Secret History of Rama's Appearance in Babri Masjid*. New Delhi: Harper Collins.

Kabir, Humayun. 1969. 'Islam in India', in Suresh K. Sharma and Usha Sharma (eds), *Cultural and Religious Heritage of India: Islam'*, Mittal Publications, New Delhi.

Khalidi, Omar. 1995. *Indian Muslims since Independence*. New Delhi: Vikas Publishing House.

———. 1997. 'From Torrent to Trickle: Indian Muslim Migration to Pakistan 1947–1997', *Bulletin of the Henry Martyn Institute of Islamic Studies*, 16(1–2): 32–45.

———. 2004. 'Indian Muslim Society and Economy', *Oriente Moderno*, 23(84): 177–202.

Khan, Kishwar Shabir. 1991. *Brassware Industry of Moradabad and its Muslim Artisans*. Aligarh: Aligarh Muslim University.

Khan, Rafiq and Satyaprakash Mittal. 1984. 'The Hindu–Muslim Riot in Varanasi and the Role of the Police', in Asghar Ali Engineer (ed.), *Communal Riots in Post-Independence India*, pp. 305–12. Hyderabad: Sangam Books.

Khan, Rasheedudin. 1968. 'Modernization', *Seminar*, no. 106, June, 25–31.

Kochanek, Stanley. 1976. 'Mrs Gandhi's Pyramid: The New Congress', in Henry C. Hart (ed.), *Indira Gandhi's India: A Political System Reappraised*, pp. 93–124, Boulder: Westview Press.

Kriplani, J.B. n.d. *Minorities in India*. Calcutta: Vigil Office.

Krishna, Gopal. 1967. 'Electoral Participation and Electoral Politics.' *Economic and Political Weekly*, Annual Number, February: 179–90.

———. 1972. 'Muslim Politics', *Seminar*, no. 153, May, 18–21.

Kudaisya, Gyanesh. 2007. 'Constructing the "Heartland" Uttar Pradesh in India's Body Politic', in Sudha Pai (ed.), *Political Process in Uttar Pradesh Identity, Economic Reforms and Governance*, pp. 3–31. New Delhi: Pearson Longman.

Kumar, Anand. 2010. 'Understanding Lohia's Political Sociology: Intersectionality of Caste, Class, Gender and Language', *Economic and Political Weekly*, 45(40): 64–70.

Lerche, Jens. 1998. 'Agricultural Labourers, the State and Agrarian Transition in Uttar Pradesh', *Economic and Political Weekly*, 32(13): A29–A35.

Lieten, G.K. 1996. 'Inclusive View of Religion: A Rural Discourse in Uttar Pradesh', *Economic and Political Weekly*, 31(23): 1411–16.

Lieten, G.K. and Ravi Srivastava. 1999. *Unequal Partners Power Relations, Devolution and Development in Uttar Pradesh*. New Delhi: Sage.

Low, D.A. (ed.). 1968. *Soundings in Modern South Asian History*. Berkeley: University of California Press.

Lutgendorf, Philips. 1991. *The Life of a Text: Performing the Ramcaritmanas of Tulsidas*. Berkeley: University of California Press.

Madhok, Balraj. 1970. *Indianization*. Delhi: S. Chand Publishers.

Madsen, Stig Toft. 1991. 'Clan Kinship and Panchayat Justice among the Jats of Western Uttar Pradesh', *Anthropos*, 86(4–6): 351–65.

Mander, Harsh. 2016. 'Muzaffarnagar Three Years Later', *The Indian Express*, New Delhi, 7 September.

Manjul, Tarannum. 2009. 'BJP's Azamgarh Candidate: History-sheeter Ramakant Yadav', *The Indian Express* Archives, Lucknow, 31 January.

Masih, Niha. 2017a. 'Anti-slaughterhouse Drive in Yogi Adityanath's UP Based on Half-truths, Rumours', *Hindustan Times*, New Delhi, 7 April.

———. 2017b. 'No Meat in this Drive', *Hindustan Times*, Jalandhar, 2 April.

Metcalfe, Thomas. 1979. *Land, Landlords and the British Raj Northern India in the Nineteenth Century*. New Delhi: OUP.

Milli Gazette. 2002. 'Mau Cloth Industry Facing Serious Crisis', available at http://www.milligazette.com/Archives/01062002/0106200256.htm, accessed on 3 January 2017.

Mishra, Amaresh. 1992. 'Count Down to Kar Seva', *Economic and Political Weekly*, 27(48): 2582.

Mishra, Ish, Mohan Rao, Pragya Singh, and Vikas Bajpai. 2014. 'Fact Finding Report: Independent Inquiry into Muzaffarnagar "Riots"', *Economic and Political Weekly*, 49(2).

Mishra, Pankaj. 2017. *Age of Anger: A History of the Present*. New Delhi: Jaggernaut Books.

Mishra, Salil. 2001. *A Narrative of Communal Politics: Uttar Pradesh 1937–39*. New Delhi: Sage.

Misra, Amaresh. 1998. *Lucknow: The Fire of Grace*. New Delhi: Harper Collins.

Mohan, Vishwa. 2017. 'No Sale of Cattle for Slaughter at Animal Markets', *The Times of India*, New Delhi, 27 May.

Moore, F.J. and C.A. Freydig. 1955. *Land Tenure Legislation in UP*. Berkeley: Berkeley Institute of East Asiatic Studies, University of California.

Morris-Jones, W.H. 1957. *Parliament in India*. London: Longmans Green and Co.

Mukul, Akshaya. 2015. *The Gita Press and the Making of Hindu India*. New Delhi: Harper Collins.

Mustafa, Faizan. 1996. 'Muslim Women's Right to Inherit Agricultural Land', *Radiance*, 14–20 April: 14–15.

Narain, Harsh. 1993. *The Ayodhya Temple–Mosque Dispute: Focus on Muslim Sources*. New Delhi: Penman Publishers.

Narayan, Badri. 2009. *Fascinating Hindutva Saffron Politics and Dalit Mobilization*. New Delhi: Sage.

———. 2014. 'Communal Riots in Uttar Pradesh', *Economic and Political Weekly*, 69(37): 29–32.

Neale, Walter. 1962. *Economic Change in Rural India: Land Tenure and Reform in UP 1800–1955*. New Haven: Yale University Press.

Noorani, A.G. 2003. *The Babri Masjid Question: A Matter of National Honour*, Vol. 1. Delhi: Tulika Books.

———. 2014. *Destruction of the Babri Masjid: A National Dishonour*, Vol. II. Delhi: Tulika Books.

Pai, Sudha. 1993. *Uttar Pradesh: Agrarian Change Electoral Politics*. New Delhi: Shipra Publications.

———. 1998. 'New Political Trends in Uttar Pradesh: The BJP and the 1998 Lok Sabha Elections', *Economic and Political Weekly*, 14 July: 1841–6.

———. 1999. *State Politics New Dimensions: Party System, Liberalization and Politics of Identity*. New Delhi: Shipra Publications.

———. 2002a. 'Politics of Language: Decline of Urdu in UP', *Economic and Political Weekly*, 6 July, 2705–8.

———. 2002b. *Dalit Assertion and the Unfinished Democratic Revolution: The BSP in Uttar Pradesh*. New Delhi: Sage.

——— (ed.). 2007. *Political Process in Uttar Pradesh Identity, Economic Reforms and Governance*. New Delhi: Pearson Longman.

———. 2013a. 'The Backsliders', *The Indian Express*, New Delhi, 6 September.

———. 2013b. 'Muzaffarnagar Memories', *The Indian Express*, New Delhi, 12 September, available at http://indianexpress.com/article/opinion/columns/muzaffarnagar-memories/.

———. 2014. 'Uttar Pradesh: Competitive Communalism Once Again', *Economic and Political Weekly* XlIX(15): 16–19.

———. 2017. 'How Adityanath Made It to Where He is', *thewire.in*, available at https://thewire.in/117655/yogi-adityanath-uttar-pradesh-bjp/.

Pai, Sudha, and Avinash Kumar. 2015. 'Understanding the BJP's Victory in Uttar Pradesh', in Paul Wallace (ed.), *India's 2014 Elections: A Modi-led BJP Sweep*, pp. 119–38. New Delhi: Sage.

Pai, Sudha and Ravi Srivastava. 2013. 'Muzaffarnagar Memories', *The Indian Express*, New Delhi, 12 September.

Pai, Sudha and Sajjan Kumar. 2017a. 'Saharanpur Protests Herald New Phase in Dalit Politics', *thewire.in*, 24 May.

———. 2017b. 'How Adityanath Made It to Where He is', *thewire.in*, available at https://thewire.in/117655/yogi-adityanath-uttar-pradesh-bjp/.

Pandey, Gyanendra. 1989. 'Ayodhya and the State', *Seminar*, no. 364 (December).

———. 1990. *The Construction of Communalism in Colonial North India*. New Delhi: Oxford University Press.

Pant, Niranjan. 2004. 'Trends in Groundwater Irrigation in Eastern and Western UP', *Economic and Political Weekly*, 31 July: 3463–8.

Papola, T.S. 1989. 'Uttar Pradesh', in M. Adiseshiah (ed.), *Economies of the States of the Indian Union*, pp. 63–70. New Delhi: Lancer International.

Parashar, Arpit. 2017. 'UP Slaughterhouse Crackdown: Yogi Adityanath Govt Taking Political Advantage of Negligent Local Authorities', *First Post*, 5 April, accessed on 10 April, 2017.

Patnaik, Prabhat. 1988. 'Capitalist Trajectories of Global Interdependence and Welfare Outcomes: The Lesson of History for the Present', available at http://www.networkideas.org/ideasact/dec11/pdf/Utsa%20_Patnaik.pdf, accessed on 21 March 2016.

Pradhan, Prasad H. 1966. 'The Phenomenon of Disguised Unemployment', *Indian Economic Journal*, 14(1): 18.

PTI. 2007. 'UP Has the Highest OBC Population in All Indian States', *Times of India*, available at http://timesofindia.indiatimes.com/india/UP-has-the-highest-OBC-population-in-all-Indian-states/articleshow/2012439.cms, accessed on 18 May 2017.

———. 2016a. 'UP Govt Must Take Action if Kairana Incidents True: Rajnath', 19 June, available at http://indiatoday.intoday.in/story/up-govt-must-take-action-if-kairana-incidents-true-rajnath/1/695479.html, accessed on 16 May 2017.

———. 2016b. 'Uttar Pradesh: Quami Ekta Dal merges with Samajwadi Party', 21 June, available at http://indianexpress.com/article/india/india-news-india/uttar-pradesh-quami-ekta-dal-merges-with-samajwadi-party-2867232/, accessed on 12 May 2015.

———. 2016c. 'Uttar Pradesh Polls: Jailed Mukhtar's Party Merges with SP, Opposition Hits Out at Government', *Indian Express*, 22 June, available at http://indianexpress.com/article/india/india-news-india/2017-uttar-pradesh-polls-jailed-mukhtars-party-merges-with-sp-oppn-hits-out-at-govt-2867909/, accessed on 15 June 2015.

———. Quraishi, Zaheer Masood. 1968. 'Electoral Strategy of a Minority Pressure Group: The Muslim Mujlis-e-Mushwarat', *Asian Survey*, December.

———. 1971. 'Emergence and Eclipse of the Muslim Majlis-e-Mushawarat', *Economic and Political Weekly*, 1 June: 1229–34.

Rai, Santosh. 2012. 'Muslim Weavers' Politics in the Early 20th Century Northern India Locating an Identity', *Economic and Political Weekly*, 47(15): 61–70.

Rai, Vibhuti Narain. 2014. *Shahar Mein Curfew Tatha Anya Chaar Upanyas*, 2nd edition, New Delhi: Vani Prakashan.

Rajgopal, P.R. 1987. *Communal Violence in India*. New Delhi: Uppal.

Ramjilal (ed.). 1988. *Communal Problem in India: A Symposium*. Haryana: Dyal Singh College.

Rawat,V.B. 2016. Dynamics of Communal Politics in Eastern Uttar Pradesh, available at http://manukhsi.blogspot.in2005/06/communalism-in-uttar-pradesh-html, accessed on 15 September.

Robinson, Francis. 1973. 'Municipal Government and Muslim Separatism in the United Provinces, 1883 to 1916', in Anil Seal, John Gallagher, and Gordon Johnson (ed.), *Locality, Province and Nation in Indian Politics 1870 to 1947*, pp. 389–441. Cambridge: Cambridge University Press.

———. 1975. *Separatism among Indian Muslims: The Politics of the United Provinces' Muslims, 1860–1923*. New Delhi: Vikas Publishing House.

Roy, Tirthankar. 1996. 'Home Market and the Artisans in Colonial India: A Study of Brass-Ware', *Modern Asian Studies*, 30(2): 357–83.

Rudolph, Lloyd and Susanne Rudolph. 1981. 'Transformation of the Congress Party: Why 1980 Was Not a Restoration', *Economic and Political Weekly*, 16(18): 811–13.

Saberwal, Satish and Mushirul Hasan. 1984. 'Moradabad Riots, 1980: Causes and Meanings', in Asghar Ali Engineer (ed.), *Communal Riots in Post-Independence India*, pp. 210–27. Hyderabad: Sangam.

Sayeed, S.M. 1989. 'Role of Muslim Majlis in UP Politics', in Verinder Grover (ed.), *Political System in India: Party System and Political Parties*. New Delhi: Deep and Deep Publications.

Seal, Anil. 1968. *The Emergence of Indian Nationalism: Competition and Collaboration in the Late Nineteenth Century*. Cambridge: Cambridge University Press.

Sen, Sukla. 1998. 'BJP's Real Agenda', *Economic and Political Weekly*, 7 February: 303–4.

Seth, Maulshree. 2017. 'Looking for Yogi', *The Indian Express*, 26 March.

Shahabuddin, Syed. 1986. 'Rejoinder: Darkness Gathers on the Horizon', *Illustrated Weekly of India*, 10 August: 4.

Shakir, Moin. 1988. 'Rise of Fundamentalism', in Ramji Lal (ed.), *Communal Problem in India: A Symposium*. Haryana: Dyal Singh College.

Shankar, Kripa. 1993. 'Agricultural Labourers in Eastern UP', *Economic and Political Weekly*, 28(24): 1211–14.

———. 2007. 'Finances of the Uttar Pradesh Government: An Analysis of the Debt Trap', in Sudha Pai (ed.), *Political Process in Uttar Pradesh Identity Economic Reform and Governance*, pp. 295–307. New Delhi: Pearson Longman.

Sharma, Pankul. 2016. 'BJP MP Gives List of 346 Families who Left Kairana to Support His "Exodus" Claim', *The Times of India*, Meerut, 8 June.

Sharma, Udayan (ed.). 1978. *Violence Erupts*. New Delhi: Radha Krishna.

Sheth, D.L. 2009. 'Political Communalization of Religions and the Crisis of Secularism', *Economic and Political Weekly*, 44(39): 71–9.

Siddiqui, Furqan Ameen. 2013. 'UP Turns Its Back on Muzaffarnagar's Gang-rape Victims', *Hindustan Times*, 4 December.

Siddiqui, Kalim. 1997. 'Credit and Marketing of Sugarcane: A Field Study of Two Villages in Western Uttar Pradesh', *Social Scientist* 25 (1–2): 62–93.

Siddiqui, Majid Hayat. 1978. *Agrarian Unrest in North India: The United Provinces 1918–2*, New Delhi: Vikas Publishing House.

Sikand, Yoginder. 2004. *Struggling to be Heard South Asian Muslim Voices*. New Delhi: Global Media Publications.

Singh, Binay. 2009. 'Mau Leaves Nightmare of 2005 Behind.' *TNN*, 9 April.

Singh, H.D. 1996. *543 Faces of India: Guide to 543 Parliamentary Constituencies*. New Delhi: Newsman Publishers.

Singh, Jagpal. 1992. *Capitalism and Dependence in Western UP*. New Delhi: Manohar.

———. 2016. 'Agrarian Transformation and Politics Communal Violence in Muzaffarnagar', *Economic and Political Weekly*, 51(31): 94–101.

Singh, Manoj. 2016. 'Ye Hain Hindutva ke Nay Angry Young Man' [Here is Hindutva's New Angry Young Man!], available at http://www.bbc.com/hindi/india/2016/03/160303_yogi_adityanath_profile_rd, accessed on 11 November 2016.

———. 2017. 'Before the Rise of Hindutva, Gorakhnath Nurtured Muslim Yogis.' *thewire.com*, 27 March.

Singh, Mohinder. 1947. *The Depressed Classes their Economic Conditions*. Bombay: Hind Kitabh.

Singh, Rajendra. 1974. 'Agrarian Social Structure and Peasant Unrest: A Study of "Land Grab" Movement in District Basti in East U.P.', *Sociological Bulletin*, 23(1): 44–70.

Singh, V.B. 1971. 'Jan Sangh in Uttar Pradesh Fluctuating Fortunes and Uncertain Future', *Economic and Political Weekly*, Annual Number 6(3–5): 307–16.

Singh, Ajit K. and Santosh Mehrotra (eds). 2014. *Land Policy for Equity and Growth: Transforming Agrarian Structure in Uttar Pradesh*. New Delhi: Sage.

Sinha, Arunava. 2014. 'Peace Party to Contest on All 80 Lok Sabha Seats in Uttar Pradesh', available at http://timesofindia.indiatimes.com/city/lucknow/Peace-Party-to-contest-on-all-80-Lok-Sabha-seats-in-Uttar-Pradesh/articleshow/28691759.cms.

Siraj, Maqbool Ahmad. 1993. 'Muslims Lost Millions', *Saudi Gazette*, 1 February, p. 4.

Smith, Wilfred Cantwell. 1946. *Modern Islam in India: A Social Analysis*. London: Victor Gollacz.

———. 1965. *Modernisation of a Traditional Society*. Mumbai: Asia Publishing House.

Spear, Percival. 1967. 'The Position of the Muslim Before and After Partition', in Philip Mason (ed.), *India and Ceylon: Unity in Diversity*, pp. 30–50, London: Oxford University Press.

Srivastava, Amitabh. 2011. 'Minority Rapport', *India Today*, December, available at http://indiatoday.intoday.in/story/up-polls-2012-india-today-opinion-poll-minority-mohammad-ayub/1/163602.html, accessed on 12 December 2014.

Srivastava, Ravi. 1994. 'Planning and Regional Disparities in India: The Uneven Record of Change and Growth', in T.J. Byres (ed.), *The State and Development Planning in India*, pp. 147–219. New Delhi: Oxford University Press.

———. 1995. 'India's Uneven Development and Its Implications for Political Processes: An Analysis of Some Recent Trends', *Social Change and Political Discourse in India: Structures of Power, Movements and Resistance*, 2: 219–47.

———. 2016. 'Once Upon a Time in Gorakhpur …', available at http://timesofindia.indiatimes.com/city/lucknow/Once-upon-a-time-in-Gorakhpur-/articleshow/11533376.cms, accessed on 10 November 2016.

Srivastava, Saraswati. 1967. 'UP, Politics of Neglected Development', in Iqbal Narain (ed.), *State Politics in India*, 322–69, Meerut: Meenakshi Publications.

Srivastava, Sunil. 1991. *The Disputed Mosque: A Historical Inquiry*. New Delhi: Vistaar Publications.

Stokes, Eric. 1978. *The Peasant and the Raj: Studies in Agrarian Society and Peasant Rebellion in Colonial India Cambridge South Asian Studies*. Cambridge: Cambridge University Press.

Suroor, Hasan. 2014. *India's Muslim Spring Why is Nobody Talking About it?* New Delhi: Rupa.

Tehelka. 2013a. 'Curfew in Force, Toll in Muzaffarnagar Climbs to 28', 9 September.

———. 2013b. 'Everybody Loves a Good Riot', 18 September.

Thakur, Ramesh. 1993. 'Ayodhya and the Politics of India's Secularism: A Double Standards Discourse', *Asian Survey*, 33(7): 645–4.

Thapar, Romila. 1989. 'Imagined Religious Communities? Ancient History and the Search for a Hindu Identity', *Modern Asian Studies*, 23(2): 209–31.

The Hindu. 2015. 'BJP Leader's Son Held in Dadri Lynching Case', October 2015. Retrieved 15 May 2017.

The Indian Express. 2013. 'Conditions at Relief Camps Appalling: NHRC', New Delhi, 22 October.

———. 2014. 'Dalit–Muslim Divide Deepens, Goes Rural', New Delhi, 7 August.

———. 2015a. 'Dadri Outrage after Mob Lynches Man for Allegedly Consuming Beef', New Delhi, 1 October.

———. 2015b. 'Mob Lynching in Dadri: Kin of Accused Attack Journalists Over Bias', 4 October 2015. Retrieved 15 May 2017.

———. 2017a. 'UP Election 2017: PM Talks about "Kabristan" and "Shamshan," We Talk about Laptop and Smartphone, says Akhilesh', New Delhi, 17 February.

———. 2017b. 'In Saharanpur, Another Youth Shot at, UP Govt Suspends DM and SSP', New Delhi, 25 May.

The Times of India. 2013. 'Muzaffarnagar Violence: Over 10,000 Displaced; 10,000 Arrested', 12 September.

———. 2014. 'How a Pauri Youth Turned into a Yogi.' 4 September, New Delhi.

Times News Network (*TNN*). 2017. 'Disband Anti-Romeo Squads: Activists.' 5 April, available at https://timesofindia.indiatimes.com/india/disband-anti-romeo-squads-activists/articleshow/58033629.cms accessed on 23 May 2017.

Tolpadi, Rajaram. 2010. 'Content, Discourse and Vision of Lohia's Socialism' *Economic and Political Weekly* 45(40).

Turner, A.C. 1933. 'Census of India, 1931', *United Province of Agra and Oudh, Part-I Report*, Allahabad: Superintendent, Print, and stationary.

Tyabji, Badruddin. 1971. *The Self in Secularism*. Delhi: Sterling Publishers.

Udaykumar, S.P. 1997. 'Historicizing Myth and Mythologizing History: The "Ram Temple" Drama', *Social Scientist* 25(7–8): 11–26.

Van de Veer, Peter. 1994. *Religious Nationalism: Hindus and Muslims in India*. Berkeley: University of California Press.

Varshney, Ashutosh. 2013. *Ethnic Conflict and Civic Life Hindus and Muslims in India* (Fourth Impression). New Delhi: Oxford University Press.

Verma, A.K. 2006. 'Uttar Pradesh Formation of Muslim Political Fronts', *Economic and Political Weekly*, 41(40): 4241–3.

Verma, Lalmani. 2017. 'RSS Red-flags Growing Hindu Yuva Vahini Clout to Adityanath', *The Indian Express*, New Delhi, 16 May 2017.

Vernier, Giles. 2017. 'Upper Hand for Upper Castes in House', *The Indian Express*, New Delhi, 20 March.

Wilkinson, Steven I. 2004. *Votes and Violence: Electoral Competition and Communal Riots in India*. Cambridge: Cambridge University Press.

Index

Wilkinson, Steven I. 2008. 'Muslims in Post-Independence India', in John L. Esposito, John Voll, and Osman Bakar (eds), *Asian Islam in the 21st Century*, pp. 177–8. New York: Oxford University Press.

Wood, Jolie F. 2014. 'Weavers Unravelled: Comparing Associationalism among Handloom Weavers and Boatmen in Varanasi, India', *Journal of South Asian Studies*, 37(1): 43–59.

Wright, Theodore. 1977. 'Muslims and the 1977 Indian Elections: A Watershed?', *Asian Survey* 17(12): 1207–20.

———. 1989. 'Muslims as Candidates and Voters in 1967 General Elections', in Verinder Grover (ed.), *Political System in India: Elections, Electoral Mechanism and Behaviour*, Vol. 6. New Delhi: Deep and Deep.

———. 1997. 'A New Demand for Muslim Reservation in India', *Asian Survey*, 37(9): 852–8.

Wright Jr, Theodore P. 1979. 'Inadvertent Modernization of Indian Muslims by Revivalists', *Journal of Muslim Minority Affairs*, 1(1): 80–9.

Zee News. 2015. 'When Muslim Dies They Give 20 Lakhs, but Hindu Doesn't Even Get 20,000: Sakshi Maharaj', 4 October, available at http://zeenews.india.com/news/india/when-muslim-dies-they-give-20-lakhs-but-hindu-doesnt-even-get-20000-sakshi-maharaj_1805764.html, accessed on 15 May 2017.

About the Authors

Sudha Pai was professor at the Centre for Political Studies, School of Social Sciences, and rector (pro vice-chancellor) at Jawaharlal Nehru University, New Delhi, India. She was senior fellow at the Nehru Memorial Museum and Library, New Delhi, India, from 2006 to 2009. Some of her publications include authored books such as *Developmental State and the Dalit Question in Madhya Pradesh: Congress Response* (2010) and *Dalit Assertion and the Unfinished Democratic Revolution: The BSP in Uttar Pradesh* (2002); and edited volumes such as *Political Process in Uttar Pradesh: Identity, Economic Reforms and Governance* (2007), *Handbook on Politics in the Indian States: Regions, Political Parties and Economic Reforms* (2015), and *Indian Parliament: A Critical Appraisal* (with Avinash Kumar, 2017).

Sajjan Kumar has a PhD from Centre for Political Studies, School of Social Sciences, Jawaharlal Nehru University, New Delhi, India. He is associated with various research institutions like Peoples Pulse, Hyderabad; Lokashraya Foundation, New Delhi, and Institute for Governance, Policies & Politics, New Delhi. His research interests include Indian politics, statecraft, agrarian politics, communalism, cultural politics, state politics, homeland security, and research methodology. He is an avid field researcher and has travelled extensively throughout north Indian states such as Bihar, Uttar Pradesh, Jharkhand, Uttarakhand, Himachal Pradesh, Punjab, Haryana, Rajasthan, and Delhi. He has contributed articles to scholarly journals and regularly writes for national newspapers, namely, *New Indian Express*, *Indian Express*, *Deccan Herald*, and also writes for *thewire.in*.